Voltaire in Exile

Voltaire in Exile

The Last Years, 1753–78

IAN DAVIDSON

GROVE PRESS
New York

First published in Great Britain in 2004 by
Atlantic Books, an imprint of Grove Atlantic Ltd.

Printed in the United States of America

FIRST GROVE PRESS PAPERBACK EDITION

Library of Congress Cataloging-in-Publication Data

Davidson, Ian, 1935–
    Voltaire in exile / Ian Davidson.
        p. cm.
    Originally published: London : Atlantic Books, 2004.
    Includes bibliographical references and index.
    ISBN-10: 0-8021-4236-2
    ISBN-13: 978-0-8021-4236-8
    1. Voltaire, 1694-1778—Last years. 2. Voltaire, 1694-1778—Exile—
Switzerland—Geneva. 3. Authors, French—18th century—Biography.
I. Title.
PQ2106.G4D38 2005
848'.509—dc22   2004054102

Designed by Nicky Barneby

Grove Press
an imprint of Grove/Atlantic, Inc.
841 Broadway
New York, NY 10003

06 07 08 09 10   10 9 8 7 6 5 4 3 2 1

GROVE PRESS
New York

To Jennifer, who made this book possible, and sustained my enjoyment in its research and writing.

Contents

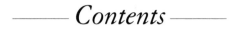

List of Illustrations

Acknowledgements

I am deeply grateful to Anne and Rachel, who were generous enough to help me make this book better than it might have been. All the remaining defects, errors and omissions are mine.

Introduction

Voltaire, as everybody knows, was one of the most famous writers of the French eighteenth century. The paradox is that, although his name is still internationally renowned, his life and work are now comparatively unfamiliar. Everyone knows that Voltaire was famous, but not everyone has a clear idea of what he was famous for, and many of the most commonly held ideas about him – for example, that Voltaire was a cynic and an atheist – are simply wrong.

There is a simple explanation for this situation: Voltaire's work is unfamiliar because most of it is no longer read; and it is no longer read because most of it is no longer readily accessible in print.

In a good English bookshop, you might expect to find Voltaire's most famous work, his satirical tale *Candide*; you might even hope to find his *Letters Concerning the English Nation* (also known under its French title *Lettres Philosophiques*); but that would be about the end of it. In France, of course, Voltaire is much better known, but even in a French bookshop, the choice would not be much greater: *Candide* (in many, many rival editions), and perhaps a collection of Voltaire's other satirical tales; the *Lettres Philosophiques*; and possibly the *Dictionnaire Philosophique*. But you would be lucky to find much else.

So you might be surprised to learn that Voltaire was mainly famous during his lifetime as the leading French author of neo-classical verse dramas, including twenty-seven tragedies and a dozen comedies. Not only did he write more plays than Shakespeare, and not only were his plays highly admired by all the most exacting critics; they were also extraordinarily popular. At the Comédie Française in

Paris, his dramatic works were performed more often than those of Corneille and Racine combined, not just occasionally, but consistently over several decades. In fact, during the middle to late eighteenth century, Voltaire's plays were the leading money-earner for the Comédie Française.

Voltaire's second claim to fame in his lifetime was as a poet: in 1723, when he was only twenty-nine, he achieved an international literary reputation with the publication of *La Henriade*, an epic poem celebrating the French King Henri IV and his efforts to end the French wars of religion between Catholics and Protestants. And just as contemporary critics compared Voltaire the playwright favourably with Corneille and Racine, and even with Sophocles, so they compared Voltaire the epic poet with Virgil.

The third strand of Voltaire's literary fame in the eighteenth century was as the author of half a dozen weighty volumes of history. These included a history of the reign of Louis XIV in the seventeenth century (*Le Siècle de Louis XIV*) and of Louis XV in the eighteenth century (*Précis du Siècle de Louis XV*), a history of Russia under Peter the Great (*Histoire de l'Empire de Russie sous Pierre le Grand*), and a history of civilisation (*Essai sur les Mœurs*).

All three components of Voltaire's literary fame during his lifetime are now largely neglected or forgotten. His plays are no longer performed, and his poems and histories are no longer read. Voltaire scholars generally concede that his plays have not worn well: that Voltaire was trying to breathe new life into dramatic conventions which were already dated in his lifetime; and that if his plays have not remained in the repertoire, it is because they do not deserve to. In fact, the last time one of his tragedies was put on at the Comédie Française was in 1965, and that was not by popular request but by presidential demand, for the entertainment of a visiting political delegation from China.

Of course, Voltaire also owes his reputation to the fact that he was a leading member of the French Enlightenment, a so-called *philosophe*, and a contributor to that great iconic enterprise of the Enlightenment, the *Encyclopédie*. Yet it was typical of Voltaire's character as an individualist and an outsider that he was in some sense a dissident *philosophe:* he contributed for a while to the *Encyclopédie*, but he disagreed with the way it was edited and eventually produced his own *Dictionnaire Philosophique*.

Even if large swathes of Voltaire's huge output are now, perhaps deservedly, overlooked, there are three elements of his legacy which were important in his lifetime, and which remain important today.

The first of these is, of course, the story *Candide*, the product of a late flowering of Voltaire's genius, when he was sixty-five, and generally recognised as his greatest and most enduring masterpiece. Fortunately, *Candide* is still universally admired, permanently popular, and always in print.

The second element in Voltaire's legacy which remains important today is the story of his personal life as he told it in his own words, in fascinating detail, in his letters. Voltaire was a tireless writer of letters: to friends and enemies, to women and doctors and priests, to bankers and debtors, to judges and lawyers, to actors and actresses and playwrights, to politicians and statesmen, to publishers and administrators; all in all, during his lifetime he wrote letters to about 1,500 different people. And since Voltaire was probably the most famous as well as the most amusing letter-writer in Europe, his letters were regularly discussed and copied and eagerly passed from hand to hand between friends and acquaintances.

As a result, there were in existence a very large number of Voltaire's letters, either carefully filed away by their recipients, or more generally in circulation, in France or elsewhere in Europe, some of them in more than one copy. When Voltaire died, his literary executors, led by the French dramatist Beaumarchais and the *philosphe* Condorcet, appealed for the return of as many letters as possible, in order to include them in the first posthumous edition of his complete works. In response, they received over 6,000 letters, of which they published around 4,500. Over the next two centuries, many more of Voltaire's letters emerged, some as recently as the 1950s. Today, the complete edition of Voltaire's correspondence in print totals 15,284 letters.

The importance nowadays accorded to Voltaire's letters can be gauged by the list of his works chosen by the French publisher Gallimard for their prestigious India-paper edition La Bibliothèque de la Pléiade. The series includes three volumes containing *Candide* and all the tales, some (but not all) of the historical works, and some (but not all) of the miscellaneous works; but thirteen volumes containing all of the letters.

Voltaire would no doubt find it richly ironic, and perhaps even amusing, that the serious literary works by which he set such store, over which he laboured so hard and so long, and on which his fame was then mainly based, should now to a large extent be neglected; and that his letters, those spontaneous outpourings in response to day-to-day events, should be regarded as a major, even perhaps a central, part of the legacy of his literary and intellectual *œuvre*. And yet Voltaire's letters are so numerous, so informative, and so compellingly entertaining that they can be considered not just as a useful supplementary source of biographical information, but even in some sense as an unplanned meta-autobiography.

This meta-autobiography is especially voluminous during the last twenty-five years of his life, for as time went on, Voltaire wrote more and more letters every year. In his forties, he wrote about 130 letters a year, whereas in his sixties and seventies, he was writing around 550 letters annually. In total, three-quarters of his letters, 11,644 out of 15,284, were written between 1754 (when he was sixty) and 1778 (when he died, aged eighty-four).

The main explanation for this asymmetry is that, during the last twenty-five years of his life, Voltaire was banished by Louis XV from Paris and Versailles, and was living in exile on one of the furthest frontiers of France, just outside Geneva. If he wanted to communicate with his friends and acquaintances, he could no longer visit them, so he had to write.

Precisely why Louis XV banished Voltaire was never made clear. Throughout his life, Voltaire's iconoclasm had frequently got him into trouble with the authorities of Church and State. In 1754, the reason for his banishment may simply have been that he was held to have disgraced his status as an official office-holder at the court of Versailles (Gentleman in Ordinary of the King's Chamber) by accepting employment as Chamberlain at the court of Frederick II at Potsdam. But that is just a plausible presumption: Louis XV never gave his reasons.

At all events, it is during these last twenty-five years that we learn so much more about Voltaire's personal life, because he tells us so much more. And what we learn is not just that Voltaire was a man of extraordinary vitality and multifarious interests, but that during his sixties and seventies he also went through a remarkable process of moral development. Most of his life, Voltaire had been almost exclusively preoccupied with his literary career, with his friends, and with his comfort, in that order, and he showed little or no sign of anything resembling a social conscience, let alone of concern for the welfare of the lower orders. In this respect, exile changed Voltaire for the better. When he acquired the château of Ferney, just outside Geneva, his immediate purpose was to make his exile as comfortable, as secure, and as independent as possible. But the château came with an estate, and for the first time in his life Voltaire found himself faced with responsibilities for tenants and peasants and servants, not to mention relations with neighbours. He responded immediately to the challenge, and it is extraordinary to witness how this embodiment of social and literary egotism threw himself into an energetic programme of economic development and the alleviation of poverty.

The third element in Voltaire's life which remains important today is closely connected to the second. Over a period of twenty years, almost until his death, he embarked on a series of one-man campaigns to combat or reverse flagrant and scandalous miscarriages of justice which were inflicted on complete strangers. Exactly why he did so is a fascinating question, since he had not previously shown any interest in the justice system. However, in his sixties, he started to become concerned, first, about a number of individual victims of injustice, then about the general defects in the functioning of the judicial system.

There were seven main cases in which Voltaire campaigned, either to prevent injustice, or for the reversal of an unjust verdict. The most famous of these was that of Jean Calas, a Protestant from Toulouse who was condemned to death allegedly for having killed his own son, in order to stop him from converting to Catholicism.

Voltaire heard about the case too late to prevent Calas's execution; but he did succeed in forcing the authorities to review and finally to reverse the verdict.

What was spectacular about these campaigns, in the context of eighteenth-century France, was that an individual Frenchman dared to take on the repressive, ramshackle, and barbaric power of the judicial and penal system, presided over by the absolute French monarchy and buttressed by the superstitions of the Catholic Church. Even more remarkable, in some ways, was the fact that Voltaire conducted his campaigns entirely by letter. Two factors made this possible: first, he was very rich, so he could hire any number of the best lawyers; second, he was probably the best-connected letter-writer in the whole of Europe, with an address book which gave him access to kings, emperors, princes, statesmen, politicians, churchmen, academics, businessmen, writers and intellectuals.

In only one of the seven cases did Voltaire actually succeed in preventing a miscarriage of justice. Yet the fundamental question, even at the time, was not whether his specific campaigns succeeded or failed, but whether he could in some measure challenge the autocratic regime, help shift the balance of opinion against the forces of state repression and religious superstition, and lever open the door to the recognition of some principles of reason and reasonableness. Today, it is widely accepted that Voltaire's individual campaigns, together with the development of his thinking about the general principles and practices of the French justice system, were landmarks in the history of penal reform in France and Europe. This aspect of his life and work, which powerfully struck the imagination of the ordinary people of France at the time, may be among Voltaire's most enduring achievements.

A question of terminology: when referring to Voltaire's campaigns, either on behalf of specific victims of injustice, or in favour of more general penal reforms, I shall from time to time have recourse to the term 'human rights'. This is, of course, an anachronism: Voltaire did not have in mind the full range of rights and liberties that we might nowadays associate with the term. At the same time, however, it is clear that, once Voltaire started to take an interest in penal issues, his moral position, in contrast to the backwardness and repression that characterised the justice system in France in the eighteenth century, was very much at the 'human rights' end of the spectrum, and that over time he moved unequivocally further in that direction.

As its title indicates, this book is mainly concerned with the last twenty-five years of Voltaire's life. In many respects, this is a narrative in which the multiple and varied threads of the story of the years of Voltaire's exile unfold within the logic of a self-contained period. On the other hand, there are a number of key features of his life in Geneva and Ferney which cannot be properly understood without some explanation of events which took place many years earlier. For this reason, the book opens with a Prologue in which I give some idea of the general shape of Voltaire's life up to the time of his exile, and describe some of the key events within it. This account will necessarily be extremely compressed, not to say skeletal, since it is hardly possible to do anything like justice to the first sixty years of Voltaire's life in the space of a few pages, but I hope it will help to make the main narrative more readable and more comprehensible.

Voltaire in Exile

I

Prologue

1694–1750

Voltaire was born in Paris in 1694, the third child of François Arouet, a well-connected professional notary from the upper bourgeoisie. Voltaire's legal name was therefore François Marie Arouet; he assumed the name 'Voltaire' in 1718, when he was twenty-four, shortly after the success of his first tragedy *Oedipe*. One theory is that he abandoned the name Arouet because he believed that he was the product of an affair between his mother and a man who was not his legal father.

Voltaire did not get on with his older brother Armand, who was a fundamentalist Catholic. However, he was fond of his sister Marguerite Catherine, who married a certain Pierre Mignot, and very fond of her three children: Marie Louise, the eldest, who became the wife and then widow of Nicolas Denis and was to become a very important part of Voltaire's life in later years; Marie Elisabeth, who became the wife and then the widow of Nicolas Fontaine; and Alexandre Mignot, who took minor holy orders as an abbé.

Voltaire was educated at the Jesuits' Collège de Louis-le-Grand, then as now one of the top secondary schools in Paris. There he learned a lot of Latin and little Greek, and acquired a taste for theatre. In later life he became fluent in Italian, Spanish and English, though he never mastered German.

Voltaire's father made repeated efforts to persuade or even force him to settle down as a lawyer; but Voltaire was determined to try his luck as a writer in the rakish salon world of literary Paris. After scoring a hit with *Oedipe*, he scored another in 1723 with his epic poem *La Henriade*. But these triumphs tempted him to take scandalous risks above his station, and he was twice locked up in the Bastille. He was first imprisoned in 1717, for writing some verses which displeased the Prince Regent, and again in 1726, for trying to pick a fight with an arrogant young nobleman, the chevalier de Rohan.

Voltaire was only released from his second term of imprisonment on condition that he go into exile, and he chose to go to England, where he stayed for two years. It was an experience which left an indelible imprint on him: he immersed himself in English life, and he was deeply impressed by the liberty and pluralism of English society, political, social, commercial and religious. In the process, he became fluent in English (partly by the assiduous study of Shakespeare), so fluent that at one point he considered remaining in England as an English writer. Voltaire wrote up his observations of English life in a book called *Lettres Philosophiques*, most of which he wrote directly in English under the title *Letters Concerning the English Nation*.

On his return to Paris, in 1728, Voltaire resumed his life as a literary careerist. His main problem was shortage of money, aggravated by the fact that he was unable to lay his hands on his inheritance from his father (who had died in 1722). Many people assume that the immense popularity of his writings must have made him prosperous, but this is a misapprehension. At that time, and until the Revolution of 1789, there was no copyright law in France, and any author was at constant risk of having his works pirated and pillaged by unscrupulous publishers and booksellers. In the case of a writer as famous as Voltaire, this was not just a risk but a dead certainty. Moreover, much of Voltaire's writing was scandalous or subversive; in these cases, not only did he not claim commercial ownership but he even denied authorship of works which everybody knew were written by him.

Voltaire should have been able to make money out of his plays. During much of his life, he was the most popular author at the Comédie Française, the leading officially authorised theatre in Paris, and in principle he would have been entitled to claim an author's percentage. But Voltaire gave his plays to the actors at the Comédie Française for nothing; he hoped that they would reward his generosity by treating his texts with scrupulous respect, since they had a deplorable habit of rewriting scenes which they thought needed 'improvement'. Unfortunately Voltaire's calculation did not work out: the *comédiens* welcomed his plays, kept his share of the profits, and continued to rewrite them regardless.

In 1728, therefore, Voltaire decided to look for another way of making money, and he found it spectacularly later that year. The key event was the discovery, by one of his friends, the mathematician Charles Marie de La Condamine, that the authorities had made a major blunder in setting the terms of a state lottery. In order to promote the sale of tickets, they undertook to subsidise the prizes. What they did not realise, apparently, was that the prizes they were offering were significantly greater than the maximum revenue from ticket sales. It was possible, therefore, to make a guaranteed and entirely legal fortune by cornering the market, and buying up all the lottery tickets. Condamine and his friends put together a syndicate, in which Voltaire was included, and they made a large profit, month after month, for at least a year. It is not clear exactly how much Voltaire made out of this operation, but it must have been a very large sum, possibly half a million francs. Soon after this, he invested heavily in a speculative share operation launched by the duc de Lorraine, and sold out immediately at a large profit. By the time he was thirty-six, he had accumulated assets which may have amounted to about a million francs.

It is difficult to express Voltaire's wealth in modern monetary terms because the scale of values then was so very different from what it is today. His biographer Theodore Besterman has suggested that one franc might have been roughly equivalent to one US dollar, but this seems a serious under-estimate. We should probably not try to reckon what one eighteenth-century franc would represent today, but rather what it represented then. In this perspective, it has been suggested that a man with an annual income of 15,000 francs (or livres) would have been wealthy, and one with an income of 30,000 francs would have been very wealthy. By this measure, Voltaire was very, very wealthy.

Voltaire sometimes talked in terms of livres, and sometimes in terms of francs; these were in fact alternative words for the same thing. The franc or livre (meaning 'pound') was divided into 20 sous (plural of sol), and the sol was divided into 12 deniers; the symbols for livres, sous and deniers were therefore £. s. d. The similarities with the English currency, until decimalisation in 1972, are striking. Moreover, although the English used the words pounds, shillings and pence, they employed the Latin-derived symbols £. s. d. for the different units. In French, the currency symbols matched the words.*

Now that he had acquired a large fortune, Voltaire was in a position to rub shoulders with the big players in the world of finance, and be admitted to some of their major operations. At that time, the French armed forces were supplied with provisions by private entrepreneurs, and the contract for this supply was currently held by the Pâris-Duverney brothers. Voltaire invested in their operation and, after just one season, this brought him profits of 600,000 francs. He was now seriously rich, and the following year he at last secured his inheritance, of nearly 153,000 francs.

Voltaire distributed his new-found wealth among a wide variety of investments: public lotteries; bank deposits; French state debt; French army supplies; and the trading operations of the French *Compagnie des Indes* (French India Company), which he normally referred to as 'Cadiz', since that was its main port of operations. But above all, and increasingly over time, he invested his money in loans to dukes and princes.

When he was younger, he lent money to French dukes and princes, like the duc de Richelieu and the family of the prince de Guise; on his return to France from Prussia, when he was fearful of the vengeful hostility of Versailles, he preferred to lend to German dukes and princes, like the Elector-Palatine or the duke of Wurtemberg, especially when they had estates in France, which (Voltaire believed) could be mortgaged to him for greater security.

These personal loans were normally in the form of a *rente viagère*, meaning a 'loan for life', which was cancelled when the lender died. The rate of interest varied according to the age of the lender: an eld-

---

*The French currency also included the louis, a gold coin worth £24; the écu, a silver coin worth £6; and the petit écu worth £3.

erly lender could expect to negotiate a higher rate of interest on the assumption that the loan would be extinguished sooner. But Voltaire defied the expectations of his borrowers by living to a great age, and was able, for many years, to demand an interest rate of 10 per cent, which was far above the normal banking deposit rate of 3 to 5 per cent. These loans were not risk-free, however, because the dukes and princes had a distressing tendency to fall behind with their payments, sometimes for years on end.

Over time, however, Voltaire became richer and richer, and his wealth gave him a crucial element of personal independence, without which he would scarcely have dared to challenge some of the worst aspects of the *ancien régime*.

In 1733, Voltaire became the lover of Émilie, marquise du Châtelet, a remarkable feminist exemplar of the Enlightenment, a mathematician and scientist, the wife of an amiable and complaisant army officer. She was twenty-seven, Voltaire nearly forty. This was to be his first long-term emotional attachment, and it marked him for life.

When Voltaire's *Lettres Philosophiques* was published in 1734, it caused a massive scandal, since its praise of English liberty and tolerance was widely, and correctly, perceived as an attack on French absolutism and religious dogmatism. Voltaire fled Paris once again and took refuge in Émilie's château at Cirey in eastern France, where she soon joined him. They spent most of the next ten years together, mainly at Cirey, and formed a curious intellectual quasi-matrimonial *ménage*. They would pass mornings and afternoons reading and writing in their separate studies, and they would meet at meal-times. Émilie translated Newton's *Principia Mathematica* and she inspired Voltaire to write an interpretation of the *Eléments de la Philosophie de Newton*; but he never persuaded her of the interest of history, which she regarded as little more than gossip.

Voltaire remained deeply committed to Émilie until her death in 1749. But after living with her for ten years, he began to tire of her possessiveness and he longed once more for the bright lights. In 1744 he returned to Paris and chased preferment at court, for which he was rewarded with the post of Royal Historian. In 1746 he received the title Gentleman in Ordinary of the King's Chamber, and was elected to the Académie Française, the prestigious official club of leading intellectuals. In later life he would say that, of all the time he had wasted in his life, the periods he most regretted were those he had spent as a courtier.[1]

In Paris, Voltaire took a new mistress: his eldest niece, Marie-Louise Denis. He was fifty, she was thirty-two. During his lifetime, the real nature of Voltaire's relationship with Mme Denis was a closely guarded secret, and his close friend Charles Augustin de Ferriol, comte d'Argental, was one of the few people who knew the truth. Positive evidence was missing until 1957, when Theodore Besterman discovered and published a series of very explicit love letters between Voltaire and Mme Denis.

In December 1745, he wrote to her from Versailles: 'I don't know when my affairs will allow me to leave a place I abhor. The court, society, the great ones of the earth bore me. I shall be happy only when I can live with you. Your company, and better health would make me happy. I kiss you a thousand times. My soul kisses yours, my prick, my heart are in love with you. I kiss your pretty arse and all your enchanting person.' (*Vi baccio mille volte. La mia anima baccia la vostra, mio catzo, mio cuore sone inamorati di voi. Baccio il vostro gentil culo e tutta la vostra vezzosa persona.*)[2] Many of the most explicit love-letters between Voltaire and Mme Denis were written in Italian, possibly in the belief that this would protect their privacy from prying eyes.

In October 1746, he wrote to Mme Denis: 'I want to drink [a] health with you. But I beg you to be sober, and to keep me sober. I ask your permission to let me bring my limpness. It would be better to have a hard-on, but whether I do or not, I shall always love you, you will be the only consolation of my life'. (Original in Italian)[3]

In July 1748, he wrote to her: 'If the poor state of my health permits, I shall throw myself at your knees and kiss all your Beauties. Meanwhile I place a thousand kisses on your round breasts, on your enchanting arse and on all your person which has so often given me a hard-on and plunged me in a river of delight.' (Original in Italian)[4]

*

In 1748, partly no doubt as a result of Voltaire's neglect, Émilie du Châtelet had a passionate affair with the marquis de Saint-Lambert: she was now forty-two, he was ten years younger. Unfortunately she became pregnant by him, and died after childbirth in 1749. Voltaire was devastated and sank into a deep depression; he returned briefly to Paris and installed Mme Denis, ostensibly just his dear niece, in the house in the rue Traversière which he had previously shared with Mme du Châtelet. But evidently he had to get away from the reminders of Émilie, and instead of pursuing life in Paris with Mme Denis, he decided to move to Potsdam, the second royal residence of Prussia where the court of Frederick the Great was based.

Frederick had been flirting with Voltaire long before he came to the throne in 1740. It was only after another ten years of urging that he finally persuaded Voltaire to accept the post of Chamberlain and poet-in-residence. Voltaire arrived at Potsdam on 21 July 1750, and at first he was delighted with his new position: his main official task, helping to polish Frederick's French prose and verse, took only a few hours of each day, and he was exempted from most courtly duties, apart from intimate suppers with the King. He thus had plenty of time for his own writing, which at this time was focused mainly on the research for his major historical work, *Le Siècle de Louis* XIV.

But his stay soon turned sour. Voltaire may have hoped to be the tutor of the 'philosopher-King' of Sans-Souci; but Frederick, though in some ways fascinated by Voltaire, in practice treated him as little more than a trophy intellectual, the most celebrated poetry sub-editor in Europe. Many years later, Voltaire quoted the bitter little anecdote, current at the time, in which Frederick had said, to an anxious rival jealous of Voltaire's privileged position: 'Don't worry: we shall squeeze the orange, and then, when we have swallowed the juice, we shall throw it away.' From that moment, Voltaire was resolved to protect the orange peel. [5]

In Potsdam, Voltaire managed to get into a personal feud with Pierre Louis Moreau de Maupertuis, the (French) President of the Berlin Academy of Sciences and Belles-Lettres (and Voltaire's predecessor in the bed of Émilie du Châtelet). This quarrel brought

Voltaire's position at Potsdam to breaking point. In December 1752 he published a vitriolic pamphlet, denouncing and deriding his opponent; it caused a major scandal at court.[6] The King was enraged, and had the pamphlet seized and ceremonially burned by the public executioner. Voltaire concluded that it was time to leave.

But when he attempted to resign, he found that he was not a free man; the King regarded him as a courtier and servant, and refused to let him go. When, however, a new pamphlet against Maupertuis (but not written by Voltaire) was published in London, in the middle of March 1753, the King sent him a brutal letter of dismissal. Ten days later, Voltaire left Potsdam for good, and set off for France. He was not to know that his return to France would not be any kind of home-coming, but that he would be met with a life sentence of banishment from which there would be no appeal; let alone that, on the way, he would have to endure a shocking lesson in the power and brutality of eighteenth-century despotism.

2

Money

1750–53

On 26 March 1753, Voltaire left Potsdam in a large, comfortable, well-suspended carriage, with two large trunks on the back. Voltaire carried with him several portfolios of manuscripts, and a case containing money, letters of credit and jewels. He was accompanied by Cosimo Alessandro Collini, his twenty-six-year-old Florentine secretary. They travelled slowly, making prolonged stays at Leipzig, Gotha and Cassel. This was partly because Voltaire always enjoyed being fêted – he was lavishly entertained for a month by the duke and duchess of Saxe-Gotha – and also because he was waiting for some indication from Paris as to how he would be received on his return. As a result, Voltaire and Collini did not reach their hotel, Le Lion d'Or, in Frankfurt until 31 May. They were in for a terrible shock.

The next morning, just as Voltaire was getting ready to set off again, he was confronted in his hotel by Baron Franz von Freytag, official representative (*résident*) of the Prussian authorities in Frankfurt. Freytag told him that he had orders to require him to hand over a book of poems by King Frederick, and he made it clear that until this happened he would impose virtual house arrest on Voltaire, by force if necessary. Voltaire explained that this book of poems, which had been given him by the King, was in a large trunk following on behind; he agreed to give instructions that it should be sent to Frankfurt. But Freytag was not satisfied, and insisted on going through all Voltaire's belongings. At the end of this bruising and degrading confrontation, which lasted from nine in the morning till five in the afternoon, Freytag took away an unopened package, a poem by Voltaire, two packets of personal papers, the

Chamberlain's key, and the cross and ribbon of the Prussian Order of Merit. Freytag gave Voltaire a written promise that he would be free to go as soon as he received the book of poems.

Voltaire now settled down to await the arrival of the trunk, and to work on his next history book, *Les Annales de l'Empire*. He also wrote some letters, including two to his close friend, the comte d'Argental; curiously, he did not mention the fact that he was under house arrest, and merely pretended that he was delayed by swellings in his legs and hands.[1] It was not until 5 June that he started appealing to influential friends and contacts across Europe for help against Freytag.

Meanwhile Mme Marie-Louise Denis, Voltaire's eldest niece, had left Paris to come and meet him on his journey home. Her original plan had been that she would join him in Strasbourg, to escort him home, or at least tell him how the political land lay at Versailles. When she learned of his predicament, she travelled on to Frankfurt; but when she arrived there on 9 June 1753, she was caught in the same trap as Voltaire.

The days passed; Voltaire, Collini and Mme Denis remained under house arrest until, on Sunday 17 June, the trunk with the book of poetry finally arrived. Voltaire assumed he would now be allowed to go but Freytag refused to open the trunk until he had received fresh instructions from the King, which he expected the following Thursday, 21 June. Never a brave man, Voltaire now began to get seriously worried, and he panicked. On the Wednesday afternoon, carrying only his manuscripts and his money box, and accompanied by Collini, he left the hotel and attempted to leave the city by a public coach. But the alarm was quickly raised and they were stopped at the city gates and taken into custody. This time it was no longer a question of house arrest; they were taken to a low-life tavern and locked up in separate rooms with a detachment of twelve soldiers on guard.

Meanwhile, Herr Dorn, Freytag's secretary, went to fetch Mme Denis from the Lion d'Or hotel and dragged her to the tavern under armed escort. Dorn then installed himself in her garret bedroom for the night, had dinner sent up, drank many bottles of wine, and, according to Voltaire, was only prevented from inflicting the worst importunities on Mme Denis by her cries for help.

The next day, 21 June, Freytag received new instructions from Potsdam: he was to release Voltaire and his companions, provided Voltaire gave a written promise to return Frederick's book of poems. But Freytag did not carry out these instructions. Collini and Mme Denis were released from their rooms, but kept under house arrest; Voltaire remained locked up. Just why Freytag disobeyed orders is not clear; perhaps he had spotted Voltaire as a rich man, and planned to relieve him of some of his money, ostensibly as payment for the cost of his detention. Voltaire and his party were still under arrest two weeks later when, on 5 July, a fresh letter arrived from Frederick, in response to the widespread public outcry at Voltaire's arrest. He rebuked Freytag for having arrested Mme Denis, and ordered the immediate release of Voltaire and his companions. Again Freytag disregarded the orders; it was not until 7 July that Voltaire and Collini were allowed to make a hurried departure from Frankfurt. Before they left, Freytag's secretary, Dorn, confiscated Voltaire's money box. Mme Denis left for Paris the following day.

Voltaire did not go straight home to France, however, for he still did not know if he would be permitted to return. He may have doubted it, for the word was already out that he was in disgrace in Versailles for having accepted an appointment at the foreign, rival and potentially enemy court of Frederick the Great. So far, however, he had heard nothing official either way. Another cause of delay was that he was so angry at his intolerable treatment by Freytag and his accomplices that he was determined to try to get some justice against them. But his efforts to get Freytag and company punished were brushed off by the Frankfurt authorities, and it was not until many weeks later, on 13 September, a month after Voltaire had returned to France, that he got any of his money back: just 1,000 francs.

In any case, Voltaire never could resist an opportunity to enjoy the hospitality of the great and the good. Just as he had made extended stays at Leipzig, Gotha and Cassel before reaching Frankfurt, so now, after leaving Frankfurt, he spent three weeks at Mainz, where he stayed with the worldly Prince-Bishop, and two weeks at Schwetzingen, the summer home of the Elector-Palatine, where he was entertained with a constant round of parties and theatre performances.

On 5 August 1753, Voltaire wrote to Mme Denis in Paris:

It's been some time since I wrote to you. But it's not entirely my fault, my dear child. I was ill at Mainz, but every day, every hour I planned on leaving, as soon as I should have the strength ...

From Mainz I went to Mannheim, and fell ill again. But it was an indispensable duty for me to pay my respects to their Electoral Highnesses, and thank them for the extreme kindnesses with which they have honoured me. All that I lack is the health to enjoy all the pleasures on offer. Comédie-Française, Comédie-Italienne, Italian grand opera, opera buffa, ballets, plenty of food, conversation, politeness, grandeur, simplicity, that's the Mannheim court for you.[2]

Six days later, on 11 August 1753, he wrote to her again:

I am still, my dear child, the Elector-Palatine's patient. His countryside is delicious, his company even more. There is everything here, and nothing in excess. They have put on *Alzire* and *Nanine* [two of Voltaire's plays] for me. The troupe of actors is fairly good. You will admit that one cannot entertain an author better than by putting on his own works ... I still say that I shall leave tomorrow, or the day after ...

[PS] They are keeping me here until Tuesday: they are putting on for me *Zaïre* and *L'Indiscret* [another two of Voltaire's plays] ... And yet without health, and without you, there are no fine days.[3]

Now the Elector-Palatine's lavish entertaining did not come cheap; in fact, he was ruining himself with his extravagance and he took advantage of Voltaire's visit to borrow 100,000 francs from him. It was to be the first of many such transactions, until the closing years of Voltaire's life.

In the summer of 1753, however, Voltaire's overriding preoccupation was not with his finances, but with where he was going to live. On 15 August he reached Strasbourg, where he anxiously waited for news from Mme Denis in Paris. He had the sense that he would not be welcome at court; as he wrote to her on 17 August:

'I have thus returned to France, but only seek an exile there ...'[4]

The bad news came soon enough. In January 1754, Mme Denis wrote that she had seen Mme de Pompadour, the King's mistress, and that she had told her that the King would not allow Voltaire to return. In his reply, Voltaire described her news as 'an overpowering thunderbolt';[5] a few days later he said that 'the bomb which has fallen on my head, has upset my plans and my hopes'.[6] He asked her to find out if he would be allowed to live near Auxerre (in northern Burgundy) or elsewhere. 'I suppose that, having received no positive order, I can choose my own exile.'[7]

For most of the rest of that year, Voltaire hung about near the French frontier, trying to decide what to do next. One reason for his indecision was that the message from Mme de Pompadour had not specified the terms of his exile. Exile was a frequent instrument of repression by the French court, but when it was decreed in an official document such as a *lettre de cachet,* it would often lay down the terms, such as exile of so many leagues from Paris, or to a particular place, or for so many months or years. In this case, Voltaire's exile was simply expressed by word of mouth via Mme de Pompadour: she gave no reference to a formal document or decree, and did not specify the terms of it. Many years later, court officials were unable to prevent Voltaire's eventual return to Paris, under Louis XV's successor, because they could not find the exile document. In fact, there had never been such a document: the sentence of exile was just an oral message from the late King. But for the moment, Voltaire did not know whether his sentence of exile was irrevocable, or whether the King might yet relent.

Another factor in Voltaire's indecision, however, was uncertainty over his relationship with Mme Denis. In the 1740s, they had been passionate lovers; but when Émilie du Châtelet died and Voltaire moved to Potsdam, Mme Denis remained in Paris. Voltaire wrote to her frequently from Potsdam; but they were no longer love-letters. He regularly promised her either that he would be returning to Paris very soon, or that he was making preparations for her to join him; in practice he did neither, and he stayed away for two and a half years.

Their brief reunion in Frankfurt, in mid-1753, evidently re-ignited their sexual fires: for in September, after her return to Paris, Mme Denis told Voltaire that she was pregnant. Perhaps it was in response to this news that he returned to the erotic charge with a letter from Strasbourg later that month: 'Me not love you! My child, I shall adore you until the tomb. I wish I could be the only one to have the happiness of fucking you, and I wish now that I had never had any other favours but yours, and had never discharged except with you. I have a hard-on as I write, and I kiss a thousand times your lovely tits and your lovely arse.'[8]

Besterman dismisses the story of Mme Denis's pregnancy as pure fiction: 'She even pretended to be pregnant by Voltaire, and Voltaire pretended to believe her.'[9] Well, it may have been pretence on her part, but it obviously was not on Voltaire's. During the following weeks, he repeatedly asked her for news of her pregnancy and her health, with concern and delighted anticipation at the prospect of a child. 'I really hope that your suspicions about Mme Daurade [his flippant code-name for Mme Denis] are true. Is it true that she is pregnant? I should really like a little Daurade, but tell the mother to look after herself.'[10]

A month later, however, in mid-October 1753, Mme Denis wrote to inform Voltaire that she had had a miscarriage. 'The misadventure of Mme Daurade pierces my heart,' he replied. 'One instant has destroyed everything.'[11] The brevity of the comment, and the fact that he spent the rest of his letter writing at length about other things, could imply that he was relatively indifferent to the news. But a week later he returned to the subject. 'You cannot believe how deeply I regret what Mme Daurade had promised me. That is something one cannot do whenever one wants, and I am afraid that it is an irreparable loss. You do not seem upset enough. How can we repair this loss?'[12]

So far as is known, Voltaire never had children; and before 1753, he does not seem to have wanted children. He never married; and despite his long liaison with Émilie du Châtelet, his deep personal commitment to her seems always to have remained well this side of parenthood.

After 1753, however, there seems to have been a real transformation in Voltaire's attitudes towards home, family and children. In Paris, he had long had a house in the rue Traversière, but it was not until he moved to Geneva in 1754, that he acquired, for the first time, a genuine home in the sense of a place that was the centre of his life: first in the country house of Les Délices, later in the estate of his château de Ferney. One of the consequences of having a home, was that Voltaire delighted in gathering round him members of Mme Denis's family: Mme Fontaine, her sister; the abbé Mignot, her brother; and Alexandre d'Hornoy, her nephew. In addition, there was a whole series of episodes over the next few years strongly indicating Voltaire's desire for children in the house.

In 1757, one of Mme Denis's former chambermaids, by the name of Pichon, died in Paris, leaving two orphan sons. Voltaire arranged for one of them, ten-year-old Mathieu, to be brought to his home near Geneva. Later that year Mathieu fell ill and Voltaire administered a purgative, which showed that he had worms. Voltaire sought medical advice: 'Since he has expelled these worms, he has not been to the cloakroom. I go into all these details only because I wish to save this little boy.'[13] Whether he did save him, is not known.

Another illuminating incident occurred early in 1758, when a young seamstress in Voltaire's household, Catherine Borri, was found to be pregnant by a servant boy called André. Voltaire tried to arrange for young Catherine to be looked after by some good woman in Lyon, so that she could have her baby in safety and away from family scandal. He added, as an afterthought, a comment of touching regret: 'Is it not abominable that these clowns should have a pleasure that I cannot have?'[14] He was obviously referring to the pleasure of having children.

In later years, he made up for this lack with surrogate children: the eighteen-year-old Marie-Françoise Corneille, whom he legally adopted in 1760, before marrying her to Claude Dupuits; and the beautiful nineteen-year-old Reine Philiberte Rouph de Varicourt, whom he absorbed into his household in 1776 before marrying her to the marquis de Villette.

Voltaire's regret at not having children comes out explicitly in a letter he wrote in 1765 to his old friend Nicolas-Claude Thieriot, to congratulate him on the marriage of his daughter. 'You have a great advantage over me, that you are marrying a daughter whom you made. You have tasted the pleasure of being a father, while I have been useless in the world, and it's not my fault. I console myself as well as I can, with the insipid pleasure of building and planting'.[15]

In 1753–4, Mme Denis was evidently undecided whether to join Voltaire, or to stay with the bright lights of Paris society. In some ways, Paris was an attractive option, since she knew that Voltaire would continue to support her in considerable comfort. But the question of how much comfort she had a right to expect was, and remained, a regular subject of disagreement between them. When she drew 4,800 livres from his banker over the space of about ten days, Voltaire seems to have complained of her extravagance. She reacted violently to his reproaches, accusing him of avarice: 'The love of money torments you. Avarice stabs you. In your heart you are the worst of men.'[16]

Her attack seems to have led to some kind of showdown on the question of money, for in the middle of March 1754 Voltaire set out an account of the state of his finances which, he said, 'would enable me to live with Mme Denis in a manner which would be agreeable to her'.[17] By the end of that month, Mme Denis was persuaded, and indicated that she was thinking of spending her life with him.[18] He replied: 'Your letter of April 6 overwhelms me with joy ...'[19] Finally, in late July 1754, Mme Denis joined him in Colmar, and with the exception of a dramatic period of separation, she remained his companion for life.

Mme Denis has sometimes had a bad press. For one thing, her extravagance regularly caused money worries for Voltaire. For another, she was a glutton; in her youth she was quite pretty and coquettish; in later life, she became a fat old woman, yet still coquettish. On the other hand, she had good points which suited Voltaire. She absolutely loved amateur dramatics; she was always ready to learn a part, and to dress up for it, especially if she could order the costumes from Paris. She was musical, and could sing and play the harpsichord; Voltaire, by contrast, was not at all musical. She loved entertaining, organising plays and parties and balls on a lavish scale; when visitors came in droves, Voltaire knew that he could stay in his study and rely on her to look after the guests.

In day-to-day terms, Mme Denis and Voltaire seem to have negotiated a strong quasi-marital partnership, in which she managed the household, he managed the income (of course), she managed the expenditure (of course), he managed the development of the estate, she managed the entertainment of local society, and they both managed the amateur dramatics.

Mme Denis clearly played a central role in Voltaire's life, yet it is not easy to form a confident picture of the nature of their evolving personal relationship. In the 1740s, they had obviously had a passionate sexual encounter, lasting several years. After 1754 the question becomes more difficult to answer. The best evidence of their passion comes from their letters, during the times when they were younger and apart; during the times when they were older and together, there is a tantalising silence.

3

Geneva

1754–5

The essential point about Voltaire's stay in Prussia, and his humiliating exit, was that it marked a fundamental watershed in his life. From this moment on, he was about to embark on many years of permanent and unwilling exile. Yet against all expectations, these years of exile turned out to be the happiest and arguably the most productive of Voltaire's life. In 1753–4, he viewed the prospect of permanent disgrace, and banishment from his friends and the rest of the world, with deep anxiety. But when he finally embraced it, he found that he really liked the new life better than the old. Time and again, over the next twenty-five years, he declared to all and sundry that he was really happy, and that his happiness dated from his involuntary retirement.

For several months, in the autumn of 1754, Voltaire remained uncertain how to proceed or where to go. At one moment, he considered moving to somewhere just a few leagues outside Paris; at another, he wondered about Lausanne, and enquired about the property laws there; he also thought, about Lyon, or Burgundy, Bayreuth and even Gotha.

One important consideration was that he was still writing prolifically. Having suffered over many years from the buccaneering business methods of unscrupulous booksellers in distant parts of France and Europe, Voltaire was tempted by the idea of being able to live in a place where he could supervise the output of a respectable local publisher. This led him to consider Geneva as a possible resting place, since it was the home of the brothers Gabriel and Philibert Cramer, well-known and politically prominent printers. He may have felt even more favourably inclined towards Geneva after Philibert Cramer travelled to Colmar especially to see him, in August 1754, and offered to publish a complete edition of his works.[1] When he did move to Geneva, his friendly and enduring relationship with the Cramers was to be an essential and reassuring element in his productivity. It lasted for much of the rest of his life, until the winter of 1775–6, when they gave up their printing business.

Two developments in early December 1754 helped Voltaire to make up his mind in favour of Geneva. First, Mme Denis's younger sister, Marie-Elisabeth de Fontaine, told him that a certain baron de Prangins (whom she knew in Paris) was offering to let Voltaire and Mme Denis live in his château de Prangins, on the north shore of the Lac Léman, not far from Geneva, at least until Voltaire should have found a longer-term solution. Voltaire was clearly relieved: 'My dear niece, you render me the most essential service. I shall never forget it ... It was a great comfort for me, and it will be even greater if he comes to his estate in May, and stays a few days with us, until we shall have taken a suitable decision.'[2]

But it was on a trip to Lyon later that month that Voltaire decided, quite suddenly, that he would move to Geneva. His old friend the duc de Richelieu, great-nephew of the great Cardinal, had planned to travel south from Paris, and he summoned Voltaire to meet him in Lyon. Voltaire arrived at the Palais Royal inn on 15 November, ill and out of sorts. He grumbled to one of his friends: 'It is too much of a bad joke for a sick man to have to travel 100 leagues just to have a chat with M le maréchal de Richelieu. He never made any of his mistresses travel so far, though he always led them a fine dance.'[3]

During his stay in Lyon, Voltaire met Jean-Robert Tronchin, a prominent local banker and a member of one of Geneva's leading patrician families, and it was this meeting which finally seems to have made up Voltaire's mind. He and Tronchin obviously hit it off at once, for Voltaire immediately opened an account with him; and on 6 December 1754 he instructed his man of business in Paris to send £50,000 for deposit with the firm of Tronchin & Camp in Lyon. (Ami Camp was a cousin of Jean-Robert Tronchin and his junior partner in the Lyon bank.) Three days later Voltaire referred to Tronchin as 'my banker at Lyon', and described him as 'my friend and perfectly honest man'.[4] From this moment, Jean-Robert Tronchin became, and for the next few years remained, Voltaire's main banker and financial adviser.

On 10 December 1754, Voltaire and Mme Denis left Lyon for Geneva, where they arrived two days later. As a result of meeting Jean-Robert Tronchin in Lyon, Voltaire now met several other members of the Tronchin 'tribe', as he called them, who were all leading figures in Geneva's oligarchy. On the first night he was invited to stay with Jean-Robert's younger brother François Tronchin, one of the city's most influential politicians and a fellow theatre enthusiast, who hosted a select dinner for him and Mme Denis. The next day, he was invited to dinner by Théodore Tronchin, a cousin of Jean-Robert and one of the most celebrated doctors in Europe. It seems likely that it was the charm and sheer usefulness of the various Tronchins which finally clinched Voltaire's choice of Geneva.

In particular, Voltaire was attracted by the prospect of having a famous (and friendly) doctor within easy reach, since he suffered from chronic ill-health and regularly regaled his friends with morbid details of his symptoms. In 1754 he described his pitiful condition: '... white hair, colic, some hydropsy, and scurvy'.[5] The following year he had a new problem: 'It is rare that milk is suitable to somewhat dried-up temperaments like ours. It so happens that our stomachs make bad cheese which stays in our poor bodies, and which becomes an unbearable weight. It then goes to the head. The cursed animal functions don't work; and one is in a deplorable state.'[6]

The most regularly recurring complaint of Voltaire (and of Mme Denis) was constipation, and Voltaire, Mme Denis and Théodore Tronchin each seem to have had different ideas about how to deal with it. Sometimes Voltaire's preferred solution was rhubarb. In April 1755 he wrote to Jean-Robert: 'I beg you, Sir, to send half a pound of the best rhubarb that Chinese Tartary ever produced.'[7] But this did not go down well with Théodore. A month later Voltaire wrote again to Jean-Robert: 'Mme Denis and I send you again all our thanks. Everything you have sent has been approved, except the rhubarb. Your cousin the doctor gives such a strong preference to cassia, that it is quite impossible to speak of rhubarb in his presence.'[8]

In December 1755, Voltaire wrote to Théodore Tronchin:

Mme Denis is unwilling to purge herself without your instructions; but that is what she needs, for though she is doing well in the dining department, she is doing badly in the cloakroom department [i.e. the lavatory]; and for her constipation and her swelling she requires a certain very agreeable and very efficacious medicine that you have prescribed for her. This medicine was a beverage which she would take in three or four cupfuls. There you are, Sir, as regards Mme Denis. As for my particular case, I am faithful to cassia, manna and oil.

(He did not dare mention rhubarb to Théodore.)[9]

Voltaire did not linger in the city of Geneva: by 14 December 1754 he was already installed in the large château de Prangins, perched above the shores of Lac Léman, and he wrote to an acquaintance: 'Good heavens, how delightful all the Tronchins are; we are very glad to have got to know them. We were wonderfully received in Geneva; they were even kind enough to keep open the city gates for us until 6.30 p.m., which they normally never do.'[10] And to Théodore Tronchin he wrote: 'I do not know how I can thank all who bear the name of Tronchin, and especially you, Sir, who have been willing to help me with so many kindnesses. As soon as my stomach has recovered and I have some horses, I shall come to tell you how much you have attached me to you. Permit me to enclose a little note for that member of the Tronchin tribe who gave me indigestion with a good supper, whereas you were giving me good advice.'[11]

Voltaire was plainly delighted by his new friends, and it is hard to overstate the importance of the influential Tronchins in helping Voltaire settle down in Geneva. He quickly became as dependent on Jean-Robert for the management of his finances as on Théodore for the management of his health. More so, in some ways, since Voltaire treated Jean-Robert not just as his banker, but virtually as his personal mail-order supplier of anything and everything. In later years,

Voltaire's relations with the family were overshadowed when political conflict broke out between the social classes in Geneva. But for now, he was on good terms with all of them.

Voltaire was also delighted with Prangins, which he described as 'the most beautiful situation in the world, a magnificent château, with trout which weigh ten pounds, and I who weigh scarcely more, seeing that I am more skeletal and more moribund than ever.'[12] Mme Denis quickly set about sending for furniture and clothes, and hired an excellent cook and some other servants. One of these was a fifteen-year-old local boy, Jean-Louis Wagnière, whom Voltaire took on to help Collini in his secretarial tasks; he had well-formed handwriting, and a taste for literature, and Voltaire gave him Latin lessons. When Collini left Voltaire's service, in 1756, Wagnière took over as the principal secretary until the end of Voltaire's life, loyal to the point of unconditional fidelity.

Voltaire soon found that the château of Prangins was too large for him, and he detested the cold that came from the fierce winter winds which beat upon it. So, without waiting for the baron to visit him in May, he set about looking for a warmer and more permanent home of his own. It did not take him long; by 23 January he told Jean-Robert that he had found what he was looking for.

A few days ago I saw a country house near Geneva, which belongs to M. Mallet: it is the palace of a philosopher, with the gardens of Epicurus; it is a delicious retreat; and I think it would suit you one day. You know how difficult it is for a foreigner, and for a good Catholic like me, to acquire property in the land of the people of God [Protestant Geneva]. Your brother has suggested that I could be your concierge until my death. You would buy the estate with money which I would provide. I have offered 80,000 French livres; we could go as high as 90,000. On my death you could reimburse 50,000–60,000 livres to Mme Denis, my niece.[13]

In other words, Voltaire and the Tronchins were cooking up a plan, which the Tronchins cleared with their friends in the Geneva establishment, to help Voltaire get round the law which banned Catholics from owning property in the republic. Jean-Robert would be the front-man in buying the house, with money put up by Voltaire; when Voltaire gave up the property, or died, it would revert to Jean-Robert, in exchange for a partial reimbursement of the original purchase loan. Such a deal would be an excellent investment for the worldly Tronchins, not least because Voltaire was to spend substantial sums on improving the place.

Within a couple of weeks, Voltaire agreed to pay 87,200 livres for the villa, which was called Saint-Jean, and which he promptly renamed Les Délices; in the meantime, he had taken a lease on another country house, called Montriond, just outside Lausanne which, he said, would be warmer than Geneva in winter. This seems implausible. It is more likely that he had a premonition about the potential risks of being totally dependent on the benevolence of the authorities of one very small autocratic Calvinist state, and he therefore wanted to spread his risks between two Calvinist states. (He called Geneva *la république parvulissime*, meaning 'the tiniest republic'.*) In any case, Lausanne was less rigidly Calvinist, less autocratic and more worldly than Geneva, and therefore more relaxed about Voltaire's theatrical activities. Voltaire tended thereafter to divide his time, summer and winter, between Geneva and Lausanne; and when he later gave up his lease on Montriond, he took a lease, for a while, on another house in Lausanne, called Le Grand Chêne (The Great Oak).

Voltaire took possession of Les Délices early in March 1755. But even before moving in, he decided that he must make substantial changes to his new home. Writing to Nicolas-Claude Thieriot, one of his oldest Paris friends, to urge him to visit, he commented that Les Délices was 'a pretty house, whose gardens are comparable to the most beautiful near Paris. The great misfortune of this house, however, is that it was apparently built by a man who thought only of himself, and who completely forgot about any convenient little apartments for his friends. I shall immediately rectify this abominable defect.' He added that the excellent cook whom he had had at Prangins was unfortunately staying there. 'I don't really mind; but Mme Denis, who is very greedy, is making a capital fuss out of it.'[14]

*parvulissime: no doubt a satirical antitheseis to Venice, known as La Serenissima.

Immediately after moving into Les Délices, Voltaire rushed into a hectic programme for the improvement and remodelling of the house and garden. He was in a hurry to construct his new life, and he wrote to his friend Charles Augustin de Ferriol, the comte d'Argental:

Here we are, my nurse [i.e. Mme Denis] and I, on the shores of the Lake of Geneva and of the Rhône. At least I shall die in my own home. It will undoubtedly be very agreeable to live in this house, which is charming, convenient, spacious, and surrounded by delicious gardens; but I shall live without you, and that is really living in exile. Our place is costing us a lot of money and a lot of trouble. I speak to no one except masons, carpenters, gardeners. I am having my vines and trees pruned. I am busy making a chicken run.[15]

On the same day he wrote to a business friend of the Tronchins, asking for five cart-loads of wine for the twenty-odd servants and workmen, for a yellow marble chimney-piece, for a fine iron grille, and for some cloth samples promised to Mme Denis.[16]

As Voltaire pressed on with doing up Les Délices, his correspondence became most intense with Jean-Robert, as the official owner of the house, as his banker, and as his supplier of everything from wine and seeds and trees and medicines to horses and paint and soft furnishings. He wrote to him pretty well every week, sometimes several times a week; and sometimes he wrote to him from his bed, for he was frequently unwell. He wrote on 17 March, twelve days after moving in:

I have abused your kindness on the question of wine. I have found some very good stuff at Versoix which I could not help buying; it is excellent and ready to drink; it is the best Burgundy, and I shall use it to supplement the two barrels of Beaujolais which you are kindly sending me. I suppose the Beaujolais is rather for laying down. We can't yet receive anyone: the house is full of workmen of every kind. M. Mallet had friends who must have liked sleeping rough, and doing without a cloakroom. I am building a small extra wing; I am putting up grilles, I am knocking down walls, I am embellishing a house which one day you will be tempted to live in.[17]

But the turmoil in the house and gardens, and the lack of a cloak-room, did not deter Voltaire from writing to Henri-Louis Lekain, the leading actor of the Comédie Française in Paris, to urge him to visit: 'If you have the courage to come here, you must also have the courage to be ill-housed and ill-bedded; my Les Délices is upside down. You will see me acting as a mason, as a carpenter, and as a gardener; only you can restore me to my original trade [as a playwright]. You can easily travel from Lyon to Geneva by the public vehicles. My house is exactly at the gates of Geneva, and I shall send a carriage which will pick you up on the road.'[18]

Lekain did come to stay with Voltaire that spring, taking advantage of the Easter holidays, when the Paris theatres were closed; and he created a local sensation when he appeared before the upper crust of Geneva society in a performance of Voltaire's tragedy Zaïre. 'We brought tears to the eyes of almost the complete Geneva Council,' wrote Voltaire; 'I have never seen so many tears; never have the Calvinists been so tender.'[19]

When Lekain left Les Délices to return to Paris, he wanted to stop off at Lyon in order to put on some freelance performances there, and earn a bit extra to supplement his meagre earnings from the Comédie Française, which amounted to barely 2,000 livres a year.[20] But the actors at the Comédie Française were not free agents: if they wanted to travel, or to act anywhere else but at the Comédie Française or at Versailles, they first had to get permission from the court, represented in rotation by one of the six First Gentlemen of the King's Chamber. This year, it was the duc de Richelieu who was duty officer, and on this occasion he did give Lekain permission.[21] But his powers over the actors were not an empty formality. Several years later, when Lekain again visited Voltaire, and overstayed his leave of absence from the Comédie Française, Richelieu flew into a rage and threatened to have him imprisoned. Such was the subservience of the theatre as a low-caste activity, in a society obsessed with rank.

The paradox was that the standing of the actors was riddled with contradictions. On the one hand, the Comédie Française was a royal foundation, set up by Louis XIV in 1680. And since theatre was the main and most regular form of public and court entertainment, the leading actors were social stars, adulated by the theatre-going public and received in the highest society. In legal terms, however, the Comédie Française was subject to the whims of the court and of the officers of the court; worse, the actors were social and political pariahs, excommunicated, deprived of any citizens' rights, and denied Christian burial. Voltaire never ceased to protest against this injustice.

A quarter of a century earlier, the most celebrated leading actress of the Comédie Française had been Adrienne Lecouvreur. She had also, probably, for a while been Voltaire's mistress. When she died, in 1730, at the age of thirty-eight, her body was buried without ceremony on waste ground. Voltaire was outraged. He frequently contrasted the barbarity of the treatment meted out to actors and actresses in France, with the honour accorded to their counterparts in England: 'The English have even been reproach'd with paying too extravagant Honours to mere Merit,' he had written ironically in his *Letters Concerning the English Nation* (1734), 'and censured for interring the celebrated Actress Mrs Oldfield in Westminster Abbey. Some pretend that the English had paid her these great Funeral Honours, purposely to make us [i.e. the French] more strongly sensible of the Barbarity and Injustice which they object to us, for having buried *Mademoiselle Le Couvreur* ignominiously in the Fields'.[22]

Over the next few months, Voltaire poured out his shopping orders to Jean-Robert in an absolute torrent. On 28 March he wrote:

Many thanks for the lavender; I promise to have it planted in all the borders of your kitchen garden. I have already planted 250 trees; I have created some avenues for you, and I am building you a little wing. Monsieur your brother has just brought me some seeds; it was the nicest present you could give me. At this moment I am sowing your Egyptian onions; even the Israelites did not like them more than me. Please send me everything you can in the way of flowers and vegetables. The garden was completely bare; we must start from scratch; I am founding a second Carthage. I embrace you tenderly.[23]

On 5 April he ordered 'artichoke bulbs, and as much as possible of lavender, thyme, rosemary, mint, basil, rue, strawberry bushes, pinks, *thadicée,* balm, tarragon, *sariette,* burnet, sage, and hyssop to cleanse our sins etc, etc, etc'; and he added, in a postscript: 'It just occurs to Mme Denis and me that we should paint all your trellises a beautiful green, all your doors white, all your tiles red, and several doors a fine yellow. [Please send] 150 pounds of green paint, 300 pounds of walnut oil, 200 pounds of ceruse white lead paint, 50 pounds of blue paint, 50 pounds of yellow ochre, 50 pounds of red paint for the floors, and 50 pounds of yellow, and 80 pounds of strong glue.'[24]

On 18 April, he ordered 'six number 4 pins, six number 18 pins, a dozen number 9, and a dozen number 14; and then you will send me a dozen times to the devil'.[25] On 6 May, he ordered quantities of carpets, and eight wing armchairs plus another sixteen ordinary armchairs, plus 'a good little barrel of really green oil, which really smells of olives'.[26] Later that month, Mme Denis was complaining that he had failed to order six arm-covers in red morocco, and six in yellow morocco, for the twelve armchairs upholstered in cane, plus two corner commodes, either in rosewood, or in walnut, or in marquetry, new or old. 'Our Délices will have the finest chicken run in the world. When will you come to eat your chickens and your eggs?'[27]

In August he asked Jean-Robert to 'have the goodness to send me a beautiful backgammon board, for we must amuse our griefs. Letters only serve to poison our lives; in fact the only good letters are letters of credit.'[28]

All these improvements were costing a lot of money. In April, Voltaire said that he had on the payroll 'two master gardeners, 20 workmen, and 12 servants'; the number of gardeners later rose to four.[29] Four months later, in August, he told Jean-Robert that his 'so-called Délices has already cost me more than 120,000 livres',[30] i.e. more than 30,000 livres on top of the purchase price, which was itself probably way above fair market value. A few days later he recalculated what he had spent at 40,000 livres.[31]

But he pressed on regardless. In October, he asked Jean-Robert to send various components for a carriage which he was having built, plus '50 pounds of the best Marseille coffee, and about 50 bottles of that good red and white Muscat wine which you let us have once before'.[32] He explained later that the carriage would be lined to keep out the draughts, but the ornamentation would be kept simple, in deference to Geneva's sumptuary laws, which banned the use of gold and silver in decoration, except in the case of buttons and uniform braid.[33]

This question of the carriage decoration was symptomatic of the potential for friction between the austere principles of the Geneva republic, and Voltaire's very different interests and lifestyle. In principle, citizens were not allowed to travel in coaches unless they were ill or going on a journey, and no one was supposed to have a carriage pulled by as many as four horses. But Voltaire's establishment at Les Délices towards the end of 1755 included a good cook, many servants and four horses in the stables; by the following spring, it had expanded to six horses, four carriages, a coachman, a postillion, two servants, a valet, a French cook, a scullery boy and a secretary. Voltaire was quite unrepentant. 'My dear colleague,' he wrote to François Tronchin, 'it is true that I have the insolence to have six horses. Mme Denis claims that six horses are necessary [to travel between Les Délices and Montriond]. Personally, I should like to have twelve of them, to come and embrace you sooner.'[34] Voltaire's characteristic flippancy towards the local mores caused a good deal of sucking of teeth among the more conservative Genevans.

A more serious source of potential conflict between Voltaire and the Genevans was his love of theatre and amateur dramatics. No public theatre was permitted inside the city, and in principle, the Geneva Protestants disapproved of Voltaire's theatrical entertainments. In practice, he had already this year attracted most of the local political elite to a popular performance of his tragedy *Zaïre*; but that event had stirred up political controversy between the clergy and the laymen in the republic.

In the spring of 1755, Voltaire's addiction to the theatre threatened to bring him into open conflict with the religious authorities of Geneva. He was working on a new tragedy; this was his seventeenth,

L'Orphelin de la Chine (The Orphan of China). When he finished it, in the summer of that year, he sent his young Italian secretary, Collini, to Paris to deliver the text to his friend d'Argental, for performance at the Comédie Française.

D'Argental, a senior lawyer (*Conseiller*) in the Paris Parlement,* was one of Voltaire's oldest friends. They had both been educated at the Collège de Louis-le-Grand, though d'Argental was six years younger than Voltaire. But what really united them was a common passion for the theatre; in their youth they had both been in love with the celebrated actress Adrienne Lecouvreur; and in later life, Voltaire relied on d'Argental, not just as his chief adviser and critic on the drafts of his plays, but also as his essential go-between in relations with the Comédie Française. Their correspondence was remarkably warm; in his letters to d'Argental, of which he wrote more than a thousand, Voltaire regularly addressed him and his wife as 'my angels' (*mes anges*).

Voltaire told d'Argental that Collini would not mind making an extra copy of the play for him, even though he must by now be tired of making copies, and even though 'he is very busy with a pretty Italian girl with whom he has travelled to Paris'.[35] In August, *L'Orphelin de la Chine* was a great success at the Comédie Française, and Voltaire started rehearsals for his own staging of the play at Les Délices, with the theatre-mad François Tronchin reading the lead part rather well.

But he soon heard echoes of disapproval from the Protestant clergy in Geneva, and he hesitated to risk local controversy. In the end he wrote to Collini: 'I think we shall not put it on. It seemed to me that our plan was upsetting the priests, and I declared that, not wanting to upset anyone, I would not perform it. Come home when you are tired of pleasures, of women, and of Paris.'[36] Voltaire was an indulgent and affectionate employer, and fond of Collini. But Collini was evidently not yet tired of pleasures, of women, or of Paris, for he did not come home until a month later.

*The French Parlements were not parliaments like the English Houses of Parliament, but law-courts with the double function of trying cases and enacting the King's decrees.

Voltaire's cancellation of his production of *L'Orphelin de la Chine* was just a tactical withdrawal, not a strategic retreat. The performance of *Zaïre* earlier that spring had been put on in amateur conditions in a large salon at Les Délices; but that summer, he and Mme Denis decided that they would build a proper small theatre.

In August 1755, five months after moving in, he wrote to his old friend Thieriot in Paris: 'You would find my retreat charming in summer. In winter one must not leave the fireside; but then, all places are the same when it freezes. But on fine days I do not know anything to compare with my situation. I did not know this new pleasure, nor that of sowing, planting and building. I would like to have you in this little corner of the earth, where I am very happy.'[37]

One immediate reason for his happiness was the pleasure he was getting from doing up Les Délices. In May 1756, he wrote from Berne to Collini at Les Délices: 'Mr Loup must get in some large gravel, which must be spread and rolled from the paving of the court-yard right up to the grille which leads to the paths to the vines. The gardeners should already have made two square lawns, on the right and left of this sandy path, while leaving three feet to be sanded at the two extremities of these lawns, as I had ordered. The servants must be sure to shake the chestnut trees, to bring down the cockchafers, and feed them to the chickens.'*[38]

One of the most frequent visitors to Les Délices over the years was Marie-Elisabeth Fontaine, the younger widowed sister of Mme Denis who lived in Paris. Voltaire was obviously very fond of her, and never happier then when he could gather all his family round him. He particularly admired Marie-Elisabeth's drawings, for which she evidently had some talent, and felt concern at her regular bouts of ill-health. But there is a curious question mark over Voltaire's relationship with her. In January 1756 he wrote to discuss the symptoms of her ill-health, for which he had asked Théodore

---

*The word Voltaire uses for 'lawn' in this letter is *boulingrin*, a Frenchified transliteration of 'bowling green'; it has been an officially recognised French word since 1663. Then, as now, French garden designers gave priority to gravel over grass; but when they used grass, the implied reference was England. The irony is that the French play *boules*, which does not need grass, but not bowls, which does.

Tronchin to prescribe some suitable treatment; and he concluded his letter: 'Adieu, my dear niece, try to come and see us, with bouncy tits and a big bum [*avec des tétons rebondis et un gros cul*].'[39] In March he wrote again about her health, and declared that Théodore Tronchin would be 'unworthy of his reputation, if he does not give you a bum and tits'. Moreover, he reverted to the subject again at the end of his letter: 'I embrace you tenderly, you and yours, and I recommend a bum and tits.'[40] Voltaire does not use this kind of language in writing to any other woman, except of course to Mme Denis, and the suggestiveness of the words fairly leaps off the page.

On 8 June Marie-Elisabeth came to stay at Les Délices, with her lover and future second husband, the marquis de Florian, and immediately found fault with the arrangements. Voltaire wrote to Jean-Robert in mock dismay: 'Mme Fontaine rightly finds my house ill-furnished. *O Heavens!*, she says; *No bidets!* She is not yet accustomed to the severe and unclean customs of the city of Calvin. Please be so good, my dear correspondent, to add to your deliveries three bidets with all the fittings. Such importunate requests! Candelabra with silver hatching, coffee, sugar, candles, gilt nails, and then bidets on top!'[41] (The two candelabra were a present for Théodore Tronchin.)

By mischance, Mme Fontaine's arrival was followed almost immediately by the sacking of Collini. He had gone to greet the new visitors, when a servant girl happened (?) to find in his room a letter which contained mocking references to Mme Denis, in which he described her as 'the louche working-woman'. The letter was shown to Mme Denis and she demanded, and got, Collini's immediate dismissal. He left Geneva four days later, on 12 June, and was succeeded by his assistant, Jean-Louis Wagnière. It seems that there was always an underlying triangular tension between Mme Denis and Voltaire's various secretaries; Voltaire spent enormously long hours dictating, at any time of day or night, which meant that there was an extraordinary intimacy between him and his secretaries, of which Mme Denis may well have been jealous.

One consequence of all the improvements to Les Délices, coupled with Voltaire's international renown and his generous hospitality, was that his home became, in short order, the place that everyone, apart from the most austere clerics, wanted to visit. Opinion in Geneva was deeply divided about Voltaire. Some of the conservatives urgently wished that he had gone to live elsewhere; some of the more worldly and cultivated laymen were fascinated by his brilliance, intrigued by his provocative liberalism, and seduced by the lavishness of his hospitality. Even the clergy were split; the most austere were hostile; but Voltaire counted quite a few pastors among his friends and frequent visitors. Lausanne was more open-minded than Geneva, with its own theatre for amateur dramatics; and some of the pastors even took part in Voltaire's theatrical entertainments there. In March 1757 he wrote to Jacob Vernes, one of the most enlightened Protestant pastors in Geneva, and a good friend: 'Yesterday we were honoured with the presence of 12 preachers, who brought with them all their novices. Moreover, we had two preachers who played the violin very well in the orchestra. Piety is not at all the enemy of honest pleasures.'[42]

Voltaire's visitors came not only from Geneva and Lausanne, but from far and wide. In April, he told Richelieu that he was visited every day by Englishmen,[43] and he added: 'I have never seen them so polite. I think they owe it all to you',[44] a sly allusion to the fact that the maréchal de Richelieu had just inflicted a serious naval defeat on the English at Minorca, at the start of the Seven Years War (1756–63). In September he wrote to his old friend d'Argental: 'I haven't a moment to myself. The long illness of Mme de Fontaine, and my own sufferings, take up at least half the day. The rest of the time has to be given to the processions of the curious who come from Lyon, from Geneva, from Savoy, from Switzerland, and even from Paris. Almost every day, I have seven or eight people come to have dinner with me.'[45] (Geneva at this time was an independent republic; it had links to Switzerland, which included Berne, Zurich and Lausanne, but did not become part of it until 1815.)

Visitors to Les Délices were not always people whom Voltaire had invited, far from it; in many cases they just invited themselves; but he was ready to take it in good part, provided he was not always compelled to entertain them himself. As he wrote to a Paris friend in July: 'The best society, of wise and enlightened people, come here almost every day, without ever bothering me. There are many English among them, and they seem more impressed by your [i.e. the French] government than by their own.'[46] The following spring (1757) he wrote that he had just put on the tragedy *Fanime* in his little theatre at Montriond: 'I have never seen so many tears. We have about 200 spectators, who are quite the equal of the people in the stalls in Paris, for they listen only to their hearts, have much wit, and have nothing to do with cabals'.[47] Some years later, when he was older and easily tired, he closed his doors against the tide of importunate voyeurs and Grand Tourists. But for the moment, he was flattered and comforted in his exile by the knowledge that, if he could not go to them, other people would come to him.

In short, Voltaire was having a wonderful time in his new home. He moaned and groaned and complained about his health, but it was mostly an act, pure façade. Gradually, and quite unexpectedly, he realised that he was enjoying real happiness, perhaps for the first time in his life.

Candide *and the English Admiral*

1753–9

Scarcely had Voltaire returned to France from Potsdam than he became involved in the *Encyclopédie, ou Dictionnaire Raisonné des Sciences, des Arts et des Métiers* (Analytical Dictionary of Sciences, Arts and Crafts). It had started out in 1745 as a project by André Le Breton, the King's printer, for a translation of the English *Cyclopaedia* of Ephraim Chambers, published in 1728. Within a couple of years, however, it had evolved into a plan for a wholly original and independent encyclopaedia in French, to chart the state of knowledge of the modern world.

The prospectus for this new *Encyclopédie* was published in 1750. It promised a work of eight volumes of text and two volumes of plates, to be jointly edited by two leading young French intellectuals, Denis Diderot and Jean Le Rond d'Alembert. It invited subscriptions of £60 in advance, followed by £280 on delivery; non-subscribers would be charged £25 per volume of text, and £172 for the two volumes of plates. (Over the years the project swelled inordinately: when it reached completion in 1772, there were seventeen volumes of text and eleven volumes of plates.)

Most people tend to think of it as 'Diderot's *Encyclopédie*', with some reason: Denis Diderot was involved in the editing of it from start to finish, whereas Jean Le Rond d'Alembert gave up less than halfway through. Since then, Diderot's name has remained better known, as a writer, philosopher and art critic, and his works are still read; whereas d'Alembert, though highly literate (he translated the Roman historian Tacitus), was by profession a mathematician and physicist, and his writings are less well known today. In the early years of the *Encyclopédie*, however, the two men were comparably brilliant and although the title page of the first volume seemed to indicate that Diderot was the senior editor, it was d'Alembert who wrote the eighty-six-page introduction, or *Discours Préliminaire*, setting out the scope and terms of reference of this vast new enterprise.

In worldly terms, d'Alembert enjoyed a more spectacular public career than Diderot: he had been a member of the prestigious Académie des Sciences since 1741, when he was twenty-four; in 1754, at the early age of thirty-seven, he was elected to the Académie Française, and thus became a colleague of Voltaire's as one of the forty members, or so-called *immortels*; and in 1772 he was appointed *secrétaire perpetuel* of the Académie. Diderot, by contrast, remained for many years largely shackled to the treadmill of the *Encyclopédie*, and never achieved the coveted membership of the Académie Française, even though Voltaire (and others) endorsed his claim.

Voltaire was obviously bound to be interested in the *Encyclopédie*, and Diderot and d'Alembert were both keen to recruit this international intellectual celebrity to their cause. By the time the prospectus appeared in 1750, however, Voltaire was already on his way to his new position as Chamberlain to Frederick the Great, and therefore not available to take part; and the first three volumes were published in 1751–3, while he was away in Potsdam. In May 1754, however, after Voltaire's return, d'Alembert contacted him in Alsace and asked if he would like to contribute. Voltaire immediately agreed, and his participation in the project was announced in the fourth volume of the *Encyclopédie*, which appeared later that year.

The *Encyclopédie* is often considered a centrepiece of the French Enlightenment or *Lumières*, and is consequently associated with the notion of *philosophie* or *les philosophes*. However, the word '*philosophie*' in the context of the French Enlightenment does not necessarily correspond with the word 'philosophy' as we understand it in English today, and it certainly did not necessarily imply a single and fully worked-out system of thought. Different *philosophes* had very different beliefs: some were atheists; Voltaire was not. What the *philosophes* mostly had in common was a belief in rationality and science. Voltaire denied the value of metaphysics, which he regarded as a subject about which we could know nothing; as far as he was concerned, the central concerns of *philosophie*, as he defined them in his *Dictionnaire Philosophique*, were with observable science, with reason, and not least with morality.[1]

D'Alembert's approach to Voltaire established a precedent for their relationship in the years to come. He had long known Voltaire and many of those in his literary and intellectual circle, including Mme du Châtelet, Voltaire's former mistress and herself a serious mathematician; he also knew, and detested, Voltaire's old friend Mme du Deffand, the prominent literary hostess, whose companion, Julie de Lespinasse, was the love of his life. There are a few letters between Voltaire and Diderot, but they are respectful and wary rather than warm or spontaneous; Voltaire and Diderot admired each other, but in general the two men did not really relate, neither did they ever meet, until right at the end of Voltaire's life, when Diderot probably called on him in Paris, once or possibly twice. Between Voltaire and d'Alembert, however, there was an instinctive rapport; d'Alembert became, not just Voltaire's main contact with the *Encyclopédie*, or just his closest ally in the struggle of the *philosophes* in favour of reason and against the forces of darkness, but also one of his warmest friends.

It is possible that Voltaire may have felt a special personal bond with his young colleague, in as much as d'Alembert was illegitimate, and Voltaire suspected the same of himself. As was the custom with illegitimate children at the time, d'Alembert's surname, 'Le Rond', came from the name of the church, Saint-Jean-Le-Rond, where he had been abandoned in infancy; while 'd'Alembert', like 'Voltaire', was an assumed name.

As soon as Voltaire agreed to contribute to the *Encyclopédie*, d'Alembert assigned him twenty-five articles, and Voltaire set to work with a will, though he warned the Cramers, his publishers, that this work on the *Encyclopédie* would delay his other writing.[2] Voltaire's attitude to the *Encyclopédie* was always deeply serious and respectful: he described it as 'a great and immortal edifice'.[3] But he was surprisingly unassuming about his own contributions, and considering his international eminence, he accepted without demur that these were liable to be edited, altered or rejected by those whose task it was. He complained that the editors seemed to want articles which were much too wordy, whereas he would prefer items that were as succinct as possible, with short definitions and a few examples. 'I'm sorry that they want such long articles. But I shall make the article *Literature* as boringly useless as they could wish. If I were on the spot, I would willingly be an artisan in their workshop.'[4]

Characteristically, he could not resist making little jokes about his articles. Towards the end of 1755, he wrote to d'Alembert: 'I shall send you my ideas, and you will rectify them as you see fit. I should gladly take on *History*, and I think I could include fairly interesting things in it. As for *Fornication*, I am all the more entitled to develop this subject, in that I am unfortunately entirely disinterested. A propos the article *Fornication*, there was another *F* which has a certain merit, but I do not think it is up to me to speak of it.'[5] (*Foutre* (fuck) was presumably what he meant; with close friends, Voltaire was much given to ribald remarks.)

In late December 1755, he sent a further batch of articles to d'Alembert: 'Here is *Figured*, corrected; *Force*, of which you will take what you want; *Favour* ditto; *Frankness* and *Flowers* ditto. I add *Fornication*; I can neither do nor say much on this word. I shall shortly send you the history of the *Flagellants*.'[6] And indeed, Voltaire's submission for Fornication was very short: d'Alembert supplemented it with a much longer appendix of his own; the combined entry makes mordant fun of two of Voltaire's favourite targets, Catholic theologians and the ancient Hebrews.

Voltaire's frequent denunciations of the barbarity of the ancient Israelites are sometimes confused with his anti-Semitism. Voltaire's anti-Semitism is surprising, and sad, considering that he was in so many respects rational and free from vulgar prejudices. But it was undeniable: he frequently referred to Jews as avaricious, calculating, money-mad. In 1765, he described a grasping Geneva businessman as 'more Jew than Calvinist'.[7] By contrast, his denunciations of the ancient Hebrews were really indirect attacks on the superstitions of the Old Testament precursors of Christianity, and thus on the sources of Christianity itself. In his search for such subversive weapons to attack Christianity, Voltaire acquired an encyclopaedic knowledge of the Bible.

Voltaire's serenity in his new-found Geneva retirement was brutally, if briefly, shattered towards the end of 1755 by the news of the massive earthquake which, on 1 November, had destroyed the city of Lisbon, killing around 30,000 people. This was one of the most violent earthquakes of modern history; and it marked a turning point in Voltaire's philosophic and moral outlook.

The Lisbon earthquake set off a major debate across Europe on the question of the problem of evil: if God was good, how could He permit such a catastrophe? It may be hard for us, today, to grasp the intensity of that debate. Nowadays, we are aware that earthquakes are natural phenomena, which occur quite frequently, and almost predictably, in certain parts of the world, for scientifically explicable reasons. But science was much less developed in the eighteenth century, and the question of how to reconcile God and science was one of the major philosophical issues of the day.

The seventeenth-century German mathematician and polymath philosopher Gottfried Wilhelm Leibniz (1646–1716) had tried to produce an answer to the problem of evil, as well as a resolution of the apparent antithesis between God and science, by arguing that, since God was good, this must be the best of all possible worlds; an argument that was subsequently simplified and popularised by Alexander Pope in his *Essay on Man*: 'Whatever is, is right.'[8]

Because of the widespread international controversy precipitated by the Lisbon earthquake, prompting a wave of commentaries by hundreds of authors, the world waited impatiently for Voltaire to pronounce. He only learned of the earthquake with certainty on 23 November 1755 and at first he thought there had been 100,000 casualties. By the first week of December, he had written his *Poème sur le Désastre de Lisbonne*, consisting of a preface and 234 alexandrine verses.

Many people expected that he would use the earthquake as a pretext to compose an anti-religious diatribe, and to attack those pietists who claimed that the disaster was a punishment from God for man's wickedness, and who therefore preached repentance. In fact, Voltaire devoted just six lines to the question of revealed religion. The main burden of his *Poème* was an attack on the fashionable and pseudo-rational philosophy of Leibniz, which had become popular under the neologism 'optimism'.

The day after he learned the news, Voltaire wrote to Jean-Robert Tronchin, his banker in Lyon: 'There, Sir, was a really cruel physical event. One would be quite embarrassed to guess how the laws of movement bring about such frightful disasters in the *best of all possible worlds.*' And to another friend, a Protestant pastor in Berne, he wrote: 'You know about the horrible events at Lisbon, Seville and Cadiz. There is a terrible argument against *optimism.*'[9]

The reader will recognise here a pre-echo of the recurrent theme in the satirical tale *Candide*, which Voltaire was to write a few years later, with its ironic ridicule of Panglossian 'optimism'.

Yet even the shocking tragedy of the Lisbon earthquake could not really spoil Voltaire's new-found happiness. In 1756 he wrote to his old Paris friend Nicolas-Claude Thieriot: 'If I live in opulence, it is only for other people, for thus I defy ill-fortune, and enjoy a very pleasant and very free situation, which I owe only to myself. When I have spoken, in verse, about the sufferings of my fellow human beings [i.e. in the *Poème* on the Lisbon earthquake], it was purely out of generosity; for apart from my failing health, I am so happy that I am ashamed of it.'[10]

Nevertheless, despite his irrepressible happiness, the Lisbon earthquake and the *Poème* it inspired are more significant in Voltaire's development than just as a literary pre-echo of a later masterpiece; they represent a milestone in the evolution of his sensibility and his attitude to human suffering. From this moment on, Voltaire became increasingly concerned with the problem of evil, and with the allied problem of man's inhumanity to man. The Lisbon earthquake can even be seen as a preparation for his later preoccupation with human rights.

But philosophy had to coexist with everyday life, and Voltaire could not remain solemn for long. Shortly after finishing his *Poème,* he wrote to Jean-Robert: 'You will have heard that we too have been honoured with a small earthquake. It cost us a broken bottle of Muscat wine which fell from a table. We were lucky to get off so lightly. But while waiting for the end of the world, I am again forced to importune you, Sir, for some of the knick-knacks of this life. Our saddler had forgotten to ask you for 10 yards of large braid, similar to the sample I enclose. And the insatiable Mme Denis swears that you will not refuse her four thousand gilt nails for the armchairs. It seems to me that we need rather a lot of things to live in a land of heretics."[11]

In the summer of 1756, d'Alembert paid a visit to Voltaire at Les Délices. The general reason for his visit was to cement relations with a fellow member of the Académie Française and fellow spirit of the Enlightenment, as well as to discuss Voltaire's collaboration with the *Encyclopédie*. But his more specific and immediate purpose was to research and write (with Voltaire's help) an article about Geneva for the *Encyclopédie*. It turned out to be a momentous event, a turning-point both in the battle between the *philosophes* of the Enlightenment and the forces of obscurantism which opposed it, and in Voltaire's relations with the Geneva authorities.

It was with impatience that Voltaire awaited d'Alembert's arrival on 10 August 1756. D'Alembert stayed for three weeks, until 30 August, and met many people in Geneva, including some open-minded Protestant pastors; and of course he was also heavily briefed by Voltaire himself. But when d'Alembert's article *Genève* appeared in November of the following year (1757), in the next published volume of the *Encyclopédie*, it caused a major scandal in Geneva, as well as in Paris. For although the article was generally compliment-ary on Geneva's political and social arrangements, it detonated two explosive controversies. The first came from d'Alembert's interfering recommendation that the Genevans should give up their Calvinist ban on theatres and theatre-going. As we have seen, some Genevans were only too ready to enjoy and even take part in Voltaire's private theatricals; but the clerics did not care to be lectured on morals by an outsider.

The second problem was much more serious; it was d'Alembert's suggestion that, while Geneva's Protestants may have believed in

God, many of them did not believe in the divinity of Jesus Christ. The clear and scandalous implication was that the Genevans were not really Christians at all, but just Socinian heretics or even deists.* The most orthodox representatives of Genevan society found d'Alembert's insinuation offensive, and they blamed Voltaire for stirring up subversive trouble; they were all the more incensed because he was suspected by some of being an atheist.

D'Alembert's article *Genève* had wider consequences, and ones that were especially serious for the fraternity of the *philosophes* and for the whole *Encyclopédie* project. For in Paris, the most orthodox representatives of the *ancien régime* were even more outraged than the Genevans, since they took d'Alembert's article to be an attack, not just on the Christianity of Protestantism, but on Christianity in general; by extension, they concluded that the article was confirmation that the *Encyclopédie*, under the cloak of science and rationalism, was really part of a campaign against true religion. From this moment on, there was a deep and unbridgeable rift between the *ancien régime* and the *philosophes* of the *Encyclopédie*.

In November 1756, however, the explosion was still a year away, and Voltaire, comfortably secure and unaware in his lakeside retreat, was still living life to the full. He tried to interest Richelieu in his idea for a battlefield tank, but failed;[12] he later hawked the same idea to Frederick and to Catherine the Great, with equally little success. He ordered more supplies from Jean-Robert Tronchin: wine, candles, sugar, coffee, paper, and two wheeled stoves because two of the fireplaces at Les Délices smoked;[13] then Beaujolais, lavender water, Parmesan cheese, six pounds of chocolate, and two dish warmers; then a large quantity of sugar.[14] He agreed that Jean-Robert should pay him an interest rate of 4 per cent on his savings account balance of £400,000; and that for running expenses, he should keep a current account balance of £20,000.[15]

All this while Voltaire was busily writing and sending d'Alembert contributions to the *Encyclopédie* – ten articles, from *Gazette* to

*After Lelio Socini, a sixteenth-century Italian Protestant, who denied the Trinity and the divinity of Christ.

Grave – and still trying to persuade him that the editors should impose brevity and succinctness on the contributors: 'I see how difficult it is to be both short and full, to discern nuances, to say nothing too much, but leave nothing out. The most general complaint is the length of the monologues; we need method, truth, definitions, examples; one would wish each article to be treated like those written by you and M. Diderot.'[16]

At the turn of the year, however, Voltaire's jolly and industrious little retreat was shaken by two echoes of distant gunfire. First, on 5 January 1757, Robert François Damiens, a lowly servant in the Paris Parlement, attacked Louis XV with a penknife at Versailles, inflicting a superficial wound on his ribcage; on 2 March he was condemned to a regicide's death; and on 28 March he was executed in circumstances of unspeakable horror.

Second, on 27 January the English admiral John Byng was condemned to death by court martial for having been worsted in a naval engagement by the French. Voltaire's interest in John Byng went back to 1726–8, the years of his first exile, in England, when he was in his early thirties and Byng in his early twenties. There he met both John Byng, at the time a young naval captain, and his father, Admiral George Byng, who was then First Lord of the Admiralty, with the title Viscount Torrington.[17] Now, at the start of the Seven Years War in 1756, John Byng was promoted to admiral, and sent with a poorly equipped squadron to relieve the English-held fortress of Port Mahón on the island of Minorca, which was being threatened with a blockade by a French fleet. This was the first major engagement of the war, and Voltaire followed events closely, not least because his friend the duc de Richelieu was the army commander in the French blockading force.

In April he wrote to Richelieu that he could not imagine that the English squadron would reach Minorca in time to head off the French expedition, and in June he went further: 'Take Port Mahón, my hero, I've got money on it. Do you know that a mad Englishman is offering odds of twenty to one that you will be taken prisoner to England in less than four months? I am sending an order to London, to lay out twenty guineas against this extravagant fellow, and I hope to make four hundred pounds sterling, with which I shall give a fine fireworks display.'[18]

In fact, even as he wrote, the story was already over. Byng had reached Minorca on 19 May and was defeated by the French fleet the following day. On his return to England, Byng was relieved of his command and imprisoned at Greenwich. He was later charged with cowardice. Minorca fell to Richelieu on 28 June.

On 4 December 1756, a new English government was formed under William Pitt. Four days later his brother, Thomas Pitt, visited Voltaire at Les Délices, and told him about the trial which was due to open later that month. Thomas Pitt happened to be a friend of Byng, but the Pitts also had a political motive for supporting his cause. Public opinion had been inflamed by the defeat at Minorca, and this had contributed to the fall of the previous government under the duke of Newcastle. If Byng could be exonerated, the blame for the defeat would shift to Newcastle.

On 20 December, Voltaire wrote to Richelieu: 'I said to him [Thomas Pitt] that you had told me that this sailor was not at fault, and that he had done what he could. He replied that a word from you could exonerate him, and that if I would transcribe the favourable words that you wrote about Byng, he would send them to England. I ask your permission.'[19]

Richelieu gave his permission, and his testimonial was wholly favourable: 'All the manoeuvres of Admiral Byng were admirable, according to comments of all our sailors. There has never been a more glaring injustice than that which is threatening Admiral Byng.'[20] It was duly sent to Byng in England. Théodore Tronchin had warned Voltaire that a French testimonial risked doing more harm than good; it is hard to know if he was right. Byng was acquitted of cowardice or disaffection, but found guilty of neglect of duty and condemned to death. On 14 March he was shot by a firing squad in Portsmouth harbour on the deck of HMS *Monarque*. Before he died, Byng wrote Voltaire a letter of thanks, in which he described Richelieu as 'so generous a soldier' and which his sister forwarded to Les Délices.[21]

Two footnotes need to be added to this account of the Byng case.

The first is that the fall of Minorca was the exception which proved the rule: after it, the English did much better and the French much worse. The English achieved superiority at sea, and by the end of the Seven Years War had secured a major consolidation and expansion of their empire, in India and North America, mainly at the expense of France. Unfortunately, England's gain was Voltaire's loss. Voltaire had invested substantial sums in French overseas trade via the brothers Gilly at Cadiz, notably in the Compagnie des Indes, and was earning vast profits in return. In 1756, for example, he sent Jean-Robert five instalments of income from Cadiz, four of which totalled £34,893; for the fifth instalment, he does not state the sum, so the total for the year was even more. But in 1757 he complained ceaselessly about his losses: 'the English have taken a ship'; 'another big ship taken'; 'I have lost a lot'; 'the English have taken 25 merchant ships'.[22] As a result, his earnings from Cadiz that year fell to £14,752, plus one small unidentified sum. In 1758 it got worse: no receipts until April, and then only for £600.[23]

The second footnote is that, even though Voltaire had failed to save the life of John Byng, he immortalised his death for ever in the pages of *Candide*, written the following year and published to massive international acclaim in 1759:

As they talked, they docked in Portsmouth; a multitude of people covered the shore, and looked attentively at a fairly large man who was on his knees, his eyes blindfolded, on the deck of one of the vessels of the fleet; four soldiers, posted opposite this man, each fired three balls into his skull as peacefully as possible, and all the audience went home extremely satisfied. *'What is all this?'* said Candide, *'and what devil is at work?'* He asked who was the large man, who had just been killed with such ceremony. *'It is an admiral,'* they replied. *'But why kill this admiral?'* *'It is,'* they told him, *'because he has not had enough people killed; he gave battle to a French admiral, and people thought he had not got close enough to him.'* *'But,'* said Candide, *'the French admiral was just as far from the English admiral, as he was from him.'* *'That is incontestable,'* they replied; *'but in this country it is good to kill an admiral from time to time to encourage the others.'* (*pour encourager les autres*).[24]

In the case of Robert François Damiens's knife attack on Louis XV, Voltaire's immediate reactions were violent, punitive and reationary. This is what makes them worth examining. They are interesting for the light they shed on the contrast with the later development of his thinking on the problems of crime and punishment.

The attack took place in the courtyard of the palace of Versailles, just as the King was about to get into his carriage to go to the Trianon. The King was accompanied by the Dauphin, and surrounded by a number of senior officers. It was around six o'clock in the evening, the light had faded, and it was extremely cold; all were wearing heavy greatcoats. Damiens managed to squeeze through the surrounding officers and guards, and drew a spring knife which had a long blade on one side, and a small four-inch penknife blade on the other. He lunged at the King with the small blade, inflicting a minor superficial wound. Some scholars say the King was wounded in the arm; according to Voltaire, he was wounded near the fifth rib. Damiens put the knife back in his pocket, and just stood there. The King felt the blow, and turned round. Seeing the unknown man, who was conspicuous because he was still wearing his hat, he said: 'This is the man who struck me. Arrest him, but do him no harm.'[25]

When Voltaire heard of the attack eight days later, he immediately assumed that it had been inspired by some fanatical Catholic sect. He wrote to a friend: 'Did you think to see such crimes in our enlightened time? Was it Jansenism which produced this monster? Or Molinism?* I thought these two sects were just ridiculous, yet like the others they spread the most sacred blood.'[26] And to Thieriot: 'Enlightened times will only enlighten a small number of honest men; the common people will always be fanatical.'[27]

It may seem that Voltaire was leaping to conclusions on the basis of little or no evidence; and of course he was. His excuse was that

*Jansenism was a revivalist and ascetic Catholic sect, deriving from the teachings of the Dutch theologian Cornelius Jansenius (1585–1638). Molinism was a Jesuit sect derived from the teachings of the Spanish Jesuit Luis Molina (1536–1600). These two sects were in permanent conflict with each other in France at this time, ostensibly over their differing teachings on divine grace, in reality as a struggle for influence in the *ancien régime*.

Henri III and Henri IV had both been assassinated by religious fanatics, and that it was the murder of Henri IV which had put paid to that King's efforts to end the long-drawn-out wars of religion between Catholics and Protestants in France. Throughout his life, Voltaire was haunted by the images of the horrors of the Saint Bartholomew's Day massacre, of 24 August 1572, in which thousands of Protestants were killed in Paris and many thousands more in the provinces in succeeding weeks.

By now Voltaire was referring to Damiens as 'a mad dog', 'a criminal idiot' and 'a crazy monster'. Three days later, Mme Denis wrote, more sinisterly: 'It is highly desirable that they make this monster talk. He is certainly a mad fanatic, but if he has accomplices, it is essential to know who they are.'[28] In other words, she (and perhaps Voltaire as well) expected and wanted Damiens to be tortured. Torture was systematically used in the French judicial system to secure confessions and/or to discover the names of accomplices. As Voltaire's thinking evolved in later years, he came to have serious reservations about the use of torture; though in fact he never ruled it out absolutely.

Needless to say, Damiens was tortured. He revealed nothing comprehensible about his motives; he said the strangest things about the King, God and the Parlement; he probably had no rational motives. He revealed nothing about his accomplices either; almost certainly he had had none. In fact, he was obviously unbalanced, if not certifiably deranged. As Voltaire said: 'All his replies were those of a madman, like his actions'.[29] Nevertheless, Damiens was condemned to die a regicide's death.

Voltaire did not, of course, himself witness the execution, which took place on 28 March 1757, but here is the account which he published over a decade later in his *Histoire du Parlement de Paris*.

After the reading out of the sentence, in the presence of five princes of the blood, twenty-two dukes and peers, twelve senior judges, seven honorary judges, four senior lawyers [*maîtres des requêtes*], and nineteen judges of the Grand Chamber, he was put to the question [i.e. torture] by wedges forced between the knees [and the other joints] and two planks tied together.

The preparation of the torture of this miserable creature, and of his execution, was accompanied by an unprecedented ceremony and solemnity. A space of a hundred feet square had been surrounded by palisades, right up to the great door of the Hôtel de Ville. This space was surrounded, inside and out, by all the police of Paris. The French Guards occupied all the avenues, and the Swiss Guards were spread throughout the city.

The prisoner was placed, around five o'clock, on a scaffold eight and a half feet square. They tied him with heavy cords held by iron rings which immobilised his arms and his thighs. They started by burning his hand in a brazier filled with burning sulphur. Then they took red-hot pincers, and tore at his flesh on his arms, his thighs and his chest. They poured molten lead and pitch and boiling oil on all his wounds. These tortures dragged from him the most frightful screams.

Four vigorous horses, whipped on by four executioners' assistants, pulled with cords on the bleeding and flaming wounds of the [limbs of the] patient; these pullings lasted an hour. His limbs stretched, but did not part. The executioners finally cut some muscles. His limbs parted one after the other. Damiens, having lost two legs and an arm, was still breathing, and did not expire until his other arm was separated from his bleeding trunk. The limbs and the trunk were thrown on a pyre which had been prepared ten feet from the scaffold.[30]

The executions of Byng and Damiens were obviously two very different events, but together they constituted a moment which was to mark the beginning of a fundamental change in Voltaire's outlook on life. We can see this particularly clearly because his reactions to them were so totally different; and because he was obviously not yet interested in those principles of human rights which were to claim so much of his attention in later years.

In the case of Byng, he recognised the claims of a friend, or at least of a personal acquaintance; and he made efforts to intervene, by letter and intermediary, to prevent sentence and execution. In some sense, therefore, his campaign on behalf of Byng, though more personal than principled, can be seen as a precursor of his later human rights campaigns.

In the case of Damiens, by contrast, Voltaire's immediate reaction was somewhere between indifference and self-righteous indignation; he pigeonholed Damiens as a dangerous religious fanatic and a threat to law and order, and attributed to him the fanaticism of the ultra-churchmen. He saw clearly that Damiens was in some sense deranged, if not actually insane; but he did not discuss whether such a man could be responsible for his acts. And he expressed no revulsion at the frightful tortures inflicted on Damiens in the name of expiation and the protection of the sacred monarchy. In this case, Voltaire's concern was not with justice, or penal reform, nor whether the use of torture was justifiable, but only with the stability of the State.

Readers familiar with Michel Foucault's *Discipline and Punish*[31] will recall that it opens with a shocking chapter describing the execution of Damiens. In some ways it is even more gruelling than the Voltaire passage just quoted, because it is so much more detailed, consisting of a series of contemporary eyewitness reports of the scene. Foucault's aim was to illustrate dramatically his central point: that, at least until the late eighteenth century, the purpose of state punishment was to inflict physical pain on convicted criminals – in the case of extreme crimes like regicide and parricide, the maximum possible pain and with the maximum publicity – and to envelop it with the presumption that the pain was expiation being inflicted in the name of God.

In his retrospective account of Damiens's execution, Voltaire did not make any comment or pass any moral judgement; he intended it as a work of history, not as a polemical pamphlet. Nevertheless, this execution marked him profoundly, and was to feature repeatedly in his later writings. By the time he wrote his account, he had for several years been personally engaged in a number of individual campaigns against miscarriages of justice, and was deeply immersed in a general rethinking of his attitudes on crime, punishment and human rights. So if the defence of human rights became the dominant concern in the later years of his life, that process started some time after January 1757. And if the civilised world has moved on from the barbaric notions of physical punishment which were then so characteristic, it is to a significant extent because of Voltaire's thinking and writing when he was in his seventies and eighties.

But that came later. In the early months of 1757, Voltaire was busier than ever, and the visitors kept coming to see him in his winter home at Montriond, just outside Lausanne: 'I give them dinner, and supper, and sometimes a bed.'[32] In March he wrote that

Zaïre has been better performed here, all things considered, than in Paris. It drew tears from all those Swiss eyes. Mme Denis may not have such beautiful eyes as Gaussin [an actress at the Comédie Française], but she acts better. People come from thirty leagues around to hear us. We eat hazel grouse, and capercaillies, and trout which weigh twenty pounds, and when the trees have resumed their green livery, we shall return to Les Délices. Don't you feel sorry for us?[33]

In February of that year the Empress Elisabeth Petrovna invited Voltaire to visit Russia in order write a history of the reign of Peter the Great. Voltaire did not make the journey, but he quickly agreed to write it, if the Russians would send him all the necessary archive material. As usual, he was a fast worker. In August he sent off eight draft chapters to Catherine's chamberlain, Count Shouvalov, but proposed to rewrite the terms of his commission, for he did not want to put the emphasis on wars or on Peter's private life:

You know, Sir, that my principal object is to recount everything that Peter I did which was beneficial for his country, and to paint those happy beginnings which are being perfected every day in the reign of his august daughter. It seems to me important not to call this work the *History* or *Life of Peter I*. Such a title would necessarily commit the historian to leave nothing out. He is then forced to tell odious truths, or if he does not, he dishonours himself without doing honour to his employers.[34]

In short, Voltaire was recoiling, a bit late in the day, from telling the whole truth about Peter. He did not want to go too deeply into why Peter's son, the Tsarevitch Alexis, was murdered in 1718, and by whom, and would therefore rather make no reference to it.[35] Voltaire tried to dispose of the problem by arguing that his *History of Russia under Peter the Great* would be a book which would praise and therefore promote elements of the Enlightenment in Russia. But he knew that his Russian commission was required to be a one-sided history and might even be described as shifty propaganda. The trouble was that Voltaire could not control his courtier's instinct to bow and scrape to despots, even allegedly enlightened despots, whether Frederick, Elisabeth Petrovna or, a few years later, Catherine the Great. Just as he did not want to tell 'odious truths' about Peter, so, in the reign of Catherine the Great, he would not want to look closely at why her husband Peter III was murdered in 1762, and by whom; nor at the circumstances of the murder of the imprisoned ex-Emperor Ivan VI in 1764.

Even before the publication of volume VII of the *Encyclopédie*, and with it the explosive article *Genève*, Voltaire's relations with the Geneva authorities started to go downhill. In the spring of 1757, he wrote a letter to his friend Nicolas-Claude Thieriot, in which he referred to the 'wicked soul' (*l'âme atroce*) of Jean Calvin.[36] Wicked, because in 1553 Calvin had caused a dissenting preacher, Michel Servet, to be burned at the stake. Unfortunately this phrase found its way into the public prints, as Voltaire's bon mots so often did; Voltaire tried to rectify matters, but the Geneva authorities were furious, and angry letters were exchanged between Voltaire and several of his Protestant friends, including Théodore Tronchin and the pastor Jacob Vernes.

Matters became even more heated in November of that year, when d'Alembert's article *Genève* appeared, which not only accused the Genevan Protestants of being deists, and therefore heretics, but also reiterated Voltaire's phrase about Calvin's 'wicked soul', and for good measure attributed it to Voltaire by name. The Geneva clerical authorities demanded that d'Alembert withdraw his article (he refused), and they appointed a commission, under the theologian Jean-Jacob Vernet, and with Théodore Tronchin as its secretary, which set about refuting d'Alembert's thesis by drafting a Protestant declaration of faith. Voltaire wrote to d'Alembert: 'I have just read and re-read your excellent article *Genève*'; and he went on to express his rage against all religious fanatics: 'Papist fanatics, Calvinist fanatics, all are moulded from the same sh ..., and soaked in corrupted blood' [*tous sont pétris de la même m* ...].[37] But when the commission finally reported, its declaration lacked any clear-cut assertion that the Protestants believed in the divinity of Jesus; in effect, the Calvinists were tacitly admitting exactly what they had so angrily denied only a few weeks before. Voltaire drily commented that even the heretic Michel Servet could have signed it.[38]

The reaction of the authorities in France was just as severe as in Geneva: the court at Versailles turned irrevocably against the *Encyclopédie*, and removed the previous official authorisation for its publication. This caused a deep and permanent rift between its two editors. D'Alembert resigned from the *Encyclopédie*, on the grounds that it was impossible to continue work under the harassment of official persecution. Diderot soldiered on alone, and eventually brought the great project to completion. Voltaire instinctively sided with d'Alembert against the censorious State, and at first demanded that all the *philosophes* associated with the *Encyclopédie* should either go on strike together, to assert their solidarity, or else move their operations to Lausanne, where he would finance them. But Diderot was determined both to continue, and to stay in Paris, and d'Alembert was determined to withdraw.

Voltaire himself veered erratically from one side to the other: at first he announced that he was cutting all connection with the *Encyclopédie*, and demanded that his articles and letters be returned to him; then he resumed contact; but by the summer of 1758 he had ceased to be a contributor. Yet he continued to lament, on this as on later occasions, that the *philosophes* were weakened by their divisions.

Voltaire concluded from this crisis that he could no longer live at ease with the Genevan authorities. At first, he explored the idea of moving to Lorraine, which was closer to Paris but still quasi-independent of the French Crown. Stanislas Leszczynski, twice deposed as King of Poland, had been compensated with a life tenancy of the duchy of Lorraine. Stanislas would have liked to have Voltaire as an intellectual ornament at his court in Lunéville, but first he had to sound out Louis XV, who was his son-in-law. After all, he was not really independent; when he died, Lorraine would become part of France. The answer came back immediately: Louis would not be happy if Voltaire moved to Lunéville. Voltaire was shaken. He wrote to d'Argental: 'Your letter, which was waiting for me, doubles the only grief that remains to me, in taking away the hope of embracing you.'[39]

It was probably only now, five years after his return from Prussia, that Voltaire finally accepted that his exile from Paris was likely to be permanent. It was only now, therefore, that he started to look for a permanent home that really belonged to him. In Lausanne, he was merely the tenant of the country house Montriond, and also, since the previous year, of the town house Le Grand Chêne. In Geneva it was Voltaire's money which paid for Les Délices, but the house really belonged to Jean-Robert Tronchin, so Voltaire's position depended on being on good terms with the Tronchin clan and the rest of the Geneva oligarchy. He could not stay in Geneva; he could not return to Paris; he could not move to Lunéville; he did not want to live far from his friends in Lausanne; he did not even want to live far from his friends in Geneva; so he had to move a very short distance, just across the French frontier, which would be far enough from Paris to be secure from the repression of the court, and far enough from Geneva to be secure from the conservative ideologues.

Later that autumn, 1758, Voltaire found what he was looking for: the château and village of Ferney, since renamed in his honour Ferney-Voltaire; and shortly afterwards, the neighbouring but separate estate of Tournay. But first he started writing his story *Candide*. He may have began working on it at the end of 1757, at the height of the crisis over *Genève*. He was certainly writing it in the summer of 1758, while on a visit to the Elector-Palatine at Schwetzingen, a visit for which, such are the curious contradictions of despotism, the King of France provided him with a passport. Voltaire's main reason for visiting the Elector-Palatine was to lend him £130,000, at a suitably rewarding rate of interest; readers will recall that Voltaire had already lent the Elector-Palatine £100,000 in 1753, so he clearly believed that this was a valuable financial relationship. During the three weeks he spent in Schwetzingen, it seems that he regularly read aloud, to the Elector-Palatine, the latest extracts from his work in progress. Voltaire also sent *Candide*, chapter by chapter, to the duc de La Vallière, the King's Grand Falconer and one of Voltaire's most loyal admirers, as well as a familiar of Louis XV and Mme de Pompadour.

The work was published pseudonymously, on 15 January 1759,[40] in three places simultaneously, for Voltaire knew that it would scandalise: in Geneva (by the brothers Cramer), in Paris (supervised by La Vallière in person), and in Amsterdam. Ostensibly, the tale was represented as having been written by a certain Mr Le Docteur Ralph and translated from the German, but Voltaire's authorship was soon exposed; and yet the world was astonished that this seasoned, familiar, rather old-fashioned sixty-five-year-old writer could have produced this youthful new voice. The authorities immediately tried to suppress the book by seizing printed copies, the French in Paris on 25 February 1759, the Genevans on 26 February. Voltaire continued to deny that he had anything to do with the book. He wrote to Jean-Robert Tronchin in early March: 'As I find that this work is very contrary to the decisions of the Sorbonne, I maintain that I have no part in it. I am still building an even more beautiful château than that of M. the Baron of Thunder-ten-trunckh. It is ruining me, but I hope that the Bulgars won't come.'*[41]

The repressive efforts of the authorities were overwhelmed by the success of the work, which was instantaneous and Europe-wide. On 10 March 1759, Voltaire told Cramer that 6,000 copies had been sold in Paris,[42] which suggests that there must have been two or three immediate reprints since print runs in those days were rarely more than two or three thousand. In the whole of 1759, there were over twenty editions of the work, six or seven in Paris, two in Lyon, one in Avignon, one in Liège, one in London (in French), plus three translations into English and one into Italian. All told, *Candide* sold at least 20,000 copies in 1759 alone, and perhaps as many as 30,000. This, in eighteenth-century terms, made it a massive bestseller.

It is easy to see why *Candide* was so popular with ordinary readers

---

*In *Candide*, the château of Thunder-ten-trunckh was overrun by the invading Bulgars. Voltaire's 'Bulgars' were in fact code for the Prussians, in an allusion to Frederick's homosexuality: Bulgars = bougres = buggers.

and so unpopular with the authorities. It is a highly entertaining little tale, at once so pessimistic and so gay, which through the medium of a knowingly unrealistic and picaresque international travel adventure, makes sceptical fun of the pretensions of all the institutions of Church and State, starting with the theologians, metaphysicians, Jesuits and inquisitors. Its most central theme is the contrast between the blind 'optimism' of Dr Pangloss (who repeatedly claims, like Leibniz, that this is the best of all possible worlds) and the many horrors, natural and man-made, of real life. In a sense, it is a re-run of Voltaire's earlier attack on Leibnizian 'optimism' in his *Poème sur le Désastre de Lisbonne*, but this time as comedy and in prose. It has been continuously popular over the past 250 years. Voltaire wrote some fifty other short tales and fictions, but by common consent it is *Candide* which is held to be his masterpiece.

Voltaire designed it to be not just iconoclastic, but short, light, rapid and humorous, and therefore readable and entertaining. He regularly complained that the articles of the *Encyclopédie* were too long and boring; two years later, in reaction, he would write his own *Dictionnaire Philosophique Portatif*, which was meant to be short, brisk and accessible.

You could say that *Candide* is a masterpiece because it marks a brilliant moment of transition from Voltaire's courtly and literary voice, his plays, his poems and his histories, aimed at the restricted audience of the courtly and literary establishment, to his populist voice, aimed at public opinion in a broader sense. In any event, it certainly added to his popular credibility when he came to engage in his later human rights cases.

There are several famous tags from *Candide*, starting with *'pour encourager les autres'*, quoted earlier in relation to Admiral Byng. Perhaps the most famous is the sign-off line at the end of the book: '*That was well said*,' replied Candide, '*but we must cultivate our garden.*'[43] The phrase is usually understood as a metaphor, as if to say: we should concentrate our attention and our efforts on simple, local things where we have some chance of doing good. No doubt this metaphorical sense is an important, even central, part of what Voltaire meant. But it seems clear that he also meant it literally: for

Voltaire, *'il faut cultiver notre jardin'* was a personal imperative in so far as it referred to his own life. He had discovered for himself the pleasures and the virtues of gardening and planting and sowing and building in the home he created at Les Délices, and he would re-enact them, with greater enthusiasm and on a much larger scale, in the new home which he was to create at Ferney.

5

L'Infâme

1758–61

When, in the autumn of 1758, Voltaire found himself faced with a choice between the château de Ferney and the château de Tournay, two estates virtually adjoining one another just outside the territory of Geneva, he decided to take them both.

Voltaire found Ferney in October, and buying it was quick and trouble-free. It was for sale freehold, and Voltaire rapidly reached agreement on a price of £130,000. The total cost would eventually be much greater, partly because he also bought other parcels and enclaves of land to round out the estate, but mainly because the château was old, ill-maintained and inconvenient, and he decided substantially to rebuild it. All told, he reckoned in a letter to Jean-Robert Tronchin in December, the overall cost would be £333,000.[1] Final signature on the contract was delayed until early February 1759, but well before then Voltaire had moved in and started improving the estate.

Voltaire had already found Tournay in September, but buying it turned out to be a tiresome haggle with its formalistic and disputatious owner. Président Charles de Brosses was a senior judge at the Parlement of Dijon and a moderately distinguished writer; but as Voltaire soon discovered, he was also by nature incurably pernickety and difficult, and his insistence on driving a hard bargain verged on the dishonest. The root of the problem was that de Brosses was only offering a life tenancy in Tournay, and while he imposed various obligations and restrictions on Voltaire's use of the estate, he also made promises, explicit or implied, which he did not fulfil. Some people have suggested that de Brosses' combative character had something to do with the fact that he was very short in stature: when defending his doctoral thesis, he had had to stand on a stool to be able to look over the edge of the lectern.[2]

During the weeks of bargaining, de Brosses drove up the price of the château de Tournay from £30,000 to £35,000 and, in addition, he imposed the condition that Voltaire spend £12,000 on repairs. The final haggle was over the *chaîne du marché*,* the symbolic present which the purchaser of a property was expected to give to the wife of the vendor. Voltaire offered to give Mme de Brosses a sowing plough (*charrue à semoir*); this was an ultra-modern agricultural tool which in one operation turned the earth, sowed the seeds, covered the furrow, and harrowed it; it was Voltaire's latest passion in his enthusiasm for cultivating his new fields and gardens. No doubt the offer was tongue-in-cheek; de Brosses turned it down, but settled for £500 in cash.[3] Terms of sale were finally agreed in December 1758;[4] but all this negotiating left a nasty taste. As Voltaire wrote to de Brosses in January: 'I read and I re-read your contract, and the more I re-read it, the more I see that you have dictated your law as a conqueror. But that is all right. I like to improve the places where I live, and what I am doing will benefit you and please me.'[5]

But Voltaire's resigned acceptance of the onerous contract soon turned to fury. De Brosses had told him that Tournay was exempt from various heavy taxes and he had clearly implied that this tax exemption went with the property;[6] Voltaire claimed that de Brosses had given him such a promise in writing. But once the contract was signed, de Brosses told Voltaire that the exemption was personal to him and therefore not transferable. For the next six months he raged at de Brosses over what he saw as his double dealing.[7] In May 1759 he wrote to him: 'I have embellished Tournay, I have improved the land; but I shall burn everything, if the least of my rights were stolen from me. I am not reasonable when I am vexed. It was only on this condition, that I should enjoy all the tax exemptions, that I settled with you. You know it, you guaranteed it in writing.'[8] But after a while he accepted that de Brosses was impervious and immovable, and he tire-

*i.e., the chain of the deal

lessly and shamelessly lobbied his court contacts at Versailles until eventually his friend the little duc de Choiseul (who was effectively prime minister) secured him the tax exemptions he was demanding – for Ferney, though not for Tournay.[9]

Unfortunately, this was only the first of several quarrels with de Brosses over the terms of Voltaire's tenancy. One of the bitterest was over five loads of firewood. Voltaire claimed that de Brosses had agreed that he could take a dozen loads of firewood from the estate, free of charge. Then it emerged that de Brosses had a previous standing arrangement with Charles Baudy, a local café owner, by which Baudy sold firewood on his behalf. So Baudy demanded that Voltaire pay him for fourteen loads of wood. The total sum at stake was somewhere between £50 and £150, depending on the number of loads. But Voltaire resisted the claim, and de Brosses persisted in pressing it, for another two and a half years, and in the process the quarrel got quite venomous. On 20 October 1761 Voltaire wrote to de Brosses:

So, Sir, you only offered your friendship in order to poison the end of my life with law-suits ... I warn you, Sir, that you will not succeed in this odious enterprise. I bought a life-interest in your little estate of Tournay, at the age of 66, on the terms you wanted. I trusted your honour, and your probity; you dictated the contract, and I signed, blindly ... You demanded £35,000, I paid cash. You wanted me to spend £12,000 on repairs during the first three years; I spent £18,000 in the first three months, and I have the receipts. I have made this uninhabitable hovel very comfortable, I have improved and embellished everything ... But I cannot stand that you should take me to court for £200, after having received from me more money than your estate was worth ...[10]

After years of argument, the legal tussle over the firewood ended in a draw, when de Brosses offered to drop the case if Voltaire would agree to give £281 as a charitable gift to the local poor. Conventional wisdom has it that this firewood episode shows Voltaire in a poor light, cheap and mean-minded; but de Brosses behaved much worse, with ill will and bad faith, and that cannot be said of Voltaire. In fact, de Brosses' behaviour seems to have been typical of the man; he seems not to have calculated that there could be a price to pay for constantly doing Voltaire down.

Many years later, Voltaire had his revenge when de Brosses campaigned to get himself elected to the Académie Française. Voltaire had been a member of the Académie for many years, and he lobbied virulently against de Brosses. He told d'Alembert that he would resign if de Brosses were elected; but he told the other members that he would bring a court case against him, to expose and punish him for his disgraceful behaviour over the Tournay lease.[11] De Brosses was duly rejected by the *immortels*. In 1758, he must have thought that he had driven a wonderful bargain in the Tournay life tenancy, since Voltaire was already sixty-four and must surely die soon; in fact, Voltaire had the last laugh, since he outlived de Brosses, if only by a year.

Until his acquisition of Ferney and Tournay, Voltaire had shown no interest in the well-being of the lower orders; his only concerns had been with his own comfort and convenience, with the cultivation of those in positions of power, and with the pursuit of his very hard-working and successful literary career. His new situation as a landed proprietor brought about a profound transformation in his feelings and attitudes, as is clearly indicated in the following letter written on 18 November – after he had surveyed his estates but before he had legally taken possession of them.

[This] area was very depopulated, very miserable, without industry, without resources. My land is excellent, and yet I have found 100 *arpents* [roughly 50 hectares] belonging to my inhabitants which remain uncultivated. The [previous] tenant farmer had not sown half of his fields. It is seven years since the curé celebrated any marriages, and no children have been born, since we only have Jesuits in the neighbourhood, and no Franciscans ...*
The most dreadful calamity is the rapacity of the tax farmers† and the brutality of their employees. Poor people who have scarcely even any black bread to eat, are arrested every day, stripped, and imprisoned, for having

---

*A typical Voltaire joke: he implies that the Franciscans were liable to father children on local girls, but not the Jesuits.
†Private financiers to whom the King subcontracted the collection of taxes.

put on this bread a bit of salt which they have bought near their cottages.* Half the inhabitants die of poverty, and the other half rot in prison cells. One's heart is torn when one witnesses so much misery. I only bought the Ferney estate in order to do a bit of good . . .'[12]

These are sentiments which Voltaire had never expressed before, but he soon acted on them. Within weeks he was starting what became a long-running campaign on behalf of the poor peasants, to protect them against a violent and rapacious local curé who was using the law-courts to extort massive arrears of tithes, and who was given to employing thugs to beat up his parishioners.[13]

In September of the following year,1759, Voltaire wrote to his old friend Thieriot: 'I must visit my smallholdings, I must look after my peasants and my cattle when they are ill, I must find husbands for the girls, and I must improve fields abandoned since the Flood. I see all round me the most frightful misery, in the midst of a smiling countryside. I put on a show of trying to remedy a bit of the evil that has been done over the centuries. When one is in a position to do a bit of good to a half-league of country, that is rather honourable.'[14] And to de Brosses he wrote in November: 'Most of [my] income goes to relieve many unhappy people, both at Tournay and at Ferney. The misery was horrible in all this region, and the fields were not sown. Thank God, now they are.'[15] And at the end of that year, he embarked on a campaign to buy off the tax farmers' stranglehold on salt and tobacco for the whole of the province centred on the local town of Gex. In fact, this was to be the start of a series of campaigns whose ultimate aim was to banish the tax farmers entirely from the province.[16]

Voltaire's sudden and unexpected compassion for the peasants of Ferney and Tournay was not just a passing whim or a literary indulgence; it was his acceptance of a whole new moral dimension that he had not acknowledged before. While he had been appalled by the Lisbon earthquake of 1755, and by its implications for the problem of evil, his dismay at that distant event was more philosophical and

---

*The salt trade was strictly controlled and heavily taxed.

abstract rather than concrete or deeply felt. It was only now, after looking closely at his new estates, that he began to feel that the problem of evil was not some large and dramatic catastrophe in a faraway country but was here and now in the everyday sufferings of the poor and downtrodden; moreover, he realised that he now had a personal responsibility for trying to alleviate it on his own estates, as well as the means to do so. Not only was this new sense of responsibility a key moment in Voltaire's evolution; it remained with him for the rest of his life, and informed his attitude both towards his own properties and towards events in the wider world.

Voltaire's first step was to make long overdue improvements to his estates. The château de Tournay, Voltaire told d'Argental, 'is a hovel made for the owls, a county* to make you laugh, a garden where there was nothing but snails and moles, vines without grapes, fields without wheat, and cow-sheds without cows.'[17] But he reassured de Brosses: 'Don't worry about your château or your forest; I am building more than I am destroying, I am planting more than I am pulling up ... I am becoming a patriarch.'† A couple of weeks later, in December 1758, almost before the ink had dried on the contract, he told him: 'I already have twenty workers who are repairing the broken-down vines; we shall repair your château right away; your forest was in a frightful state, I shall put it right, everything is settled. Let me have 4,000 vine stocks, or rather 5,000.'[18] In January 1759 he wrote again to de Brosses: 'Send me the vine stocks. They will be planted with the same despatch as your staircase has been shifted, as the fields have been repaired, the hedges restored, the ditches cleaned and widened, and the field beyond the forest ploughed for the first time in its life. I shall populate the country of Gex with partridges; I should like to populate it with people.'[19]

Voltaire's enthusiasm for cultivating his garden was wholehearted and practical: this was not an operation which he managed from behind a desk in his study. He visited the cow-sheds and examined

*Tournay carried with it the feudal title of 'Count'.
†After his move to Ferney, Voltaire regularly referred to himself, and was described by others, as a 'patriarch'.

the animals himself. 'I love my bulls,' he says, 'I stroke them, and they make eyes at me.'[20] To walk about the farm he had some clogs made, and he even set aside one field for himself, whose cultivation he personally supervised.[21]

In April 1759 Voltaire he announced that he was 'a great partisan' of the new sowing plough which he had just acquired, and which had five blades and five seed drills, and that he was looking into a new and more convenient grape press.[22] By now he regularly had up to a hundred people working for him, and by May he was bringing in extra families from Switzerland, since he did not have enough farm-hands to cultivate the fields; in July he said that he had 'eighty persons and eighteen horses to feed'.[23] Not content with all this hectic activity, in which he was very much his own master-of-works, Voltaire continued to add to his landholdings. In May he told Jean-Robert Tronchin that he was buying two parcels of land between Tournay and Ferney, but he added in mock humility: 'I must end this letter, for fear of having to tell you about more land that I am buying'.[24] In August he was again acquiring several small pieces of land.[25]

During the summer 1759, Voltaire had also embarked on horse breeding. He wrote to Jean-Robert:

As for the mares which I had the honour to ask for, I should explain my policy. I use all my horses, except for two that are privileged, for pulling either a carriage, or a cart, or a plough. I choose my mares the way one should choose a wife, not too beautiful nor too ugly, but capable of bearing children; and I want my mares to bear children, since my serving women do not; so if you find two creatures which would suit my seraglio, black and young like Solomon's mistress, you would do me great pleasure if you would send them at your convenience, especially if they are not too dear.[26]

But two weeks later, he told Tronchin that he had just come across a good mare, and had bought her. 'You won't guess who she's for: she's for me. I want to ride. I have a little horse which is scarcely bigger than a donkey, and which will help the circulation of the blood.'[27] Voltaire was obviously very taken with his new horse, for he wrote again a few days later: 'Do you want to know, my dear correspon-

dent, the size of my pony?* Imagine a lovely she-donkey, like Bal-
aam's ass, and from that you can measure the height of the prophet's
arse.'²⁸ Voltaire was less than five foot six inches tall, and skeletal
into the bargain, so he did not need a big horse to carry him.

The château of Ferney needed substantial rebuilding, and
Voltaire threw himself into it with gusto. In July 1759 he wrote to
d'Argental: 'You would be enchanted with my château, it's of the
Doric order, it will last for a thousand years. I shall put on the frieze
Voltaire fecit. Posterity will take me for a famous architect.'²⁹ (Three
weeks later Voltaire said the façade was Ionic,³⁰ while others
described it as Palladian. He had little taste in visual aesthetics: for
the interior decoration of his home, he ordered pictures by the
square yard.)

By the autumn of that year, the heavy building work was largely
complete at both Ferney and Tournay. In October, Voltaire wrote to
Jean-Robert asking for some wine ('Have you no nectar from
Beaujolais, really tasty, full of sap? Three barrels would do nicely')
and he continued: 'I have already had some fruit from the trees I
planted at Les Délices less than three years ago. Everything is going
well. We are making some new bedrooms in the outhouses. Tournay has become an agreeable château, Ferney is rebuilt, and people
even say that it is really handsome. But nothing will compare with
the garden at Les Délices when the terrace was finished. Won't you
come and see our little kingdom next year? You will see the happiest
of men.'³¹

Naturally, Voltaire's improvements were costing a lot of money.
In April he had complained that his resources were 'reduced to a
narrow span by so many new acquisitions'.³² In May, in a letter to
Jean-Robert, he reckoned up his finances: 'The little patriarch from
Gex province can see, my dear correspondent, that he now has more
bulls, cows and sheep, than you have bags of his money.' He calculated his outgoings at £286,150 and went on: 'In these circumstances,

*The word Voltaire uses for his pony was *haquenée*, a Frenchified transliteration
of the English word 'hackney', which itself comes from the London borough of
Hackney, long celebrated for its horses. *Haquenée* has been an officially recognised
French word since 1360.

I do not see how I could ask you for another thirty-two thousand livres to round out my estates. It seems to me that I should have nothing left, or almost nothing.'[33] A week later he promised Jean-Robert that he would go on an economy drive. 'Your advice will be followed. No more orders for 16 or 17 thousand livres; I shall prune everything, even my orders for uniform braid. Everything which was to have been crimson will now be green instead, and the decorations will be smaller, and especially cheaper.'[34] In August 1759 he moaned to Jean-Robert that he was much less wealthy than before: 'My dear correspondent, we are no longer as great a seigneur as we used to be. We used to reckon by five hundred thousand livres; but now we are reduced to reckoning by 200 thousand, and thanks to the Ionic façade of my château, to the water basins, to the fountains, to the land which costs a lot and brings in little, and to the sixty-plus people I have to feed every day, you may expect that soon we shall be reduced to reckoning in fifty thousand écus.'[35]

It is not clear whether Voltaire was really worried about his finances or whether he was making a half-lamenting, half-exulting joke about the sheer scale of his spending. Over the years, he went through quite frequent cycles of money worries, but on this occasion, his financial anxieties, whether real or not, soon evaporated, for in September he wrote to Jean-Robert: 'Despite my cost-cutting rules, I admit that if I found two pretty silver sauce boats ready made, I should take them. But do not think you have to send any gold, for we have some. In fact, we are overflowing with it.'[36] And so was Jean-Robert, for it appears that he held £500,000 on account for Voltaire.[37] A few days later Voltaire wrote again to Jean-Robert: 'Having visited my cash-box and my wallet, I have the boldness to send you £14,062 10s., instead of the weakness to ask you for £12,000. You see that I am adding to the loot instead of taking from it.'[38]

You might think that Voltaire would be fully occupied by this hectic programme of improving his new estates; not a bit of it. In June 1759, he was suddenly inspired to write a new tragedy, *Tancrède*, and he boasted to d'Argental that, as with his earlier tragedy *Zaïre*, he had written it in three weeks flat: 'We have witnesses,' he declared proudly.[39] What inspired him was, at least in part, the news from Paris that there had been a revolutionary change at the Comédie Française. For many years, the management of the theatre had sold seats actually placed on the stage. Inevitably these seats severely restricted the space for stage action, but they brought in extra revenue and the theatre could not afford to get rid of them. Two months earlier, Voltaire had learned that the marquis de Lauragais had persuaded the Comédie Française to remove the seats, in exchange for a gift of £30,000. Voltaire wrote to d'Argental: 'I am overcome with feelings of the noblest zeal when I learn that the white-powdered wigs and the red heels will no longer mingle with Augustus and Cleopatra. For in that case the Paris theatre will change its appearance. Tragedies will no longer be conversations in five acts, at the end of which one learns that there had been a bit of blood spilled. People will want pomp, spectacle, noise. Plays like *Fanime* are a bit too much rose water: you will have something a bit stronger.'[40] The 'something stronger' was to be *Tancrède,* a patriotic and tearful melodrama of medieval chivalry.

Naturally, Voltaire wanted to see his new play performed. So even before the structural work at Tournay was complete, he planned to build a private theatre inside the château. It would be a miniature affair, in a gallery, capable of holding a hundred spectators, but Voltaire was quite excited about it. In August 1759 he told Jean-Robert: 'My little Punch-and-Judy theatre will not cost much. I shall make the theatre all by myself. It's not my fault if the generous Président de Brosses does not have a gallery which is longer and wider. I am sorry that the height from floor to ceiling in my theatre is only eight foot, but all we have to do is act well, and then one forgets where one is. These are performances between friends. It is as if one were reading beside the fire.'[41]

By October his 'green and gold' theatre was already in use.[42] After a performance of *Tancrède*, Voltaire wrote to d'Argental: 'My Punch-and-Judy theatre is very small, I admit, but yesterday, my divine angel, nine of us were quite comfortable in a semicircle on stage. Moreover, we had lances and bucklers, and we had green shiny batons for pilasters. A troupe of violin scrapers and Saxon horn blowers made up the orchestra. How handsomely we were dressed! Madame Denis gave a superior performance. All in all, I only wish that the play could be played as well in Paris as in my hovel at Tournay.'[43] In November he boasted that he had put on three performances of *Tancrède* and one of *Mérope* before an audience from Geneva, Switzerland and the country round about.[44]

Tancrède was performed at the Comédie Française in Paris on 3 September 1760, and it was a great popular success. But though Voltaire continued to write dramas until the end of his life, some of them were never staged at the Comédie Française, and others were flops. *Tancrède* was Voltaire's last really successful play: if his *philosophie* was ahead of its time, his neo-classical verse formulae belonged to an earlier age and seemed to have been increasingly out of tune with changing French tastes.

While the building work was going on at Ferney and Tournay, Voltaire divided his time between his three homes, but he lived mainly at Les Délices. In April 1759 he wrote to Gabriel Cramer, his publisher: 'M de Voltaire will return on Saturday evening to Les Délices, so as not to be present in his Parish of Ferney on Sunday, but above all to see Monsieur Gabriel Cramer, whom he begs to come to supper on Saturday and stay the night.' He urged Cramer to be more diligent over some proofs, 'for, as the man said [*comme disait l'autre*], I spew the luke-warm out of my mouth[45] ... Dictated in the middle of my ruins, on a step-ladder in the attic of our palace for bats, in the midst of the masons who prevent me from sleeping and are ruining me.'[46] In September 1760 he described how he used his three homes: 'God has given me, barely a quarter of a league from Les Délices, a château where I have transformed the great hall into a theatre. We can get there on foot. We have supper there; and the next day we go to Ferney, which is a fine estate.'[47]

Voltaire's theatre at Tournay quickly became a popular draw attraction.[48] In September 1760 he wrote: 'Tomorrow we are performing *Alzire* at Tournay, and then *Tancrède* and then *Mahomet* and then *Les Ensorcelés*; we have spectators who have come over 100 leagues to see us, including the duc de Villars.'[49] According to Voltaire, the duke was an excellent actor, though for the sake of his noble reputation he only performed in private. 'M. le duc de Villars is getting dressed to play Genghis Khan behind closed doors; La Denis is primping herself; these are two great actors, I might say. My bonnet is being readjusted ...'⁵⁰ A week later: 'We have to put on a play twice a week. In our little hole we have had 49 persons to supper, and all of them talked at once ... It rather interrupts the continuity of my studies.'⁵¹ In fact, what really interrupted Voltaire's studies was that he could not get at his library since it was in a part of the house now occupied by the visiting duc de Villars.⁵²

By now he was planning to rebuild the church at Ferney, and in the spring of 1760, when the interior decoration and furnishing of the château were complete, he told d'Alembert that he had decided to move his main home there from Les Délices. 'Write to me by the post, and address it boldly: *To Voltaire, gentleman in ordinary of the King, at the château of Ferney, via Geneva*; for it is at Ferney that I shall live in a few weeks. We have Tournay for putting on plays, and Les Délices will be the third string for our bow. Philosophers should always have two or three underground holes, against the dogs which run after them.'⁵³ Voltaire and Mme Denis moved permanenently to Ferney in December that year.

Yet despite the success of the little theatre at Tournay, within twelve months Voltaire decided to build a bigger one, this time at the château de Ferney. As he wrote to his other niece, Mme Fontaine, in the autumn of 1760: 'The Tournay theatre will in future be at Ferney. I shall build an auditorium despite the hardness of the times [i.e. the Seven Years War]. But if I damn myself by building theatres, I am earning salvation by building a church; I must hear Mass there with you, after which we shall perform some new plays.'⁵⁴ By October of the following year, 1761, the new church and the new theatre had both been built at Ferney.⁵⁵ The theatre was constructed in a large barn close to the château, with seating for three hundred spectators; the church bore the famous inscription: *Deo erexit Voltaire.*⁕⁵⁶ Voltaire kept Les Délices for several more years, but in most respects

---

⁕Latin, meaning: 'Voltaire built it for God.' The visual impression, from the relative sizes of the letters used for 'Deo' and 'Voltaire', was that Voltaire was more important than God.

Ferney was now his main home, and he was to live there almost without interruption for the next eighteen years.

His happiness continued. In September 1759 he wrote to a friend: 'Four years ago I was getting ready for death, but now I find I am stronger than I have ever been, building, planting, versifying, and writing the history of the Russian empire.'[57] In October 1759 he wrote to his old friend Mme du Deffand, the Parisian literary socialite: 'To have pleasure, you need a bit of passion, a great and interesting purpose, a determined desire to learn, which occupies the soul continuously. It is difficult to find, and does not come without effort.'[58]

He pursued the same theme the following April, in another letter to Mme du Deffand: 'I have never been less dead than I am at present. I haven't a free moment. The bulls, the cows, the sheep, the pastures, the buildings, the gardens, all take up my mornings; the afternoons are for study; and after supper, we rehearse the plays which we perform in my little gallery theatre. This way of life makes me want to live. When you get down to it, I am a decent fellow, and my priests, my vassals and my neighbours are all pleased with me.'[59] And in the autumn of 1760 he wrote to his other niece Mme Fontaine: 'I am quite amazed to find that I have been happy here for the past five years. I have made a little sovereign state for myself, pushing out my frontiers to left and right. I have done everything I wanted. It is good that there should be people like me in this world. But to play this role, one must be old, rich, free, bold, and in good standing at the court, but without ever going there.'[60]

Voltaire was now in his mid-sixties, but his energy seems to have remained boundless, and inspired him to embark on a two-phase campaign on behalf of Enlightenment and *philosophie*, and against repression. The first phase took the form of an attack against the forces of superstition and darkness, which he encapsulated in an idiosyncratic personal slogan directed against '*L'Infâme*', or 'The Horror'. His first reference to it came in a letter to French writer Mme d'Epinay in June 1759: 'We must drive out l'Infâme.' In later letters to close allies like d'Alembert, the slogan became 'Ecrasez l'Infâme' (Crush the Horror), often abbreviated after 1763 to the virtual password 'Ecr l'Inf'. Some commentators have debated long and hard over the exact definition of L'Infâme, but Voltaire's general meaning is clear: his targets included superstition, theological repression, Jesuits, monks, fanatical regicides, and the Inquisition in every shape and form; in short, all facets of the dark and regressive alliance between the Catholic Church and the French State.

Some of Voltaire's friends, like Diderot and the philosopher d'Holbach, were atheists, and some of his enemies accused him of atheism; but in fact, Voltaire was not an atheist, as he constantly made clear. He was quite distinctly and unmistakably a deist: he believed in a single all-powerful and all-virtuous God, though not in the story of Christianity or in Christianity's God.[61] His enemies were the institutions which used religion and superstition to inflict evil, and many of his *philosophe* friends agreed with him. Nevertheless, some of them were alarmed that he should be so outspoken, since his letters were in permanent danger of being opened by the authorities, and in any case regularly got into general circulation. One of these was d'Alembert, who wrote to Voltaire in some concern in May 1761: '*Écrasez l'infâme; écrasez l'infâme!* That is easily said when one is a hundred leagues from the bastards and the fanatics, when one has an independent income of a hundred thousand livres, and when one has become independent by reputation and fortune. But a poor devil like me does not tread on the serpents, for fear that they should twist their heads and sting him on the heel.'[62]

Soon after his arrival at Ferney, Voltaire met four Jesuit fathers in the little local community of Ornex, and in April he asked Jean-Robert Tronchin for two folding chess-boards so that he could play chess with theJesuits.[63] Voltaire appears to have taken a liking to one of the Ornex Jesuits in particular, the fifty-four-year-old Father Antoine Adam, whom he described early in 1759 as 'a pretty decent devil'.[64] Adam was a keen chess-player, and it is quite likely that it was mainly for games with him Voltaire needed his folding chess-boards. Voltaire later invited Adam to move in as his personal priest, as he mentioned in 1765: 'I have a [Jesuit] in my house, who says Mass most properly, and who plays chess very well; he's called Adam, and though he is not the First Man, he has merit.'[65] Father Adam stayed for many years as a permanent part of the household, conducting church services, playing chess, and conversing with Voltaire.

The second phase of Voltaire's Enlightenment campaign started in February 1760 when he began work on his *Dictionnaire Philosophique Portatif*. Voltaire planned this as a brisk, accessible alphabetical guide to Enlightenment thinking and attitudes, and it was his answer to what he saw as the interminable prolixity of the *Encyclopédie*, to which he had by now ceased to contribute. Several years later he was to claim that the great *Encyclopédie* was bound to be harmless both because it was so large and because it was so expensive: 'I should like to know what harm could come from a book which costs 100 ecus. A work in twenty folio volumes will never make a revolution; it's the little books costing 30 sous which are to be feared. If the New Testament had cost 1,200 sesterces, the Christian religion would never have been established.'[66]

In addition to his building and estate management, in addition to his history of Peter the Great, in addition to his play-writing and play-acting, in addition to his *Dictionnaire Philosophique*, in addition to his campaign against *L'Infâme*, and in addition to his voluminous letter-writing, Voltaire managed to keep up with a wide range of literature. In September 1760 he wrote to an Italian acquaintance, partly in French, partly in Italian, partly in English: 'Have you read Tristram Shandy? T'is a very unaccountable book; an original one. They run mad about it in England.'[67] In fact, the first volume of Sterne's *Tristram Shandy* (out of nine) had only just been published in England. The previous year Voltaire had encouraged Mme du Deffand to read the Old Testament, which he said was more entertaining than *Tom Jones*. He had also urged her to learn Italian so that she could read Ariosto, and suggested that she re-read Rabelais which he used to despise but now enjoyed greatly, despite its excessive vulgarity; and recommended the writings of Jonathan Swift: 'Let it please God, Madame, for the good I wish you, that there be a faithful copy of the *Tale of a Tub* by Dean Swift! It is a treasure-house of entertainment, of which no one else has any idea. Pascal is only amusing at the expense of the Jesuits; Swift entertains and informs us at the expense of the human race. How I love the English boldness! How I love people who say what they think! People who only half think are only half alive.'[68]

The only thing that was missing in the life of Voltaire and Mme Denis when they moved into their spacious and newly rebuilt château of Ferney in December 1760 was children; but Fate almost immediately gave them a surrogate daughter.

6

The Adoption of Mlle Corneille
1760–63

In October 1760, shortly before moving to Ferney, Voltaire learned from the poet Echouard Le Brun of the existence of a teenage girl who was a descendant of Pierre Corneille, the great tragedian, and that she (and her father) were living in Paris in great poverty. Her name was Marie-Françoise Corneille, and her father, Jean-François Corneille, was a lowly, almost illiterate employee of the postal system, barely surviving on £50 a month. Voltaire at first believed she was the great Corneille's granddaughter; in fact, she was a more distant relative, a first cousin twice removed, from a parallel branch of the family. Voltaire believed she was sixteen; she was in fact eighteen. He decided almost immediately that he would rescue her from poverty, take her into his family, and educate her. Later he also decided to adopt her.

Within days he was making arrangements for her to travel to Ferney. He wrote to Brun:

It is fitting that an old soldier of the great Corneille should try to be useful to the granddaughter of his general. I am old, I have a niece who loves all the fine arts and who does well in some of them; if the young person of whom you speak wished to accept a decent education from my niece, she would take care of her as of a daughter; I should seek to be a father to her. Her own father would have nothing to pay. We should pay for her journey as far as Lyon. At Lyon she would go to M. Tronchin, who would provide a carriage right to my château, or else a woman would go to fetch her in one of my vehicles. Part of the education of the young lady would some-times be to see us act the plays of her grandfather.[1]

Matters were quickly arranged, and Marie-Françoise was soon on the road; by 16 December Voltaire reported that she was already at Lyon with Jean-Robert. 'They will probably introduce her to Mme de Groslée, who will not fail to feel her tits, according to her laudable custom. It's an honour that she does to all the girls and women introduced to her.'[2] Unfortunately Marie-Françoise had received virtually no formal education, and on the same day Voltaire wrote to a friend in Lausanne, in search of a tutor for her:

She is coming here. She has learned to read and write a bit, by herself. They say she is amiable. If you know of some poor man who knows how to read and write, and who may even have a smattering of geography and history, or who is at least capable of learning some, and of teaching the next day what he had learned the day before, we will house him, heat him, launder him, feed him, water him, and pay him, but pay him very modestly, for I have ruined myself in building châteaux and churches and theatres.[3]

Four days later, Marie-Françoise Corneille arrived, and Voltaire reported that they were delighted with her. 'We find her natural, gay and true, with a charming little face, lovely eyes, beautiful skin, a large mouth, rather attractive, with two rows of pearly teeth. If anyone has the pleasure to get his teeth close to hers, I hope it will be a Catholic rather than a Protestant. But on my word of honour, my divine angels, it will not be me: I'm 67 years old.'[4]

But Voltaire himself embarked on Marie-Françoise's education within a day of her arrival, without waiting for a tutor. 'I am teaching her spelling, but I shall never make an intellectual of her. I want her to learn how to live in the world and be happy there.'[5] In January her lessons became more systematic:

We are taking care of all the parts of her education, until a worthy tutor arrives. She is learning spelling; we make her write, and you can see that she forms her letters well, and that her lines don't go diagonally like some of our Parisiennes. She reads with us at regular hours, and we make sure that she understands the meaning of the words. After her reading, we talk to her about what she has read; and thus we teach her, indirectly, a bit of history. All this happens quite gaily, without the smallest sense of a lesson.[6]

Note that Voltaire said 'we', implying that the education of Marie-Françoise was a joint enterprise between himself and Mme Denis.

We may wonder about the real nature of Voltaire's intimate relationship with Mme Denis, partly because he was now in his late sixties, but more especially because some of his infrequent references to her are quite disobliging, to say the least. In practical terms, it seems that Voltaire and Mme Denis mostly rubbed along pretty well together in their respective roles. 'I have only had an idea of happiness since I have been in my own home in retirement; but what a retirement! I sometimes have fifty persons at my table; I leave them with Mme Denis, who does the honours, and I shut myself away. I have built what the Italians would call a *palazzo*, but I only like my study.'[7]

With regard to their new charge, it appears that Voltaire and Mme Denis were at one in their shared delight. Marie-Françoise may have been no intellectual, but she was obviously a charming girl:

We do not cease to give thanks for this treasure we now possess. Her heart seems excellent, and we have every hope that, even if we do not make an intellectual of her, she will become a very lovable person with all the virtues, the graces, and the naturalness which make the charm of society. What I like especially about her, is her attachment to her father. She has been given a chamber maid, who is delighted to be with her. She is loved by all the servants; everyone competes to serve her little whims, though her whims are certainly not very demanding. It is too soon to hire any tutors, apart from myself and my niece. We don't let her get away with bad words nor vicious pronunciations. Habit is everything. I must not leave out the fact that I take her myself to the Parish Mass: we have a duty to give a good example, and we give it.[8]

Voltaire and Mme Denis evidently entered wholeheartedly into their new parental roles; it was from this time on that Voltaire increasingly referred to Mme Denis as 'maman'.

What Voltaire did not mention, at first, was that Marie-Françoise was rather childish, since she still played with dolls,[9] or that she was physically somewhat malformed, since she suffered from the aftermath of childhood rickets (no doubt due to poverty and malnutrition). It was not until nearly two years later that he referred explicitly to her physical condition, in a letter to his doctor, Théodore Tronchin: 'Mlle Corneille was once knotted [*nouée*, a locution for rickets]. Her spirit is now unknotting itself, and her body unknotted itself first. She sometimes feels the consequences of this old conformation. Weakness and pain in the hip, vague and rheumatic pains in the side near the afflicted hip. In a word, she hobbles and she suffers. What is to be done?'[10]

Voltaire was clearly enchanted with the unfamiliar duties which he had taken on in his new role as a surrogate father. A month after her arrival, in January 1761, he wrote to d'Argental: 'I am weighed down by so many frightful tasks. My most difficult duty is teaching grammar to Mlle Corneille, who has no disposition for this sublime science.'[11] But he told Mme du Deffand that Marie-Françoise was 'gentle and gay, good, true, grateful, affectionate without guile but by inclination; she will have good sense; but as for good taste, she will have to get it where she can.'[12]

In fact, Voltaire's pleasure at the arrival of Marie-Françoise only added to his enormous ebullience in dealing with all his other newly acquired roles: as semi-feudal landowner, moderniser and benefactor. He wrote to d'Argental: 'Yes, I serve God, for I have a horror of the Jesuits and the Jansenists, for I love my country, for I go to Mass every Sunday, for I am setting up schools, for I am building churches, for I am going to set up a hospital, for there are no longer any poor on my estates, despite the efforts of the salt tax inspectors. Yes, I serve God, I believe in God, and I want it known. My only sadness in this world is not being with you in your study to eat Parmesan, and to drink, for I like drinking (as you know).'[13] A few weeks later Voltaire told d'Argental that he intended to take communion at Easter, with Mme Denis and Mlle Corneille; 'and you can call me a hypocrite as much as you like'.[14]

But he never forgot that his happiness depended crucially on his wealth. He wrote to Jean-Robert Tronchin in January, 1761:

My dear correspondent, I was born fairly poor, I have spent my life in a beggar's trade, as a scribbler on paper, and yet here I am with two châteaux, two pretty houses, 70 thousand livres of income, and two hundred thousand livres in cash. Sometimes I take all my happiness for a dream. I should find it quite difficult to say just how I have managed to be the happiest of men. I just stick to the fact, without reasoning.

And to increase my happiness, you should soon receive a partridge pâté with truffles from Angoulême, which I ask you to send on to Les Délices, where we are for some time, because your frightful Geneva plasterers have made fireplaces at Ferney which smoke.[15]

A few days later, this partridge pâté, a gift from the marquis d'Argence, arrived safely: 'Thanks to the prudence of your cook, and four fingers of lard placed between the partridge and the crust, your pâté arrived fresh and excellent, and we have been eating it for the past eight days; we have greatly toasted your health, glass in hand.'[16] This cook was not always so successful in the pâté department. In January 1765, when the marquis d'Argence again sent Voltaire a partridge pâté, he wrote: 'We have just received your pâté. The pâtissier will deserve every compliment if his partridges have arrived without a beard, in the rotten weather we've been enduring ...' [later:] 'My dear warrior philosopher, don't send any more pâté; it's too far from Angoulême to Ferney.'[17]

By May 1761, the education of Marie-Françoise had been extended to include arithmetic, and she soon started to show some natural talent for acting small parts in Voltaire's plays.[18] But she felt no affinity for the dramas of the great Pierre Corneille and it was only with difficulty that Voltaire at length persuaded her to read Corneille's *Le Cid*.[19] He soon concluded that there would be strict limits to what he could expect of her education: 'This young person is as naïve as Pierre Corneille was great.'[20] The best thing for this charming girl, he thought, would be to find her a husband. But a husband would require a dowry, and Voltaire hit on a scheme for financing this: he would write an extensive and erudite commentary in a new edition of the works of Corneille; he would get it endorsed by the Académie Française; he would publish it in a luxurious and expensive multi-volume edition; he would persuade the great and the good throughout Europe to subscribe to it; and the proceeds would go to Marie-Françoise.

This idea first occurred to him when he learned that the Académie Française was planning a series of editions of the works of classic French authors. He wrote to Charles Duclos, *secrétaire perpetuel* of the Académie: 'It seems that Mlle Corneille would be entitled to sulk at me if I did not take on the great Corneille as my share of the project.'[21] Three weeks later he wrote again to Duclos, and asked that Corneille should be the first in the series, 'since it was he who first made our language respected among foreigners.'[22] He proposed that the edition should be opened to subscription, to which the greatest nobility, and even the royal family, should be invited to subscribe for a few copies; and he asked that the Académie Française should endorse his proposal. Voltaire's bubbling enthusiasm was irresistible; three weeks later, the Académie Française approved his plan.

Voltaire's rationale for undertaking the Corneille project was explicitly nostalgic, since he believed that the great age of French civilisation was the seventeenth century.[23] 'It seems to me that we should regard him as the Greeks regarded Homer, the first in his line, and unique, even with his faults.'[24] Since then Voltaire believed there had been a decline into decadence, and he hoped that his commentary would in some sense help to fix the rules of the French language. 'My dear and respectable colleague, I believe it is a question of the honour of the Académie and of France. We must fix the language, which 20,000 brochures are now corrupting'.[25] Such a belief in fixed rules was, of course, entirely consistent with the thinking behind the rule-based Académie Française, as well as with Voltaire's views of the rules of stagecraft. The paradox, though, is that modern French was created at least as much by Voltaire as by Corneille, and not by rules, but by the rapidity and simplicity of his diction. Today, Dr Johnson's English seems stilted and formalistic, whereas Voltaire's colloquial French is astonishingly modern.

Voltaire got down to his editing task almost immediately, but even before that, he set about rustling up a list of subscribers. He wrote to a Dijon friend: 'I trust that the King will head the list. I shall subscribe for six copies [in fact he took a hundred],[26] several members of the Académie Française will do as much; I shall tax M. de Brosses for two copies at 40 livres apiece, that's reasonable for an estate which he sold me a bit dear. Our colleagues in the Paris Académie must take more copies than other people, for they have still to expiate their servility to cardinal Richelieu and their censure of Le Cid.'[27]

(*Le Cid* had been a triumphant popular success when it was first performed in 1636; but in 1638 Cardinal Richelieu, the King's chief minister and founder of the recently created Académie Française, compelled the Académie to pass a formal censure on the play, for having failed to observe the neo-classical rules of the three unities.)

The King, urged by Mme de Pompadour and the duc de Choiseul, duly put his name down for two hundred copies; the Tsarina Elisabeth Petrovna also asked for two hundred, the Empress Maria-Theresa for a hundred; but Frederick the Great for only six. Yet Voltaire tried to prevent any unduly vulgar marketing of the subscription lists; early in 1763 he urged that Philibert Cramer be discouraged from hawking subscription forms at the theatres and on the promenades, 'as if they were tickets for green oysters'.[28] Nevertheless, the subscription list ended up with 1,176 names, for a total of 4,009 copies.[29]

At first Voltaire planned to limit his commentaries to the best of Corneille's tragedies, since he thought some of them were really not very good. He wrote to an old schoolmaster friend: 'My undertaking, my dear Master, attaches me more and more to the great Corneille. [But] Corneille wrote far too much that was bad, and I do not mean just unworthy of him, but absolutely unworthy of the theatre. So I shall not comment on any of the comedies, except *Le Menteur*, nor on any of those tragedies which have dropped out of the repertoire.'[30] But he soon found himself reluctantly dragged by a sense of duty into working on all Corneille's plays, including the bad ones. He moaned to d'Argental: 'Just think: I have 32 plays to comment on, of which 18 are unreadable. Pity me, encourage me, don't scold me.'[31] Three weeks later, Pierre Corneille's scorecard had got markedly worse: by now, the number of plays which Voltaire thought were 'unbearable and do not deserve to be read' had gone up from eighteen to twenty-two.[32]

And yet Voltaire sympathised with Corneille's personal plight when his plays started to go out of fashion. 'He had no consideration, people laughed at him; he went on foot, he arrived at the theatre from his publisher all covered with mud; they hissed his last twelve plays; he could scarcely find actors who deigned to perform them. Don't forget, I was brought up by people who had long known Corneille. My father used to drink with Corneille. He told me that this great man was the most boring mortal he had ever seen, and the one with the lowest conversation. Yet they want commentaries on those works which should never have seen the light of day. All right then, they will have their commentaries, and I shan't complain of my trouble.'[33] By the end of January 1762, just nine months after his approach to Duclos, the first volume of Voltaire's commentaries went into production.

Meanwhile, Voltaire's theatre entertainments, with their attendant dinners and dances, were becoming increasingly popular. In March 1762 there was a run-through of *Cassandre*, in front of three hundred people; a few days later there was another performance, with two hundred spectators, followed by a ball. Official Huguenot opinion in Geneva still officially disapproved of Voltaire's dramatics, and the Geneva preachers did not dare to come themselves; but, as Voltaire exultantly pointed out, they sent their daughters instead.[34] All these people needed refreshments, so Voltaire ordered 'the most enormous cart-load' of wine. 'The *vin ordinaire* will be for the guests, and the better stuff, if you please, will be for me. A little barrel of this better stuff, containing about 240 pints, will do nicely.'[35] In April Henri Lekain, the star of the Comédie Française, came to stay and took the lead in *Tancrède* and *Alzire*. By the end of that year, Voltaire's theatre at Ferney was giving performances every week.

All this was costing a lot of money, so Voltaire decided that the time had come to impose some discipline on his expenditure. That meant imposing some discipline on Mme Denis, as he wrote to Jean-Robert Tronchin on 10 January 1762:

Mme Denis and Mlle Corneille need some amusements; they deserve it, for their goodness in living in Gex nine months of the year. But I should like to put a bit of order into the pleasures and the affairs of Mme Denis. I have reckoned that, having paid all the debts of the household, having made considerable settlements of every kind on her, having handed over to her all the income from the Ferney estate, she should be able to cover all the household expenses with an extra hundred louis per month, including the various trifles she may order from Lyon. By this arrangement, I should put a certain and unchanging order in my little fortune.*[36]

But it soon became clear that Voltaire's well-meaning efforts at financial discipline were not working. In May he told Ami Camp: 'As for the other amusements you have been kind enough to send Mme Denis, we shall make a separate account at the end of the year, which will be deducted from the 1,200 louis that I give her for the management of the house.'[37] Later that month, Voltaire was again insisting, to Ami Camp that 1,200 louis a year was plenty for Mme Denis to run a fairly large house, 'if she knows how to control herself'. And soon afterwards: 'I cannot stop the torrent of our expenses, but we shall ruin ourselves if we want.'[38] By August 1762, Voltaire had increased Mme Denis's monthly allowance from 100 to 120 louis and agreed to pay for everything she had ordered from Lyon until then; but in future, anything else she ordered would be deducted from her increased allowance.[39] In future . . .

In May 1762, Voltaire fell seriously ill, and retreated to Les Délices, which was closer to Geneva, so that he could be nearer his doctor, Théodore Tronchin. 'I am still very weak', he wrote to a friend, 'M. Tronchin claims that he will pull me through. I hope so, for I should be very embarrassed to die before completing my work.'[40] A few days later he felt a bit better. 'I was on the point of going to see if one commits as many stupidities in the next world as in this. Tronchin and nature made me postpone the journey.'[41] But he was still rather feeble, and said that he had been told he must stop working. 'Work, which was my consolation, has been forbidden me.

*1 louis = £24.

I am getting weaker. But the Corneille edition will continue as before.'[42]

Voltaire admitted to Charles Duclos, *secrétaire perpetuel* of the Académie Française, that his comments on Corneille were rather harsh. 'You will no doubt find the commentaries a bit severe, but I have to tell the truth. During my lifetime, people will say that I am very insolent, but after my death they will say that I am very fair; and since I shall die soon, I have nothing to fear.'[43]

In the end d'Alembert and the Académie Française persuaded him to tone down his criticisms, but the final impression was almost as much a denunciation of Corneille's defects as an exposition of his virtues.[44] When the edition appeared in 1764, there was an indignant public outcry in defence of Corneille, but Voltaire had the satisfaction of knowing that it had been a great publishing success, bringing in £40,000 for Marie-Françoise.

Voltaire's health, never good, deteriorated around this time, and he again moved back to Les Délices, so as to be nearer to Théodore Tronchin. In May 1764 he wrote to a friend: 'For the past two months I have found myself absolutely incapable of writing or of moving. I have been obliged to transport myself to Les Délices, near M. Tronchin, even though I know very well that the journey to the temple of Epidaurus cannot restore health. I only speak to my doctor out of consideration for my family. I should have to be mad to imagine that one man could cure the age and the weakness of another man, and even madder not to submit to fate with good grace.'[45] This particular crisis proved short-lived. On 23 June Théodore Tronchin wrote to one of their mutual friends: 'Voltaire's health could not be better. I met him yesterday, between the two bridges over the Rhône, driving a cabriolet, harnessed to a two-year-old pony. I shouted to him through the window: "*Old baby, what are you up to?*"' Voltaire immediately wrote him an urgent disclaimer: 'The spectacle of a young pedant of seventy years old, driving a cabriolet, does not come along every day. My dear Aesculapius [Greek god of medicine], I was coming to see you. I had something to say to you. I had no carriage horses, and I decided to go to see you, as if I were a little dandy. Do not go and draw your cruel conclusions, that I am in good health, that I have a body of iron, etc. Do not slander me any more, but love me.'[46]

Voltaire did not say in his letter what it was that he had wanted to tell Tronchin; perhaps the truth was that he just enjoyed driving his cabriolet. At all events, he continued driving and on Christmas Day 1764 he told Cramer of a little upset he had had:

My very dear Caro, you remember that when Luc [his monkey] bit me on the leg, I said that it was I who was at fault. I owe the same justice to Collete [his mare]. We were busy, Wagnière and I, plumping up our cushion, and we had let go of the reins, Collete came upon a milestone and made the cabriolet go over it, we all fell one on top of the other, that's to say, Wagnière, Collete, the cabriolet and me; and we got up as best we could; Collete asked me a thousand pardons, and made me the most charming faces, and we continued our promenade very gaily.[47]

By one test, however, Voltaire was clearly not inventing his ill-health: he found that he could no longer act in his plays. 'These past few days, they wanted me to play the part of an old man in my little theatre; but I found that I was in fact so old and so feeble, that I could not even portray a character which should come so naturally to me.'[48] Instead, he lent Les Délices to two visitors, the ducs de Lorges and de Randan, who were bringing a company of actors to put on some plays at Ferney.[49] He said that he was only too willing to hand over the theatre to them, on one condition: 'Provided I am not in the cast. That's all done with. I have given up the theatre. One must know when to take one's leave, when one is over 71.'[50] A week later, Voltaire wrote to d'Alembert: 'I let Mme Denis lay on meals for 26 guests, and put on plays for dukes and presidents and governors, and passers-by whom we shall never see again. Amidst all this hubbub, I go to bed, and I shut the door.'[51]

Despite Voltaire's complaints at the drudgery of his Corneille edition, nine years later, in 1773 (when he was seventy-nine), he brought out a second edition, which was 50 per cent larger than the first.[52] According to the Voltaire scholar René Pomeau, it was over a hundred years before Corneille's reputation really recovered from the impact of Voltaire's critical onslaught.[53] But recover it did, and today Corneille's plays are still performed, whereas Voltaire's are not.

By December 1761, long before the completion of the Corneille commentaries, Voltaire had already provided generously for Marie-Françoise, so that she would never be in need.[54] All that was missing was a suitable husband. In December 1762, a young man, Colmant de Vaugrenant, presented himself, and Voltaire was quite taken with him. But he soon discovered that Colmant was in debt and was after her dowry. Fortunately Marie-Françoise did not care for him at all and in January the engagement was called off.

The aftermath of this episode was particularly revealing of Voltaire's social reflexes. He wrote to d'Argental: 'My divine angels, the marriage between M. de Colmant and our little marmotte has been struck off. Lekain has written to us that she should marry an actor, and offered his congratulations. Now I respect actors when they are good, I want them to be neither infamous in this world, nor damned in the next; but the idea of giving a cousin of M. de la Tour du Pin to an actor is a bit revolting.'[55] Voltaire protests often and noisily at the iniquity of the pariah status of actors, by which they were excommunicated and denied Christian burial; but when it came to his adoptive daughter marrying one, well, it seemed there were limits.[56]

But all turned out for the best, for within two weeks it was decided that Marie-Françoise was to marry Pierre-Jacques-Claude Dupuits de La Chaux, a twenty-three-year-old cornet of dragoons. This young man was already well known to Voltaire, who had lent him £9,000 to enable him to buy a company of dragoons: 'A very pleasant gentleman, with charming manners, good-looking, loving, loved, fairly rich. We all agreed, in a moment, without discussion, as if we were arranging a supper party. Yesterday, it seemed that the two parties love one another. If I could, I would hold the marriage tomorrow. There's no point in delaying, life is too short.'[57] The best part of it, for Voltaire, was that since Dupuits was a local boy and an orphan, the married couple could live at Ferney, and Voltaire could keep Marie-Françoise near him. 'We shall house the two orphans; they love each other passionately, and that cheers me. I wish that Pierre [Corneille] could come back to see all that, and witness Voltaire leading to church the only person left with his name. Mlle Corneille, with her little face, and two dark eyes which are worth a hundred times the last dozen plays of uncle Pierre. Have you seen her? Do you know her? She is a gay child, sensitive, honest, gentle, the best character in the world.'[58]

Voltaire's conservative social instincts immediately asserted themselves. He sent some money (25 louis) to François Corneille, the father of Marie-Françoise, but in instalments so that he could not throw it all away at once. And then he tried to see if François could not be found a new job outside Paris, for example as manager of a tobacco warehouse or some other similarly dignified post. 'You know how disagreeable it must be for a gentleman and an officer to have a father-in-law who is a little postman trotting along the streets of Paris.'[59] But at all costs Voltaire was determined that François must be kept away from the wedding: 'I gather that the first thing the father will do, as soon as he has received some money, will be to come to Ferney. Heaven preserve us! His person, his conversation, his job would not go down well with the family into which Mlle Corneille is marrying. M. le duc de Villars and the other French guests at the ceremony would make nasty jokes at his expense. As for me, I should have no repugnance; but not everyone is as philosophical as your servant.'[60]

Marie-Françoise Corneille was married very quietly in mid-February 1763. 'My angels, Maman Denis is still unwell, and I am blind [because of the snow], and the tutor of M. Dupuits is deaf. All these things rather spoiled our little fête: we didn't fire any cannon, *maman* did not come to supper, and the marriage took place without ceremony.'[61] Nevertheless, 'the two lovers are very happy, the parents are enchanted [meaning himself and Mme Denis], and apart from the snow, everything is as good as possible.'[62]

Word about Marie-Françoise Corneille and her good fortune got around, and in 1763, a month after her marriage, there turned up at Ferney *another* young Corneille, hoping to pick up a share of Voltaire's largesse. This was Claude-Etienne Corneille who was a direct descendant of Pierre Corneille, whereas Marie-Françoise was only a distant relative. But Voltaire was having none of him; one adopted child was enough, and besides the Corneille edition was already sewn up in favour of Marie-Françoise. He thought he could get rid of Claude-Etienne by giving him a little bit of money.[63] Voltaire wrote to his Paris friend Etienne-Noël Damilaville: 'Please tell me just how many other little Corneilles there are in the world. One has just turned up here who really is great-grandson of Pierre, and therefore a real gentleman. He has come on purpose, so that I can marry him off; but I do not think I shall arrange his wedding any time soon.'[64]

Voltaire had great wealth, two chateaux with their estates, great fame and inexhaustible creative energy; now he had a delightful daughter, a delightful son-in-law, and the hope of delightful grandchildren. His personal life had reached a new zenith of contentment.

7

The Calas Affair

1761–5

Following the happy marriage of Marie-Françoise, Voltaire had every reason to take life more easily. After all, he was nearing seventy. Yet he became busier than ever, for he was already embarked on a new vocation, as a campaigner for justice. This was not a vocation that he willed or consciously chose; on the contrary, it came to him out of the blue, and he showed at first every sign of preferring to avoid it. But it claimed him irresistibly, and when he finally responded, he engaged in it with wholehearted commitment until the end of his life.

Voltaire's campaigns were triggered by his indignation at specific cases of miscarriages of justice. In most cases, he was too late to prevent the injustices; in three of the most celebrated instances, his aim was to secure the posthumous rehabilitation of the victim. In one of these three cases, he secured a complete rehabilitation. In the second, he eventually learned of the possibility of rehabilitation, but only on his death-bed. In the third, he failed; but the French Revolution subsequently changed the relevant law.

Over time, Voltaire's perspective broadened, from concern for particular individuals in particular cases, and from the specific details of each miscarriage and the holes that he could pick in the unjust legal process, to a consideration of the defects of the French justice system and, eventually, to a consideration of the principles of justice in general.

The first three cases were those of François Rochette; Jean Calas and his family; and Pierre-Paul Sirven and his family. They can be grouped together, because they have much in common. The victims were all Protestants; the cases were all concerned with the persecution of Protestants by the Catholic State, and the superstitious tensions that existed between the Catholic and Protestant populations; the cases all took place in or near Toulouse, in the Languedoc, a region with a relatively large Protestant population; and they all took place in quick succession within a few months during the winter of 1761–2.

First, a word about the position of Protestants in eighteenth-century France. The Edict of Nantes, which Henri IV issued in 1598, had been intended to bring an end to the French wars of religion, and it gave French Protestants considerable security to practise their reformed religion, as well as a number of defended strongholds as a guarantee of their physical security. In the following century, however, it became clear that this settlement was really just an unstable truce. This truce progressively broke down, leading to widespread Catholic campaigns of intimidation in the 1680s against Protestants in the Poitou, the Béarn and the Languedoc. In 1685 Louis XIV revoked the Edict of Nantes, subjecting Protestants once more to far-reaching official persecution: more than 200,000 French Protestants emigrated, to Holland, Germany, England, Geneva. In 1724 Louis XV reaffirmed this policy of repression: Protestant services of worship were forbidden, male offenders were liable to a life sentence in the galleys, female offenders to life imprisonment, and preachers to execution. The only valid marriages were those sanctified by the Catholic Church, and all newborn children were required to be baptised and brought up as Catholics. Many professions, including that of the law, were open only to those who could prove they were practising Catholics. Protestant families were required to employ Catholic servants.

Naturally, the Catholic policy of repression did not drive out Protestantism: in the mid-eighteenth century there were still around 300,000 Protestants in France. Some were forced by discrimination and persecution to convert to Catholicism; many pretended outwardly to conform and were able to lead honourable, even prominent public lives, including in liberal professions like the law. But many remained Protestant at heart and in private, and continued to attend illegal religious services in the remote countryside ('in the desert', as it was known); they remained in permanent danger of imprisonment or execution.

Why these three cases occurred within a few months of each other in the Languedoc is an interesting question. The usual explanation hinges on the fact that they all took place in the closing years of the Seven Years War, which was generally perceived as a war between Catholic France and Protestant England; that France had suffered a series of major defeats at the hands of the English; and that French Catholics therefore looked upon French Protestants as the representatives of an enemy power, even though an area like the Languedoc was comparatively remote from any theatre of the war. Whether or not this explanation is valid, there seems to have been an easing of Catholic–Protestant tensions when the Seven Years War came to an end in 1763.

François Rochette was arrested on the night of 14 September 1761, near Montauban, on suspicion of being a thief. He openly declared that he was a Protestant minister, and he was imprisoned in the town of Caussade. The following day was market day in Caussade and many people were in town. Civil unrest gave way to spontaneous agitation when word spread among the Catholics that the Protestants were planning an attack. Three Protestant brothers, named Grenier, who were gentlemen glass-makers, attempted to free Rochette and were themselves arrested. They and Rochette were hauled off for trial in Toulouse.

A certain Jean Ribote-Charron, a young Protestant merchant, fearing for the safety of Rochette and the three brothers, and knowing of the liberal reputations of Voltaire and the Genevan writer Jean-Jacques Rousseau, wrote to each of them asking them to intervene. Rousseau simply brushed off his appeal, claiming that he had no power to do so. Voltaire informed Ribote-Charron, on 5 October, that he had written to the duc de Richelieu, and believed that the men's release could be arranged. But he could not resist adopting a sarcastic and condescending tone: 'I hope you will have confessors, but not martyrs; it's very ridiculous to go to heaven, by way of a ladder [i.e. the ladder of the gallows].'¹ Voltaire was equally dismissive when he wrote again to Ribote-Charron at the end of November:

M. le maréchal de Richelieu tells me, Sir, that he can do nothing for your minister and his followers so long as they are in the hands of the Parlement of Toulouse. I hope I can trust the clemency of the King when the case is heard. You must not doubt, Sir, the indignation of the Court [i.e. Versailles] against public demonstrations. Jesus Christ said that he would always be there where two or three were gathered together in his name;² but when there are three or four thousand, it is the devil who is there.³

Voltaire apparently believed that the agitation in Caussade had been close to an uprising. On the same day, he wrote to Richelieu: 'Whether they hang the preacher Rochette or make him an abbot, will make no difference to the prosperity of the kingdom of the Francs. But I think that the Parlement should condemn him to be hanged, and that the King should pardon him. Such humanity will make him loved more and more.'*⁴

Three months later, at the beginning of March 1762, Voltaire heard that the Parlement of Toulouse had sentenced Rochette to death; yet in a letter to d'Argental he still made a supercilious joke of the affair. 'The Parlement of Toulouse has just condemned a minister to be hanged, three gentlemen to be decapitated and five or six bourgeois to be sent to the galleys, and all for having sung some of the psalms of David. This Parlement of Toulouse really does not like bad verses.'⁵ In fact, the sentence had already been carried out. On 19 February François Rochette, clad in a white shirt, walked barefoot through the streets of Toulouse to the place of execution; there he prayed, sang psalms as he mounted the scaffold, and was hanged. The three Grenier brothers, by virtue of their privilege as noblemen, were beheaded.

The Rochette case does not normally figure prominently in accounts of Voltaire. This is no doubt because it does not fit in with the canon of his later, more heroic campaigns; it is one of a number of

---

*Louis XV was sometimes known as 'le bien-aimé, 'the well-loved'.

cases which he knew about, but did not take up. But in certain ways it is particularly interesting, since it gives a vivid picture of some of Voltaire's habitual feelings and attitudes just *before* he started to change his mind on a series of issues relating to human rights.

Up until about 1762, when he was sixty-eight, Voltaire had three main fears or hatreds. His first and main *bête noire*, as in his campaign to 'écraser l'infâme', was the nexus between the Catholic Church and the repressive French State, and their joint manipulation of popular superstition. His second aversion, springing from the first, was the fanaticism of deranged individuals, like Damiens; he was equally likely to distrust the fanaticism of intense Protestants, as we saw in his hostile contempt for the prospective 'martyrdom' of Rochette. His third anxiety was about the danger of breakdowns in public order, which could result from eruptions of fanaticism. This was implicit in his assumption that Damiens's attack on Louis XV might have been part of a larger conspiracy against the State, and in his consequent acceptance that Damiens should be tortured to reveal his fellow conspirators. It also prompted his reflex condemnation of what he believed, mistakenly, to have been a mass demonstration at Caussade in favour of Rochette.

This triangle of fears is obviously in some sense internally contradictory: Voltaire detested the repressive French State, but he feared any rebellion against that State. And when he joked that it did not matter whether Rochette was hanged or made an abbot, he was clearly implying that the claims of realpolitik outranked those of justice. Over the next few years, as a direct result of his campaigns for justice, his thinking on these issues changed fundamentally, to the point where he came to see that the claims of the rights of ordinary people had inherent validity even against those of the State.

Jean Calas was a prosperous cloth merchant who lived with his wife, Anne-Rose Cabibel, over their shop in Toulouse. They were both Protestants, and they had four sons and two daughters. Louis, the third son, and a convert to Catholicism, had left home; Donat, the youngest son, was serving an apprenticeship at Nîmes; and the two daughters, Rosine and Nanette, were away from home, staying with friends. So the family circle, on the evening of 13 October 1761, consisted of Jean Calas and his wife, their two eldest sons, Marc-Antoine (almost twenty-nine) and Pierre (twenty-eight), and their Catholic servant, Jeanne Viguière. There was also a visitor with them at the supper table, young Gaubert Lavaysse, a friend of Pierre and the son of a prominent local lawyer.

After supper Marc-Antoine went downstairs, apparently intending to go for a walk; the rest of the party stayed upstairs, talking, until Gaubert Lavaysse said he had to go home and Pierre took a light to show him out. When they got downstairs, they found Marc-Antoine in the shop, apparently dead. A doctor was called but could do nothing. The Calas family alerted the town authorities, and the magistrate David de Beaudrigue arrived on the scene; he arrested the entire Calas family, on suspicion that they were responsible for the death of Marc-Antoine.

This Beaudrigue was a brutal and a hasty man. His assumption, based on gossip overheard that evening on the street, was that Jean Calas, with the help of his family, must have murdered his oldest son in order to prevent him from converting to Catholicism. To us this may seem preposterous; but at that time mutual ignorance and superstition was such that ordinary Catholics apparently believed that Protestants would go to any lengths to prevent their children from abandoning their faith. David de Beaudrigue does not seem to have taken any account of the fact that the third son, Louis Calas, had in fact already converted to Catholicism without being murdered. But his suspicions were increased when the Calas family changed their story: at first they had said that they had found the body of Marc-Antoine lying on the ground, but later that they had found it hanging by a noose between a pair of double doors connecting the shop and the storeroom behind. Their explanation for the change of story was that they had at first wanted to conceal the fact of suicide – if such it was – since a suicide would be denied honourable burial and dragged on a hurdle through the streets to be abandoned on the city dumping ground; but that they had then realised they must tell the truth. Which of these stories was true? Either way, it did not look good for the Calas family.

We still do not know exactly how and why Marc-Antoine Calas died. The modern consensus is that he was almost certainly not killed by his family; his sixty-two-year-old father would not have had the strength to do it on his own, and a joint murder by several members of his family is frankly unbelievable, not least because the Catholic servant would have had to be part of the conspiracy. In any case, David de Beaudrigue was simply clinging to his first assumption: he never succeeded in producing any evidence to support it. But the main interest of the Calas case lies not in its potential as a detective story, but rather in some aspects of the unfolding of the trial, and in Voltaire's subsequent reactions to it.

The first phase of the trial of Jean Calas took place before the magistrates or *Capitouls* of Toulouse, and one of their first steps, according to the custom of the time, was to enlist the help of the Catholic Church in the police enquiry. They issued a nine-point summons or *monitoire*, which was posted up in every parish church in Toulouse, and read out on three occasions by the parish priest at the service of Mass, summoning the (Catholic) faithful to testify against the (Protestant) Calas family. Witnesses were called for, to confirm, 'on the basis of hearsay or otherwise', among other things, that Marc-Antoine had been about to convert to Catholicism; that a meeting held in a Protestant house had decided on his death; and that this execution had been carried out on 13 October, whether by hanging or strangulation.[6]

This device of the *monitoire*, linking Church and State against evil-doers, was consistent with the customary trial process of the time, which was heavily rigged in favour of state repression. The accused was allowed a lawyer, who could make representations on his behalf outside the courtroom; but the lawyer was not permitted to be present at the questioning of the accused, which took place behind closed doors. The accused was not given any advance notice of the questions, nor of the evidence or witnesses arrayed against him, and he might even not know the details of the offence he was charged with. This procedure would seem extraordinary today, but the mainstream assumption at the time was that anyone who was accused must almost certainly be guilty, and that the purpose of a trial was not to discover the truth, but to prove guilt, if possible by confession. The *monitoire* failed to produce any hard evidence against the Calas family, apart from gossip, guesswork and hearsay. Nevertheless, it seems that many ordinary Catholics in Toulouse were convinced both that Marc-Antoine had been planning to convert and that the Calas family were guilty of his murder. No one could be found with first-hand evidence (as opposed to rumour and hearsay) that Marc-Antoine really intended to convert to Catholicism, let alone any priest able to testify that he had actually done so. Nevertheless, the *Capitouls* prejudged the conversion of Marc-Antoine, and therefore the guilt of Jean Calas, by ordering that Marc-Antoine should receive a Christian burial in consecrated ground. The Catholic Church then raised the stakes by giving Marc-Antoine a martyr's funeral, accompanied by forty-six clerics and a barefoot procession of the White Penitents, one of several lay Catholic brotherhoods in Toulouse.

This public fervour among the Catholic population regarding the presumed guilt of the Calas family, urged on by the Catholic hierarchy , seems to have created an atmosphere of hysteria which in turn exerted enormous influence on the judicial process. On appeal, the case was transferred from the *Capitouls* to the Parlement, whose judges decided to renew the *monitoire*, this time accompanied by a 'fulmination', that is, a threat that anyone who withheld the required evidence would be excommunicated. Still no hard evidence was forthcoming. The attorney-general demanded that Jean Calas and his son Pierre should first be broken alive on the wheel, and that Mme Calas should be hanged; all three should be tortured. Judgement on Gaubert Lavaysse and Jeanne Viguière should be delayed. The judges hesitated, then decided to confine themselves to the case of Jean Calas, postponing a verdict on Pierre Calas and his mother. By a narrow majority vote the court decided, on 9 March 1762, that Jean Calas should be broken on the wheel, exposed for two hours, then strangled and thrown on a burning pyre. Why? Because this punishment, they said, was 'a reparation owed to religion, for the son's happy conversion, which had probably (*vraisemblablement*) been the cause of his death.'[7]

Jean Calas had still not confessed, so on the day of his execution, 10 March, he was subjected, in the presence of David de Beaudrigue, to two forms of torture. In the first, known as the *question ordinaire*, his arms and legs were stretched on the rack; in the second, known as the *question extraordinaire*, he was compelled to drink ten jugs of water, not once but twice. Still there was no confession.

Jean Calas then walked barefoot in a white shirt to the scaffold in the place Saint-Georges in Toulouse. He was tied face up on the wheel, and his arms and legs were broken with an iron bar; priests begged him to confess his crime and his sins; but still he did not confess. After two hours, he was strangled, and his body burned.

In the absence of any confession, the confidence of the judges of the Toulouse Parlement was now thoroughly shaken, and they recoiled from proceeding on the same basis with the trial of the other members of the Calas family. They condemned Pierre to banishment, but they freed Mme Calas, young Gaubert Lavaysse, and the servant Jeanne Viguière, though without declaring them innocent. Mme Calas's two daughters were locked up in different convents, even though they could not possibly have had anything to do with the death of Marc-Antoine. Public opinion in Toulouse was outraged; it had been looking forward to further persecution of the Calas family.

As we have seen, Voltaire was aware of the Rochette affair even though he showed little interest in it; but he made no reference to the Calas case at this time, so may have known nothing about it.

One reason why he was not paying as much attention to outside events as usual is that he was too busy managing his amateur dramatics. His new, larger theatre at Ferney had been in operation since the previous October, and now, on 8 March 1762, he wrote to d'Argental, exulting in the spectacular success of his latest theatre party:

I am exhausted; I have just come from a ball; I can no longer call my head my own. '*A ball, old fool? A ball in your mountains? And for whom have you given it? For the badgers?*' Not at all, if you don't mind: for a very fine company of people, for these are the facts. Yesterday we played *The Rights of the*

Seigneur [by Voltaire], and that in a theatre which is certainly more beautiful and more brilliant than yours [the Comédie Française]. You perhaps
imagine that we were playing to an audience of primitive provincials; not
at all, but to people of very refined taste ... Yes, *The Rights of the Seigneur*
enchanted 300 spectators, of every age and condition, gentry and farmers,
believers and dandies. They came from Lyon, from Dijon, from Turin.
Would you believe that Mlle Corneille won all the votes? How natural she
was! Lively! Gay! How she was mistress of the theatre, stamping her foot
when she was prompted out of turn! There was one place where the audience forced her to repeat a scene. I played the bailiff, and, if you don't mind,
fit to make them burst out laughing. But what is one to do with 300 people,
in the middle of the snow, at midnight, when the show is over? We had to
give them all supper, and then we had to make them dance. It was a pretty
well turned out party. I was only expecting fifty people. But enough of that,
I mustn't boast. We play *Cassandre* in eight or ten days, and afterwards I
shall tell you how it went.[8]

Cassandre was Voltaire's latest tragedy, which he subsequently
renamed *Olympie*.

Voltaire's first reference to the Calas affair came a few days later,
on 22 March 1762, in a sardonic throwaway paragraph at the end of
another letter about his amateur dramatics.

I believe, Sir, that the travellers whom you had the goodness to send on to
us, may have been a bit astonished by the confusion which they found in our
hermitage which ought to have been consecrated to repose. We gave them
a play and a ball, but your relative had quite some trouble finding a bed.
They were so ruffled by our disorder, that I heard no further mention of
them. I am very sorry. Your relative, Sir, seemed to me infinitely amiable, in
the press of people; and I could glimpse that in society he must be the best
company in the world ... You have perhaps heard of a good Huguenot
whom the Parlement of Toulouse has had broken on the wheel for having
strangled his son. Yet this reformed saint thought he had done a good deed,
seeing that his son wished to become a Catholic, and that it was to prevent
an apostasy. We may not be worth much, but the Huguenots are worse, and
in addition they preach against play-acting.[9]

(Voltaire also says in this letter that he has rented out his Tournay estate, to put an end to friction with de Brosses.)

From Voltaire's initial summary of the Calas trial, it seems clear that at first he knew few or none of the details of the case, and couldn't have cared less. But within three days his attitude changed totally: he abandoned his mocking, disdainful tone of voice, and instead became, first, intensely anxious about the basis for the conviction, and then gradually convinced that Jean Calas had been the victim of a great injustice.

This is one of the most dramatic turning-points in Voltaire's life, and a key moment in the history of penal reform in Europe. One day he was brimming with self-confidence, supercilious, condescending, uninvolved; three days later, he was anxious, emotional, uncertain, and quivering on the edge of horror and indignation.

On 25 March he wrote to Cardinal Bernis, the French ambassador to the Vatican in Rome and a fellow member of the Académie Française:

May I beg your eminence to tell me what I should think of the frightful adventure of this Calas, broken at Toulouse for having hanged his son? What they claim here [in Geneva] is that he is totally innocent, and that he called God to witness as he expired. They claim that three judges protested against the sentence. This adventure grips my heart; it casts sadness over my pleasures and corrupts them. We must regard either the Parlement of Toulouse or the Huguenots with horror.'[10]

On the same day he wrote in much stronger terms to a close friend:

There has just taken place, in the Parlement of Toulouse, a scene to make the hair of one's head stand on end. Perhaps people in Paris do not know about it, but if my information is correct, I defy Paris, frivolous and opera-comic as it is, not to be struck with horror. The Calas father took God to witness as he died, entrusted his judges to the judgment of God, and wept on the wheel for his dead son. Two of his children are in this neighbourhood, and they fill the country all about with their lamentations. I am beside myself. I am concerned as a man, and a bit also as a *philosophe*. What I want to know is, on which side is the horror of fanaticism.[11]

Exactly what made Voltaire change his mind so suddenly and so radically is not clear. We know that he talked with a Protestant merchant from Marseille, who knew the Calas family well, and argued for their innocence; his Protestant acquaintances in Geneva would undoubtedly have discussed the case, and some of them may also have had information about it. But what seems to have clinched matters for Voltaire was an extended personal interview, the first of many, with twenty-two-year-old Donat Calas, the youngest of Jean Calas's four sons. At the time of his brother's death, Donat had been an apprentice in Nîmes; when he learned of the tragedy in Toulouse, he made his way immediately to safety in Protestant Geneva. Voltaire summoned him to Ferney, and was won over. Three years later, in a retrospective account, he described that meeting:

I had expected to see a roustabout, such as you sometimes find in the country. I saw a child, simple, innocent, of the gentlest and most interesting physiognomy, and who, as he spoke to me, made vain efforts to hold back his tears. I asked him if his father and mother were of a violent character: he told me that they had never beaten a single one of their children, and that there had never been more indulgent or more tender - parents. I confess that I needed no more to presume strongly the innocence of the family.[12]

From the moment of his first meeting with young Donat Calas, the Calas affair became for Voltaire a virtual obsession. Between 25 March 1762, when he wrote his first anxious letter to Cardinal Bernis, and the end of the year, Voltaire wrote over a hundred letters which were in whole or in part about the case, and about his efforts to challenge the verdict; this is more than a quarter of all the 390 letters he wrote during the nine-month period. In the first three months of 1763, he wrote another thirty-eight letters wholly or partly about the Calas case.

If Voltaire now instinctively presumed the innocence of Jean Calas, he needed more information on which to base a reasoned conviction. But his attempts to get at the facts met with serious obstruction: the processes of a French trial were intensely secret; they were not intended to be transparent or open to challenge; and the Toulouse authorities stubbornly resisted the release of any information about the procedures of the case. 'People cry that we [the French] are an odious people, intolerant, superstitious, as atrocious as we are frivolous. The silence of the Parlement, in a case where it ought to publish the reasons for its sentence, shuts the mouth of anyone who wishes to endorse the equity of its judgement'.[13] In another letter he wrote: 'If there is anything which can stop the frenzy of fanaticism, it is publicity.'[14] Publicity was exactly what the Parlement wanted to avoid, precisely because it had no proof of Calas's guilt; but Voltaire concluded that this would be his best weapon for forcing the authorities to act and the Parlement to submit.

He soon learned, not only that the death sentence was passed by a majority of the Toulouse judges, but by the narrowest of majorities, writing to d'Argental on 27 March:

You may ask, my divine angels, why I am so strongly interested in this Calas. It is because I am a man, because I see that all foreigners are indignant at a country which breaks a man on the wheel without any proof. I was mistaken on the number of judges: there were thirteen of them, and five consistently declared Calas innocent. If there had been one more vote in his favour, he would have been absolved. Does a man's life hang by so little? And such horrible tortures? It is not up to me to condemn the Parlement of Toulouse, but in fact there were no eyewitnesses. The fanaticism of the people may have been communicated to complicit judges, for several of them were members of the White Penitents.[15]

The point about the vote is that the death sentence required a majority of two; at first the bench had been split seven to six, putting the necessary majority out of reach, until one of the judges changed sides.

By 4 April, Voltaire was categorically asserting, to his close friends at least, his belief in the innocence of Jean Calas. 'My dear brothers,* it is recognised that the judges of Toulouse have broken the most innocent of men. Almost the whole of the Languedoc groans with horror at it. Never since the day of Saint Bartholomew has anything so dishonoured human nature.'†[16] On 17 April, Voltaire summarised the preliminary conclusions he had drawn, from four legal opinions which he had commissioned: that it was quite impossible for Jean Calas, an enfeebled old man of sixty-nine, to have hanged his vigorous twenty-nine-year-old son; that even with the help of other members of the family it would have been extremely difficult; and that he had 'certain proofs' that Marc-Antoine had had no desire to convert to Catholicism.[17] In fact, Jean Calas was sixty-four, not sixty-nine. No matter. Voltaire's central point is obviously true: that a vigorous young man would be extremely difficult to hang (or strangle) against his will. Voltaire does not say what his 'certain proofs' were.

By 15 May Voltaire felt sure, first that the Parlement had no hard evidence against Calas, but had sentenced him solely on the basis of pure conjecture; and second that the Parlement now saw that it had made a terrible blunder, and wanted at all costs to prevent the truth coming out.[18] But Voltaire's confidence in his position was shaken when he got what he described as a 'very strange letter' from his friend the duc de Villars, one of the six First Gentlemen of the Chamber at Versailles, expressing complete confidence in the Parlement and its verdict, and claiming that it was only the clemency of the judges which had spared the rest of the Calas family.[19] Voltaire began to fear that there was a closing of ranks between the authorities in Toulouse and the hierarchy in Versailles.

---

*Voltaire addressed this letter to Etienne-Noël Damilaville. But he starts it with 'My dear brothers' because Damilaville, Jean Le Rond d'Alembert and Nicolas-Claude Thieriot were all close friends, and often passed Voltaire's letters round between them.
†On 24 August 1572, the feast-day of Saint Bartholomew, some 3,000 Protestants were massacred in Paris, and the killing continued in the provinces until October. Voltaire was so horrified by his knowledge of the event that he was regularly ill each year on 24 August. See Letter 11381, 30 August. 1769.

Voltaire could now see that a serious challenge to the Calas verdict would meet great resistance; and that if his challenge was to be effective, it would have to be conducted with a much stronger legal and factual brief. On 5 June he wrote to Jean Ribote-Charron in Montauban: 'For two months I have made the greatest efforts with the leading persons of the kingdom, in favour of this unhappy family, which I thought innocent. But they believe them all guilty; they hold that the Parlement administered both justice and mercy. M. Ribote should go to Toulouse, to throw light on this horrible adventure. He must discover and inform me of the truth.'[20] One of the key questions Voltaire wanted answered was: Did the Calas family remain together in the same room after supper, or not? Everything, he said, depended on this 'great truth'.[21] For if the answer to the question was yes, then it was impossible that Jean Calas alone could be guilty of the murder of his son. Six days later, he sent Ribote-Charron a serious chaser: 'It is now almost two months that I have been waiting for a detailed report, and it hasn't come. This nonchalance in an affair which requires the most urgent application is unforgivable.'[22]

At home, Voltaire's amateur dramatics were becoming increasingly popular and time-consuming, with performances and dinners and balls, but they were no longer at the centre of his thoughts, as he told d'Alembert in July: 'I am at present preoccupied with a more important tragedy, that of a hanged man, of a man broken on the wheel, of a family ruined and scattered, and all for the sake of holy religion. I urge you to cry out loud, and make others cry out. Do you see Mme du Deffand and Mme de Luxembourg? Can you stir them up? Farewell my great philosopher, *Écrasez l'Infâme*.'[23]

Voltaire's strategy for his Calas campaign developed on three fronts: digging out the facts of the trial; pulling strings with all the influential people he knew at court; and mobilising public opinion. The first two of these fronts were predictable; and with his manifold high-level contacts, Voltaire could be expected to try to influence leaders of the establishment behind the scenes. Much more interesting, and surprising, was his declared objective of influencing the authorities through public opinion, or as he put it, making 'a public outcry'.

Of course, Voltaire did not understand 'public opinion' in anything like the sense it has today; on the contrary, he rejected the idea that society at large could have a valid opinion. Several years later, in the context of a very different human rights case, he explicitly addressed this issue: 'When I say *"the voice of the public"*, I do not mean that of the population at large, which is almost always absurd; that is not a human voice, it is a cry of brutes; I mean the collective voice of all the decent people who think, and who, over time, reach an infallible judgement.'[24] Nevertheless, there is a world of difference between trying to influence individual members of the political establishment one by one (which is what Voltaire had always done in the past) and trying to influence the political establishment collectively. It is a measure of Voltaire's ambition in his human rights cases, and of his understanding of the power of public communication, that he saw his writings as a way of exerting leverage on the authorities through the society in which they were embedded.

Getting the facts proved difficult, because the Parlement at Toulouse was totally recalcitrant. 'What do we ask?' Voltaire wrote to d'Argental.

Nothing more than that justice should not be as dumb as it is blind, that it should speak, and say why it condemned Calas. What horror is this, a secret judgement, a condemnation without explanations! Is there a more execrable tyranny than that of spilling blood on a whim, without giving the least reason? '*It is not the custom*,' say the judges. Hey, monsters! It must become the custom! You owe an accounting to men for the blood of men. As for me, I do not ask anything more than the publication of the trial procedure. People say that this poor woman [Mme Calas] must first get the documents sent from Toulouse; but where will she get them? Who will open the clerk's den? In any case, it is not just she who interests me, it is the public, it is humanity. It is important for everybody that such decisions should be publicly justified.[25]

In other words, Voltaire was by this time no longer motivated primarily by his pity for Jean Calas, though that obviously came into it, nor by sympathy for the family, though that too played a part, but by consideration of larger principles of State, society and humanity. Later that year he wrote: 'It is in the interest of the State that we discover on which side is the most horrible fanaticism.'[26] And again: 'Please note that the reason which should influence the King's Council to procure the documents, is not the memory of Jean Calas, about which the Council cares very little, but the public good; it is humanity that the Council should consider.'[27] It would obviously be stretching things to suggest that Voltaire was promoting 'human rights' in the modern sense of the term, but he was starting to move in that direction, and he would move further in the years to come.

Voltaire faced deadlock on his first two fronts: the Parlement refused to release the evidence and the trial records, and the King's ministers refused to exert pressure on it to do so. Pierre Mariette, one of the lawyers hired by Voltaire, 'tells me that he can do nothing without a summary of the evidence. What! Does that mean we cannot demand justice without having the weapons which our enemies deny us? So people can spill innocent blood with impunity, and get away with it, by saying they do not want to say why they spilled it? Ah! *Quelle horreur!*'[28] As for the great and good at court, Voltaire said that he must knock on every door; in fact, he had already knocked on several very important doors, including those of Richelieu and Villars, but so far he did not have enough allies to tip the balance.

There remained public opinion. In early July 1762 Voltaire wrote: 'Only the ultimate intervention of the King can force this Parlement to reveal the truth; we are doing our utmost to secure it; and we believe that a public outcry is the best way to do so.'[29] To secure the kind of public outcry that would exert pressure on the King and his ministers, Voltaire published a pamphlet which he called *Pièces Originales* [Original Documents]. This purported to be letters from Mme Calas and depositions from her sons Donat and Pierre Calas, telling their version of what happened on the night of 13 October 1761. It also included an ostensible appeal from Donat Calas to the chancellor and to the King-in-Council to investigate the case and make the truth known. These documents were, of course, all written by Voltaire himself, and they argued the innocence of Jean Calas and that of his family; but, in addition, they constituted an indictment of several aspects of the French judicial system, above all its secrecy, in contrast with the relative openness of the English system.

The pamphlet *Pièces Originales* was widely distributed in Paris, especially to key figures at court, to the duc de Choiseul, the prime minister, to René Charles Maupeou, the Chancellor, and to Mme de Pompadour, the King's mistress and something of an ally of the *philosophes*. This document may have marked the turning of the tide of opinion: Voltaire claimed in July that it had had 'a prodigious effect' among leading figures in Paris, and he reported that the duc de La Vallière wanted to present Mme Calas to Mme de Pompadour.[30]

Crucially, the Chancellor himself called for a formal review of the Calas case. Voltaire wrote on 20 August: 'The Calas affair is going even better than I dared to hope; yes, the chancellor has called for the trial record, the whole court is stirred up, and the King is informed. We are working on a reasoned appeal, and it is my barrister at the Council who is in charge of it. So far my campaign against the most barbarous fanaticism has been very successful.'[31]

As confirmation of an important shift in opinion at court, Mme de Pompadour wrote a remarkable letter in late August to the duc de Fitzjames, commander of the province of Languedoc, and therefore partly responsible for Toulouse:

You are right, the affair of poor Calas makes one tremble. It seems impossible that he could have committed the crime of which he was accused; it is not in human nature. Yet his judges will not repent. The King's good heart really suffered when he heard this strange tale, and the whole of France cries out for revenge. The poor man will be avenged, but not brought back. The people of Toulouse are excitable, and have far more of their kind of religion than they need for being good Christians. May it please God to convert them, and make them more human.[32]

At the end of August, Voltaire's indignation against the Parlement of Toulouse rose to a new pitch. He wrote to d'Argental: 'I have seen the opinion of Pierre Mariette [one of Voltaire's key lawyers] on behalf of the Calases; and I have also seen the text of Calas's sentence. The jurisprudence of Toulouse is really very strange, for this sentence does not even say what Jean Calas was accused of. I can only regard the sentence as an assassination carried out in black robes and square hats.'[33]

In September, Voltaire's campaign at last made substantive legal progress. He wrote to Ribote-Charron in Montauban:

By now they must know in Toulouse that the widow Calas's request for a review of the case has been accepted, that the *rapporteur* for the case has been named, and that fifteen leading barristers in Paris have signed the opinion which calls for vengeance, that this opinion, and the report of the advocate to the King's Council [Mariette], have been printed, and that this widow, as respectable as she is unfortunate, is not short of help. The little preliminary documents [the *Pièces Originales*] which have inspired the public with pity for innocence and indignation at injustice, have been translated into English, German and Dutch.[34]

In December 1762 Voltaire was becoming increasingly optimistic. He wrote to Philippe Debrus, a Geneva merchant:

Believe me, everything depends on the *rapporteur*, and I think we can have confidence in him. The bench which will judge the case is composed of enlightened and honourable judges, who will not be at all afraid to offend the Parlement, and who will hand down the most exact justice, just as the public desires it. The good side of the delays we have suffered is that the judges will be better informed, and we shall have more time to enlighten their justice and excite their zeal. We must deal mainly with the lawyers* in this affair. Women and ambassadors are useful for influencing the general public, but only the lawyers are useful for influencing the judges.[35]

---

*The expression Voltaire uses is 'gens de robe', a generic term for lawyers and judges. There was a customary antithesis between the *noblesse de robe* (those who had acquired, often by purchase, titles as lawyers, judges or other civil servants of the State) and the *noblesse d'épée* (those with ancient feudal titles, or who had received titles for military services).

As for the women of the Calas family, Voltaire argued that their plight must be exploited for the maximum emotional effect: in January 1763 he wrote that the widow Calas and her two daughters 'will soon go, all three of them, to display their mourning weeds and their tears to the gentlemen of the Council of State, whom M. de Beaumont [another of Voltaire's leading barristers] has so well persuaded of Calas's innocence.'[36]

The Toulouse Parlement continued to drag its feet, but Voltaire was well on the way to winning. Shortly before the session of the King's Council in early March 1763, Mme Calas surrendered to prison in Versailles. This was customary: a person seeking to overturn a trial verdict had to surrender to prison beforehand, as a sign of readiness to accept a new trial and a new verdict. But all proceeded smoothly: the appeals committee of the King's Council formally endorsed the admissibility of the Calas appeal, and on 7 March 1763 the King's Council in formal session, presided over by the chancellor, and with three bishops and a hundred judges in attendance, acting unanimously, ordered the clerk of the Toulouse Parlement to submit the record of the trial of Jean Calas, and the attorney-general of the Toulouse Parlement to submit the reasons for the verdict.[37]

Voltaire was overjoyed. He wrote to the duc de Richelieu at the end of March 1763: 'Our victory in the Calas case is much greater than you have been told; not only have they ordered them to submit the trial record, they have also called on the Parlement to give a justification of its verdict. This last demand is already a sort of reprimand.'[38] But he was becoming more and more aware that there were systemic reasons for the malfunctioning of the judicial system in Toulouse. He wrote to Damilaville: 'Let me repeat my congratulations on the success in the Calas case. But I have just learned one of the reasons for the Toulouse verdict which will astonish you. These Visigoths have a maxim that four quarters of a proof, and eight eighths of a proof, make two complete proofs, and they give to hearsay the weight of quarters and eighths of proof. What do you think of this manner of reasoning and judging? Is it possible that the life of men can depend on such absurd people?'[39]

In this particular case, the battle was virtually over; but the formalities would take another year. [40] First, the Toulouse Parlement demanded that Mme Calas pay the exorbitant sum of £1,500 for the costs of making a copy of the records. Voltaire was enraged: 'The Parlement was ordered to send the trial records to the King, not to the widow, so it is not up to her to pay for the obedience which the Parlement owes the King.' But he submitted, and proposed that he and other Calas supporters should jointly contribute. [41] The money was handed over on 24 May 1763, but still the Parlement delayed, until several weeks past the deadline set by the King's Council. Voltaire wrote on 12 July: 'The records of the Calas trial only reached Paris last week. [They show that] the Toulouse attorney-general had had the infamy to suppress the requests, which poor Calas had put forward, for the court to hear witnesses who were likely to testify in his favour. We shall push forward this affair with the greatest warmth.' [42]

What Voltaire meant was that he now intended to use the Calas case as a way of raising much broader issues: not just whether, in this particular case, Jean Calas did or did not murder his son, but more generally the role played by the fanaticism of the Catholic Church, and the pervasive superstition and prejudice of the Catholic population, in bringing about an iniquitous and wholly unproven guilty verdict.

Voltaire opened this new phase of his campaign with his ninety-page pamphlet, the *Traité sur la Tolérance* (Treatise on Tolerance). In December 1762 he gave Damilaville an oblique hint that he was working on something important but that it would only be published after the Calas case was heard in the King's Council. [43] By late January, the *Traité* was taking shape, and Voltaire made clear, in a letter to Damilaville, that he was rather pleased with it: 'My dear brother, we can no longer prevent Jean Calas from being broken, but we can make his judges hated. [Look out for] a little work on tolerance which will soon appear. There are passages which make one shudder, and others which make one burst out laughing; thank God, intolerance is as absurd as it is horrible.' [44] On 13 April 1763, the *Traité* was printed and a small number of copies circulated privately to key social and political figures, including Mme de Pompadour, the Ministers of State, some of the members of the *Conseil d'Etat*, as well as King Frederick and some of the German princes. 'I shall include a circular letter,' wrote Voltaire, 'in which I shall beg them to ensure that it is only read by sensible people, and to make sure that their copy does not fall into the hands of a publisher.'[45]

With the opening words of the *Traité sur la Tolérance*, Voltaire threw down a challenge to the regime, brutal in its frankness. 'The murder of Calas, committed in Toulouse with the sword of justice, on 9 March 1762, is one of the most exceptional events which deserve the attention of our age and of posterity.' There followed a recapitulation of the Calas affair and of Voltaire's case against the legal procedures of the Toulouse Parlement which had made possible the death of a man like Calas. 'If an innocent father of a family is delivered into the hands of error, of passion, or of fanaticism; if the accused has no defence except his own virtue; if the arbiters of his life run no other risk in killing him, than that of making a mistake; if they can kill with impunity by a simple decree; then a public outcry is raised, every man feels he is in danger, one can see that no one's life is in safety in the face of a tribunal set up for watching over the life of the citizens, and all voices in unison demand vengeance.'[46]

Voltaire's primary thesis in the *Traité sur la Tolérance*, apart from the innocence of Jean Calas, was that the practice of religious intolerance and the persecution of non-believers were unique to Christianity, whereas all other civilisations, past and present, had been tolerant of religious pluralism.

We know enough about the price that has been paid since Christians first quarrelled over dogma: blood has flowed, either on the scaffold, or on the battlefield, from the fourth century until our own day.[47]

I say it with horror, but with truth: it is we Christians who have been persecutors, executioners, assassins! And of whom? Of our own brothers. It is we who have destroyed a hundred cities, with the crucifix or the Bible in our hands, and who have not ceased spilling blood and lighting pyres, since the reign of Constantine until our own day.[48]

And yet Jesus himself did not preach intolerance: 'Almost all the words and actions of Jesus Christ called for gentleness, patience, indulgence. I ask if it is tolerance or intolerance which is the divine law? If you want to resemble Jesus Christ, be martyrs, but not public executioners.'[49] By contrast, the pamphlet claims, religious tolerance was the norm among the Greeks and the Romans, and in India, Persia, Tartary, China and Japan.

Voltaire also compares the religious persecution of Protestants in France and other Catholic countries with the relative toleration towards Catholics in the Protestant countries of Europe: Germany, England, Holland. And he proposes that Protestants should be accorded a similar degree of toleration in France as Catholics enjoyed in England: the protection of natural law, the legal validity of Protestant marriage, security for Protestants and for their children, the right of inheritance. Voltaire's recipe for legal toleration was quite restrictive: Protestants would not be allowed to gather in public places or to attend public forms of worship, nor would they be allowed to hold municipal offices or to receive public honours or any special privileges, or to have special strongholds (as provided for in the Edict of Nantes). In other words, Protestants would enjoy greater religious freedom, though still heavily qualified, but not equality with Catholics. This very modest suggestion made no headway: the legal position of Protestants remained unchanged for another twenty-four years, until the Edict of Tolerance of 1787, nine years after Voltaire's death and two years before the French Revolution.

Voltaire's second thesis, much more insidious in its implications for the Catholic Church, is his deistic claim that all civilisations really believe in the same virtuous God. One of the key chapters in the *Traité* is a 'Prayer to God', in which Voltaire addresses 'God of all beings, of all worlds, of all times'. He goes on: 'Let us use the instant of our existence to bless, in a thousand different languages, from Siam to California, your goodness which gave us this instant.' The logical implication of his notion of a universal deism is that Christianity is not the only true religion and that many of the specifically Christian elements of Christian doctrine are not, or at least are probably not, true.

The *Traité sur la Tolérance* was not formally published in Geneva until November 1763, and at first Voltaire believed it was doing well. In December he wrote to Gabriel Cramer: 'I can see from the success it has had, and from the approval of the ministers, that if you had run off four thousand copies, you would still not have printed enough. But this work is not a bird of passage, it seems it is one for all seasons.'[50] He told d'Argental: 'The duc de Choiseul tells me that he is enchanted with it, and so is Mme de Gramont, and so is Mme de Pompadour.'[51] Voltaire was not exaggerating: he had received a letter from Choiseul, who told him: 'Everyone who has read it, tells himself: we must agree that he is right; I've always thought so myself.'[52]

But even if the *Traité* was privately admired by the duc de Choiseul and by Mme de Pompadour, even if it quickly became an enormous, and enormously influential, popular success, Voltaire soon learned that it was officially regarded by the authorities as a dangerous and seditious work. Choiseul, though a genuine friend of Voltaire and a man of tolerance, ostensibly refused to accept a single copy, and the state postal service intercepted all the copies sent from Geneva that it could. This came as no surprise to Voltaire, who had written earlier that year: 'There is no way of sending printed matter by post these days. They open and confiscate all packets which contain any kind of printed material. Thus they cut off the nourishment of the soul.'[53] In theory, Voltaire pretended that he was no longer particularly disturbed by the dangers of state censorship, for he wrote to Damilaville: 'In truth, I do not much mind whether the book is condemned or not. They have burned so many books, good and bad, so many bishops' instructions, so many works, pious and impious, that it no longer causes the slightest sensation. Books survive if they can.'[54]

But by the end of 1763, Voltaire was again worried by the intensity of the censorship crackdown. 'I am a bit upset that they have confiscated, at the Paris post office, two copies [of the *Traité*] sent by Cramer. Perhaps the precaution I took, of circulating it at court before releasing it to the public, may have done more harm than good.'[55] In January 1764, he wrote to Mme du Deffand: 'These days, no book can enter France by post, without being seized by the officials, who for some time have been building up a rather fine library, and who will soon become in every sense men of letters. We no longer even dare send books care of ministers.'[56]

Voltaire advised Cramer to lock up his next consignment for Paris, 'with a hundred keys', for a month or six weeks, until the storms had died down.[57] But the storms were slow to subside. On 1 February 1764, Voltaire wrote to d'Argental: 'It seems (and I am very well informed) that there are great alarms in Versailles about the *Tolérance*, even though all those who have read the work have been very pleased with it. You may easily imagine that these alarms have spread to me.'[58] Voltaire went on to urge that Damilaville in Paris should be told not to release any more copies of 'this diabolical work, which proves that all men are brothers'.[59] And yet in a letter to Damilaville himself, on the same day, Voltaire told him that if he would 'take a dozen copies, and circulate them with [his] usual prudence to people who are safe and reliable', he would render a great service to honest people.[60]

By March 1764 Voltaire became more cheerful, partly because the storm over the *Traité sur la Tolérance* seemed to be dying down.[61] He wrote to d'Alembert: 'Today they are quite disposed to allow this book to get out into the public with a certain discretion, and I should like brother Damilaville to let you have half a dozen copies, which you could give to honest people, who would let it be read by other honest people, and the vine of the Lord would be cultivated. This tolerance is an affair of state, and it is certain that those who are at the head of the kingdom are more tolerant than people have ever been; a new generation is rising which has a horror of fanaticism.'[62] A fortnight later, Voltaire was urging Damilaville to get hold of another twenty-odd copies of the *Traité* from Antoine de Sartine, which he could distribute to his friends, and to the friends of friends; but he reckoned that it was too early to think of a Paris edition.[63] A month later, however, Voltaire heard that a pirate edition of the *Traité* had come out in Paris, and in June that 'lovely editions' had appeared in Liège and in England.[64]

Voltaire's reference to de Sartine throws a tantalising shaft of light on the internal contradictions of the *ancien régime*. Antoine-Raymond-Jean-Gualbert-Gabriel de Sartine had previously been the chief police officer in Paris; in 1763 he was put in charge of the state publishing directorate (*Directeur de la Librairie*). This very senior position meant that he was charged with the responsibility for controlling book publishing, in line with French censorship policy; in particular, it meant that he would repress all dangerous or seditious books. But it is clear, from Voltaire's reference, that de Sartine was in fact acting as Voltaire's depository in Paris for copies of the highly controversial *Traité sur la Tolérance*, imported from Geneva. In other words, the *ancien régime* managed to combine a general system of autocratic repression, in this case of censorship, with flexible and ad hoc practices of collusion with people who were outside the system, or even opposed to it.

Sartine was not a unique case. Another official who helped Voltaire in a similar way was François-Louis-Claude Marin, previously when he had been the royal censor, and from this year (1763) when he was *Secrétaire Général de la Librairie*. Voltaire was dismayed when he discovered later that Marin was betraying him, and playing not just a double but a triple game, selling on one of his forbidden manuscripts to a pirate publisher. But Voltaire's influential friends, like d'Argental, urged him not to make a fuss because Marin might still be useful, even if he was a double-crosser.

These practices of double-dealing were symptomatic of the internal contradictions of the French *ancien régime* in its later years. Voltaire evidently had some premonition of the turbulence that lay ahead, for in April 1764 he wrote to Bernard-Louis Chauvelin, French ambassador to Turin: 'Everything that I see sows the seeds of a revolution which will come without fail, but which I shall not have the pleasure to witness. The French arrive late for everything, but they do arrive at last; the light has spread so much from man to man, that there will be an outbreak at the first opportunity, and there will be a fine row; the young are lucky, they will see such beautiful things.'[65]

Voltaire does not explain why the revolution will come, or what form it will take; his tantalising words appear abruptly in the letter, without context or explanation; we can only guess. But it is surprising that he should imply that the revolution would be beautiful, for elsewhere his views seem strongly anti-revolutionary, and he appeared to believe firmly in the rights and responsibilities of a quasi-feudal order.

In the case of his own community at Ferney, he wrote to d'Argental in March 1764:

Everyone gets married here, we are building houses on every side, we are clearing land where nothing has grown since the Flood, we are sprucing things up, we are fertilising a barbarous country; and if we were absolute masters, we should do even better. I detest feudal anarchy, but I am convinced by my own experience, that if the poor masters of the châteaux were less dependent on our masters the governors, they could do as much good to France as the governors sometimes do harm, considering that it is quite natural that a master of his château should regard his vassals as his children.[66]

Voltaire's paternalism, which was diametrically opposite to Rousseau's democratic inclinations, comes out in another letter around this time. He complained that 'one of our scourges is that the peasants are abandoning the plough, to go and work in Geneva as jewellers and watchmakers. [This is] a very useless craft'; and he sought a decree which would forbid the peasants to leave the land.[67] It may be that Voltaire believed that job mobility would be a threat to political stability, as he obviously thought that it would be to the rural economy. The irony is that Voltaire would, within a very few years, completely reverse his country-versus-town dialectic, and would promote and finance a watchmaking industry in Ferney, with worldwide sales.

One of the indirect consequences of the publicity surrounding the pamphlet *Traité sur la Tolérance* was that Voltaire was stirred up to campaign on behalf of those Protestants who had been condemned to a life sentence in the galleys.* In January 1764, Louis Necker, a

---

*In reality, the galleys no longer existed literally: condemned Protestants were simply imprisoned. But they were still known as *galériens*.

merchant at Marseille,* appealed to Voltaire to help with the case of an individual *galérien,* a cobbler called Claude Chaumont, who had been imprisoned since 1751. Voltaire wrote to Choiseul to appeal for Chaumont's release, and the following month he asked Necker to send him a list of the names, nicknames, trades and prison numbers of all the *galériens,* and to mark in the margin the merits of each case.[68]

By early March, Choiseul had ordered the release of Chaumont; Voltaire said that this made him 'fairly happy', but he did not hold out much hope that he could render the same service to the other *galériens.*[69] A few days later, Claude Chaumont visited Ferney to thank Voltaire for his help, but once in his presence he found himself completely tongue-tied with shyness. Voltaire was not impressed. 'I have seen your cobbler. Really, he is an imbecile. If his comrades are as poor-spirited as him, as I assume they are, then they are just as sure to go to paradise in the next world, as to the galleys in this one.'[70]

Voltaire made one last attempt to help the *galériens.* The duc de Choiseul had for some time been pondering a scheme to populate the French colony of Guiana, in South America, at least partly to compensate for the loss of Canada to the English. Voltaire suggested that one solution would be to release the *galériens* from prison, on condition that they agree to go out to Guiana. But the idea did not get very far: it turned out that the *galériens* would rather stay in prison in France than risk the unknown in Guiana.[71] 'Would you believe,' Voltaire asked d'Argental rhetorically, 'that those clowns behaved like the companions of Ulysses, who preferred to remain as pigs, rather than become men again?'[72]

Thereafter, Voltaire rather lost interest in the *galériens,* though this was mainly because the Calas affair reached a new climax. On 4 June 1764, after a long legal palaver, the case was finally brought before the King's Council; it decided unanimously to annul the verdict and sentence of the Toulouse Parlement. Voltaire wrote to Damilaville: 'You can imagine how much the quashing of the Toulouse verdict

*The elder brother of Jacques Necker, the Swiss Protestant financier who later became finance minister to Louis XVI.

revives me. There we have fanatical judges confounded, and innocence publicly recognised. But what more can we do? Can we get expenses, damages and interest? Can we bring a suit against Master David [de Beaudrigue]? I can see that it is much easier to break a man than to make reparation. I embrace you tenderly.'[73] And to Cramer he wrote: 'The sentence, by which Calas was broken on the wheel, has been quashed unanimously. But the bones of poor Calas have not been any less broken. What damages will the family have? If Mme de Pompadour were still alive, the poor widow and her daughters would have a pension.'*[74]

After the quashing of the Toulouse verdict, a new trial had to be to held, to reach a new verdict; and the critical question, which could determine the final outcome, was: Before which court would this trial be held? If the case was retried in Toulouse, there was a danger that the previous verdict might be confirmed. When Voltaire heard that the retrial was to take place in the Paris appeals court, he was relieved and delighted.

A much more interesting thing is that the Calas case has been sent to be heard by the Requêtes de l'Hôtel [Appeals Court], that is to say, before the same judges as have quashed the Toulouse verdict. This horrible adventure of Calas has opened many people's eyes. The copies of the *Tolérance* have spread throughout the provinces, where people used to be pretty stupid. The scales are falling from people's eyes, the reign of truth is near. My angels, let us bless God.[75]

---

*Mme de Pompadour (1721–64), mistress of Louis XV and a friend of the *philosophes*, died 15 April 1764.

8

The Swiss Marmot

1764–5

Even before the final resolution of the Calas case, Voltaire was hard at work finalising one of his most controversial works, his *Dictionnaire Philosophique Portatif*, which he started to circulate in July 1764. He claimed that it was intended to be a brisker and briefer alternative to the *Encyclopédie*. But the most important characteristic of the *Dictionnaire Philosophique*, compared with the *Encyclopédie*, was not just its witty brevity, but its overt anti-clericalism. The *Encyclopédie* had set out to be a comprehensive survey of the current state of knowledge in the arts and crafts and sciences; the *Dictionnaire Philosophique* did not even attempt such a factual survey. The majority of its articles dealt, directly or indirectly, with questions of morality and of society, and in particular with those relating to Christianity, usually in critical, sceptical or derisory terms. To give a small flavour of Voltaire's approach, here are a few examples.[1]

Anti-Trinitarians: To explain their sentiments, it is enough to say that they maintain that nothing is more contrary to right reasoning than what is taught among the Christians about the Trinity of Persons in a single divine essence; that this incomprehensible doctrine cannot be found in any place in the Scriptures; and that to maintain that there are several distinct persons in the divine essence, is to introduce in the church of Jesus Christ the grossest and most dangerous error, since it is an open encouragement of polytheism.

Christianity: Several scholars have expressed surprise not to find anywhere in the works of the historian Josephus any trace of Jesus

Christ. Josephus was of priestly descent, a relative of the queen Mariamne, wife of Herod; he goes in great detail into all the acts of this prince; and yet he does not say a word about the life or death of Jesus; and this historian, who does not hide any of the cruelties of Herod, does not speak of the massacre of the infants.

Divinity of Jesus: The Socinians, who are regarded as blasphemers, do not recognise the divinity of Jesus Christ. They dare to claim that the idea of a man-God is monstrous, and that it is impossible that the infinite, immense, eternal Being could be contained in a mortal body. They cite Saint Paul, who never calls Jesus Christ God, and who often calls him man. They push their audacity to the point of declaring that the Christians spent three centuries building little by little the apotheosis of Jesus, and that they only raised up this astonishing edifice in the manner of pagans, who turned mortals into gods.

Tolerance: Of all religions, the Christian religion is no doubt the one which should inspire the most tolerance; and yet, up till now, the Christians have been the most intolerant of all men. It would be easy to show how far the Christian religion of today differs from the religion that Jesus practised. If we really look closely, the Catholic religion, apostolic and Roman, is, in all its ceremonies and all its doctrines, the opposite of the religion of Jesus. If it were permitted to reason coherently about religion, it is clear that we should all become Jews, because Jesus Christ our Saviour was born a Jew, lived as a Jew, and died as a Jew, and he said explicitly that he was accomplishing, that he was fulfilling the Jewish religion.

Torture: The Romans never used torture except on slaves, but then slaves were not regarded as men. Nor does it appear that a judge in the criminal court regards as a fellow human being a man whom they bring to him haggard, pale, defeated, eyes downcast, the beard long and dirty, covered with the vermin that gnawed at him in his cell. He gives himself the pleasure of applying the great and the little torture, in the presence of a doctor who takes his pulse, up to the point where he could be in danger of death, after which they start again; as they say, 'It helps to pass an hour or two.'

The grave magistrate who has bought, for a certain amount of money, the right to carry out these experiments on his fellow-man, will tell his wife at dinner what happened that morning. The first time, Madame was revolted; the second, she acquired a taste for it, for after all women are curious; and then the first thing she says to him when he comes home in his judicial robes is: 'My little heart, haven't you had the question applied to anyone today?' The French, who pass, I do not know why, for a very humane people, are astonished that the English, who have had the inhumanity to take from us the whole of Canada, should have given up the pleasure of applying the question.

As so often with his controversial works, Voltaire published the *Dictionnaire Philosophique* anonymously, in Geneva in 1764. He vigorously and repeatedly denied to all and sundry that he had had anything to do with what he describes as 'this abominable little dictionary, a work of Satan',[2] but it immediately got him into trouble: the book was condemned and publicly burned in several European capitals, starting with Paris. But Voltaire remained unrepentant. He brought out a new and expanded edition in 1765, with two more reprintings that year, another expanded edition in two volumes, a sixth expanded edition in two volumes in 1767, and yet another edition in two volumes in 1769, reissued twice in 1770, once in 1773, and twice in 1776. In parallel, he launched an analogous dictionary work called *Questions sur l'Encyclopédie*, which he brought out in nine volumes from 1770 to 1772.

Voltaire's denial of the authorship of the *Dictionnaire Philosophique* was important in legal terms, since it should have protected him from prosecution, even if it did not protect the book; but it fooled no one. The prime minister, the duc de Choiseul, wrote to him:

Why in the devil's name are you agitating so much, you Swiss marmot? No one says anything to you, and certainly no one wants to do you any harm;

you disavow the book even though no one has spoken to you about it, so much the better; but you will never persuade me that it is not by you. Silence about this work would have been more prudent; your multiple letters are an extra proof that it is by you, and that you are afraid. Stay calm, and everything will be calm for you; but don't take us for idiots, or for persecutors; in my case, think of me as the marmot's servant.[3]

When the Geneva authorities took steps to censor the *Dictionnaire* in September, Voltaire at first made light of the matter. He wrote to Damilaville, all wide-eyed innocence: 'It's a work which seems to me pretty strong. I had it bought for me in Geneva, there were only two copies. The consistory of the pedantic priests brought it before the magistrates, so then the booksellers ordered many more copies. The magistrates read it with edification, and the priests were quite astonished to see that something which would have been burned thirty years ago, is today well received by everybody.'[4] In fact, the Geneva authorities brought a prosecution against the book, and in late September it was publicly lacerated and burned by the public executioner. But in private they let Voltaire know that he should not be too worried; they wanted to remain on good terms with him. 'A magistrate came to ask me politely for permission to burn a certain *Portatif.* I said to him that his colleagues were the masters, provided that they did not burn me in person, and that I had no interest in any *Portatif.*'[5]

Voltaire was much more concerned by the hostile reactions that were building up in Paris, for despite the reassurances of Choiseul, he had learned that there was a serious danger that the *Dictionnaire Philosophique* might be burned by order of the Paris Parlement. He wrote to d'Alembert in October 1764, 'I have just learned that storms are brewing against the *Portatif.* The situation is very serious ... but why attribute it to me?'[6] And then a few days later: 'You ask why I worry so much about a book which is nothing to do with me. It is because it is attributed to me; it is because, by order of the King, the attorney-general is currently preparing a prosecution; it is because at the age of seventy-one, ill and almost blind, I am preparing to suffer the most violent persecution.'[7] And, indeed, the *Portatif was* burned in Paris in the spring of the following year, 1765, an event which would return to haunt Voltaire a year later, in the case of the chevalier de La Barre.

By August 1764 Voltaire was reasonably confident that the legal review process would eventually end in a total posthumous rehabilitation for Jean Calas. 'The Calas affair is going well, and it will continue to go very well. We shall have complete justice; but we shall not have it in one day. It is easier to break a man than to condemn a Parlement.'[8] So it was to prove, and final victory was delayed for another six months. On 9 March 1765, forty senior barristers (*maîtres de requêtes*) recommended the posthumous exoneration and rehabilitation of Jean Calas, and their recommendation was formally enacted by the *Hôtel des Requêtes* on 12 March. This was almost exactly three years after the barbarous death sentence passed on Jean Calas by the Parlement of Toulouse. Voltaire wrote to d'Argental a few days later: 'A young Calas was with me when I received your letter and that of Mme Calas, and that of Elie de Beaumont [one of Voltaire's leading barristers]), and of so many others. We wept tears of tenderness, young Calas and I. And yet it was *philosophie* alone which carried off this victory.'[9]

But Voltaire did not rest here. He reported with delight that David de Beaudrigue, the Toulouse *Capitoul*, had been stripped of his position, and he called for a ban on the festival staged each year in Toulouse, in which the Catholics celebrated the massacre of several thousand Protestants on 17 May 1562, ten years before the much bigger and more notorious massacre of Saint Bartholomew.[10] He wrote to Théodore Tronchin later in March 1765: 'Let us both congratulate ourselves on living in an age where fifty *maîtres de requêtes* can be found to appeal to the King, to beg him to abolish for ever the fête in which the town of Toulouse used to thank God for having once cut the throats of three or four thousand of their brothers. It is a long time since I tasted a joy so pure.'[11]

At the same time Voltaire stepped up the pressure for financial compensation for Mme Calas and her family. He wrote to d'Argental on 1 April: 'The poor widow Calas has not yet received from the King any damages for the breaking of her husband on the wheel. I do not know the exact value of a wheel, but I believe it must be expensive. Some people advise her to bring a case against the Toulouse judges, others not. My opinion is that she should sound out the Vice-Chancellor and the Contrôleur Général [finance minister], for fear of taking a step which could upset the Court and weaken the King's good-will."[12]

Fortunately, even without the influence of Mme de Pompadour, Louis XV proved generous. On 11 April he gave the Calas family £36,000 from the royal purse: £12,000 to Mme Calas, £6,000 to each of the daughters, £3,000 to each of the sons, and £3,000 to the family servant, Jeanne Viguière, plus £6,000 to cover legal and travel expenses.[13] Voltaire wrote to Damilaville: 'I forgot all my ills when I learned of the King's generosity; I felt young and vigorous again."[14]

Later that month, a plan was floated in Paris for making a commemorative print of the Calas family, to be sold for their benefit. Voltaire wrote to Damilaville: 'The idea of a Calas print is marvellous. Please put me down as a subscriber for twelve prints."[15] The print, by Louis de Carmontelle, shows, on the right, Mme Calas seated in prison, flanked by her two daughters and her servant, Jeanne Viguière, while on the left Gaubert Lavaysse and Pierre Calas read out the final submission by their lawyer, Elie de Beaumont. Thereafter, Voltaire always kept a copy by his bedside.[16]

The case of Pierre-Paul Sirven was in one important respect the most successful of Voltaire's human rights campaigns: it was the only one in which he was able to prevent a massive miscarriage of justice. The story of Jean Calas is the one for which Voltaire is most remembered, largely because his success in securing a complete posthumous rehabilitation for Calas set a spectacular and groundbreaking precedent. Pierre-Paul Sirven, by contrast, was able to escape with his wife and family before he could be arrested. He was nevertheless tried and condemned to death in absentia; Voltaire's great achievement was to secure the quashing of the verdict against him, and to rehabilitate Sirven and all of his family.

In many respects, the two cases were remarkably similar. Pierre-Paul Sirven was a master land surveyor and tax assessor, living near

Castres in south-west France, with his wife Toinette, and their three daughters, Jeanne, Elisabeth and Marie-Anne. The Sirvens were ostensibly converts to Catholicism, but in reality were still Protestant, and known to be so; locally, in Castres and nearby Mazamet, Protestants constituted about half the population.

Elisabeth Sirven, the second of the three daughters, was mentally unstable. On 6 March 1760 she disappeared from home; she was twenty-three years old. It turned out that she had been virtually abducted, on the instructions of the local Catholic bishop, and held in the Convent of the Black Ladies in Castres; the story the bishop told Pierre-Paul Sirven was that Elisabeth had asked to convert. In the convent, her mind became more disordered; but she refused to convert to Catholicism. After seven months she was returned to her parents, in a state of serious psychological and moral distress; in June 1761, a doctor was called, and declared that she was mad.

On the night of 15 December 1761, Elisabeth again disappeared from home. Two weeks later, on 3 January 1762, her body was found, drowned in a local well.

At this time, the trial of Jean Calas and his family was already under way in Toulouse, and the authorities in Mazamet immediately assumed that, just as Jean Calas must have murdered his son Marc-Antoine to prevent his conversion, so Pierre-Paul Sirven must have murdered his daughter Elisabeth for the same reason; and this despite the fact that there were no traces of violence on her body.

On 20 January 1762, the authorities issued warrants for the arrest of Jean-Paul Sirven and his entire family. But they were forewarned, and had fled on foot the previous day. Eventually, after five months, the Sirvens found their way by various different routes to safety in Protestant Lausanne. Meanwhile, in Mazamet, the trial against them proceeded slowly in their absence. Two years later, on 20 March 1764, the court condemned Pierre-Paul and his wife to be hanged, and their two daughters to be banished. Six months later, on 11 September, Pierre-Paul Sirven and his wife were hanged in effigy.

Voltaire first heard of the Sirven affair early in December 1762, but he did his best to keep it quiet, for fear that the coincidence of two cases alleging murder by Protestants of their children might seem to strengthen the credibility of both. 'Above all,' he wrote, 'let us say nothing about the Sirven affair.'[17] In March 1763 he was alarmed when he learned that the Protestant writer Antoine de Court was about to publish his book *Lettres Toulousaines*, publicising the two cases.

The *Lettres Toulousaines* go on at length about the story of Sirven and his daughter. This could finish our chances. The Sirven case has not been judged yet. The Toulouse Parlement will link these two cases together, and will justify the one by the other. I had expressly recommended to our three barristers [Elie de Beaumont, Pierre Mariette and Loyseau de Mauléon] never to talk about the Sirven affair, and they have kept their promise. If you could persuade the author to delay publication, until the end of our trial, we shall be saved.[18]

By the end of the month, Antoine de Court had agreed to hold back his book, and Voltaire offered to pay him compensation for his trouble: 'M. de Court has written with only the best of intentions in the world. I think it would be wrong to upset or discourage him. We should console him with a little present, to compensate for the delays and the corrections. I think a present of 10 louis should be enough; I offer to pay a quarter of that.'[19]

Voltaire put off from campaigning on the Sirven case for another two years, until early 1765, by which time he was virtually certain of complete victory in the Calas affair. In any event, there was no great urgency, since the Sirven family had escaped execution in Mazamet, and were in a place of Protestant safety. But in late February 1765, in a letter to the barrister Jean-Baptiste-Jacques Elie de Beaumont, congratulating him on the success of his efforts on behalf of the Calas family, Voltaire also urged him to take on the Sirven case: 'My eyes can scarcely see to read, Sir, but they can still weep, as you have made me realise. The whole of this affair has covered you with glory ... Now, has M. Damilaville spoken to you of another family of Protestants, executed in effigy at Castres, fugitives in Switzerland, and sunk in poverty?'[20]

Voltaire followed up his commitment to the Sirven case, in

September 1766, with a new campaigning pamphlet: *Avis au Public sur les Parricides imputés aux Calas et aux Sirven* (Notice to the Public, on the Parricides imputed to Calas and Sirven).[21] This was ostensibly a recapitulation of the stories of the Calas and Sirven cases and of the reasons for believing in their innocence. At the same time, it was an attack on fanaticism and bad jurisprudence in general. But the most immediate purpose of the pamphlet was to appeal for financial help for the Sirven family, who had been languishing in poverty since their escape from Languedoc four years earlier, in 1762. Sirven's assets had consisted of £19,000, not counting his salary of £1,500 a year,[22] but one important consequence of their condemnation for parricide was that these had automatically been confiscated by the authorities.

Voltaire sent obsequious begging letters, together with his *Avis au Public*, to many of his rich, noble and powerful friends, mainly, as he said, to those living outside France: Catherine the Great, Frederick the Great, Frederick of Hesse-Cassel, and others.[23] When writing to kings and princes, Voltaire's penchant for grovelling flattery knew no shame and no restraint. His letter to Catherine the Great gives some idea of the tone.

It is now towards the Star of the North that all eyes must turn. Your Imperial Majesty has found a path to a glory unknown, before her, to all other sovereigns. None had thought to spread benefits to seven or eight hundred leagues of their estates. You really have become the benefactress of Europe; and you have gained more subjects by the greatness of your soul, than others can conquer by force of arms.

There is perhaps indiscretion in daring to implore the support of Your Majesty for the Sirvens, after all the kindnesses with which she has overjoyed the Calas family. I know how much Your Majesty has done that is great and useful for her peoples. It would be culpable to beg you to divert, for an unhappy family of the Languedoc, part of the source of the benefits that you spread in Russia. I only take the liberty to write to you, Madame, to beg you to moderate your goodness. The smallest help will suffice us. We only ask for the honour of placing your august name at the head of those who help us to crush fanaticism, and to render men more tolerant and more human.[24]

Voltaire's begging seems to have worked: Catherine the Great, as well as the other kings, counts and princes, duly coughed up varying amounts of money for the Sirven cause.

But Voltaire's attempt to relaunch the Sirven campaign got off to a slow start, for his leading lawyer, Elie de Beaumont, was not enthusiastic, and proved lamentably dilatory in producing his legal opinion. When he did so, in December 1766, it was endorsed by nineteen barristers; but the first appeal, to the King's Council, was rejected, on the technical ground that, since the original judgement came from the court in Mazamet, any appeal should strictly be heard at the next higher level in the hierarchy, that is, at the Parlement in Toulouse.

It took another five years, after interminable foot-dragging by the law courts in the Languedoc, before Voltaire was able to secure justice for Sirven and his family. The strengths of the Sirven case, compared with that of the Calas family, were that there was no evidence of violence on the body of Elisabeth Sirven, no real evidence that the Sirven parents had murdered their daughter, and no contradictions in the evidence given by the family. The danger for the Sirvens was that the Parlement of Toulouse might display the same anti-Protestant prejudice as it had in the case of the Calas family.

In November 1769, five years after the original conviction, the Parlement in Toulouse was finally compelled to quash the old sentence. Yet it stopped short of formally acquitting Sirven. Instead, it adopted a new verdict which corresponded roughly with 'not proven', and in effect saddled him with the costs of the trial. With Voltaire's help, Sirven launched a new appeal against this verdict; but it was not until two years later, in November 1771, after the Parlement which had condemned Sirven in 1764 had been replaced by new judges in a new Parlement, appointed by the new Chancellor René Maupeou, that Pierre-Paul Sirven won a complete victory of rehabilitation, including substantial costs and the restoration of his confiscated property.

It had been an abysmally long struggle for justice. As Voltaire commented after his sensational victory over the archaic French penal justice system: 'It took only two hours to condemn this virtuous family to death; nine years to give them justice.'[25]

Between them, the Calas and Sirven cases left an indelible mark on Voltaire's life, on his attitudes, and on his reputation. Previously, he would never have thought of campaigning on behalf of some wretched victim of injustice; from now on, he was regularly engaged in a succession of such campaigns. Previously, he had not thought much about the principles of justice or the interests of society; from now on, he was increasingly interested in justice and social reform. Previously, he was famous, mainly among high and literary society, as a literary intellectual, France's leading writer of neo-classical verse tragedies; from now on, he also became famous among the common people as a champion of the downtrodden. And of all the 'human rights' cases which Voltaire took on, the Calas affair stands out, for this was the case which marked his name in the popular consciousness. When he finally returned to Paris, thirteen years later, ordinary people in the street referred to him as 'The Man of the Calas'.

9

Ferney

1765

Two months before his final victory in the Calas case, Voltaire made one of the key life choices of his retirement: he decided to give up Les Délices, and hand it back to its real owners, the Tronchins; from now on, he would live wholly at Ferney. On 10 January 1765, he wrote a formal one-sentence letter of renunciation to Jean-Robert Tronchin: 'I surrender to M. Robert Tronchin the house on the territory of Saint-Jean called Les Délices, with all its outhouses, according to the agreement made between us.'[1]

Voltaire gave varying reasons for his decision. To a Protestant pastor in Geneva, he implied that he was in a financial squeeze: 'It is true, my dear philosopher, that I am giving up Les Délices, the state of my affairs does not allow me to keep it. I have suffered some little setback in my fortunes, and it is not up to me to have as many houses as the sun [= zodiac].'[2]

Finance may well have played some part in Voltaire's decision. His income depended, to a considerable extent, on the interest on a large loan to the duke of Wurtemberg. The previous summer (July 1764) the duke had suspended all payment of interest on money he owed, and since these payments included £28,000 a year to Voltaire, he could reasonably be said to have 'suffered some little setback' in his fortunes. By February 1765, Voltaire was telling Richelieu: 'I am getting rid of Les Délices because, having the largest part of my assets dependent on M. le duc de Wurtemberg, and my affairs with him not being completely settled, I have feared to die of hunger as well as of old age.'[3]

To Damilaville, by contrast, he suggested that he was giving up Les

Délices for different reasons: 'I have become so old and so feeble that I can no longer have two country houses. So I shall give up Les Délices, if I can come to a reasonable arrangement, which is still very difficult.'[4] The previous November, Voltaire had written to an English friend, George Keate: 'I have an amusing fate, my dear Sir: I am almost completely blind for four or five months of the year. It is hardly fair that, being so far from equalling Milton, I should be as completely blind as he. I am only blind when the snows cover the Alps and the Mont Jura. I shall soon be obliged, I believe, to leave these Délices. In spring, summer, and autumn, I must live at the Ferney estate, which I am improving, and in winter all I need is a really warm room.'[5]

So many different explanations – his finances, his blindness, his age, and his feebleness – strongly suggest that they were all at least partly pretexts. It seems likely that the real reason for his decision to leave Les Délices was that he was becoming disenchanted with Geneva and the chronic friction with its political institutions. As he wrote to d'Argental: 'I have lost my taste for Les Délices. The troubles of Geneva no longer interest me, and having perceived that I have only one body, I have concluded that I did not need two houses; one is quite enough. After all, there are people who are worth more than me, and who have no house at all.'[6]

In short, the carping criticisms of the Geneva authorities, their disapproval of his amateur dramatic entertainments, and their censorship of his controversial writings were becoming increasingly irksome to Voltaire. No doubt his irritation with the Genevans was reciprocated and may well have affected Voltaire's relationships with the Tronchin clan, key members of the Geneva political establishment. For when Voltaire did start proceedings for relinquishing his lease on Les Délices, Jean-Robert Tronchin took a position on the terms of the handover that was at best pernickety, at worst decidedly unfriendly.

As it happened, Jean-Robert was no longer based in Lyon, since he had moved to Paris, on his appointment by the French government as a tax farmer (*fermier-général*) in 1762. For practical purposes, therefore, he had effectively ceased to be Voltaire's personal banker. For a while longer, Voltaire continued to do banking business with Ami Camp, a cousin of Jean-Robert Tronchin and his junior partner in the bank in Lyon; but the personal relationship was not as close, and after a time Voltaire made other arrangements. Voltaire remained on friendly terms with François Tronchin, Jean-Robert's brother, a fellow theatre enthusiast and a frequent visitor. But his links with the rest of the Tronchin family were further weakened a few months later, at the beginning of 1766, when his doctor, Théodore Tronchin, left Geneva to set up a fashionable practice in Paris.

Before Voltaire could give up Les Délices, he had to agree terms for its surrender with the Tronchins. When Voltaire had 'acquired' Les Délices ten years earlier, he had been disqualified, as a notional Catholic, by the property laws in Protestant Geneva from buying it himself. It had therefore been bought for him by the Tronchin clan, with money provided by Voltaire, for him to occupy as a tenant; when the property reverted to the Tronchins, they would reimburse him an agreed proportion of the purchase price.

Unfortunately, the Tronchins (or perhaps it was just Jean-Robert) insisted on a formal inventory to assess the state of the property; and they appointed Jean-Louis Labat, a Geneva businessman, to act as their representative in the negotiations. He proved very tiresome. Voltaire complained to François Tronchin: 'My dear friend, Mme Denis has been a bit annoyed with M. Labat, who has not accepted any arrangement. M. Labat told our representative that if we have changed chimney-pieces of plaster into chimney-pieces of marble, we must pay the cost of the plaster. That was not the spirit of our deal. As far as I am concerned, I only need your orders to complete everything to your satisfaction.'[7] Labat – whom Voltaire later described as 'more Jew than Calvinist'[8] – was extremely difficult over the state of the house and gardens, even demanding compensation for the large terrace which Voltaire had built.

By 4 February, Voltaire was telling François Tronchin that Mme Denis was now extremely angry with Labat:

It has been pointed out to me that not only has there been no deterioration in the transformation of a poor vineyard into a field planted with wheat, but if there had been deterioration it would be M. Tronchin who would have caused it, since it was he who proposed the terrace, of which he paid a quarter, myself another quarter, and the republic a half. M. Tronchin is begged to consider that it is difficult to say that a house has deteriorated, when it is worth much more when it is handed back than it was worth before.[9]

Voltaire's architect calculated that the value of the improvements made by Voltaire, such as the stables, the outhouses, the attics, the servants' rooms, the new kitchen garden, the rainwater barrels, the water pipes, etc., outweighed the value of any deteriorations in a ratio of eight to two. 'This should put a stop to any small desire M. Labat may have had to place us in an embarrassing position.'[10]

Just why the Tronchins should have allowed or encouraged Labat's petty trouble-making is a mystery. Ostensibly they were all friends of Voltaire; they were very prosperous patricians; and Voltaire had spent large amounts of money improving the estate, which they were now on the point of recovering much sooner than they might have expected. And yet it even seemed possible at one point that the Tronchins might resort to lawyers and court proceedings against Voltaire.

Fortunately, on 14 February François Tronchin (who was to be the new occupier of Les Délices, and would therefore be Voltaire's neighbour), decided to end the conflict: 'My dear friend, no judge or arbitrator will decide between you and my brother. For myself, I can tell you that I am ready, on his behalf, to receive Les Délices in whatever state you think fit to hand it over to me, entrusting myself perfectly and solely to you alone and your good niece.'[11] On 5 March Voltaire wrote to François Tronchin: 'My dear friend, it is with great regret that I have left Les Délices. The state of my affairs forced me to this sacrifice, but it is with great pleasure that I see you as the new owner.'[12]

From this point on, the handover went smoothly. On 21 March Voltaire signed a letter of authorisation for Mme Denis to complete the formalities, and 'negotiate over those pieces of furniture which belong to me, and receive from Jean-Robert and François

Tronchin £38,000 in letters of credit', the reimbursement due on the surrender of the lease.[13] He wrote to Jean-Robert: 'Mme Denis today completed the arrangements of Les Délices with your brother. There has not been the shadow of a difficulty, and I cannot conceive how M. Labat had imagined to make any. My niece thinks it was a joke.'[14]

On 2 April 1765, Voltaire left Les Délices for good: 'We have carried to Tournay the few pieces of furniture we could find. But we won't be able to avoid being a bit embarrassed this summer, for Ferney will be crowded right up to the roof.'[15]

Ferney would be 'crowded right up to the roof' because Voltaire would no longer have Les Délices as an overflow hostel for all his visitors. These visitors were of every kind and condition: local friends and acquaintances from Geneva and Lausanne; friends and acquaintances from further afield, Lyon, Dijon, Turin, Paris; casual passers-by who expected to be fed, as well as entertained with a sight of the great man; travellers on the Grand Tour who increasingly treated Voltaire as an essential stopover; spectators for his tragedies; and in later years, troops of soldiers who were billeted on him. As he wrote to Mme du Deffand: 'I happen to live in a part of the country situated right in the middle of Europe. All the passers-by come to my house, I have to deal with Germans, with Englishmen, with Italians, even with Frenchmen, whom I shall never see again.'[16]

Despite his advancing age and chronic ill-health, Voltaire ran a very open house, even if many of his visitors were people he would not necessarily have chosen to invite. In March 1764 he wrote, tongue-in-cheek, to Damilaville:

I believe that [Jesuit Father] Berthier passed nearby today, on his way to Soleure [location of a noted Jesuit church]. I was very sorry not to have given him dinner. I had a few Englishmen with me, who would have increased the pleasure of the meeting. We were fifteen at table, and I noted with pain that none of us was a Christian, apart from me. This happens every day. It is one of my great griefs. You would not believe how far this cursed *philosophie* has corrupted the world. My brother, *écr l'inf.*[17]

In June he wrote to d'Argental: 'Today I had the honour of seeing Mme de Pusigneu [one of d'Argental's relatives]. She insisted that I receive her, even though I was in my nightcap and dressing gown. My inflammation has slightly eased from my eyes, but spread to all the rest. I am a man of sorrows, but I suffer everything quite gaily.'[18]

One of Voltaire's most notable visitors was James Boswell, the future biographer of Samuel Johnson, who solicited an invitation to Ferney in December 1764 during his travels in Europe on the Grand Tour. Boswell was twenty-four at the time, whereas Voltaire was now seventy, and he left a vivid picture of his encounter with the great man.

He was all brilliance. He gave me continued flashes of wit. I got him to speak English, which he does in a degree that made me now and then start up and cry, 'Upon my soul this is astonishing!' When he talked our language he was animated with the soul of a Briton. He had bold flights. He had humour. He had an extravagance; he had a forcible oddity of style that the most comical of our *dramatis personae* could not have exceeded. He swore bloodily, as was the fashion when he was in England. He hummed a ballad; he repeated nonsense. Then he talked of our Constitution with a noble enthusiasm. I was proud to hear this from the mouth of an illustrious Frenchman.

At last we came upon religion. Then did he rage. The company went to supper. Monsieur de Voltaire and I remained in the drawing room with a great Bible before us; and if ever two mortal men disputed with vehemence, we did … He went too far. His aged frame trembled beneath him. He cried, 'Oh, I am very sick; my head turns round', and he let himself gently fall upon an easy chair. He recovered. I resumed our conversation, but changed the tone. I talked to him serious and earnest. I demanded of him an honest confession of his real sentiments. He expressed his veneration – his love – of the Supreme Being, and his entire resignation to the will of Him who is All-wise. He expressed his desire to resemble the Author of Goodness by being good himself … I was moved; I was sorry. I doubted his sincerity. I called to him with emotion, 'Are you sincere? Are you really sincere?' He answered, 'Before God, I am. I suffer much; not as a Christian – but as a man.'[19]

Boswell wrote Voltaire a thank-you letter from Italy, and Voltaire replied in February, 1765, in his best English:

My distempers and my bad eyes do not permit me to answer with that celerity and exactness that my duty and my heart require. You seem solicitous about that pretty thing call'd soul. I do protest you I know nothing of it. Nor whether it is, nor what it is, nor what it shall be. Young scholars, and priests know all that perfectly. For my part I am but a very ignorant fellow. Let it be what it will, be assured that my soul has a great regard for your own, and if you should turn aside into our deserts, you shall find me (if alive) ready to show you my respect and obsequiousness.[20]

But Voltaire's eyesight and his faculties of recognition were now becoming somewhat impaired. In July 1765 he wrote to Fyot de la Marche, one of his oldest friends:

I must tell you, my dear and respectable magistrate, that two days before receiving your letter, they came to tell me, in my dirty study, at about two o'clock, that there were, in my little pocket-handkerchief of a salon, a dozen Englishmen and Englishwomen, who had come to dinner. I received them in the English manner (*à l'anglaise*), with little fuss, a few arguments about Shakespeare, some vague small-talk. Then, looking at one of the ladies, insofar as my feeble eyes can look, I said to one of my nieces: '*There is an Englishwoman who looks very like M. le président de la Marche; I could take her for his daughter, if I didn't know that she comes from London.*' She overheard my remark, and she told me that she didn't come from England, but from Lyon, and that she was your niece. M. de Longecour, whom I had taken for an English officer of dragoons, informed me that he was related to you. I suddenly found I was surrounded by your family. My heart trembled; I forgot my Englishmen and Shakespeare and Milton, and even all the ills which weigh me down.[21]

Since Voltaire's hospitality was so often involuntary, exacted by self-appointed visitors, it is not surprising that his manner of providing it was sometimes brusque and cavalier. In October he wrote to d'Argental, who had implied that Voltaire spent all his time hobnobbing with the grandees of Geneva:

> I can assure you that I have never lived with the members of the Council of the Littlest [*parvulissime*] Republic of Geneva. Except for the Tronchins and two or three others, that whole set-up consists of sixteenth-century pedants. There is much more wit among the other citizens. Besides, comes to me who wants, I don't beg anybody; Mme Denis does the honours, and I remain in my room, condemned to suffer, or to scribble on paper. Visits would make me waste my time, so I never pay any. The beauties and grand ladies, the peers, even the governors, have got used to my rudeness. It is not in my power to live any other way, thanks to my old age and my illnesses.[22]

In reality Voltaire was much less curmudgeonly than he pretends. That same month he wrote to a friend: 'I am not one of those old men who, unable to have any pleasure themselves, do not want others to have pleasure either. I can't digest, but I want others to have good food; I can no longer act, but I want others to act; in short, I want them to do everything that I can no longer do.'[23] And yet even here Voltaire is putting on a bit of an act: in reality he takes a great interest in his food. He wrote to a friend:

> If you could have come here this autumn, I should have tried to provide you with good food, simple rather than delicate. There are dishes which are very traditional and very good. You like them, and I should eat them gladly with you, though I admit that my stomach cannot get used to *nouvelle cuisine*. I can't stand sweetbreads (*ris de veau*) swimming in a salty sauce which rises an inch above the little *ris de veau*. I cannot eat a mince combining poultry (*coq d'Inde*) with hare and rabbit, which they want me to take for a single meat. I do not like pigeon *à la crapaudine*,* nor bread without crust. I drink moderately, and I find very strange people who eat without drinking, and who do not even know what they are eating.
>
> I won't even hide from you that I do not at all like private conversation at table, in which one says what one has done yesterday, to one's neighbour,

---

*a recipe in which the pigeon is spread-eagled like a toad (*crapaud*).

who couldn't care less. I do not disapprove the saying of grace, but that should be the limit, because if one goes any further there is no agreement, and the company becomes an uproar, with a new disagreement before every dish. As for cooks, I cannot bear essence of ham, nor too many morels [*morilles*] or mushrooms, nor too much pepper or nutmeg, with which they disguise dishes which are in themselves very healthy, and which I only wish they wouldn't overdress. A supper without too much elaboration, such as I suggest, gives one hope of a sweet and deep sleep, untroubled by any disagreeable dreams.[24]

Even before announcing the surrender of Les Délices, Voltaire decided to build more bedrooms at Ferney, in order to be able to welcome more guests. This would involve dismantling the theatre, but that did not matter so much because Voltaire was now too old to act; or so he said. The people he wanted to convince that he was doing the right thing were his allies in the theatre world: the duc de Richelieu, who could determine the repertory at the Comédie Française, and therefore the performances of Voltaire's plays there; and the comte d'Argental, his closest theatrical adviser, critic and friend, and in some sense his go-between with the company at the Comédie Française.

On 21 January 1765, Voltaire wrote to Richelieu:

I have the honour to tell you that I am so disgusted with the stage, that I have got rid of my own. I have dismantled my theatre, and with it I am making bedrooms and ironing rooms. I find I am so old that I am giving up the vanities of this world. All that remains is for me to become pious, to be able to die with all possible propriety. I have with me, as I think you know, a Jesuit [Father Adam] who was deprived of his right to perform religious services, as soon as they found out he was living in my profane hovel. His bishop has been badly advised, for he risks making me die without confession, a misfortune for which I shall never be consoled.[25]

Evidently, Richelieu was not persuaded. In March, Voltaire wrote to a friend:

If M. le Maréchal de Richelieu regrets my little theatre at Ferney, I regret it too; but when a priest can no longer say Mass, there is no point in having an altar. I am losing my sight, I no longer have any voice, I am condemned to suffer, I am starting my seventy-second year, there is no way of amusing the Genevans. Besides, I no longer write tragedies, nor act in any; and in place of a theatre, I am building two wings for the château of Ferney.[26]

Voltaire's building ambitions had now gone well beyond his initial plan to convert his theatre barn into bedrooms and ironing rooms.

But it was the reaction of d'Argental and his wife which most concerned him. He wrote to them on 23 February:

My divine angels: I saw, a few days ago, a letter from one of you in the hands of Mme Denis. That letter did not convey total approval of my decisions relating to my theatre and to Les Délices. But consider, I beg you, that I am, whatever they say, in my seventy-second year, that Mme Denis has started her fifty-sixth, and that at this age you must be possessed [*avoir le diable au corps*] to act in a play. It seems to me that one must know how to grow old, and that the flowers of the spring are not made for the winter.

This letter ends with a deeply felt reproach, oblique but poignant, to d'Argental for never, ever visiting Voltaire in his exile, either at Les Délices or at Ferney. 'I am having built some new cells for visitors to my convent. If you had ever been able to come to Lyon, and from there to Ferney, I should certainly have preserved my theatre.'[27] It recalls Voltaire's sharp but touching complaint in a letter he wrote to d'Argental in 1755: 'You only love me as a maker of tragedies; I do not want to be loved like that.'[28] Unfortunately, that was a large part of how and why d'Argental loved Voltaire.

In the spring of 1765, Voltaire became concerned about a tightening of censorship in France, which he described as 'a very severe inquisition into books'.[29] In principle, ministers, diplomats and other state officials were exempt from censorship, and Voltaire regularly drew on his contacts in the world of the great and the good, to use them as postboxes for evading it. But this device worked less and less well as the century wore on, and as the underlying confrontation between the *ancien régime* and the rationalising pressure of the *philosophes* became more and more intense. In July 1765 Voltaire wrote to d'Argental:

Your package, addressed to M. Camp, arrived in Lyon. The postal authorities had stopped it, and countersigned it in Paris in a new manner, putting in large letters on the envelope and in red ink '*Suspect Package*'. I think, then, that since you will only have honest packages to send me, the best way is to put them with dispatches for the French Resident in Geneva; you can let me know you have sent them, with a simple letter, by post, to Wagnière, without any other envelope.[30]

When Voltaire discovered how comprehensively his correspondence and that of his friends had been penetrated by the state security services, he wrote to d'Alembert to warn him:

Most letters are opened by the postal service. Yours have been for a long time. A few months ago you wrote to me: '*What would you say of the ministers who are your protectors, or rather your protégés?*', and the passage did not sing their praises. A fortnight later, a minister wrote to me: '*I am not ashamed to be your protégé, but . . . etc.*' This minister appeared to be very irritated. It is also said that people have seen a letter from you to the empress of Russia, in which you said: '*France is like a viper, all of it good, except the head.*' They also say that you have written in similar terms to the King of Prussia.[31]

The 'very irritated' minister in question was almost certainly Voltaire's friend, the duc de Choiseul, the prime minister. The inference is that Choiseul had written to Voltaire, to warn him that d'Alembert must in future be more careful about what he wrote.

One reason for d'Alembert's outspoken irritation with the authorities was that the Académie des Sciences had recommended him for a state pension, but that it had still not been granted. He wrote to Voltaire at the end of June 1765:

I know that the Minister has not yet given a definitive response; but to make me wait and justify what should be my due, is an outrage almost as great as to refuse me outright. I am nearly fifty, I was counting on the pen-

Voltaire is arrested in Frankfurt on his way home to France, on the orders of Frederick II, 1753. Undated illustration after a painting by Jules Giradet.

The château de Ferney, Voltaire's main home during his long years in exile. Voltaire's bedchamber and study were located at the rear of the château, with a view of the Alps.

Voltaire would dress in the morning while his secretary Jean Louis Wagnière took dictation. Oil painting by Jean Huber.

Voltaire and Mme Denis.
Crayon on paper by
Charles Nicholas Cochin II.

Marquis de Condorcet.
Engraving by Jean Jacques Frilley.

Jean le Rond d'Alembert.

The Philosophers' Supper: a purely fictitious scene, depicting Voltaire
dining with fellow intellectuals d'Alembert, Marmontel, Diderot, La Harpe,
l'Abbé Maury and Father Adam. Engraving by Jean Huber.

The agony of Damiens, before
the judges at the Châtelet, Paris,
March 1757.

Seated statue of Voltaire in
marble by Jean-Baptiste Pigalle,
now in the Louvre.

Jean Calas being broken on the wheel after being pronounced guilty of murdering his son, March 1762.

Mme Anne-Rose Cabibel Calas, in prison, learns of the rehabilitation of her late husband, Jean Calas. She is seated with her daughters Rosine and Nanette. Her son Pierre reads out the decree; behind him the young Gaubert Lavaysse. Centre, standing, the servant Jeanne Viguière. Voltaire hung a version of this scene above his bed at Ferney. Engraving by Carmontelle after de la Tour.

Voltaire at breakfast with the banker Jean-Joseph Laborde. Mme Denis is sitting next to Voltaire. Father Adam and a servant are in the background. Engraving dated July 1775.

Voltaire playing chess with Father Adam.
Oil painting by Jean Huber.

The old invalid of Ferney.
Etching by Jean Huber or possibly Jacques
Cassin after Huber.

Homage to Voltaire on stage at the Comédie Française,
30 March 1776, after the sixth performance of *Irène*. Engraving by
C E Gaucher after J M Moreau le Jeune.

Voltaire in his box being crowned with
a laurel wreath in the presence of
Mme Denis and 'Belle et Bonne', the
Marquise de Villette.

The elderly Mme Denis with Voltaire's
laurel wreath in her hands. Oil painting by
Joseph Siffred Duplessis.

In 1791 the Revolutionaries claimed Voltaire as a
supposed precursor, and on 11 July his ashes were transferred to
the Panthéon. Engraving by Berthault.

The seated Voltaire in the
upstairs bar at the Comédie
Française, scene of his
long career as France's most
famous playwright of
the eighteenth century.
Marble statue, by
Jean-Antoine Houdon.

sion from the Académie as my only resource in my old age; if this resource is taken from me, I shall have to think how to secure something else, for it is frightful to be old and poor. Without the pension from the King of Prussia, I should have been obliged to retire to the country or to the provinces, or even to live abroad.[32]

In fact, d'Alembert's pension from the Académie des Sciences had merely been delayed, and it brought him a yearly stipend of £2,400. In addition, he had an annuity of £1,200 left him by his father, a pension of £1,200 from Louis XV, a pension of £1,200 from Frederick the Great, and an annuity of £600 from Mme Geoffrin, the literary hostess and supporter of the *Encyclopédie*, plus book royalties and some funding from the Académie Française, of which he had been a member since 1754, and of which he was promoted *secrétaire perpetuel* in 1772.[33]

Voltaire reversed his plans to dismantle his theatre barn when he heard that Mlle Clairon, the star actress at the Comédie Française, might be coming to Geneva. The main reason for Mlle Clairon's visit was her increasing ill-health and the fact that the doctors were forbidding her to undergo the stress of public performance. Voltaire wrote to d'Alembert in late May: 'People would have me believe that Mlle Clairon may come to consult Tronchin; in that case, I shall have to get my theatre rebuilt; but I have become so old, that I can no longer play even the role of an old man.'[34] In late June 1765, he wrote to d'Argental: 'As for Mlle Clairon, it seems decided that, despite the severe injunctions of the doctor, she will perhaps deign to display her talents in our marionette theatre, which Mme Denis has had rebuilt almost despite me.'[35]

By the following month Voltaire's theatre was at least partly restored, but on a much smaller scale: the auditorium now held only twenty-five seats.[36] 'I think I told you that Mme Denis had asked me for a large hall for ironing her washing, and I gave her the theatre auditorium; but after having thought about it deeply, she concluded that it would be better to put up with dirty linen, and perform some plays. She has had the theatre rebuilt, and tomorrow we shall put on *Alzire*, while waiting for Mlle Clairon, who perhaps will never come.'[37] But come she did, at the end of July, and stayed for three weeks. Because of the banging and hammering of the masons who were building the new wings at Ferney, and because she was not in good health, she opted to stay instead in the château of Tournay, which Voltaire had handed over on indefinite loan to his publisher Gabriel Cramer, who used it to give gaudy parties.[38]

In August, Voltaire wrote to d'Argental:

Mlle Clairon will perform in my little theatre at Ferney, which we have restored, as you wanted. This is against the express orders of Dr Tronchin, who says he will not answer for her life if she makes any efforts, and who absolutely insists that she give up acting in tragedies. So she has been obliged to promise him that she would never go back on the stage in Paris, which would put strains on her voice, and require vigorous acting, which would inevitably make her succumb.[39]

Two days later, they put on *Oreste* in Voltaire's rehabilitated theatre, with Mlle Clairon in the starring part. That evening, after the show, Voltaire hurried back to his study, to finish dictating a letter he had started earlier that day. 'I have just come from it [the play], I have been in heaven for the past two hours. There have been many great talents in France, but none in her line have reached her degree of perfection. I am beside myself. I am sure that she has never made a stronger impression than in my primitive hovel, where I had gathered about 150 people, most of them worthy to hear her.'[40] (Given the tiny size of the restored auditorium, most of the audience must have been standing, or perhaps only a small minority were admitted to the show.)

Mlle Clairon had once been one of the many mistresses of Richelieu, and in a letter to him Voltaire adopted a suggestively leering tone. 'I received Mlle Clairon, as you wished, and as she deserved. She was honoured, and fêted, and serenaded. All that was missing was the little attention with which you honoured her a few years ago; but there is no way that I could be as polite as you. I can assure you that she would have been badly caught out if she had expected the same civilities from me.'[41]

Mlle Clairon's visit inevitably disrupted Voltaire's normal routine, but it also disturbed his ideas on drama and acting.

Mlle Clairon's stay has a bit upset me. I knew nothing of her merit; I had no idea that acting could be so animated and so perfect. I had become accustomed to the cold declamation of our cold theatres, and I had only ever seen actors reciting verses to other actors, in a little circle surrounded by dandies. Mlle Clairon told me that she had never explored the range of acting which is possible on stage, until M. le comte de Lauragais had rendered, to a fairly ungrateful public, the service of restoring, with the gift of his money, the freedom of the theatre and the beauty of the spectacle.[42]

Voltaire harped with increasing frequency on the coldness of theatre in France, and on the contrast with the more lively, but unbearably vulgar English theatre. In 1764 he wrote: 'The English, who come here in great numbers, say that all our tragedies are icy; there may be something in it; but theirs are diabolical.'[43] And yet Voltaire was aware that it was he who was becoming out of date. In late 1766 he wrote to an acquaintance, who had asked him for some theatrical advice: 'I am very little suited to decide, in my retirement, whether a play is likely to be successful in Paris. They say that the taste of the public has completely changed. Mine, which hasn't, is too superannuated and out of fashion.'[44]

A part of Voltaire still adhered to his austere seventeenth-century ideals of a noble and high-minded theatre, and yet another part was increasingly aware that the old model was over-formal and lacking in vitality. In 1766 he wrote to Thieriot: 'I was becoming tired of always seeing princes with princes, and of hearing nothing but talk of thrones and politics. I thought that one could give a broader scope to the picture of Nature, and that with a bit of art one could put on stage the lowest forms of life with the most elevated. This is a very fertile field, which others, more capable than me, will open up.'[45] A few days later he wrote in a similar vein: 'I thought it would be agreeable to put on the same tragic stage, a princess darning her shirts, and people with no shirt at all. It seemed to me that all the conditions of life could be treated without vulgarity.'[46] Paradoxically, this was precisely what Shakespeare had done; but in his case Voltaire did not like the result.

Mlle Clairon stayed for three weeks, and returned to Paris on 20

August 1765. Ten days later, Etienne Noël Damilaville arrived, and he stayed for about five weeks, until 8 October. Damilaville was one of Voltaire's closest and most loyal friends, and in certain practical respects one of the most useful. Born in 1723, he had had a patchy education, and went on to be a soldier and royal bodyguard, and as a member of the elite cavalry *gardes du corps* he fought in many of the campaigns of the War of the Austrian Succession. After his discharge he became an attorney, but he soon gave up the law and went to work for the Finance Ministry (*Contrôle Générale des Finances*); for the past ten years he had been a senior civil servant (*premier commis*) in the office supervising the tax known as the *Vingtième* (Five Per Cent). But he did not like his work and felt he had been unfairly passed over for promotion.

As a poor man, and as a salaried state functionary, Damilaville was much less brilliant than Voltaire's brilliant friends, but he was indispensable in carrying out errands for Voltaire, he was a tireless supporter of Voltaire's campaigns, especially the Calas and Sirven cases, and his official position gave him the enormously useful privilege of free access to the postal system.

In April 1765, Voltaire asked Damilaville to collect a consignment of copies of the *Dictionnaire Philosophique* and to distribute them discreetly to reliable friends.[47] When the parcels had still not arrived in Paris two weeks later, he started to get worried. 'You have not yet acknowledged receipt of the package which should have been handed over to you. Has it not yet arrived in Paris? Or if it has, some misfortune must have befallen it. The package is rather important. *Écr l'Inf.*'[48] Evidently the package did arrive safely because a few days later Voltaire told Damilaville to deliver one copy of the *Dictionnaire* to Mme la marquise du Deffand, and two to Mme la marquise de Coaslin, and enclosed some documentation for the Sirven case to be delivered to the lawyer Elie de Beaumont.[49]

The conventional picture of Damilaville is not exactly flattering. His contemporary, baron Melchior von Grimm, one of the *philosophes* and the editor of the journal *Correspondance Littéraire*, found his personality as defective as his mind: 'He had neither grace, nor mental wit, and he lacked that worldly savoir-faire which makes up for it. He was sad and heavy, and his lack of basic education always showed through. Since he had not done any studies, he had no opinion of his own, and he repeated what he heard others say.'[50] Grimm's damning appraisal has been echoed by modern scholars. René Pomeau says Damilaville had 'something of the military mind, a certain stiffness, and zeal in carrying out orders ... A conscientious bureaucrat, he lacked brilliance ... Untalented ... An unsubtle mind.'[51] Peter Gay has described Damilaville as one of those 'privates of the movement, the hangers-on, consumers and distributors rather than producers of ideas'.[52]

Such disparaging assessments may reflect a part of the truth, but they are obviously not the whole truth. In the first place, Damilaville was a friend and regular drinking and dining companion of Denis Diderot, and gave him some help with the editing of the *Encyclopédie*, besides contributing two or three articles. No doubt Diderot, too, was glad to take advantage of Damilaville's readiness to provide a free and discreet postal service for his correspondence with his mistress, Sophie Volland. But his friendship seems to have been more than cupboard love; he wrote to Damilaville: 'I am sincerely glad to have found you. It is one of the happy events of my life.'[53] Damilaville was also a close friend of d'Alembert. It is unlikely that these two friendships would have endured if Damilaville had been as dreary as Grimm suggests.

Moreover, of all Voltaire's friends, Damilaville was the one whom he loved most deeply and most intensely, almost as if he were a surrogate son. The conventional view among Voltaire scholars is that his closest and most intimate friend was d'Argental, followed by d'Alembert in the younger generation, whereas Damilaville was mainly a useful and unconditional errand boy. But while it is undeniable that Damilaville was not Voltaire's equal in the same way as d'Argental and d'Alembert – the former in the theatrical world (though he was not a playwright), the latter in the intellectual world – it is also clear, from the most casual reading of his letters, that Voltaire would not have recognised the damning picture of Damilaville conventionally handed down. On the contrary, the depth and warmth of Voltaire's feelings for him, as expressed in his letters, were unequalled in any of his other friendships.

One indication of the closeness of the relationship between Voltaire and Damilaville is the sheer volume of their correspondence. To d'Argental, the most frequent addressee, Voltaire wrote some thousand letters; but he received only two-hundred letters in reply, and their correspondence was spread over sixty years. To Damilaville, Voltaire wrote at least 539 letters; but these were essentially concentrated in the eight years from 1760 to 1768. In the first half of 1765, Voltaire wrote Damilaville 61 letters, that is, an average of one letter every three days. And it was a symptom of his sympathy and trust in Damilaville as one of the inner band that ever since 1762, when he first invented the phrase, Voltaire regularly signed off his letters to Damilaville with the words 'Écrasez l'Infâme' or *Écr l'Inf*, as the password and battle cry of the *philosophes*. Perhaps the most surprising thing about this very warm and trusting friendship was that it was built, for the first five years, exclusively on their correspondence: Voltaire and Damilaville did not meet until the latter's visit to Ferney in August 1765.

Another indicator of Voltaire's feelings for Damilaville, even before they met, was his unmistakable concern over his friend's health. In March, hearing that Damilaville had a sore throat, Voltaire sought advice from Théodore Tronchin: 'My dear Aesculapius, my best friend among the philosophers begs you, as I do, to be kind enough give him your advice.'[54] He then wrote to Damilaville: 'My dear brother, I do not think that I will be able to send the response of M. Tronchin until Wednesday the 6th. I should be very surprised if he prescribed for you anything other than soothing potions (*des adoucissants*) and a diet, but what is quite sure, is that he will be very interested in your health. Do not have a sore throat, my dear brother. *Écr l'Inf*.'[55]

In May Voltaire noted, with regret, that Damilaville's sore throat was 'stubborn', and by June, when it seemed clear that it was not getting better, Voltaire started to suggest that he should come to Geneva to consult Théodore Tronchin in person. 'I have received, my dear friend, your letter for Dr Tronchin. He says you should continue the regime which he prescribed. If it is possible that the care you owe your health should lead you to Geneva, and that I should have the pleasure of embracing you and of opening my heart to you, I should think the end of my life very happy.'[56]

By July, Voltaire was increasingly anxious for Damilaville to visit Ferney.

My dear friend, your sore throat worries me a lot. Could it be true that you might come here to our deserts, and cross the mountains that surround us? It is a very sad state of affairs to which I should owe the happiness of seeing you; but I should be doubly consoled by the pleasure of embracing you, and by the hope that Tronchin would cure you. My cottage is nothing but a desolate hovel which has been overturned by the masons. But if I could be sure of welcoming you, I should get them to make you a cell in my little convent. You will be lodged, well or ill, my dear friend, and we shall take the greatest care of you.[57]

By the end of August 1765, Damilaville had arrived at Ferney. Voltaire wrote to his Paris friend Nicolas-Claude Thieriot: 'My old friend, the visit of Mlle Clairon, and my health which gets worse by the day, have not allowed me to write to you. I am enjoying the real satisfaction of having M. Damilaville in my hermitage. He is a real philosopher; he's not like Rousseau, who does not even know how to put on the mask of philosophy.'[58] In September, Voltaire described Damilaville as 'a friend with whom I should like to pass the rest of my life', and he wrote to d'Alembert: 'I love my *philosophe* Damilaville more and more every day; Tronchin has given him a fever to make him better. I hope he will stay a long time in his care, and I really wish you would come and join him.'[59]

A fortnight later, Damilaville still had not left for Paris. Voltaire wrote to Thieriot: 'My old friend, I am starting to be as lazy as you. I was counting on writing to you by M. Damilaville; happily he has from day to day postponed his return to Paris. I shall give him my letter, and it will reach you as well as it can. Two things charm me in this M. Damilaville, his reason and his virtue. Why must a man of his merit languish in the tax collector's office of the *Vingtième?* It's a trade which is quite unworthy of him.'[60]

On 8 October 1765, after having been, as Voltaire says, 'for a few months the consolation of my life',[61] Damilaville left Ferney to return to Paris. Voltaire wrote to him there on 16 October:

I passed lovely days with you, my dear brother; I have regrets at your departure, but I also have the sweetness of my memories, and the hope of seeing you again before I die. What would prevent you, for example, from coming back one day with M. & Mme Florian? [Voltaire's other niece and her new husband] You know how much they love you, for you have won over every heart ... I am beginning to read today the Italian book *On Crimes and Punishments* [by Cesare Beccaría]. One can tell at a glance that it is philosophical; the author is a brother. Adieu, you who will always be mine, adieu, my dear friend, perish the infamous prejudices which dishonour and brutalise human nature, long live reason. Adieu once again.[62]

Damilaville's sore throat still did not get better and Voltaire wrote to him on 25 November: 'Your sore throat and your loss of weight displease me greatly. You know how interested I am in your well-being and your long-being. Our Aesculapius, Tronchin, does not cure everybody. Whatever he does, my dear friend, nature knows more than medicine. Philosophy teaches us to submit to the one, and do without the other. That's the position I have adopted.' And in December:

My dear friend, I must tell you: if you are unwell, I am deeply saddened. Tronchin will not cure either you or me. But you will cure yourself by your diet: it is the true medicine in all ordinary cases. It is possible, however, that since the swelling in your throat has not suppurated, the infection [*l'humeur*] may have spread to the blood; in that case you would be obliged to add to your diet some gentle laxatives [*détersifs*]. Perhaps a little sage with a bit of milk would do you good. The foods and the drinks which can be used as remedies are the only things which have kept me alive; and I know no doctor who is better than experience.[63]

Of course, Damilaville's sore throat did not get better, for it was really cancer of the throat. He had another three years to live, and died towards the end of 1768. Voltaire suffered acutely with him in spirit, though his cynical wit never deserted him. In September of that year he wrote to Mme Denis (who was at that time in Paris): 'I should not be surprised if Tronchin were mistaken on Damilaville. He had condemned Daumart to die in two days, but there he is, for his misfortune, still alive nine years later. When Tronchin is mistaken, he has the glory to be more mistaken than all his colleagues; no one makes greater strides on the road of error; sometimes he hits the mark, but when he goes astray, it is by a hundred leagues.'[64]

Charles-Hyacinthe Daumart, a young cousin of Voltaire, had been injured in a riding accident in 1758 at the age of seventeen. The following year, Théodore Tronchin operated on his legs, and at the time Voltaire thought he had performed 'a miracle'.[65] But after a few weeks he was still limping, and a year later, in 1760, he could no longer walk, even with crutches. In 1761, Voltaire consulted another distinguished doctor, but by now Daumart was confined to his bed and completely paralysed.[66]

Voltaire's comments on the effects of Théodore Tronchin's medical treatment were now becoming increasingly caustic. He wrote to his other niece, Mme Fontaine: 'Daumart has been in bed for the past five months without being able to move. In your case, Tronchin cured you, because he did nothing. But in Daumart's case, he did something, and this poor boy will die of it, or else his life will be worse than death.'[67] A year later, Daumart was still totally paralysed, and Voltaire was starting to warn Damilaville that he no longer hoped that Théodore Tronchin would be able to help him; on the contrary, he implied that it was Tronchin who had maimed Daumart. By 1763, Daumart could no longer move any part of his body, and was expected to remain paralysed for the rest of his life.[68]

The rest of Daumart's life was not long, for he died in 1769 at the age of twenty-eight. But the point of the story about the unhappy Daumart is not just that medical science in the eighteenth century was primitive, nor that Théodore Tronchin's reputation may have been inflated, but that Voltaire cared for Daumart throughout his last ten years of sickness and paralysis, and that he was obviously deeply upset by his cousin's sufferings. Here is his testimony to Daumart in 1764, in a letter to Mme du Deffand, the blind literary hostess, who lived in a fine apartment inside the Convent of Saint-Joseph in Paris.

I agree with you that life is very short, and fairly unhappy; but I must tell you that I have in my house a 23-year-old relative, handsome, well built, vigorous, and here is what happened to him.

One day while hunting he fell from his horse, he bruised his thigh a bit, they made a little incision, and there he is, paralysed for the rest of his days; not paralysed in part of his body, but so paralysed that he does not have the use of any of his limbs, he cannot raise his head, with the complete certainty that he can never have the least relief; he is accustomed to his state, and he is madly in love with life.

It is not that there is no good in nothingness [*le néant*], but I think it is impossible truly to love nothingness, despite its good qualities.

As for death, let us reason a bit, if you please: it is very certain that one does not feel it, it is not a painful moment, it is as like sleep as two drops of water, it is only the idea that we shall never wake up that causes us pain, it is the apparatus of death which is horrible, it is the barbarity of extreme unction, it is the cruelty with which they warn us that everything is over for us. What good is it to come and pronounce our sentence? It will be executed anyway, without the notary and the priests getting mixed up with it. If they had the least charity for us, they would let us die without saying anything about it.

Farewell, Madame, let us bear our life, which is not much, let us not fear death, which is nothing at all, and please believe that my only grief is not to be able to talk with you.[69]

By late November 1768, Voltaire knew that Damilaville's end was near. He told Mme Denis: 'The state of Damilaville overwhelms me with grief. I believe it may be necessary to collect those of my letters which are no doubt at his home, almost all written in the hand of friend Wagnière. Here is an irreparable loss for people who think. I shall never be consoled.'[70]

On 13 December 1768, Etienne Noël Damilaville died in great agony or, as Voltaire put it, in 'an abominable trial'.[71] In late January 1769, Voltaire wrote to Thieriot: 'I have lost my dear Damilaville, whose firm and courageous friendship had long been my consolation. He never sacrificed his friend [i.e Voltaire] to the malice of those who would impose themselves on the world. He was brave, even with those people on whom his fortune depended. I cannot regret him too much, and my only hope in my last days is to find him again in you.'[72]

Voltaire never ceased to mourn Damilaville, and with an intensity which he never expressed for any of his other friends. Eight years after Damilaville's death, in 1776, when he was eighty-two, Voltaire wrote to Denis Diderot, who had been another of Damilaville's dearest friends: 'I once had a friend, who was also your friend, and who never let me lack my daily bread in my solitude. No one has replaced him, and I am dying of hunger. This friend knew that we [i.e. Voltaire and Diderot] were not so far apart, and that all it needed was a conversation for us to understand each other; but one can't find just anywhere people one can talk to.'[73]

Beccaria and the Commentaire

1765–6

After 1765–6 Voltaire started to direct his critical gaze, not just at specific instances of miscarrages of justice but at the defects of the penal justice system itself.

The central problem of the judicial system in France, and in many other Continental European countries, was that the rationale of criminal law was confused with the rationale of social hierarchy, and both were confused with the rationale of religious dogma. Equality before the law was unknown, both socially and geographically; an offence against a nobleman was more severely punished than an offence against a common person; and some laws only applied to ordinary commoners, not to nobles or churchmen; moreover, the law in one part of France was likely to be quite different, for traditional reasons, from that in another part. As Voltaire frequently commented, as one travelled across France, the law changed as often as one changed horses.[1]

In 1670 the French politician Jean-Baptiste Colbert had introduced the first attempt at a codification of French criminal law; but in some cases the new code specified no penalty, and in others it gave judges wide latitude to choose a punishment. Worse, criminal law was pervaded by theology and religious bigotry, so that offences against society or one's fellow men were confused with offences against God, and the punishment of such offences became intertwined with confession to a priest and expiation before God. The converse was also true: criminal cases were tried as if they were theological cases, and the method of trial was closely related to that of the Inquisition. Criminal prosecution of witches and sorcerers had largely disappeared by the mid-eighteenth century, but these imaginary offences remained on the French statute book until the Revolution. The death penalty and bodily mutilations were common punishments, even for crimes of a quite trivial nature, and in France the death penalty came in many versions: burning alive at the stake, quartering, breaking on the wheel, hanging, strangling and beheading.

The main features of the inquisitorial system were that it operated in private, and depended heavily on the use of torture. The real purpose of a trial was not primarily to discover and establish the facts of a case, but to prove guilt; the assumptions being that a man would (probably) not be tried unless he were guilty, and that an acquittal might be perceived as a defeat for the prosecuting authorities. The enquiry by the judge was conducted in writing and in secret; witnesses were also heard in secret and separately; a witness who changed his testimony was liable to be severely punished; the clerks of the courts were forbidden to publish any of the evidence or records of the trial. Torture, masquerading under the euphemism 'the question' (*la question*), was regularly used, ostensibly in order to compel the criminal to reveal his accomplices, in reality to try to force a confession out of him; there were several levels of torture for a judge to administer, the *question ordinaire* and *question extraordinaire*, and torture with or without a doctor present. As we have seen, Jean Calas was condemned to death without any proof of his guilt, and even as they were torturing him to death, the Church and State authorities were attempting to extract a confession out of him. Judicial practice varied from region to region. In Rouen the *question* took the form of a thumbscrew, or even a double thumbscrew, or a vice for crushing a leg; in Brittany, the victim's bare feet were slowly pushed towards a fire; in Besançon, the 'patient' had his arms tied behind his back, and then a rope was fixed to his arms, and he was dragged upwards into the air by a pulley.[2]

Voltaire played a key role in opening up the critique of the defects of the French criminal justice system, and he started to do so systematically from 1765 onwards. But we should not over-simplify; this was not a question of a sudden Damascene conversion, nor was it a matter of Voltaire inventing, some wholly new and rational ideas about penal policy reform. Many earlier political writers in Europe, from Montaigne to Grotius, from Hobbes to Locke, had criticised the defects of various aspects of received judicial practices. In Voltaire's own lifetime, a number of powerful critiques of the subject had been published before Voltaire embarked on his own, including those by Montesquieu, in his *Lettres persanes* (1721) and his *L'Esprit des Lois* (1748), and by Helvetius in his *L'Esprit* (1758), as well as by the *Encyclopédistes*.

Well before 1765, Voltaire had made many critical comments about various aspects of the French judicial system, and about its functioning. He was scathing about the practice by which a judge's seat on the bench could be bought and sold, and could be passed down from father to son as a hereditary possession. He was even more scathing about the bizarre French legal calculus which claimed that there could be mathematical fractions of a proof, 'so that four hearsays on one side, and eight popular rumours on the other, add up to two complete proofs, equal to two eyewitnesses'.[3] He was fiercely critical of the secrecy of French judicial processes, which enabled the Toulouse Parlement to obstruct his campaign for the revision of the Calas and Sirven cases. He believed that punishments should be proportional to crimes, and that there should be fewer death penalties. And he systematically contrasted the inquisitorial, priest-ridden, secretive, inconsistent and arbitrary justice system in France with the relatively more open, non-clerical and adversarial system in England.[4] Two years earlier, in the *Traité sur la Tolérance* (1763), Voltaire had opened a new social and moral critique, by arguing the connection between impartial justice in the law-courts and tolerance and pluralism in society. But it was not until the autumn of 1765, by which time he had launched his campaign on the Sirven scandal, so similar in many respects to the Calas scandal, that Voltaire really started to address the systemic problems of the French penal justice system.

This comes out clearly in a key letter written in September 1765 to Elie de Beaumont, his lead lawyer in the Calas case, and now re-enlisted as leading lawyer in the Sirven case.

You are undertaking, Sir, a task worthy of you, in trying to reform the criminal jurisprudence. It is certain that the French system sets too little store by the life of men. It is assumed, apparently, that the condemned, if properly confessed, go straight to paradise. England is almost the only place I know where the laws seem designed more for sparing the guilty than for sacrificing innocence. You should believe that everywhere else the criminal procedure is completely arbitrary.

The King of Prussia has made a little code entitled the Code according to Reason, as if our laws were made according to madness. The best usage established in Prussia, as in the whole of Germany, is that no one is executed without the express permission of the sovereign. This custom used formerly to be established in France. But now your [i.e. the French] people are a bit too hasty: they break a man on the wheel just like that, at the drop of a hat [*de broc en bouche*, literally from the spit to the mouth], even before the neighbourhood has been informed; and the most pardonable cases slip past the humanity of the sovereign.[5]

Voltaire's interest in the general question of penal reform was further aroused the following month, October 1765, when he told Damilaville that he had started reading the Italian book *On Crimes and Punishments*.[6] The author, Cesare Bonesana, marchese de Beccaría, was a young Milanese nobleman, born in 1738, who had studied law at Pavia and then turned to journalism and the study of the French *philosophes*. In 1761, when he was twenty-three, he became friendly with the brothers Pietro and Alessandro Verri, whose home in Milan was a centre of literary and philosophical study and debate. Beccaría was both shy and lazy, and Pietro Verri encouraged him to write his first book, on currency reform, which appeared in 1762; he also played a large part in persuading him, in 1763, when he was just twenty-five, to turn to the study of the principles of penal justice.

By the end of that year (1763), Beccaría had completed this new book, *Dei Delitti e delle Pene* (On Crimes and Punishments), advocating a root-and-branch rethink of penal principles on humanitarian, rational and utilitarian lines. It was to prove a landmark in the history of penal reform. The first edition, published anonymously in

January 1764, was immensely successful and was quickly followed by a second edition that year, and a third in 1765. By 1766, it had been through six editions in Italian. It also attracted international attention, notably among the French *philosophes*.

Considering its pioneering place in the history of penal reform, *On Crimes and Punishments*[7] is a surprisingly short and simple book: it is barely eighty pages long, and its forty-seven chapters are correspondingly brief. Some of Beccaría's key principles are worth summarising, however briefly.

- The law should promote the greatest happiness of the greatest number.
- Justice is part of the social contract.
- Since the law's only purpose is the preservation of the social contract, it can have no business punishing offences against God: 'What insect will dare to supplement divine justice?'.
- Punishments should be prescribed by law, not by judges.
- All punishments are unjust if they are more severe than is necessary to preserve the social contract.
- Laws should apply equally to all, whether noble or commoner.
- The punishment must be proportionate to the crime.
- The most serious crimes, deserving the most serious punishments, are those which most damage society.
- If large and small offences carry the same severe punishments, men will not be deterred from large offences.
- The purpose of punishment is not to inflict pain, but to deter future offences.
- The accused should be given the time and the means to conduct his defence.
- Torture is wrong; for either a man is proved guilty, in which case he does not deserve anything except the punishment prescribed by law; or else he is not proved guilty, in which case there is no basis for torturing him.
- Punishment should not be cruel, but it should be prompt and inevitable; the prompter and more certain the punishment, the greater the deterrent effect.

- Punishments should be as mild as possible.
- Crimes of violence should be punished by corporal penalties; the rich should not be able to avoid this by paying a fine instead; thefts should be punished by fines.
- There is no case for capital punishment, except where a citizen threatens the security of the state.

At the end of his book, Beccaría sums up his conclusions in one lapidary sentence: 'In order that any punishment should not be an act of violence committed by one person or many against a private citizen, it is essential that it should be public, prompt, necessary, the minimum possible under the given circumstances, proportionate to the crime, and established by law.'[8]

Not all of Beccaría's ideas were completely new; he openly acknowledged his debt to other writers, notably Montesquieu. The use of torture was already widely criticised, and had been abolished in England, Prussia and Sweden. The principle of proportionality between crime and punishment was frequently affirmed. The notion of the social contract as the basis for law could be traced to Hobbes and Rousseau. Many had long urged the importance of clarity in the law, and openness in judicial procedures.

The originality (and therefore, perhaps, the success) of Beccaría's book was precisely due to its shortness and simplicity, and to the coherence of his vision of a non-religious, moderate, open, social utilitarian system of criminal justice. Naturally, it provoked furious denunciations from the Church, the lawyers and the defenders of the status quo, but it appealed enormously to the *philosophes* and other modernisers.

Since Voltaire was reading Beccaría's book in the autumn of 1765, eighteen months after its first publication, he must have been reading it in Italian, presumably in the third edition. Considering that he was normally quick to pick up the latest literary novelties, and that he had corresponded with Beccaría about his earlier book on monetary reform soon after its publication in 1762,[9] it is surprising that it took him so long to read Beccaría's new work. In fact, Beccaría's book was brought to him at Ferney by James Macdonald, a young

Scotsman on his way home from Italy. Perhaps Voltaire had been too busy with his theatre and Mlle Clairon to send for a copy earlier; perhaps he had been too preoccupied with the Calas and Sirven cases. Or perhaps he was just getting old; a few years later, he admitted that he no longer read new books.

D'Alembert read *Dei Delitti e delle Pene* a few months earlier than Voltaire. In June 1765 he lent a copy to the abbé André Morellet, a friend and fellow *philosophe*, and urged him to translate it into French. Morellet quickly went to work, and his version (incorporating some rearrangement of Beccaría's chapters) was published in late December. When sending a copy to Beccaría on 3 January 1766, Morellet wrote: 'I dare assure you, Sir, that its success is universal. I am particularly charged to convey the thanks and the compliments of M. Diderot, of M. Helvetius, of M. de Buffon. In truth, Sir, if your affairs and your situation allow you to travel to France, you really must come here and receive the thanks and the marks of esteem which you have deserved.'[10] This French translation was even more successful than the original Italian version; in the first six months, seven editions were published. Later that year (1766), Beccaría did visit Paris at the invitation of the *philosophes*; but he was so shy, so timid and so homesick, and possibly so lovesick for his young wife at home in Milan, that his visit was not a success. He returned to Milan as soon as he decently could and, having become famous throughout Europe, spent the rest of his life in relative obscurity as an academic and civil servant.

If Voltaire was slow to read Beccaría's *Dei Delitti e delle Pene*, he was also slow to react to it in print. He admired the abbé Morellet's translation, and when Morellet visited him in June 1766, they undoubtedly discussed the book at length.[11] It may have been that visit which prompted Voltaire to think of writing something about the Beccaría book. A month later, in a letter to Damilaville, Voltaire alluded to the commentary that he was writing, and by September he had finished it, sending a copy to d'Argental.[12] It was published anonymously as a *Commentaire sur le livre Des Délits et des Peines, par un avocat de province*.[13]

Despite its anonymity, Voltaire's authorship of the *Commentaire* was quickly known, and his fame and his Commentary gave substantial new impetus to the international renown of Beccaría. In many European editions of the eighteenth century, in Italy, France, England and Germany, the two works were published together in the same volume. If the truth be told, however, Voltaire's *Commentaire* is rather an odd little book, which wanders all over the place. In fact, it is not really a commentary on Beccaría at all. Voltaire includes some respectful references to Beccaría's book and he covers some of the same points as Beccaría. But he does not follow Beccaría's method of working up from first principles to construct a rational and civilised criminal justice system, nor does he echo Beccaría's tone of voice. Where Beccaría is cool, systematic, analytical, Voltaire is polemical, discursive, historical, anecdotal and passionate. The fact is that Voltaire was not particularly suited to systematic and dispassionate analysis, and he had no interest in disguising, behind a cloak of intellectual suavity, his indignation at the crude barbarities of the French judicial system. He wanted to reform the system, and he aimed to do so by stirring up indignation in others.

On some important points of detail, Voltaire is less radical than Beccaría. Whereas Beccaría opposed all use of torture, Voltaire would in the last resort keep it as a way of discovering the identities of the accomplices of convicted regicides and parricides. Whereas Beccaría denied any legitimacy to capital punishment, unless the State was in jeopardy, Voltaire went no further than to argue that the death penalty should be replaced as far as possible by forced labour, and that no execution should be carried out unless explicitly confirmed by the King. On the other hand, Voltaire's *Commentaire* is a powerful complement to *Dei Delitti e delle Pene*; for whereas Beccaría mainly restricted himself to the discussion of the general principles of a just penal system, Voltaire vigorously attacked some of the worst procedures customary in French judicial practice. In this sense, his *Commentaire* marks Voltaire's shift of focus from the specifics of a given case to the inherent problems of the French penal system. Here is a passage from his chapter 'On Criminal Procedure':

If one day humane laws should soften some over-rigorous practices in France, perhaps they will reform the rules of procedure. In several respects the Criminal Ordinance seems to have been designed only for the destruction of the accused. It is the only law which is uniform throughout the Kingdom; should it not be as favourable to the innocent as terrible to the guilty? In England, a simple wrongful imprisonment is repaired by the minister who ordered it; but in France, the innocent who has been buried in the cells, who has been tortured, has no compensation to hope for, no damages to secure against anyone. The investigation of a crime must be rigorous, that is a war which human justice wages against wickedness; but even in war there is generosity and compassion.

Among the Romans, witnesses were heard publicly, in the presence of the accused, who could reply to them, and question them himself. This procedure was noble and frank, it breathed Roman magnanimity.

With us, everything takes place in secret. A single judge, with his clerk, hears each witness one after another. The witnesses are, usually, people from the dregs of society, and the judge, shut up with them, can make them say anything he wants. These witnesses are heard a second time, still in secret, which is called 'review' (*récolement*). But if, after this review, they withdraw their testimony, or change it in important respects, they are punished as false witnesses. So that when a simple man, who does not know how to express himself, but has an upright heart, and recalls that he has said too much or too little, or that the judge misunderstood him, withdraws what he said for reasons of justice, he is punished as a criminal, and so he is often compelled to stand by his false testimony, simply for fear of being treated as a false witness.

When the accused escapes, you start by seizing all his property. You do not have any proofs, and you start by exacting immense penalties. You say it is a punishment for his disobedience in refusing arrest. But does not the extreme rigour of your criminal practices force him to this disobedience?

A man is accused of a crime, and first you lock him up in a frightful dungeon; you do not allow him to communicate with anyone; you put him in irons, as if you had already found him guilty. The witnesses who testify against him are heard in secret; he only sees them briefly at the confrontation. If he can show that the witnesses have either exaggerated the facts, or that they have left out other facts, or that they are mistaken on certain details, the fear of torture will make them persist in their perjury. If the story of the accused is different from that told by the witnesses, that will be enough for judges, if they are either ignorant or prejudiced, to condemn an innocent man.[14]

Voltaire never moved into the camp of those who opposed all capital punishment. In 1770, when he was seventy-six, Louis Philipon de la Madelaine sent him the text of a 'Discourse on the Necessity and the Means of Suppressing Capital Punishment'.[15] Voltaire's reply was cautious and equivocal: he agreed that capital punishment should be limited, and should not be imposed on those who were mentally disturbed; but he insisted that it should be applied with all the most extreme apparatus of horror in the case of the worst criminals.

Sir: You have sent me a work dictated by humanity and eloquence. It has never been better proved that judges must start by being men, that the punishments of the evil-doers must be useful to society, and that a hanged man is no good to anyone. Undoubtedly, premeditated murderers, parricides, incendiaries, deserve a death whose apparatus must be frightful. I should without regret have condemned Ravaillac to be quartered; but I should not have imposed the same torment on a man who had not wanted, nor been able, to kill his prince, and who must obviously have been mad. It seems to me diabolical to have shot Admiral Byng, for not having killed enough Frenchmen.[16]

For Voltaire, François Ravaillac's assassination of Henri IV in 1610 was a monstrous crime, since it was a mortal blow against the King's attempt to reconcile Catholics and Protestants in France; it therefore deserved the most monstrous punishment. What is striking about the second half of this passage is that Voltaire had now changed his mind on the case of Damiens and his deranged and half-hearted attempt on the life of Louis XV in 1757. At the time, he seems to have felt nothing but indignant indifference to Damiens's extreme agony; now, it seems, he was having second thoughts about imposing excessive suffering on a man who was not responsible for his actions. Voltaire had not moved anything like as far as Beccaría on the question of capital punishment; but to the extent that he had changed his mind, it was partly, no doubt, as a result of reading *Dei Delitti e delle Pene*.

The Execution of the Chevalier de La Barre

1765–8

Even before the publication of Beccaría's *Dei Delitti e delle Pene*, Voltaire had become convinced, from his engagement in the Calas and Sirven cases, of the general and systemic defects in the French judicial system. This conviction was massively reinforced in 1766, the year following the rehabilitation of Jean Calas and Voltaire's reading of Beccaría, by the eruption of two more major judicial miscarriages in quick succession: the trial and execution, in May 1766, of Thomas Arthur Lally Tollendal, ostensibly for offences apparently including embezzlement and treason; and the trial and execution, in July 1766, of Jean François Le Febvre, chevalier de La Barre, for blasphemy and sacrilege.

Both of these executions appeared to be the result of fundamental malfunctions of the machinery of justice; and unlike the Calas and Sirven cases, neither of them could be explained away in terms of strange local coincidences, although in the trial and execution of the chevalier de La Barre, local factors and the fanatical bigotry of the Church and State hierarchy had both clearly played a critical role. These two new cases reinforced Voltaire's growing conviction that the central problem was not that French judicial processes were imperfect in certain respects, or that trials could unfortunately go wrong, or that the possibility of impartial justice could too easily be compromised by personal or popular prejudice; but that the criminal justice system was profoundly flawed.

Thomas Arthur, Count Lally Tollendal (1702–66), was a nobleman of Irish descent, whose family had followed James II into exile in France. He pursued a brilliant career as an officer in the service of the

French State and he was sent to India, early in the Seven Years War, to defend the interests of the French India Company (*Compagnie des Indes*) against the English. Voltaire, who had long known Lally personally, was aware that he was violent, difficult and headstrong; and since Voltaire had invested money in the *Compagnie*, he had worried at the time that the appointment of 'this Irish hothead' might not be good for the shareholders, and might even jeopardise his own income from the company, currently running at some £20,000 a year.[1]

After his arrival in India, Lally had at first had some military successes against the English, but his victories soon gave way to an uninterrupted series of defeats. In January 1760, he had to fall back on the French-controlled town of Pondicherry, where he was besieged. In Pondicherry, he quarrelled with the local management of the company, with his own officers, and with the leaders of the people of the town. A year later, in January 1761, the town council decided to capitulate; Lally Tollendal was taken prisoner of war by the English, along with more than two thousand officers and men of the French army. In September that year he was transferred to England.

In his absence, Lally's fellow officers, the staff of the *Compagnie*, and the members of the Pondicherry town council, all conspired to blame him for the defeat. In response, Lally persuaded the British authorities to let him return to France, on parole, to defend his honour against his accusers. When he did return home in November 1762, he was locked up in the Bastille, where he languished for the next seventeen months without being questioned or knowing exactly what he was charged with, or even whether he would be charged. But popular opinion, overheated with excitement at the prospect of punishing a scapegoat for the French defeat in India, was clamouring for a trial. At the time of the siege of Pondicherry, the father superior of the local Jesuits in the town had been a certain Father Lavaur. When he died, early in 1764, a report was found in his personal effects, cataloguing a series of complaints against Lally, including embezzlement and treason (*lèse-majesté*); and its publication prompted the French attorney-general, Maître Omer Joly de Fleury, to bring formal charges.

This Joly de Fleury (1715–1810) came from a powerful family of parliamentarians; he was a diehard enemy of the Enlightenment and the *philosophes*, and therefore an old opponent of Voltaire. It was he who had formally denounced *Candide* in February 1759, which he described as a 'scandalous brochure'. In the same year, he called for a ban on the printing of the *Encyclopédie*. In 1763 he proposed a Parlement regulation forbidding inoculation against smallpox. In 1765 he demanded and secured the Parliamentary condemnation of Voltaire's *Dictionnaire Philosophique*. Voltaire never missed an opportunity to express angry derision towards this reactionary, whom he described as neither *Homère* (Homeric) nor *joli* (pretty) nor *fleuri* (flowery).

When Lally's trial began in April 1764, he had still not received any documentation of the charges, and he was not allowed to have a lawyer to defend him. Throughout the trial, lasting two years, Lally protested his innocence and made counter-accusations against his accusers with a violence and intemperance which probably damaged his case. On 6 May 1766, he was sentenced to death for having 'betrayed the interests of the King, of the State, and of the *Compagnie des Indes*; for abuse of authority, vexations, and exactions'.[2] Three days later, after making a failed attempt at suicide in prison, Lally was gagged, to prevent him protesting his innocence, and hustled in a garbage cart to the scaffold on the place de la Grève.* The executioner's first blow only sliced open Lally's skull; he did not succeed in beheading him until the second attempt.[3]

Voltaire heard of Lally's execution a few days later, and on 17 May 1766 he wrote to Damilaville: 'I knew Lally for an absurd man, violent, ambitious, capable of pillage and abuse of power; but I should be astonished if he was a traitor.'[4] Ten days later he wrote to another friend: 'I have just been reading up the tragedy of poor Lally. I can easily see that Lally got himself detested by all the officers and all the inhabitants of Pondicherry, but in all the submissions to the trial there is no appearance of embezzlement, nor any appear-

---

*The place de la Grève in Paris was on the right bank of the Seine, just below the place de l'Hôtel de Ville. This was the traditional place of execution in Paris. It was also the place where workers would congregate to show that they were ready to be hired for work. Today, of course, to be *en grève* means to be on strike.

ance of treason. There must have been proofs against him which have not been revealed in any of the briefs.'[5]

At the end of May, Voltaire wrote again to Damilaville: 'I have received the briefs for and against the unfortunate Lally. I cannot see anything but vague insults; the substance of the charge is apparently in the questioning, which still remains secret. In France, no reasons are given for the verdict or sentence, so the public is never informed.'[6] On the same day, Voltaire wrote to Alexandre d'Hornoy, the lawyer son of his other niece, Mme Fontaine:

I am not surprised that he discovered all of a sudden the trick of making enemies of all the other officers, and of all the inhabitants of Pondicherry. I do not doubt but that he was legitimately condemned; but I confess that I do not see for what. The briefs only contain fairly vague insults, and confused accounts of military operations which even a council of war would find difficult to assess. There must have been some embezzlements, and yet his numerous enemies do not specify any. Even the term 'embezzlement' is not found in the verdict. You would give me great pleasure if you would tell me exactly what he was condemned for, and what his assets were. I presume that you won't have any difficulty finding it out from your colleagues.[7]

In June, Voltaire wrote again to Damilaville:

As for Lally, I am very sure that he was not a traitor, and that it was quite impossible for him to have saved Pondicherry. The Parlement can only have condemned him to death for embezzlement. But it would have been desirable if they had specified what kind of embezzlement he was guilty of. France, once again, is the only country where no reasons are given for verdicts and sentences, just as it is the only country where the right to judge other men can be bought and sold.[8]

Voltaire never succeeded in penetrating the Parlement's wall of secrecy. The best he was able to do was to write up the Lally case and its antecedents in an updated version of his *Précis du Siècle de Louis XV* in 1768, as well as in his *Fragments Historiques sur l'Inde* (1773).[9] In this case, his real handicap as a campaigner was that the events leading up to the trial of Lally had all taken place in a distant part of the world, and one moreover which was no longer under French control. In the Calas case, Voltaire had been able to discredit the verdict because he had managed, with the help of a team of leading lawyers and other assiduous friends, to investigate the people and the events in Toulouse on that fateful night, and thus to assemble, quite independently of the Toulouse Parlement, a dossier by which he could show that the condemnation of Jean Calas was flawed, unproved, absurd, even impossible. But not only was Pondicherry far away; many, or most, of the key personae in the siege of Pondicherry were hostile to Lally.

Voltaire still felt able to make worldly little jokes, as when he wrote of Lally: 'His character made him detested by all who had to do with him. But that is not a reason for cutting off a man's head. The briefs both for and against him, which I have read attentively, contain nothing but insults, and not the least proof.'[10]

It is hard to tell from Voltaire's correspondence at this time whether he was mainly irritated and impatient at the authoritarian secrecy of the French judicial system, or whether he already suspected a major judicial error. His letters show that, since he could find no proof of treason, he assumed that Lally must really have been condemned for embezzlement. Yet this was just an assumption, since he could not find any evidence of embezzlement either. Later he certainly came to believe, as he made explicit in the *Précis du Siècle de Louis XV*, first, that Lally had not been guilty either of treason or of embezzlement, and second, that the wording of the published verdict was not just misleading, but inherently suspicious: it asserted that Lally had 'betrayed the interests' of the King, but it did not say that he was guilty of *lèse-majesté* or high treason. Voltaire was sure that the 'betrayal of interests' was not a recognised legal concept, and must be different from outright treason. In other words, the Parlement had been making up the law as it went along.

By late June 1766, he was becoming increasingly angry about the Lally case. 'My destiny is not to be happy with the verdicts and sentences of the Parlements. I dare to be very unhappy with that which condemned Lally; the statement of the verdict is vague and means nothing. The briefs for and against are no more than insults. Finally, I cannot get used to sentences of death given without reasons. There is in this jurisprudence an arbitrary barbarity which insults human nature.'" This last sentence is a critical indicator of Voltaire's attitude at the time. Quite independently of whether the Lally verdict could or could not be justified, and he obviously doubted it, he had reached the point where he rejected the 'arbitrary barbarity' of the French judicial system. But as far as fighting the Lally verdict was concerned, Voltaire had come to a dead end, and he made no further efforts to challenge it until several years later.

Of all the cases that Voltaire took up, the one that he found most shocking and most moving, because of the contrast between the youth of the victim and the barbarity of the judicial process, was the trial and execution, in Abbeville in Normandy, of the young Jean François Le Febvre, chevalier de La Barre. The offences he was alleged to have committed were malicious damage to a crucifix, singing anti-religious songs, and showing disrespect to a religious procession. The charges were blasphemy and sacrilege. The verdict was guilty, and the sentence that he should have his tongue torn out, that he should then be beheaded, and that his body should be burned on a pyre.

The story began on the morning of 9 August 1765, when it was discovered that a crucifix, on the Pont-Neuf bridge in the middle of the town of Abbeville, had been cut about, perhaps by a sword or a knife. Around the same time, a figure of Christ in the cemetery had been soiled with filth. These events stirred up extreme emotions among the God-fearing population. The local bishop, from Amiens, leading a procession of ceremonial apology (*amende honorable*) to the crucifix, declared that the culprits 'deserved the most extreme torments in this world and eternal punishment in the next'. The stage was being set for a highly charged trial.

The two main figures in the investigation, and in the trial which followed, were Charles-Joseph Dumaisniel, sieur de Belleval, a local notable and magistrate; and Nicolas-Pierre Duval de Soicourt, mayor of Abbeville and therefore the chief investigating official in the case. It was Belleval who was mainly responsible for whipping up the judicial investigation, not simply in the line of public duty but essentially for reasons of personal vendetta.

As a result of his efforts, an enquiry was opened, and it quickly focused on a group of local adolescents, well born, but loud, turbulent, slightly but ostentatiously dissolute, a bit impious, and disrespectful of authority. They were frequently heard singing barrack-room songs, vulgar, anti-clerical, bawdy. Some of them had been seen, not long before, passing a religious procession without taking their hats off. In short, they were prominent members of the local youth.

As in the Calas and Sirven affairs, the Church and State authorities issued *monitoires* in every parish church summoning the faithful to produce evidence for the prosecution of these crimes. Their initial enquiries produced plenty of hearsay and gossip, but no hard evidence against any of the young men.

The chief suspect, and the main target of Belleval's personal vendetta, was Jean François Le Febvre, chevalier de La Barre. He was probably born in 1745, and was therefore nineteen or twenty years old at the time of these events. Voltaire variously describes him as sixteen, seventeen, nineteen and twenty-one.

It soon emerged that La Barre's dissolute friends and associates included three other young men who were uncomfortably closely related to the investigators: Dumaisniel de Saveuse, the son of Belleval; Jean-François Douville de Maillefer, the son of Duval de Soicourt, the mayor and chief investigating magistrate; and Jacques Marie Bertrand Gaillard d'Étallonde, the son of the Président de Boëncourt, a senior local judge and Duval's immediate hierarchical superior. Belleval and Duval were able to spirit away their sons before they were publicly named in the investigation; Gaillard d'Étallonde was also helped to escape, but not before he had been identified as a possible suspect, along with La Barre.[12]

Gaillard d'Étallonde, who was born in 1749, was four years younger than La Barre. Before he could be arrested, he fled to Prussia and enlisted in the army under the pseudonym Morival; on Voltaire's recommendation, in February 1767, Frederick the Great took steps to have 'Morival' located, found he was serving as a military standard-bearer, and soon appointed him an officer.[13]

When the authorities issued their arrest warrants and proceeded to trial, therefore, they could lay their hands on only two suspects: the chevalier de La Barre, and a young friend, Charles François Marcel Moisnel, sixteen or seventeen years old[14] (though Voltaire says he was about fifteen). Some evidence emerged from their interrogations that the main perpetrator of the vandalism on the crucifix on the Pont-Neuf may well have been Gaillard d'Étallonde. Perhaps it was true; but perhaps La Barre and Moisnel had been cowed, first by the intimidation of Belleval, then by the ferocious interrogations of Duval, into pointing the finger at d'Étallond; or perhaps La Barre could see that it was convenient to divert blame on to him since he had got away. Either way, Gaillard d'Étallonde could only be tried *in absentia,* just like Pierre Paul Sirven. Nevertheless, the shadow of the possible guilt of the absent Gaillard d'Étallonde was used by the prosecution to implicate his friends, and thus to secure the conviction of La Barre.

La Barre was an orphan, who had arrived in Abbeville not long before, and was living with his aunt, Anne-Marguerite Feydeau, the abbess of the convent of Villancourt. Mme Feydeau was a worldly and perhaps an attractive woman: she had been the object of the pressing attentions of the local magistrate, the middle-aged Charles-Joseph de Belleval, but after the arrival of La Barre, she rejected Belleval's advances. Belleval believed that La Barre had displaced him in the affections of Mme Feydeau, and was the cause of his rejection; so he thought that he could use the scandal of the mutilation of the crucifix to get his revenge. Belleval pursued a fierce campaign against La Barre, going from door to door to drum up evidence against him, and invoking the *monitoires* which had been issued in August, with their associated threats of excommunication. By the end of September 1765, he had secured La Barre's arrest.

As part of the enquiry, Duval de Soicourt, mayor of Abbeville and the chief investigating magistrate, searched La Barre's room in the convent and discovered a number of compromising books, including several works of erotic literature. Most compromising of all, he found a copy of Voltaire's *Dictionnaire Philosophique Portatif.* In the trial, it was argued by the prosecution that the young men had been incited to their crimes by the corrupting influence of *philosophie* in general and by the *Dictionnaire Philosophique* in particular.

On 28 February 1766, the court in Abbeville found the chevalier de La Barre guilty, and condemned him to have his tongue torn out, to be beheaded, and his body burned on a pyre; it condemned Gaillard d'Étallonde, in absentia, to have his right hand cut off, his tongue torn out, and himself to be burned alive on a pyre; and it condemned the *Dictionnaire Philosophique* to be burned on the same pyre as La Barre. La Barre's sentence was slightly less horrendous than Gaillard d'É-tallonde's because he was a nobleman and therefore entitled to the privilege of beheading. The court postponed any verdict on young Moisnel.

The sentences could not be carried out, however, until they had been confirmed by the Parlement in Paris. La Barre and Moisnel were therefore transferred, on 12 March, to the prison of the Conciergerie in the centre of Paris, where they remained for three months. (It was while they were there that the Paris Parlement condemned Lally to death, and carried out his execution on 9 May 1766.)

On 4 June, by a majority of fifteen judges to ten, the Parlement confirmed the sentence on La Barre and Gaillard d'Étallonde, as well as on the *Dictionnaire Philosophique*. The two young men remained in the Conciergerie for another three weeks, during which time various highly placed relatives of Mme Feydeau and La Barre, as well as the bishop of Amiens, appealed to Louis XV for a royal reprieve. The King refused.

On 27 June, La Barre and Moisnel were taken back to Abbeville. Four days later, on July 1, La Barre's execution took place. First, he was tortured: each of his legs was enclosed between two wooden planks, and the executioner hammered thick wooden wedges between the planks and his legs. This torture went on for an hour, during which time Duval insistently demanded a confession; in vain. La Barre was then taken in a cart to the scaffold, wearing a placard reading: 'Impious, sacrilegious and hateful blasphemer.' By all accounts, La Barre endured his torments with great fortitude and calmness; he even laughed when he saw, hanging from the gallows, a paper cutout representing the absent Gaillard d'Étallonde. According to Voltaire, he said, at the foot of the scaffold: 'I did not believe that they could make a gentleman die for such a small thing.'[15] The authorities omitted that part of the sentence requiring the tearing out of La Barre's tongue, and the public executioner – the same one who had so recently botched the decapitation of Lally in Paris – proceeded directly to the beheading of La Barre. This time he achieved it at the first attempt.[16] La Barre's body was burned on the pyre, and with it the copy of Voltaire's *Dictionnaire Philosophique*.

Voltaire was slow to hear of the La Barre case, or at least slow to comment on it. On 16 June, he wrote to Alexandre d'Hornoy, the lawyer son of his other niece, Mme Fontaine, whose country home was not far from Abbeville: 'I beg you, my dear judge, to satisfy my extreme curiosity on this adventure. Please send me the fullest details. I am afraid that people may say that those fellows were *encyclopédistes*.'[17] If Voltaire was late in learning about the La Barre case, it may have been partly because he had been exceptionally busy: with his campaign for the retrial and rehabilitation of the Sirvens; with his attempts to mediate in the political quarrels in Geneva; with the quarrels of Jean-Jacques Rousseau; with the visit of Damilaville; with his reading of Beccaría; and with the writing of his *Commentaire* on Beccaría. At all events, he alludes to several of these preoccupations, alongside a reference to the La Barre case, in a letter to Damilaville of 23 June 1766, four months after La Barre had been condemned to death.

My dear friend, I trust that I shall receive very soon the brief of our dear Beaumont [Voltaire's lead lawyer in the Calas and Sirven cases], this indefatigable defender of innocence. The little discourse which has been prepared to back up his brief [the *Avis au Public*, see Chapter 8] is absolutely only meant for a few foreigners who could protect this unfortunate family ... I have been told that the Parlement had not confirmed the verdict condemning the young idiots of Abbeville, and that it wanted to give their relatives the time to get from the King a commutation of the sentence; I hope this news is true. It is not just to punish idiocy by torments which should only be reserved for great crimes.[18]

But the Sirven case, though important, difficult and time-consuming, was not really urgent, since the Sirvens were alive and safe. Voltaire's most pressing preoccupation now was the La Barre affair, and he was not at all reassured by what he learned about the details of the case; he was especially worried, indeed alarmed, by the implications of the public condemnation of his *Dictionnaire Philosophique*. On 1 July, he wrote to d'Alembert:

Are you in a position to find out about this young idiot named M. de La Barre, and his companion, whom they so sweetly condemned to lose their fist, their tongue and their life? I have been told that they said, in their interrogation, that they were led to the acts of folly which they committed, by reading the books of the *encyclopédistes*. I can hardly believe it: idiots do not read, and certainly no *philosophe* would have advised any profanity. This is very serious. Try to get to the bottom of so odious and so dangerous a story.[19]

Voltaire did not yet know quite how serious; for on the same day, he wrote to the marquis d'Argence, his partridge-paté friend in Angoulême, in terms which implied that there was still time to avert the execution: 'They have taken the decision not to endorse the sentence, in order to be able calmly to take appropriate measures which will prevent its execution. The punishment would not have been proportionate to the offence. It is not just to punish idiocy as one punishes crime.'[20] It was too late; on that same day, 1 July 1766, in Abbeville, La Barre had already been executed.

The more Voltaire learned about the La Barre case, the more upset he became, and frightened for his own safety. He wrote to Damilaville on 7 July: 'My dear brother, my heart is withered, I am cast down. I did not imagine that anyone would blame the silliest and most unrestrained madness on people who only preach wisdom and purity of morals. I am tempted to go and die in some foreign land, where men might be less unjust. I shall be silent, I have too much to say.'[21]

But of course Voltaire was not silent, far from it, for he was becoming increasingly worked up. On the same day, he wrote to his other niece, Mme Fontaine: 'We believe you are informed of the news from Abbeville; we ask you urgently to tell us in the last detail the astonishing adventure of these young people whose heads were so horribly disoriented. Tell us their names, their age, their employment. Had they any previous outbursts of madness? Is it true that one of them was nephew of an abbess?'[22]

Given the obduracy with which the Toulouse Parlement had concealed the facts in the Calas case, it may be imagined that the villainous story behind the trial and execution of La Barre would also have remained a deep and inaccessible secret. Not a bit of it. Within a fortnight of the execution, Voltaire was so well informed that he was able to recount the story of Belleval, the abbess and the vendetta in terms that are recognisably the same as modern scholarship tells today. The speed with which Voltaire was able to gather all the information, and put it together in a lively and coherent narrative, may have been due to the fact that he had uncommonly good contacts in the legal world, notably through his great-nephew d'Hornoy; or perhaps it was that, in the tiny world of the provincial town of Abbeville, the story was almost common knowledge. It was probably a bit of both.

Voltaire dressed up the story in the form of an ostensible 900-word letter as if from some anonymous correspondent in Abbeville, and he circulated it to his friends. He wrote to Damilaville on 14 July:

You will be most astonished, you will shudder, my dear brother, when you read the account that I enclose. Who could believe that the condemnation of five young men of family, to the most horrible death, could have been the fruit of the love and jealousy of an aged villain of a magistrate of Abbeville? Did you know that several advocates have drafted a memorandum which demonstrated the absurdity of this frightful sentence? Is it possible to get me a copy of this memorandum? Please send a copy of this account to M. de Beaumont.[23]

In some ways, the most significant element of this letter was one to which Voltaire drew no overt attention: his address. He was writing it from 'The waters at Rolle in Switzerland'. Since Rolle was a spa, a little to the north of Ferney but on the same shore of the Lac Léman, he might have gone there for his health. In fact, he was scared out of his wits by the burning of his *Dictionnaire Philosophique*, and by the fear that he might now be in serious personal danger from the French authorities; so he had run away to safety in Switzerland.

The more Voltaire looked into the La Barre affair, the more scandalous problems he discovered. The case, like those against Calas and Sirven, had been based on a highly charged alliance between the bigoted Church–State machine and the superstitious local Catholic population. The evidence against La Barre was fragmentary, rumour-based, unreliable, wholly insufficient. The legal basis for the charges of blasphemy and sacrilege was questionable, unsafe, perhaps non-existent; the charges of themselves were manifestly out of proportion to the offences alleged; and if there was a legal offence of blasphemy, it almost certainly could not incur the death penalty. Worst of all, the case against the accused had been deliberately whipped on by a local magistrate for reasons of personal grudge against La Barre, quite unrelated to the ostensible charges.

Voltaire wrote to d'Argental:

I am convinced that the King would have reprieved him if he had known the whole story; but this poor chevalier de La Barre was completely disoriented, no one could defend him, they didn't even know how to refute the witnesses who had virtually been suborned by Belleval. Moreover, what is very odd is that there is no specific law for such an offence. He was abandoned to the prudence, or the caprice of the judge. Is it possible that a majority of five votes can be enough to execute, in the most horrible torments, a young gentleman who was guilty of nothing worse than folly? What more could they have done to him, if he had killed his father?[24]

Voltaire remained at Rolle for over a month, until he thought the storm had blown over. He dashed back to Ferney briefly, in order to welcome and entertain the visiting duke of Brunswick, but this was just a one-day trip; he immediately returned to Rolle, and stayed there until at least 16 August.[25]

Voltaire had scarcely finished drafting his first, very brief account of the La Barre affair, in the form of the pretend letter, before he followed it up with a much longer narrative which appeared as a twenty-four-page pamphlet entitled *Relation de la Mort du Chevalier de La Barre* (Account of the Death of the chevalier de La Barre).[26] Once again, Voltaire concealed his authorship, ostensibly representing it as if it were a memorandum from Maître Pierre Cassen, a well-known real-life Paris lawyer and a relative of Damilaville, addressed to the Marchese Cesare Beccaría, the celebrated Milanese author of *Dei Delitti e delle Pene* and pioneer of penal reform.

In this pamphlet, Voltaire explicitly laid out the details of his allegation that Belleval had engineered the investigation of La Barre for reasons of personal envy and sexual jealousy, had pressured witnesses to give evidence against La Barre under threat of excommunication, and had pressured the local mayor into holding a trial. Voltaire itemised the evidence of the various witnesses, claiming that all or almost all of it was hearsay, that the alleged offences were of the kind of trivial impiety to which wild youth is often inclined, such as the singing of vulgar songs, or disrespect to a religious procession, and that no evidence at all was produced to implicate La Barre in the vandalism of the crucifix on the Pont-Neuf. (Seven years later, in 1773, in a letter to Belleval, Voltaire retracted his accusation of a personal vendetta.[27] But the following year, after securing fuller documentation of the case, he changed his mind again, and asserted brutally that 'Two villains got up this trial solely to ruin Mme l'Abbesse de Villancour [sic], who would not sleep with them.'[28])

In his *Relation de la Mort du Chevalier de La Barre*, Voltaire underlined the fact that under French law the offence of blasphemy did not carry the death penalty. 'The legal ordinance of 1666 prescribes a fine for the first offence, a double fine for the second offence, etc., and the pillory for the sixth offence.'[29]

In the end, says Voltaire,

there was so little evidence of a substantial offence that the judges, in their sentence, employed vague and ridiculous terms as used by the common people: '*For having sung abominable and execrable songs against the Virgin Mary and all the saints*'. Are these terms compatible with the dignity of the Bench? An ancient bawdy song is, after all, only a song. It is human blood casually spilt, it is torture, it is the torment of the tongue torn out, the hand cut off, of the body cast into the flames, which is abominable and execrable.

Unfortunately, I have heard several people say that they could not prevent themselves from detesting a sect [i.e. the Catholic Church] which is only sustained by the public executioners. These people wanted to execute, with a torture reserved for poisoners and parricides, mere children accused of having sung ancient blasphemous songs. You could not believe, Sir, how much this event makes our Roman Catholic religion hateful to all foreigners. The judges say that politics forced them to act in this way. What imbecile and barbarous politics! Ah, Sir, what a horrible crime against justice, to pronounce a sentence for political reasons, above all a sentence of death! And what a death!

The sadness and horror which grip me do not allow me to say any more.[30]

Voltaire's 'sadness and horror' was not assumed; on the contrary, he was so outraged, and so fearful for his own safety, that he was even beginning to think of moving abroad, as he wrote to d'Alembert on 18 July 1766:

Our brother [Damilaville] has no doubt passed on to you the Abbeville story, my dear philosopher. I cannot understand how thinking beings can remain in a country of monkeys, which so often become tigers. As for me, I am ashamed even to be on the frontier. In truth, now is the time to break the connection, and to bear elsewhere the horror we feel. I still have not managed to get hold of the lawyers' memorandum. You have seen it, no doubt, and you have shuddered; for the time has passed for pleasantries, witty remarks are not appropriate for massacres. What! Monsters in judicial robes put to death children of sixteen years in the most horrible torments, and that in spite of ten honourable and humane judges! And the nation endures this! Is this the country of *philosophie* and civilisation? No, it is that of [the massacre of] Saint Bartholomew. Even the Inquisition would not have dared do what these Jansenist judges have carried out.[31]

Voltaire continued to think about moving abroad, especially if he could persuade his friends to move with him; after he had taken refuge at Rolle in Switzerland, he was not sure that he would ever feel safe enough to return to Ferney permanently. One indication of his anxious uncertainty about his future, and where he would find safety, was that he had with him in Rolle, not just Mme Denis, but also his adopted daughter Marie-Françoise Corneille and her husband Claude Dupuits; it was as if he had gathered all his family around him, ready to flee together at the approach of danger. In mid-August he told Damilaville that he did not know if he would return to Ferney, or if he would move instead to Mannheim, seat of his friend Charles Théodore de Sulzbach, the Elector Palatine; the attractions of Mannheim were that the Elector ran an opulent and entertaining household, including a theatre; and that he owed Voltaire £130,000.[32]

Another option that Voltaire considered, more seriously, was to move to Kleve (or Clèves, as it was known in French), one of Frederick the Great's estates in north Germany, near the Rhine and close to the Netherlands frontier. Voltaire wrote to Damilaville on 21 July:

I am not letting myself be got down, my dear brother; but my pain, my anger, and my indignation redouble every moment. So little am I letting myself be got down, that I shall probably decide to go and finish my days in some country where I could do some good. I shall not be the only one. I am persuaded that the prince who will favour this enterprise [Frederick] would find you a good position, if you wished to join us. I know you have enough courage to follow me, but you probably have commitments which you cannot break. I have already started to take steps; if you back me up, I shall not hesitate.[33]

Then Voltaire had the bright idea of trying to persuade Denis Diderot to join him in Kleve, where he could continue the work of editing his great *Encyclopédie* in safety: an idea which he expanded to become a vision of an entire colony of *philosophes*. Voltaire admired Diderot, for his learning, his eminence and his commitment, and he referred to him in private by the nickname of 'Plato', or even on occasion 'Tonpla'; but he and Diderot were not close, in fact they were not even really friends, and they had little direct contact: their correspondence over twenty-nine years amounted to six-teen letters from Voltaire and only ten replies from Diderot. Most of the communication between them passed through intermediaries, mainly Damilaville (who was a friend and drinking companion of Diderot) or d'Alembert. But at this time of emotional crisis over the execution of La Barre and the burning of the *Dictionnaire Philosophique*, Voltaire wrote directly to Diderot with an emotional appeal to join his projected little colony:

A man like you must only see with horror the country in which you have the misfortune to live. You should come to a country where you would have complete liberty, not only to print whatever you want, but to preach out loud against superstitions that are as infamous as they are blood-stained. You would not be alone, you would have companions and disci-ples. You could establish a Chair which would be the Chair of Truth. Your library would be transported by water, with only four leagues of overland travel. Finally, you would leave slavery for liberty. If the course we propose satisfies your indignation and pleases your wisdom, just say the word, and we shall try to arrange everything in a manner worthy of you, in the great-est secrecy, and without compromising you. The country we are proposing is beautiful and close to everything.[34]

Coincidentally, Voltaire had at this time a casual exchange with Frederick the Great about the Sirven family, which provoked a wave of rumours, in Paris, that he was planning to emigrate. Frederick had offered to provide asylum in Wesel or Kleve for the Sirvens, and Voltaire had idly replied that he would be tempted to escort them there. Frederick read Voltaire's letter out loud in the Prussian court, and one of those who heard it was a certain Louis-François Tronchin, the son of Théodore Tronchin and secretary of the English ambassador in Berlin. 'The little Tronchin,' wrote Voltaire later to Mme du Deffand, 'thought he understood that I would rejoin the King of Prussia. He told his father, his father talked about it in Paris, the newspapers discussed it up and down, and that's how history gets written. He does not realise that I am seventy-three years old, and that I cannot go out of doors.'[35]

Théodore 'talked about it in Paris' because he had moved there permanently in late January 1766; when, in early August that year, he taxed Voltaire with planning to emigrate, Voltaire half denied it: 'It is untrue (at least for the present) that I am thinking of leaving the agreeable house which I built.'[36] But two days later he was still pushing the plan in a letter to Damilaville:

Your friend [i.e. Voltaire] still persists in his idea. It is true, as you have said, that he would have to tear himself away from many things which console him and which he would regret; but it is better to give them up by *philosophie* than by death. The only thing that astonishes him is that so many other people have not reached this decision together. Why don't many others seize such a lovely opportunity?[37]

For four months Voltaire went on urging the attractions of his idyllic Kleve colony project. He wrote to Damilaville: 'If the modern Plato wanted to, he could play a much greater role than the ancient Plato. I am persuaded, once again, that we could change the face of things. But as has been said, it is a question of will, and people do not have enough will.'[38] Voltaire's advocacy was in vain. His Parisian friends discussed his plan among themselves, but they decided (just like modern-day Parisians) that they could not leave Paris; Diderot was the first of the *philosophes* to tell Voltaire that he would not go. Voltaire was dismayed by their reaction: 'It is inexcusable to live under the sword when one could easily secure the triumph of the truth. I cannot understand those who would prefer to crawl to fanaticism in a corner of Paris, when they could crush this monster. What! Couldn't you even find me two zealous disciples? I should only ask three or four years of health and life. My fear is that I may die before I have rendered some service.'[39]

Voltaire did not move to Kleve after all, or to anywhere else; perhaps it had always been an unrealistic pipe-dream; as he never stopped pointing out, he was seventy-three, and he had put down quite deep roots of habit and custom at Ferney. Yet the idea of a utopian colony of *philosophes* was one of those pipe-dreams he never quite abandoned, and he continued to refer to it with regret several years later.

Voltaire's noisy and eloquent public protests at the illegal barbarity of the trial and execution of the chevalier de La Barre may have had some effect on public opinion, and perhaps even on the legal establishment as well. The court in Abbeville made no attempt to resume the trials of the others accused in the La Barre affair, and young Moisnel was released. Nicolas-Pierre Duval de Soicourt, the mayor of Abbeville and chief investigating magistrate in the case, was dismissed. But La Barre was dead, and Gaillard d'Étallonde, though absent, was still under sentence of a death even more barbaric than that endured by La Barre.

Voltaire was permanently marked in heart and mind by the La Barre case, and he never ceased to evoke it, with pity and anger, as a vivid symptom of so much that was evil in the French judicial system. But after the publication of his *Relation de la Mort du Chevalier de La Barre*, he did not take any immediate practical steps to attempt to have the trial reopened or the sentence quashed. One reason for this, no doubt, was that he was already heavily occupied with his campaign for the rehabilitation of the Sirven family; and this campaign was going particularly slowly, not just because the French establishment was systemically resistant to any form of judicial review, but also because Voltaire's leading lawyer on the case, Élie de Beaumont, was chronically distracted from the Sirven case by his personal involvement in a property law-suit.

The chevalier de La Barre was the last person to be condemned to death in France for blasphemy, but his rehabilitation had to wait for the French Revolution. It was one of the demands of the nobility in their list of political complaints (*cahiers de doléances*) which they submitted to Louis XVI just before the Revolution; after the Revolution it was solemnly granted, late in the day, by the Convention that declared France a republic in 1792.

The Blockade

1765–8

One of the reasons that Voltaire gave up Les Délices in 1765, and thus shifted his base to Ferney, outside Geneva, was that the political situation inside the republic was becoming increasingly stormy, with growing conflict over the balance of power between the patricians and the rest of the citizenry. As he said in a letter written over a year later: 'When I saw all these quarrels, I sensibly left Les Délices, in accordance with the terms of the agreement I made with Councillor Mallet.'[1]

In principle, Geneva was a quasi-democratic republic; in practice, it was an oligarchy dominated by a very small number of hereditary patrician families. The patrician oligarchs were able to control affairs because the population was divided into four political classes, each of which was subordinate to the class above. At the bottom were the *habitants* ('inhabitants'), foreigners who were merely permitted to reside there, without any political rights; above them were the *natifs* ('natives'), children of *habitants*, born in Geneva and automatically entitled to live there, but also without any political rights and with quite restricted economic and social rights; next above them were the *bourgeois* ('burghers'), who had been *natifs* but had managed to buy into a more privileged status by paying a substantial fee; and finally, at the top, the *citoyens* ('citizens'), born in Geneva from other 'citizens' or from '*bourgeois*'. Only the *bourgeois* and the *citoyens* had any political rights and they also had far-reaching economic and social privileges, but together they accounted for much less than half the 25,000 population of Geneva.

The oligarchic system in the republic was in fact even more restrictive than this four-tier stratification would suggest. For within the class of 'citizens', there was a tiny group of patrician families which controlled all the real political power in Geneva, through the Council of the Twenty-Five or *Petit Conseil* (Little Council). There were two other councils, the Council of 200 and the *Conseil Général* (General Council) which was larger still (up to about 1,500 members), which were supposed to represent all the *citoyens* and *bourgeois*. In theory, political power in the republic was meant to be counter-balanced between these three institutions. In reality, however, the Little Council was all-powerful, since it controlled all public appointments, as well as the agenda of issues which could be decided, or even discussed, in the lower-level assemblies to which the other 'citizens' and 'burghers' had access.

In short, the Geneva constitution was like a series of holding companies, in which all the real power was held by the shareholders in the top holding company. The system had evolved from Geneva's history as an immigrant republic, especially after Louis XIV relaunched full-scale persecution of the Protestants in France in 1685, with the revocation of the Edict of Nantes. Geneva had grown rich through the absorption of skilled immigrant labour, and its prosperity depended in large part on the lower orders, especially in the watch-making industry. But the old patrician establishment had no wish to share power with their fellow citizens, and certainly not with the working class.

This hierarchical disequilibrium was reflected in the social geography of Geneva, which still exists today: the patricians lived at the top of the town, in the *rues hautes*; whereas the lesser orders lived lower down, in the *rues basses*.

The system was so patently unfair in its distribution of power and privilege that it was bound to provoke conflict between the haves and the have-nots; and, indeed, conflict had already broken out several times in recent memory: in 1707, in 1718 and in 1734. On the last occasion, the conflict had become so acute that it was only settled, in 1738, by the outside mediation of France, Berne and Zurich. But the 'settlement' they imposed did not in fact settle anything, and thereafter the political tension between the political orders in Geneva remained endemic.

The fuse for the latest political conflict, which erupted in earnest in 1765, can be traced back to 1762, and to the triangular quarrel between Voltaire, Jean-Jacques Rousseau and the Geneva authorities. In April 1762, Rousseau had published his revolutionary political tract, the *Contrat Social*, and the following month, his educational thesis, *Émile.** Both works were denounced by the French and Genevan authorities, the *Contrat Social* for being seditious, and *Émile* for being anti-Christian, especially in the chapter known as 'The Vicar of Savoie'. In early June that year, both books were formally condemned by the Parlement in Paris and publicly burned, and immediately afterwards condemned in the same way by the *Petit Conseil* in Geneva, which also issued a warrant for Rousseau's arrest.

Voltaire wrote to d'Alembert later that month:

Excess of pride and envy has ruined Jean-Jacques, my illustrious *philosophe*. This monster dares to speak of education!, he who would not bring up any of his own sons, and placed them all in the orphanage. I should be sorry if he were hanged, but only by pure humanity; personally, I can only regard him as Diogenes' dog, or rather as a dog descended from a bastard of that dog. I do not know if he is detested as much in Paris, as by all the honest people of Geneva.[2]

Voltaire's contempt may seem intemperate until we recall that, two years earlier, Rousseau had sent him a celebrated hate-letter:

I do not like you, Sir; you have done me ills to which I would be most sensitive, to me your disciple and your enthusiast. You have ruined Geneva, in return for the asylum you have received there; you have alienated my fellow citizens from me; it is you who have made it unbearable for me to live in my own country; it is you who will make me die in a foreign coun-

---

*In the *Contrat Social*, Rousseau argued that the sovereignty of the people was inalienable and indivisible. The individual renounces his natural freedom in return for civil liberty in the community. Rousseau favoured democracy, especially in small states. In *Émile*, Rousseau set out the successive stages of an ideal education.

try, deprived of all the consolations of the dying. I hate you, finally; you wanted it; but I hate you as a man even more worthy to love you if you had wanted it.[3]

In June 1762, Rousseau responded to the condemnation of his *Contrat Social* and *Émile* by the *Petit Conseil* with a pamphlet defending his works; this pamphlet was itself banned by the *Petit Conseil*. Rousseau then escalated his quarrel with the Geneva authorities and on 12 May 1763, he publicly and formally renounced his status as a citizen of Geneva.

This prompted a belated series of protests by members of the Geneva citizenry at his mistreatment by the *Petit Conseil*. On 30 June, Voltaire wrote to his friend the duchesse de Saxe-Gotha:

If your most Serene Highness can be pleased with the little things which affect humanity, I shall tell her that Jean-Jacques Rousseau, condemned in the city of Calvin for having depicted a Vicar of Savoie, Jean-Jacques who uncitizened himself from Geneva, has found some citizens who have taken his side. Two hundred people, including two or three clergymen, presented a petition on his behalf to the magistrate. *'We know well that he is not a Christian,'* they say, *'but we want him to be our fellow citizen.'* That's tolerance for you. God be blessed.[4]

But the *Petit Conseil* did not give way, and the protests continued. Six weeks later Voltaire reported to Damilaville:

Yesterday six hundred persons came, for the third time, to protest in favour of Jean-Jacques against the Council of Geneva, which had dared to condemn the *Vicar of Savoie*. They say that any citizen is permitted to write whatever he wishes about religion, that he cannot be condemned without being heard, and that the rights of men must be respected. People say that all this could end up with an armed uprising. I should not be sorry to see a civil war over the *Vicar of Savoie*.[5]

Still the *Petit Conseil* did not give way, and there was another large demonstration at the end of September. Voltaire wrote to d'Alembert: 'Jean-Jacques has been condemned, because he sided too much with the people against the magistrates. So the people, very gratefully, have sided with Jean-Jacques. Seven hundred citizens went two by two in procession, to protest against the judges.'[6]

The attorney-general, Jean-Robert Tronchin (not Voltaire's banker, but a cousin by the same name), attempted to justify the actions of the *Petit Conseil* in a pamphlet called *Lettres écrites de la campagne* (Letters written from the countryside). From this point on, however, the quarrel between Rousseau and the government of Geneva spilled over into a quarrel between Rousseau and Voltaire, since Rousseau believed (mistakenly) that Voltaire had conspired to engineer his rupture with Geneva; relations between the two *philosophes* soon became irreparable.

At the end of 1764, Rousseau responded to the attorney-general with a pamphlet of his own, *Lettres écrites de la montagne* (Letters written from the mountain), in which he attacked Voltaire personally, by exposing him as the author of the anonymous pamphlet *Sermon des Cinquante* (Sermon of the Fifty).[7] Voltaire was acutely sensitive to being identified as the author of this work, not just because it was scandalously anti-Christian and could get him into trouble but even more because he had recently started circulating his *Dictionnaire Philosophique Portatif*, which was destined to be much more popular and much more scandalous to the authorities. He wrote to Damilaville in December 1764:

Decent people, and especially my dear brother, should know that Jean-Jacques has written a great book against the tiny (*parvulissime*) republic of Geneva, with the intention of rousing the people against the magistrates. In this book, J.-J. accuses me of being the author of the *Sermon des Cinquante*. Such a proceeding is certainly not that of a philosopher nor of an honest man. It may be clever, but it isn't honest ... Omer [Joly de Fleury, the French advocate-general] is currently working on an indictment of the *Dictionnaire Philosophique*. People keep saying it is by me, but I have nothing to do with it.[8]

In response to Rousseau's accusation, Voltaire counter-attacked with a scurrilous pamphlet of his own, *Le Sentiment des Citoyens* (The Feeling of the Citizens),[9] in which he denounced Rousseau, and in particular revealed that Rousseau had abandoned all of the five (illegitimate) children he had had by his companion, Marie-Thérèse Levasseur. This fact was known to very few people, and Voltaire had only recently learned it.

At first the conflict in Geneva was just between the three top classes: the oligarchs in the *Petit Conseil*, the ordinary *citoyens*, and the less privileged *bourgeois*. The ordinary *citoyens* and *bourgeois* became known as the *Représentants* because they were representing their claims to a fairer deal; the oligarchs were known as the *Négatifs* because they had recently (in 1763) claimed a veto power (*droit négatif*) over all other institutions.

Inevitably this conflict of principle could not be confined indefinitely within the upper orders of society. Below them, the artisan class of the *natifs* had an even stronger moral claim for more political and social justice, since they had no political rights and yet constituted over half the population. For the moment, in this year of 1765, the *natifs* were still passive but sooner or later they too were bound to demand a fairer deal. They started to move the following year, and their demands eventually led to an unprecedented outbreak of political violence. (As immigrants, the *habitants* do not seem to have joined the agitation for political rights.)

Of course, once the *natifs* started campaigns for improved political and economic rights, the *Représentants* had second thoughts: it was one thing for the *citoyens* and *bourgeois* to demand political concessions from the patricians, quite another to share political privilege with the *natifs*. At that point, many of the *Représentants* changed sides, supporting the patricians against the *natifs*.

Voltaire started out instinctively on the side of his friends, the patricians; as time went on, he shifted to side with the *Représentants*; and as more time passed, and the *natifs* joined the struggle, he shifted again to side with them. In short, it was a textbook case of the evolution of Voltaire's political thought in a democratic direction. He was not, and had never been, a principled democrat; but the more he heard the arguments of the rival parties in Geneva, the more democratic his conclusions became. These were limited to Geneva, however; he still did not become a democrat on grounds of general principle, and he did not apply his Geneva conclusions to Russia, Prussia or France. In this case, as in so many others, he remained eclectic, pragmatic and resistant to systemic thought.

In public, Voltaire insisted that he was not taking sides and would not get involved in the quarrels of the Genevans; and at first this may have been true, at least in intention. But he could not resist the temptation to be helpful; he made repeated efforts to act the part of an initially impartial conciliator, by inviting members of the *Représentants* and of the *Négatifs* to meet socially at the château de Ferney, to talk things over. It was no doubt this process of repeatedly hearing the arguments of both sides which gradually persuaded Voltaire that the *Représentants* had justifiable claims.

During 1763 and 1764, and most of the following year, Voltaire remained loyal to his oligarchic friends; in January 1765 he wrote: 'the people are insolent, and the *Conseil* is weak'.[10] By mid-October, however, Voltaire had privately swung behind the *Représentants*. He wrote to d'Argental: 'For France, it matters very little whether Geneva should be aristocratic or democratic. I will admit that at present I incline towards democracy, despite my ancient principles, because it seems to me that the magnates have been in the wrong on several points. The twenty-five of the *Petit Conseil* have chosen to take the title of noble lords, and it has gone to their heads.'[11]

But a couple of days later, in a letter to Damilaville, he took a much more uncompromising stand.

The splits in Geneva will soon break out. It is absolutely necessary that you and your friends should put it about in public that the citizens are in the right against the magistrates; for it is certain that the people only want liberty, and that the magistrature is aiming at absolute power. Is there anything more tyrannical, for example, than to remove the freedom of the press? And how can a people say it is free, when it is not permitted to think in writing? Whoever has the power in his hands would like to put out the eyes of all those who are subordinate to him. Every village judge would like to be a despot. The madness of domination is an incurable sickness ... Today I am starting to read the Italian book *On Crimes and Punishments*. At a glance it seems to me philosophical; the author is a brother.[12]

It is perhaps not a complete accident that Voltaire's conversion to the *Représentants* should happen to coincide with his exposure to Beccaría's work on penal reform. But however that may be, it is clear that he was no longer on the side of his aristocratic friends, and he soon felt obliged to tell them something about the reasons for his change of heart, and his hopes of a compromise.

In November 1765 he was sent a pamphlet setting out the demands of the *Représentants*, and he wrote directly to Jacob Tronchin:

Immediately after having read, Sir, the new book in favour of the *Représentants*, the first thing I do is to speak to you about it. It is a collection of bitter complaints. The author is aware how much I am tolerant, impartial and a friend of peace; he must also know how much I am attached to you, to your relatives, to your friends, and to the constitution of the government.

If he thought that I would declare myself on the side of the discontented party, and that I should poison open wounds, he does not know me.

I am very far from believing that I could be useful, but I have an idea (mistakenly, perhaps) that it may not be impossible to bring minds together. There have come to my home some citizens who have appeared to combine moderation with enlightenment. Even if such a meeting should serve only to ease bitter feelings, and to encourage a necessary conciliation, that would be a great deal, and nothing but good could come of it. It is not for me to be a conciliator, I simply limit myself to take the liberty of offering a meal where people could listen to each other.[13]

For a while, Voltaire continued to observe the most scrupulous self-control in his dealings with the authorities. A week after the previous letter, he wrote to Pierre Lullin, secretary of state of the *Petit Conseil*:

Sir: This morning four citizens let me know that they wished to speak to me; I sent them a carriage; I gave them dinner; and we discussed their business. I must first bear witness that not one of them expressed a single word which could offend the magistrates. I do not believe that it can be impossible to bring minds together, but I admit that conciliation is very difficult. There are questions on which, it seemed to me, they might give way; there are others which need a wiser man than me, and more capable of persuasion.[14]

At first, the patricians notionally accepted Voltaire's efforts to be helpful and impartial. But his attempts at facilitating conciliation made no progress, and by early December 1765 he had had enough. 'My angels, I can confirm that I am tired of wasting my time in trying to pacify the Genevans.'[15]

Voltaire became so impatient with the unreasonable stubbornness of the contestants that he developed some modest proposals of his own for a compromise; and he sent them to d'Argental, to have them shown to lawyers in Paris, as well as to some of the ministers in the French government. At the centre of Voltaire's plan was the rather obvious idea that the leverage of the *Conseil Général* should be increased, and the veto power of the *Petit Conseil* reduced. He proposed that whenever a motion in the *Conseil Général* was supported by seven hundred, that is, roughly half the members, it could not simply be blocked by the *Petit Conseil*, but must be debated for action. But as Voltaire commented a little later to d'Argental: 'This number seems too high to the citizens, and too low to the magistrates. As a result, it cannot be far from a fair compromise, since the general assembly almost never has more than thirteen hundred members at most.'[16]

In addition, Voltaire recommended reforms of the legal system: the patricians had undertaken to publish all the laws governing Geneva, but had not done so, and should be required to now; moreover, the *Petit Conseil* must give up its practice of imprisoning without trial, simply by administrative fiat.

Voltaire incorporated some of these reform proposals in the short pamphlet *Idées Républicaines*, which he wrote at about this time (November 1765). Too much of the pamphlet is devoted to barbed comments on Rousseau's *Contrat Social*, or to criticisms of Montesquieu's *Esprit des Lois*, but it also contains some unexpectedly radical propositions.

- The civil government is the will of all, carried out by one man or several, by virtue of the laws which all have supported.
- In a republic worthy of the name, the freedom to publish his thoughts is the natural right of the citizen. That is the law in England, a monarchical country, but where men are freer than elsewhere because they are more enlightened.
- [In Geneva] they burned this book [the *Contrat Social*]. If the book was dangerous, it should have been refuted. To burn a book of argument is to say: *We do not have enough wit to reply to it.*
- There has never been a perfect government, because men have passions. The most tolerable of all is no doubt a republic, because it brings men closest to natural equality.[17]

For a while, Voltaire thought his proposals were making progress, but he deceived himself. The *Petit Conseil* informed him officially that it had no intention of modifying the constitution of Geneva, and rather than negotiate with the *Représentants*, it called on France to mediate, no doubt on the assumption that the autocrats in Versailles would automatically side with the autocrats in Geneva. Voltaire then declared that he was washing his hands of the conflict, especially 'when I saw that the Genevans were not seriously interested except in the pre-eminence of their *rues hautes* over the *rues basses*, and were determined to weary the French government to know if the Council of the Twenty-Five has or has not the negative power in every case'.[18]

The French government named as chief mediator Pierre de Buisson, the chevalier de Beauteville, ambassador to Berne, and in March 1766 Beauteville arrived in Geneva with an extensive retinue, including ten chefs. He started his mission of mediation in the strangest way: he required the Geneva authorities, including the consistory of the Calvinist clergy, to lift their ban on the opening of a theatre in the town. Such a provision should already have been in force, under the terms of the earlier settlement of 1738. But because it had effectively been blocked by the Calvinist preachers, the local theatre company, which was popular with the people of Geneva, was compelled to perform just outside the territory of Geneva, and therefore just out of reach of the Calvinist authorities. With Beauteville's support, this theatre company was now able to move into Geneva and perform in the heart of the city.

Voltaire was exultant, especially when, in November of that year, the actors scored a big popular success with his tragedy *Olympie*. 'The Geneva troupe, which is not totally bad, surpassed itself yesterday with *Olympie*; it has never had such a great success. The crowd watching the show demanded with loud cries that it be put on again the next day. The Genevans have gone mad for *Olympie*, they perform it every day, and at three o'clock in the afternoon all the seats are taken. Everyone has seen *Olympie* except me, for I'm in my bed.'[19]

The arrival of the mediators did not calm the political disturbances in Geneva, however, neither did it persuade Voltaire to stop his meddling. In May 1766, he reported, with indignation, an extraordinary example of the quasi-feudal pretensions of the *Petit Conseil*. 'Not long ago, the Gentlemen of the Council sent me their bull-dog, to demand that I swear my homage-liege to them, in respect of a field I own. I shall certainly make them eat all the hay of that field before I swear homage-liege to them. These people seem to me to have more wig than wit *(plus de perruque que de cervelle)*.'[20]

Meanwhile, the *natifs* had decided that the arrival of Beauteville gave them their only chance of a better political deal, and in March they started holding meetings to agree their tactics. On 2 May, Beauteville reported on the agitation of the *natifs* in a letter to the duc de Choiseul.

For some time we have noticed movement among the *natifs* of this town. As their number is much greater than that of the citizens, their frequent assemblies began to worry the government. The magistrates suspected that they had an understanding with the *Représentants*. Last month, four men came to find me. When they told me that they were *natifs*, I replied that, being in the State, but not one of the political classes of the State, they had nothing to do with the mediation. So I sent them to the magistrates, without being willing to hear them nor receive any memorandum.[21]

The *natifs* then approached Voltaire for advice, and he helped them draft a memorandum of their demands. But when the *Petit Conseil* found out about Voltaire's intervention they got quite irritated, and Beauteville sent his secretary, Pierre de Taulés, to rebuke him.

I thought I ought to complain to M. de Voltaire, for having once again put in an appearance in the disputes of the Republic. I sent M. de Taulés to Ferney. M. de Voltaire only justified himself by his consternation; he admitted everything with the greatest candour, and ended by personally handing over to M. de Taulés the papers which concerned this little negotiation.

The *Petit Conseil*, all of a-tremble, could not be calm until it knew the secret plans of the *natifs*. They had already been several times, seven or eight hundred of them, to Carouge [a suburb of Geneva] to debate and co-ordinate their conduct. Informed that a certain Georges d'Auzière was the principal leader of these movements, the *Petit Conseil* had his papers seized, and put the man in prison. It is claimed that the *natifs* hoped to secure political recognition in the Republic, and to hold the balance between the magistrates and the *bourgeoisie*; that they had been excited by some of the *Représentants*; and that M. de Voltaire had had the weakness to promise them his protection.[22]

But, in reality, Beauteville thought that Voltaire's 'absurd and ridiculous behaviour' was more deserving of compassion than anger, considering that he was nearly seventy-three years old, 'and has fainting fits every day'.[23]

By this time, all the different warring parties began to think that Voltaire was on the other side, as he told d'Argental in mid-May.

As for the comedy of Geneva, it is a cold and complicated play which is starting to bore me terribly. The *natifs* say that I take the side of the *bourgeois*; the *bourgeois* fear that I am taking the side of the *natifs*. The *natifs* and the *bourgeois* pretend that I am too deferential to the Council. The Council says that I am too friendly with the *natifs* and the *bourgeois*. I therefore declared to the Councils, *bourgeois* and *natifs* that, not being a churchwarden in their parish, it was not appropriate that I should get mixed up in their business, and that I have enough business of my own.[24]

Théodore Tronchin, though far away in Paris, strongly suspected Voltaire of disloyalty, and in September 1766 twice accused him of bias. Voltaire denied it, but evidently Théodore Tronchin was neither convinced nor mollified, for he continued to go around Paris claiming that Voltaire was on the side of the *Représentants*. Seven months later, in the spring of 1767, Théodore was heard to say to the King that he was no longer Voltaire's friend, on the grounds that Voltaire was siding with the *Représentants*, an assertion that Voltaire described as 'quite ridiculous, especially in the mouth of a doctor'.[25] It was all the more ridiculous since Voltaire was by now probably at least as much on the side of the *natifs* as on that of the *Représentants*.

But Voltaire soon found himself in the middle of a real-life drama, which had some of the elements of low farce but which threw him into a state of rising panic. This was the drama of Mme Lejeune and the contraband books.

Censorship was more severe in France than in Geneva, so enterprising Parisian booksellers would try by underhand methods to procure from Geneva (and other places) books which could not legally be printed (or sold) in France. Mme Lejeune was the wife of such a Parisian bookseller, and towards the end of 1766 she travelled to Geneva, under the pseudonym of Mme Doiret, to buy some forbidden books. The comte d'Argental discreetly supported Lejeune's activities as a bookseller in the distribution of forbidden books, including those by Voltaire, and he allowed Lejeune to claim that he was, or had previously been, a domestic servant in his household. D'Argental had written to Voltaire to tell him that Mme Lejeune would be coming to Geneva to buy books, and had asked him to help her make her way home. Voltaire naturally agreed and on 11 December 1766, he wrote to d'Argental:

This honest woman has just arrived, and you can be sure that we have welcomed her in the name of my angels. We immediately sent for her and her luggage from Geneva. We rescued her from the most expensive hostelry in Europe, where she would have been ruined. We shall put her up, and we shall take good care of her. We shall supply a vehicle to conduct her in safety as far as Dijon. The recommendations of my angels are sacred, are they not? [26]

Accordingly, Voltaire lent Mme Lejeune a carriage and horses belonging to Mme Denis, and enlisted a local customs inspector called Jeannin, from the tax office at nearby Saconnex, to escort her part of the way. Her three trunks were loaded up, and they set off in the expectation that at the French customs post at Collonges (southwest of Geneva) the trunks would be sealed and Mme Lejeune could proceed in peace. The plan went badly wrong, however, for Jeannin betrayed Mme Lejeune to the French customs officers. The trunks were opened and were found to contain, under a surface covering of old clothes, over eighty forbidden books, including Voltaire's *Dictionnaire Philosophique* and his anti-Christian *Sermon des Cinquante*. The customs officials seized the trunks and their contents, as well as the carriage and horses. Mme Lejeune panicked, and legged it across country back to Geneva.

Voltaire's initial reaction shows that he thought that the mishap at Collonges could be extremely dangerous to him personally, for it had taken place only five months after the execution of La Barre in Abbeville on 1 July 1766, and with it the ceremonial burning of Voltaire's *Dictionnaire Philosophique*. But he hoped that it might not prove too dramatic, provided his influential friends could pull the right strings in Paris. He wrote to d'Argental on 23 December:

She [Mme Lejeune] took flight through ice and snow through a fearful countryside. We don't know where she is. She has made a really cruel journey. Her flight makes her seem guilty. But of what? She does not know how to read, she was following her husband's orders, she does not know if a book is forbidden or not. I am so sorry for her, I am having her looked for everywhere, I am afraid she may be in prison. There is not a moment to be lost.

One word from a *fermier général* to the customs post at Collonges will be enough, but this word is really necessary. You must write immediately.

My worst fear is that the director of the bureau at Collonges may send the papers to the police at Lyon or Paris, and that it could become a criminal affair which could go far.[27]

Four days after his first account of the Lejeune disaster, Voltaire adopted an indignant tone of injured innocence.

Mme Lejeune is in a safe place, she has nothing to fear, she is guilty of nothing. Here is a copy of the letter which I have written today to the Vice-Chancellor [Maupeou]. We are not asking for favours, we are asking for justice. There is certainly nothing else to be done, unless you would speak to M. Maupeou and make him see the absurdity of the idea that I should sell foreign books, or that I should send fifty or sixty volumes containing ten or twelve different works, that we demand in justice the release of our stolen property. One conversation will be enough. I trust they will not bother the King with this miserable affair.[28]

On 2 January, 1767, Voltaire told d'Argental that Mme Lejeune was safe in Switzerland, and that he was taking care of her expenses. Towards the end of his letter, he mentioned that Mme Lejeune had written to him to let him know that she was returning to Paris on horseback. 'You can see how brave she is.'[29]

Voltaire's next news was more serious. He learned that Mme Lejeune had been carrying a note from her husband, signed by him and identifying him as d'Argental's *valet de chambre*, in which he included a list of the forbidden books he wanted her to buy. Unfortunately, she had mislaid this incriminating evidence while she was in Geneva. Voltaire still thought that the best course of action would be to get Vice-Chancellor Maupeou to impound the three trunks, and have the contents burned.[30]

By the New Year Voltaire was becoming desperate with anxiety, and on 9 January he wrote to Antoine Auget, baron de Montyon, the senior Foreign Ministry official who was responsible for judging contraband cases.

Sir, it is a great consolation that you should be the judge of my niece, Mme Denis; for as for me, having nothing, I have nothing to lose; I have given everything away. The château that I have built belongs to her; the horses, the carriages, everything belongs to her. It is she whom the Cerberuses of the frontier post are persecuting; we both have the honour to write to you to beg you to free us from the claws of the gatekeepers of hell.

It is absurd to suppose that Mme Denis and I should carry on a trade in foreign books. We have never known any Mme Doiret; there was a Mme Doiret who came to our part of the world in her capacity as an old clothes trader; she bought some clothes from our servants, though we never saw her; she borrowed from them an old cart and some ploughing horses from our farm, which is far from the château; we knew nothing of it until after the arrest.

Far from contravening in any way the laws of the kingdom, I have considerably improved the king's estates on the frontier where I am, clearing waste ground and building eleven houses; and, far from engaging in the least contraband, I have on three occasions armed my vassals and my servants against fraudsters. I am only occupied in serving the king, and I have found in belles-lettres my only recreation at the age of seventy-three years.[31]

It is a pitiful, wretched letter, full of lies and half-truths, pathetic denials and abject snivelling; it is very Voltaire. For if Voltaire was spiritually bold, he was not personally at all brave. To the young *philosophe* Condorcet, Voltaire was a hero; but when Condorcet wrote the first semi-official biography of Voltaire, for the posthumous Kehl edition of the complete works, he candidly expressed his regret that so great a man as Voltaire should have had this weakness of fearfulness. 'We have often seen him expose himself to the tempest with temerity, but seldom face up to it with constancy; and these alternations between boldness and weakness have often saddened his friends, and prepared undeserved triumphs for his cowardly enemies'.*[32]

*The Kehl edition, edited by Condorcet, was the first posthumus edition of all Voltaire's works, so-called because it was published at Kehl, across the Rhine from Strasbourg, and therefore outside France and out of reach of the French authorities.

In his rising anxiety about the Lejeune case, Voltaire wrote a torrent of seventeen letters to d'Argental between 11 December 1766 and 2 February 1767. But he got far fewer back, and by 12 January he began to suspect, with distress, fear and anger, that d'Argental was not trying as hard as he might to help him.

You will perhaps be impatient, my adorable angel, to receive so many letters from me; but that's because I am quite upset to receive so few from you. Please forgive, I beg you, Mme Denis's anxieties, and mine.

You have told us that the ministers had made it a rule never to compromise themselves for their friends, and never to ask favours from each other. It would certainly be a very odious rule, dictated by indifference, weakness and self-satisfied amour-propre. I cannot conceive that one can only feel warmth for tragic verses, and not also put some warmth into the concerns which most interest friends like you.

Is it possible, in such an important affair as the one which affects us both, that you never wanted to act?[33]

Coming from Voltaire, who was normally gushingly friendly to d'Argental, these accusations of indifference and neglect come across with great brutality, and bear eloquent witness to the intensity of Voltaire's fear. The next day, Voltaire wrote d'Argental another long and insistent letter about the Lejeune affair; but when he received it, d'Argental wrote coldly cutting comments on his urgings and complaints in the margin.[34]

On the same day, 13 January 1767, Voltaire wrote to Richelieu, suggesting that he might quite suddenly have to escape to Switzerland, and openly blaming d'Argental, though without naming him.

You would be quite astonished at the main reason which could, from one moment to another, force me to make this journey. It is a man whom you know, a man who has been my friend for more than sixty years, a man finally who, by the most extraordinary adventure in the world, has placed me in a strangely embarrassing position; I have compromised myself for him in the most painful manner, but the only thing I can reproach him for is having acted too limply.[35]

Voltaire's fears were intensified when he heard word, in late January, that the Lejeune case might well be referred to the court at Dijon. This prospect so alarmed him that he wondered if he could not buy off the customs office, by offering to pay them a fine to be negotiated.[36]

Then all of a sudden, the sun came out, the clouds evaporated: Vice-Chancellor Maupeou had stifled the Lejeune affair, and Voltaire's worries were at an end. He wrote to d'Argental on 2 February: 'We have learned from [Mme Lejeune] that God is just. We do not yet know the details; but we think that his justice must crush the devils, especially the devil Jeannin. I can breathe again; I shall send no more packets [of books]. I think it is appropriate that I should write a little thank-you note to M. de Montyon.[37]

When it was all over, Voltaire became quite sheepish about his terrors and his reproaches. He wrote to d'Argental on 6 February:

Your servant got away with it, my divine angels: the councillors of state, the snows, and the illnesses which come with age and the rigours of the climate, reduced me to a pitiful state. I consider that of all these scourges, fear is still the worst. It freezes the blood, it gave me a sort of apoplexy. Blessed be the Vice-Chancellor who has been my main doctor. Without him, nothing would have been done. I only had the honour to know him from having played chess with him over fifty years ago. This time he could have checkmated me with a single word.[38]

Meanwhile, in Geneva, the mediators had totally failed to bring about a negotiated settlement and by the beginning of January 1767, Ambassador Beauteville had abandoned his efforts and had secretly left Geneva; some kind of military pressure by the French was now to be expected. As Voltaire reported a few days later: 'I am patiently waiting for the large army of five or six hundred men which will pretend to beseige Geneva. The only thing the headquarters will really beseige will be Ferney; they will expect to be amused, but they will only find sadness here.'[39]

The political crisis made daily life rather difficult. As Voltaire reported:

Almost all the shops are closed, and the financial markets too. I have a large part of my assets in Geneva, but all the banks are closed. It so happens that at Tournay and Ferney I have 150 mouths to feed; but you can't keep that going with alexandrine verses and bankruptcies. The ending of almost all trade, which only now happens through smugglers; the terrible expense of foodstuffs; the doubling of guards on the farms; the multiplication of beggars; the looming bankruptcies; none of that is at all poetic. No, no, there won't be war this winter – but while waiting for the war, there is famine here, and the devil everywhere.[40]

The following day, 8 January, the troops had arrived. 'There is no longer any communication between Geneva and France. The troops are spread all along the frontier, and by a curious fatality, it is we who are being punished for the foolishness of the Genevans. Geneva is the only place where we used to be able to get butcher's meat and all the necessities of life. We are blockaded and we are dying of hunger.'[41] Voltaire added: 'Would you mind, my dear friend, sending on to M. Laleu, in an envelope, my certificate of life, since I am still alive.'[42] (Guillaume-Claude de Laleu, the King's secretary, was also Voltaire's personal lawyer in Paris. In order to continue receiving the income from his life rents, Voltaire had every year to provide proof that he was still alive.)

The next day he wrote to the chevalier de Beauteville:

They have lodged dragoons all around my hen-coop known as the château de Tournay. Maman Denis can no longer have good beef on the table; she has to send to Gex for cow-meat. I do not know how we shall manage to get the letters which arrive at the post office in Geneva. Even worse, we shall need a passport from the King to go and fetch cassia [his preferred laxative] from Colladon's [a well-known pharmacy]. Beef and partridges is bad enough, but not to be able to get cassia! It's intolerable![43]

And, indeed, Voltaire wrote the same day to the duc de Choiseul, the prime minister, to ask for a passport to allow Voltaire's servants to cross the frontier to get supplies from Geneva or Switzerland.

Voltaire's extensive contacts soon proved useful. Even before

Choiseul replied to his request for a *laisser-passer*, Pierre-Michel Hennin, the permanent French Resident at Geneva, gave him a limited passport for collecting his post. And Jean-François-René Tabareau, the director of postal services at Lyon, sent him a pair of freshly caught soles; Voltaire's letter of thanks, with its obsequious slithering into new requests, is a marvel.

Sir, we are obliged to you for having perfectly satisfied the taste of one of the mortal sins. Our greed thanks you most warmly for your soles, which were as fresh as if we had eaten them at Marseille. I am embarrassed by your offers; but if you have some agent you could recommend, we should take advantage, Mme Denis and I, of your kindness, and go as far as to send you sometimes a little list of our needs. I had just got that far, Sir, when they brought in a shad and two soles, which had just come from you; seriously, the Charterhouse of Ripaille does not eat as well as we. If Mme Denis and I were really impudent, we should beg you to get your supplier to send us this winter, by post, two pieces of poultry twice a week; that would not load him down too much, we would pay the supplier cash, and the postal costs would be taken care of; but really, we dare not be so indiscreet.[44]

But it was not so much a question of discretion as of practicability. By the end of January 1767, Voltaire wrote again to Hennin to explain his difficulties, and to ask for more passports.

We have sent to Gex for some butcher's meat, but all they could get was bad cow's meat; our people could not eat it. On two occasions we sent by post to Lyon for rations for one day, but we cannot keep doing it. We used to send to Lyon for provisions by the public carriers; but the carriers stopped running. Our almoner fell dangerously ill at Ornex; we could not get him either a doctor or a surgeon, because the carts sent to fetch them could not get through.

We do not complain of the troops; on the contrary, we would wish them to remain permanently at their posts. Not only would they put a brake on the audacity of the smugglers, often numbering as many as fifty or sixty, who cross to the territory of Geneva, and who would soon become highway robbers; but they could prevent the pernicious trade in jewellery and watches made in Geneva, which is prohibited in France, but which is mainly sustained by the inhabitants of the province of Gex, almost all of whom have abandoned agriculture to work at home on the manufactures of Geneva.

We have always secured our provisions as far as possible from France, and we would like to go on doing it; but geography does not permit it. We are therefore forced to ask for three passports: for Mr Wagnière, for Mr Faÿ, and for the postman. [Louis du Faÿ was *maître d'hôtel* at Ferney.][45]

The next day, 30 January, however, he wrote again to Hennin to cancel his request for three passports; for Choiseul had given instructions to the chevalier de Jaucourt, the local French military commander, to provide all-purpose passports for Voltaire and all his household. Now Voltaire urged Hennin to come and visit him: 'Come, come; *maman* will now be able to feed you well; we shall have good beef, not cow.'[46]

Voltaire's concern to 'prevent the pernicious trade in jewellery and watches made in Geneva' is doubly ironic. At this stage he was a vigorous, reforming, but still patriachal landowner and he hated to lose his farmworkers to the Geneva watch industry. So he regularly coupled his political advice to the Geneva dissident *natifs* with assurances that, if life got too difficult for them, he would welcome them in Ferney. Perhaps he was hoping to rebuild his agricultural labour force. But when, three years later, the political troubles in Geneva became so violent that many watchmakers fled the city and sought refuge in the frontier region in France, Voltaire quickly saw a very different opening: he organised the establishment of a new and remarkably successful watchmaking industry at Ferney.

Despite Choiseul's passports, life at Ferney remained difficult under the blockade. Mme Denis was able to buy meat in Geneva but she had to get all her other provisions by post, from Lyon, since the public carriers were still not operating.[47] As a result, Voltaire cut back on his entertainment of visitors; or at least he said he did:

Mme Denis has been very ill, they bled her twice. As for me, I bear all the burdens of old age. There are no more big suppers, either for her or for me.

We eat one pigeon between us at dinner; the Dupuits, the Racle, the La Harpe, these three households dine together with the children. Fortunately, we have closed our doors against the English, the Germans and the Genevans. One must end one's days in retirement; for me the hurly-burly has become unbearable.[48]

But the French troops kept up a perpetual commotion in the château and village: 'I write to you to the sound of the drum. I have here a complete regiment, which has been brought here by the troubles of Geneva. The officers have supper in my house while I am in my bed, and the soldiers have made a fine road, but at the expense of my wheat and my vines; but they won't defend me from the north wind, which will be my despair during the next six months.'[49]

Voltaire's determination to cut back his social life seems to have been rather changeable. In the late summer of 1767, he heard with great distress that Mme d'Argental was seriously ill. But she recovered, and a fortnight later Voltaire prepared to hold a party for her recovery. 'We are getting ready to celebrate her convalescence; we shall have a new comedy [his play *Charlot*], and then supper for eighty guests; and then we shall have a ball and fireworks.'[50] A couple of days later he wrote to his great-nephew, the judge Alexandre d'Hornoy: 'It is true that there are lots of parties at Ferney, but it is *maman* who takes care of them by herself, she runs the department of good food, spectacles, balls and ruin. As for me, I lead a life of permanent suffering and weakness.'[51]

They had another party on 4 October, the feast-day of Saint François, and Voltaire's saint's day. That same evening he wrote to Damilaville: 'We have performed *Charlot* again at Ferney, and better than it will ever be played at the Comédie Française. Mme Denis has just given me, in the presence of the Conti regiment and of the whole province, the most agreeable fête I have ever seen.'

Though Voltaire did not know it, this turned out to be the last big party at Ferney for a long time.

In November 1767, ten months after they had arrived, the French blockading troops departed. 'Ferney is deserted, for we no longer have any soldiers here. The august powers have decided against the illustrious *Représentants*, and the news of the decision has been even worse received than a new play.'[52] Voltaire elaborated on this judgement six weeks later, in January 1768: 'There is no longer any real disturbance in Geneva, but certainly a lot of ill-will, and many troublesome pamphlets. Everything has remained calm. The two opposing parties have pleaded their cases before their judges; the magistrates have won, but the *Représentants* have not accepted the judgement. People are looking for some means of conciliation.'[53]

The failure of the outside arbitrators became apparent on 6 March: 'Tronchin, the attorney-general of the little republic next door, was assailed yesterday evening in front of his house by five hundred people, of whom more than half cried that they wanted to tear him to pieces. The people's commissioners had the greatest difficulty in pulling him from their hands, and they had him guarded all night by fifty *bourgeois*. It is no longer a joke.'[54] Faced with the violence of the dispossessed, the oligarchs almost immediately offered concessions, both to the *Représentants* and to the *natifs*. Voltaire wrote to Mme Denis on 8 March: 'The Council has surrendered almost everything to the people, who have made peace as victors. It was hardly worthwhile sending an ambassador and some troops, to leave the mastery to those they wanted to punish.'[55]

Under the peace plan, the *Petit Conseil* would give up the practice of arbitrary arrest, and the *Conseil Général* would have a greater role in the election of the members of the Council of 200, as well as the power to block the election of up to four of the twenty-five members of the *Petit Conseil*. In addition, and perhaps more significantly, the new deal gave some real benefits to the *natifs*: in future they would have the right to full commercial independence as artisans, as well as the right to practise medicine, surgery and pharmacy; and the right to sit on juries. They would also have the right to purchase citizenship of the republic, if in quite limited numbers. On 11 March, this so-called *Édit de Conciliation* was overwhelmingly adopted in the *Conseil Général* by 1,204 votes to 37; the ultra-*Négatifs* refused to vote for it, however, and called it the *Édit des Pistolets*.[56]

A few days later, Voltaire reported that 'everything in Geneva was in a deep peace', and that 'several people, from both sides, are at Ferney, drinking tea together in the greatest friendship. A week ago they were preparing to cut each other's throats. Everything has finished to the satisfaction of the people.'[57]

Despite what Voltaire believed, it was not to the satisfaction of the people. Obviously, the patricians had made significant concessions; equally obviously, the balance of power was still heavily skewed in their favour against all other classes of the population. But the really serious problem was the attitude of the *natifs*. Not only were they not grateful for the unprecedented concessions they had been granted; they were deeply dissatisfied that these concessions were not greater, and bitterly resentful at their disadvantaged place in society. As so often, it was the beginning of reform which released the floodgates of revolution. The *Édit de Conciliation* turned out not to be a settlement, but just a way-station in a long-running saga of conflict between the patricians and the rest. It was the breakdown of this 'settlement' two years later, in February 1770, which paved the way for Voltaire's most extraordinary new incarnation, at the age of seventy-six, as an industrial financier, entrepreneur and international salesman to the rich and famous on several continents.

13

Solitude

1767–9

At the beginning of March 1768, Voltaire suffered a painful blow when Mme Denis abruptly left Ferney and went back to Paris. It seems clear that Voltaire and Mme Denis had, for some weeks or even months previously, discussed or quite possibly argued about the idea that she might visit Paris, almost certainly in connection with recent difficulties over Voltaire's finances. But it also seems clear that, in the days immediately preceding her departure, they had a quarrel on quite a different subject, that this quarrel must have become increasingly fierce, and that it culminated on her last night at Ferney in a violent row. So violent that Mme Denis departed the following morning, together with Marie-Françoise Corneille and her husband Claude Dupuits, without seeing Voltaire or saying goodbye to him.

Voltaire was distraught when he discovered, in the middle of the day, that she had left without a word of farewell. He wrote to her immediately, at two o'clock in the afternoon; it appears that his handwriting in this letter was unusually irregular for Voltaire, the writing, for the first time, of an old man.

No doubt there is a destiny, and often it is really cruel. I went three times to your door, you knocked at mine. I wanted to walk my pain in the garden. It was ten o'clock, I put the needle at ten o'clock on the solar globe, I was waiting until you should have woken. I met M. Mallet [a local landowner and councillor of state in Geneva]. He said he was upset by your departure. I reckoned that he had come from your apartment.

I thought that you would be dining at the château as you had said you would. None of the servants warned me of anything, they all thought I knew. I called for Christin [a lawyer friend] and Father Adam. We talked until midday. Finally, I go back to your apartment. I ask where you are. Wagnière says to me: '*Eh, what! Don't you know that she left at ten o'clock?*' I turn, more dead than alive, to Father Adam. He replies to me like Wagnière: '*I thought you knew!*' Immediately I send to the stables for a horse. There was no one there. So, in the same house, with twenty servants, we looked for each other without seeing each other.

I am in despair, and this obstinacy of my unhappiness foretells a sinister future. I know that the moment of separation would always have been frightful; but it is even more frightful that you should have left without seeing me, when we were looking for each other.

This is another proof of the persecutions of my destiny. La Harpe [a young literary protégé of Voltaire] is the cause of my unhappiness. Anyone who predicted that La Harpe would have caused me to die a hundred leagues from you would not have been believed. But finally the truth is out. Damilaville went to see Antoine in the rue Hautefeuille, and Antoine said that La Harpe was lying. There, that is the origin of my suffering.

If I die, I shall die all yours, and if I live, my life is yours. I tenderly embrace M. and Mme Dupuits. I love them, I miss them, my heart is pierced.[1]

It is obvious from the terms of this letter that Voltaire had expected Mme Denis to leave for Paris; and there is confirmation in Voltaire's later correspondence that they had discussed and planned her mission some time before. In a letter to Mme Denis, written a full year later, he says that she had left three days earlier than they had agreed. In her reply, she claims not to understand his allusion, but she virtually confirms it: 'You asked me every day if my cases were packed.'[2]

On the other hand, it is equally obvious that Voltaire had not expected that her departure would take the form of a personal rupture between them. Yet some kind of rupture there must have been, since it is striking that the letter contains no reference to the expectation or prospect of her return. In fact, Mme Denis did return to Ferney; but not until eighteen months later, after long ambivalence on her side, and perhaps also on his.

Voltaire himself never really explained the circumstances of her sudden departure. In a letter she wrote him a year later, Mme Denis asserts that Voltaire simply drove her away: 'You know, my dear friend, that you obliged and forced me to leave your house.'[3]

Such a one-dimensional construction is obviously too simplistic. Yes, it seems probable that he did, in some sense, persuade or even force her to go to Paris; but if so, the question is whether Voltaire viewed this as a limited journey for practical purposes, or whether he intended a permanent separation.

As Voltaire's secretary, Wagnière was well placed to read the situation, and he wrote to Damilaville three weeks after the event: 'I saw that his mind was made up long ago: he was weary of being an innkeeper for all the passers-by, and weary of all the expenditure. He wants to live alone; he does not want any visitors, not even his closest friends. He did not want Mme Denis to come back; he wanted to sell the estate, to live at Tournay; but he has taken no firm decision. He is very well, and very gay, though sometimes in a bad temper. He works, he amuses himself.'[4]

Some parts of this explanation seem quite plausible. First, Wagnière says that Voltaire was 'weary of being the inn-keeper (*l'aubergiste*) for all the passers-by'; one week later, Voltaire used almost exactly the same phrase, but now better honed, in a letter to Mme du Deffand: 'For the past fourteen years I have been the inn-keeper of Europe (*l'aubergiste de l'Europe*), and I have wearied of this profession.'[5] He was now seventy-four, and might reasonably have become tired of the commotion of constant entertaining.

Wagnière also says that Voltaire wanted to live alone; the question is, did Voltaire really want to live alone, or was it rather that he felt that a solitary life was unavoidable? From the beginning of their relationship, Voltaire had repeatedly questioned the compatibility between Mme Denis's need for parties and sociability and his own need for solitude and work. By now he seems to have come to feel that their lives may have diverged irrevocably from one another. In a poignant letter, written a fortnight after her departure, he concluded sadly: 'For the past fifteen years [i.e. ever since he moved to Geneva], I have really only been living by myself, even though I have been the inn-keeper of Europe; finally, I am now completely retired, and I shall stay that way, so far as I can see, until the end. At least, that's how I think right now.'[6] This could suggest that he did not expect or want Mme Denis to return.

Third, according to Wagnière, Voltaire was 'weary of all the expenditure'. Voltaire himself never really explained the circumstances of, or complex reasons for, the sudden departure of Mme Denis, even to his close friends; indeed, he explained it less to d'Argental, supposedly his closest friend, than to some others, like Damilaville. But the nearest he ever got to a credible explanation (leaving aside one absurd story, that she needed urgent treatment for her gums) was when he wrote to a friend that 'Mme Denis has gone to Paris to sort out our affairs, which had become rather damaged by suppers for 200 guests, by balls, and by plays. I have been like a little duke of Wurtemberg: I have ruined myself giving parties.'[7]

In short, it seems quite likely that Voltaire and Mme Denis were chronically at odds about money and about the cost of their lifestyle, and had been for some time. What makes this credible, in practical terms, is that Voltaire was owed large amounts of money by several French nobles, starting with the duc de Richelieu and the family of the ducs de Guise, in the form of *rentes viagères* which had been in arrears for many years; and that, since Voltaire could not go to Paris to deal with the situation, Mme Denis would have to go instead.

As he explained to d'Alembert: 'I shall perhaps sell Ferney to straighten out our affairs, which have been somewhat upset by our occupation as the inn-keeper of Europe, as well as by the parties given by *maman*. But they have been even more upset by the great lords of Paris, who owe us ten years' arrears. If she does not know how to get paid, she will be poor. If she succeeds, she will be rich.'[8] Voltaire may also have hoped that Mme Denis would have specially persuasive powers in the case, since she had at one time had a liaison with Richelieu. '*Maman*, who has lived with him a lot, will find it easier to get him to pay than would a bailiff with a tipstaff. It is true that she is no longer at an age which opens the purses of dukes and peers; but a former liaison is always respected.'[9]

Another reason why Voltaire's finances were under pressure was that he was also being squeezed by his debtors in Germany. The duke of Wurtemberg, in particular, was failing to keep up the very large payments that he owed, and Voltaire had been protesting with increasing agitation to the duke's representatives since the previous summer.[10] The duke's agents continued to drag their feet, however, and the business had still not been settled by the time Mme Denis set off for Paris on 1 March 1768.

It was because of his frustrations with the long-drawn-out negotiations with the duke of Wurtemberg that Voltaire had the idea of turning to the duc de Richelieu and other French noblemen. Early in December 1767, he had written to his grand-nephew, the lawyer Alexandre d'Hornoy, to ask him to chase up these debts.

There is a certain abbé de Blet, a Prior from I don't know where, a gentleman from the Poitou, who has long been attached to the maréchal de Richelieu. He has undertaken to sort out the affairs of the Richelieu family; he is wise, honest and punctilious. M. le Maréchal owes me a fairly substantial sum. According to M. Laleu [Voltaire's lawyer] it will be about £42,000 in January; according to M. l'abbé de Blet only about £27,000. I beg you to clear up this difficulty, and then find out from M. de Blet how, and by when, he can settle with me, with letters of credit on Lyon.

This same M. de Blet is also charged with the arrangements for the successors of the prince and princess de Guise. I contributed a great deal to the marriage [thirty-three years earlier, in 1734] of M. le duc de Richelieu to Mlle de Guise, by lending £25,000 to the prince de Guise, the deaf one, on which he agreed a *rente viagère* for me of £2,500, believing that I would die within a year. It was the deaf one who died. The august princess, his wife, on whose property my *rente* was mortgaged, died as well. Her daughter, the duchesse de Richelieu, did the same; and here am I, still alive for a few more months.

Having said that, it is clear that their successors owe me about £18,000, and in January will owe over £20,000. I mean, net of all deductions. The abbé de Blet will not refuse to discuss this with you. Please see what I can and should do; and then, if necessary, find me an advocate and an attorney.[11]

My guess is that Voltaire originally envisaged Mme Denis's trip to Paris as a short-term, practical affair; but that the violence of their quarrel in the days immediately before her departure may have changed the emotional equation. The fact that Mme Denis left with Voltaire's beloved Marie-Françoise and her husband, and the length of time that she stayed away, certainly hint at the possibility of a permanent separation.

But if this is a convincing story, as far as it goes, it does not explain the violence of the quarrel which immediately preceded her departure. For even if Voltaire expected her to go to Paris, it is dramatically obvious that the manner of her departure came as a thunderbolt. There must have been some other, emotional factor to explain the fact that Mme Denis left Ferney quite so suddenly, and without even saying goodbye to Voltaire.

This critical extra factor almost certainly came in the shape of an ambitious, moderately talented, but also moderately unscrupulous young writer, Jean François de La Harpe. He was born in 1739, so when he first came to Voltaire's notice, with his tragedy *Le comte de Warwick*, in 1763, he was only twenty-four years old. He quickly became a disciple of Voltaire, as well as a protégé, on whom Voltaire lavished admiration and affection. With his young and extremely pretty wife, he visited Ferney several times, for extended stays; and he depended heavily on Voltaire's advice and encouragement. Voltaire treated him as a favourite son, a standard-bearer for the next generation; he called him 'mon fils'. He also called him 'petit', for he was in fact unusually short of stature. But La Harpe betrayed his trust, creatively and morally. Voltaire immediately and repeatedly forgave him, as an impetuous and impecunious young man with what he hoped would be a great literary future.

Towards the end of 1766, La Harpe went to stay at Ferney, with his wife, ostensibly to work on a new tragedy under Voltaire's supervision. Three weeks after his arrival, Voltaire wrote to Marie-Elisabeth de Fontaine, his other niece: 'Little La Harpe has read his play to us. He has never done anything so bad. But I think that if we adjust his plot, we can make something really good of it. He writes verse easily;

he doesn't complain of hard work; he has wit and courage; I trust that he will succeed.'[12]

Unfortunately, La Harpe did not live up to Voltaire's hopes. He won two poetry prizes, but the tragedies he wrote were poor, and flopped; worse, he took to going through Voltaire's manuscripts on the sly, and secretly purloining those which he thought he could advantageously circulate among the literati in Paris.

One of these was particularly sensitive to Voltaire, both personally and politically. It was part of his *Guerre Civile de Genève*, a satirical poem in three cantos (later expanded to five), in which he made mock of many of the protagonists in the recent political troubles in Geneva. Voltaire had circulated the first and the third of these cantos, but he held back the second because it made fun of the Tronchins by name. Voltaire had seen La Harpe poking about in his study, but he had assumed that his favoured protégé would be loyal and discreet. He was deceiving himself. In early November 1767, La Harpe made a trip to Paris, taking with him the second canto of the *Guerre Civile de Genève*, along with other manuscripts he had filched.

Voltaire's first suspicion that something was wrong came in February 1768, when he learned that the second canto of the *Guerre Civile de Genève* was being circulated in Paris. The first person he wrote to, to express his dismay and indignation, was Damilaville:

We have here, my dear friend, a new and very disagreeable trouble that I entrust to you. You know that I had a bit of fun with the ridiculous war in Geneva. I was quite willing to let out two cantos of this little poem, in which I sharply rapped the fingers of the priests of Geneva, as well as of that madman Jean-Jacques [Rousseau], but since the Tronchins were discussed in the second canto, I never gave it to anyone. I refused to give it even to princes, it has always remained locked up in my study. La Harpe would go into this study every day, and he would ferret about in all my papers. I let him do it; I counted on his discretion, and on his sense of obligation for all I have done for him.

As soon as he reached Paris, this second canto was made public. If he had only given copies to d'Alembert and to my family, and insisted on complete secrecy, his faithlessness would have been less dangerous; but a hundred persons now have copies, and there is even one in the hands of the Tronchins.

When he returned here, and I complained of the publication of this second canto, he said nothing and blushed. Knowing that he was accused by the whole household, he went four whole days without daring to speak to me. His wife finally drove him to make his excuses to me; and he said he had the manuscript from a certain Antoine. This Antoine is a sculptor who lives in the rue Hautefeuille. It is quite certain that I never sent the manuscript to Antoine, since I do not know him.

The worst of it is that La Harpe does not seem to feel the dishonesty and turpitude of his actions. This is all the more cruel in that it comes from a man whom I loved.[13]

All this while, La Harpe was still staying at Ferney, but without coming clean to Voltaire. On the contrary:

His miserable excuse [about the sculptor Antoine], which he only invented two weeks later, merely compounded his offence.[14]

He never spoke to me of this affair, without hanging his head, and his face took on a pallor which was not that of innocence. The case against him is complete.[15]

But instead of repairing the damage he had done me, he wrote, from his bedroom to mine, a very hard letter in which he insulted me without justifying himself.[16]

Two days later, on 24 February 1768, La Harpe and his wife left Ferney for Paris, but without exchanging any words of affection, friendship or remorse with Voltaire.

Some time in the next few days, Voltaire and Mme Denis must have had their major row. As it was only five days after the departure of La Harpe that Mme Denis also left abruptly for Paris, with Mlle Corneille and her husband Dupuits, it seems most likely that the row which precipitated their departure was about La Harpe.

For even though Voltaire and Mme Denis had for some time been debating, perhaps even arguing about money, about her extravagance, and about what she should do to restore their income, it seems clear that it was *not* money which provoked the sudden violent row. If we want confirmation of this, it comes in the fact that, almost immediately after Mme Denis left for Paris, Voltaire showered her with money, as if in appeasement for a practical and low-level dispute which should never have got out of control.

For despite his financial embarrassment, or rather his feeling of financial insecurity, Voltaire was still enormously wealthy. Just how rich he was becomes clear in a letter he wrote seven weeks after Mme Denis's departure, to Guillaume-Claude de Laleu, secretary to the King and Voltaire's personal lawyer in Paris:

I send you, Sir, the certificate of the little life that remains to me; not without being extremely sensitive to all the kindness you have shown me. I have sent my family a memorandum, which I submit to your decision. It is a question of giving, during my lifetime, £20,000 a year to Mme Denis; £3,600 to MM. l'abbé Mignot [brother of Mme Denis] and d'Hornoy [Voltaire's great-nephew], that is to say, £1,800 each, which is rather little and of which I am very ashamed; about £2,700, I think, to Mme de Florian [Marie-Elisabeth, Voltaire's other niece]; about £1,300 to Mlle Corneille who is today Mme Dupuits, without counting the £400 which should belong to M. Wagnière. I shall not have much left. I count on running my household with the £3,000 that M. de Laborde, the King's banker, is kind enough to let me draw every month.[17]

In all, this amounts to largesse of £28,000 a year to Mme Denis and other members of the family, and £36,000 for Voltaire to run his establishment of twenty-seven servants or a total of £64,000. This was not counting the large arrears of the *rentes viagères* due from Wurtemberg, Richelieu, Guise and others.

And if we want confirmation that the violent row was about La Harpe, not about money, we do not have to look further than the letter which Voltaire wrote to Mme Denis immediately following her departure, and in which he refers to La Harpe 'as the cause of my unhappiness'.[18] The letter seems to imply that the quarrel between Voltaire and Mme Denis had been essentially about La Harpe's dishonesty and the theft of the second canto of the *Guerre Civile de Genève*. Five weeks later, however, in the closest he ever got to an emotionally frank account of the incident, he gave d'Alembert a version of events which suggested that the La Harpe problem went much deeper than that. In short, he effectively alleged that Mme Denis's relationship with La Harpe had been indecently close.

I have entirely forgotten the wrong that M. de La Harpe has done me; but it seems to me that he is not familiar with tender and touching expressions. He told you that he had read to Mme Denis the letter which he wrote from his bedroom to mine, and that both of them started weeping; apparently he mistook Mme Denis for his wife; and I do not see how this letter could have drawn tears from my niece. These are his own words:

You allege that you had not given it to anyone, I believe you, but what reason would you have for not believing me, when I tell you that it was in Paris that it was given to me? If you were to make damaging complaints against me, you would force me to have some sort of public trial with you.

However, far from complaining of him, I have defended him against all the imputations which the crowd of his enemies hastened to make against him.

He is the cause of my separation from Mme Denis; he is the reason why the last days of my life are deprived of all help; my only consolation is knowing that Mme Denis should be happy in Paris. I am giving her a pension of £20,000, and I have promised her £35,000.[19]

On the same day, Voltaire told a similar story to Damilaville.

He persuaded Mme Denis of his innocence. She was very angry with me for having made her lose, in Mme La Harpe, a complaisant woman who could amuse her during the winter. It is on this subject that Mme Denis treated me very cruelly; but since I forgive La Harpe, you can easily see that I forgive Mme Denis. My life is so different from hers that it is absolutely necessary that she be in Paris, where she has many friends and relatives, and that I should die in solitude.[20]

It is hard to know exactly what has been going on, but it is not too difficult to tell what Voltaire thinks has been going on: he believes that Mme Denis has been disloyal to him, siding with La Harpe against him; and he even suspects that she may have been unfaithful to him in the fullest sense. When he says that Mme Denis and La Harpe were weeping together over La Harpe's letter in the latter's bedroom, that La Harpe mistook Mme Denis for his wife, and that Mme Denis regarded La Harpe's wife as a *complaisante*, it seems clear that he believes that Mme Denis and La Harpe have been sharing a wholly improper degree of intimacy.

Inevitably, the rupture between Voltaire and Mme Denis led to recriminations and post-mortems. Some flavour of these comes out in a letter Voltaire wrote to Marie-Elisabeth de Fontaine, his other niece, a month after Mme Denis's departure.

Behold the sad consequences of ill humour. You know how much bad temper Mme Denis showed towards us. Remember the scene she inflicted on M. de Florian [Marie-Elisabeth's husband]. She made me suffer an even crueller scene. It is sad that her reason cannot put aside these violent storms, which sometimes overwhelm her, and which are so distressing to others. I am convinced that the hidden cause of this violence, which attacks her from time to time, has been her natural aversion to life in the country, an aversion which she could only overcome with crowds of people, parties, and magnificence. This tumultuous life does not suit my age of 74 years, nor the weakness of my health. Besides, I felt very constrained by the non-payment of my *rentes*, both by the duke of Wurtemberg, and by the maréchal de Richelieu and some other grand *seigneurs*.[21]

Two days later Voltaire poured out to Mme Denis herself some of his pent-up anger.

The eight-page letter I sent you spelled out my justifiable pain at the cruel ill humour that you inflicted on me several days in a row, and at the dining table, in public. I was deeply pained, and my wound bleeds still, but the sad state you have put me into will never prevent me from rendering what I owe to such a long and such an intimate friendship. Sometimes you let fly barbs which pierce the heart. It is to be believed that we shall never see each other again, and that I shall die far from you in the retirement where I shall bury myself. But be sure I shall never accept the insulting mistrust with which you have embarrassed my friendship. You have driven me to despair, but you cannot weaken my feelings for you. Think of my age, my weakness, my illness, and forgive me all of them. You will see once more how much I have been wounded, how much I love you, and how far I have carried my desire to make you happy.[22]

But if Mme Denis was sometimes ill-tempered with Voltaire, it seems clear that Voltaire was equally capable of referring to her in extremely disobliging terms. In August 1760, he had written to a not particularly close acquaintance:

Mme Denis is a fat pig, Sir, like most of your Parisiennes; they get up at midday; the day passes, they do not know how; they have no time to write, and when they want to write, they can find neither paper, pen, nor ink, so then they have to come and ask me, but now the desire to write disappears. For every ten women, nine are like this. Forgive, Sir, Mme Denis her extreme laziness; she is no less attached to you, but she would rather say it than write it.[23]

It sounds as though he was often irritated with her whole demeanour. No doubt Voltaire intended his remarks in this letter to be humorous, but the effect is not so much amusing as contemptuously waspish. We are left wondering what had become of his earlier passion.

Voltaire went on writing to Mme Denis with great frequency over the next year and a half. He took pains to ensure that she was comfortably off, and he never ceased to say how much he loved her. When she eventually decided to return, Voltaire was overjoyed. It is possible, therefore, that at the height of their quarrel, and before she left, Voltaire may have wanted to be free of her, but that he changed his mind after she had left, and wanted her back – provided, of course, that it was on his terms. Inevitably, it would be on hers.

One of the strangest things about the rupture between Voltaire and Mme Denis is that he never explained or even discussed it with d'Argental, his oldest and usually his most intimate friend. He wrote to many other friends in the days that followed her departure; in several of these letters, he mentioned that she was going to Paris to repair his shattered fortunes. To d'Argental, however, he did not write at all until six weeks later, and even then it was a very curious letter, in which he almost explicitly withheld any explanation of the break-up.

You ask, my dear angel, that one should open one's heart, and when one has opened it wide, you do not say a word to the usher. I have not talked to you about the adventure of La Harpe, whom I don't think you know, and to whom in any case I do not want to cause any pain, and who never had any intention of harming me, even though he was in the wrong. He is young, he is poor, he is married: he needs help, I did not want to undermine his reputation with you. I want Mme Denis to live happily in Paris, and I wish to die in solitude.[24]

In other words, the 'adventure of La Harpe' was none of d'Argental's business. Voltaire wrote another twelve letters to d'Argental during the next eight months, but in all of them he simply passed over in silence the question of his relationship with Mme Denis. What makes this wall of silence particularly strange is that d'Argental was one of the very few people who had been allowed by Voltaire to know the true nature of his liaison with Mme Denis.

Almost the first thing that Voltaire did, after Mme Denis's departure, was to talk of selling Ferney; the château had been bought in her name, so she would be entitled to all the proceeds of the sale. Within five days of her going, he told her that there were potential buyers who could be interested, at the right price, and he urged her to take the opportunity. 'At one o'clock today I received a letter offering to buy Ferney from you, and to pay half in cash, half in *rentes viagères*. All that remains is to settle the price. I suggest that you ask £300,000, but perhaps you should consider whether you would be prepared to go as low as £250,000.'[25] Two days later he told her (perhaps he had only just discovered) that the bidder was Jacob Tronchin, a cousin of

Jean-Robert and François and a member of the *Petit Conseil*; and since Jacob was hesitating between Ferney and another property, Voltaire urged her to drop the price to £200,000 or even £180,000.

This would give you £10,000 in *rente viagère*, and £80,000 in cash. Your health, your tastes, the sweetness of life in Paris, your relations, your friends, everything keeps you in Paris, and I count on coming to see you there as soon as I have settled my business affairs, and yours, with the duke of Wurtemberg. By July, I count on having formal and irrevocable assignments from them, which will guarantee your *rentes* and mine.

You ask me what will become of me. I answer that Ferney is odious to me without you. If I sell Ferney, I shall retire in the summer time to Tournay. But I am thinking more of you than of me. I want you to be happy, and I have had my life. I have so far kept all the servants, but I have not left my room. The thermometer has been six degrees below freezing. All the newly planted trees will die. I shall not regret them.[26]

Voltaire's project to sell Ferney can be seen as a practical response to financial difficulties. But it seems more likely that these practical and financial considerations, though meant to be taken seriously, were really a front for deeper and more important questions about the relationship between himself and Mme Denis. For if she were to go along with Voltaire's suggestion and agree to sell the estate, that would be a powerful symbolic indication that she intended their relationship, or at least her life with Voltaire, to be over for good.

In June, Voltaire told her that they had missed the chance of selling Ferney to Jacob Tronchin for £200,000, since he had bought another property, but he added: 'As for me, I should leave it tomorrow, if it weren't for the fact that I am kept here by my two centuries.' (He was working on two history books, the *Siècle de Louis XIV* (The Century of Louis XIV) and the *Précis du Siècle de Louis XV* (The Précis of the Century of Louis XV).[27] In other words, Voltaire was telling Mme Denis that he was working too hard to leave Ferney just yet.

A month later, in July, he once again raised the idea of selling the château; but he was obviously half-hearted about it, and by late August, Mme Denis told Voltaire that she did not want to sell

Ferney. For nearly six months she had hesitated. The fact that she had now decided not to sell strongly suggests, not necessarily that she had opted for a life with Voltaire but at least that she had not decided against it. Voltaire must have been acutely sensitive to these implications.

If Voltaire was depressed by his new solitude, he remained as combative as ever. At Easter 1768, shortly after Mme Denis's departure, he managed to provoke a scandal with the authorities of the Catholic Church, the vibrations of which ricocheted all the way to Versailles and back. Before Easter, he went to confession and received absolution; and on Easter Day he solemnly attended Mass and took communion, like the other parishioners, in the church he had built at Ferney. Just before the sermon, however, Voltaire stood up and, in a clear voice, called on the priest to say prayers for the Queen, who was at the time very ill; and he informed the congregation that a burglary had been committed in the parish. Wagnière described the scene in a letter to Damilaville: 'I was present at the service, and when I heard him open his mouth to harangue the congregation, my blood froze and I hid myself. This is making a frightful scandal, and is not having the effect that he had hoped.'[28]

It does not appear that there was anything particularly offensive in what Voltaire said in church that day; what caused the controversy was the fact that he, a layman, had intervened in the middle of a church service. Pious Catholics had always assumed that Voltaire's church and his church-going were no more than a cynical charade, and the rumour mills were soon putting it about that Voltaire had taken it upon himself to deliver a sermon.

Within a week Voltaire received a written rebuke from Jean-Pierre Biord, the bishop of Annecy, under the guise of a sarcastic congratulation that he had done his Easter duty:

The public will no longer be able to regard you as the greatest enemy of the Christian religion, of the Catholic Church, and of its ministers. But if, on the day of your communion, you had not been seen to intervene to preach to the people on the subject of thieving and larceny, which greatly scandalised all those present, then no one would be been able to treat as equivocal your public displays of religion.[29]

He said he would like to be able to believe in the sincerity of Voltaire's confession (clearly implying that he believed no such thing), and he went on to demand that Voltaire make a public disavowal of his attacks on the Christian religion.

Voltaire was unrepentant:

Your letter has given me much satisfaction; it also somewhat surprised me. How can you thank me for carrying out those duties on which every *seigneur* should give an example in his estates, from which no Christian is exempt, and which I have often carried out? It is not enough to draw one's vassals up from the horrors of poverty, to encourage their marriages, to contribute as far as one can to their temporal welfare; one must also edify them; and it would be rather extraordinary that a lord of the manor should not do, in the church which he has built, what all the so-called reformed Christians do in their temples in their own way.[30]

Voltaire sent the bishop a certificate, signed before a notary by several local worthies, starting with the parish priest and Father Adam, his almoner, attesting that Voltaire had not only carried out the duties of the Christian religion, but had also virtuously rendered important benefits to the local community. But Bishop Biord refused to be fobbed off by Voltaire's evasions, and he returned to the attack. The taking of holy communion, he told Voltaire, required of him a spectacular public recantation; without such a public recantation, he would forbid any priest to give him the sacrament in future.

Finding Voltaire recalcitrant, Bishop Biord alerted the authorities in Versailles, and Voltaire soon received a sharp reproof from Louis Phélypeaux, comte de Saint-Florentin, the minister of the interior: 'The King, Sir, has been informed, by the complaints which have been carried to His Majesty, that on Easter Day last you made in your parish of Ferney a public exhortation to the people, even during the celebration of the Mass. It is not up to any lay person to make any kind of sermon in the church, especially not during divine service.'[31] Voltaire continued to deny that he had done anything like deliver a sermon. 'It is rather extraordinary that, having alerted the priest in a low voice to pray for the health of the Queen, people took this act of duty of a loyal subject to say that I had given a sermon. I dare to hope, Sir, that you will inform the King of these truths.'[32]

Voltaire was determined not to be put down by Bishop Biord, and the following year (1769), at Easter-time, he was again resolved to take communion, in defiance of the bishop. He knew that Biord would prevent him from taking it in the normal way, so he pretended to be dying, in order to be able to demand that Father Pierre Gros, the local parish priest, give him the last rites in his bed. At first Gros procrastinated, and told Voltaire that he must first retract, before a notary, all his wrongdoings. But Voltaire was not to be put off, claiming that he had suffered several attacks of fever, and that in such circumstances the law required Gros to give him the last rites. He wrote to Gros on 30 March 1769:

François-Marie de Voltaire, Gentleman of the Chamber of the King in ordinary, lord of Ferney, etc., being over seventy-five years old, being of a very feeble constitution, having dragged himself to the church on Palm Sunday, despite his maladies, and having since that day suffered several attacks of violent fever, of which Mr Biagroz, surgeon, has informed M. le curé of Ferney according to the laws of the kingdom; and the said invalid, finding himself in the total incapacity to go to confession and take communion at the church for the edification of his vassals, as he should and desires, and for that of the Protestants by whom the country is surrounded, begs M. le curé of Ferney to do, on this occasion, everything that the ordinances of the King and the decrees of the Parlements command, jointly with the canons of the holy Catholic Church professed in the kingdom, the religion in which the said invalid was born, has lived, and wishes to die, and of which he wishes to fulfil all the duties, as well as those of a subject of the King, offering to make all the necessary declarations, all required protestations, whether public or private, submitting himself fully to everything that is right, not wishing to omit any of his duties whatever they may be, inviting M. le curé of Ferney to fulfil his duties with the greatest exactitude, as much for the edification of the Catholics as of the Protestants living within the household of the invalid. This present, signed in his own hand, and by two witnesses.

[Jean-Louis Wagnière and Simon Bigex, Voltaire's other secretary.][33]

There was now a prolonged tussle back and forth, in which Gros and various other priests tried to insist that Voltaire could not have absolution, and therefore could not receive communion, without a full recantation of his past impieties, and a full declaration of his Catholic faith. Voltaire drafted for them several different statements that were much less than a full declaration of faith, but avoided signing any of the texts that they put before him. Eventually, by persistence and evasion and deception and bullying, he wore them down: he demanded and received absolution from a friar, and his 'last rites' from Gros.[34] As he received communion, he said: 'Having my God in my mouth, I declare that I sincerely forgive those who have written calumnies about me to the King, and who have not succeeded in their evil plan.' After all the priests and bystanders had left, Voltaire jumped out of bed and went for a walk in the garden with Wagnière.[35]

Voltaire could pride himself on having outmanoeuvred Bishop Biord this time; but he continued to claim, indignantly, that he had only done his public duty by taking communion at Easter; and he remained angry at what he felt was his persecution by the bishop. Shortly after Easter 1769, he spilled out his rage to d'Argental:

I am a better Christian than they are; by taking communion I edify all the inhabitants of my estates and all my neighbours. Not only do I do my own duty, I also send my Catholic servants regularly to church, and my Protestant servants regularly to the temple, and I employ a school master to teach the children their catechism. I even have public readings at meal-times from the history of the Church and the sermons of Massillon.*[36]

---

*Jean-Baptiste Massillon (1663–1742), priest, professor of rhetoric and member of the Académie Française, was famous for his sermons.

Voltaire's claim that he had the sermons of Massillon read aloud at table was actually true, at least on one occasion, in the presence of distinguished visitors from the Parlement of Dijon; but it was only a part of his skirmishing with his persecutors. According to a visitor who was present, Voltaire had asked permission of the guests to follow 'the custom of the house', and have a sermon read after the soup; and he did not spare them a single syllable of it. Yet even Voltaire's combative vitality had its limits: he did not try the Easter charade again.

If the Massillon sermon was a totally insincere gesture, the fact that Voltaire had it read aloud at table was not. For in the spring of that year, he had introduced a regular routine of reading-aloud at meal-times.

I have myself read to, at dinner and supper, from good books, by very intelligent readers, who are rather my friends than my servants.[37]

In our retreat, people have nothing to say to each other; conversation is not kept going by the events of the day. Very few people have in themselves a fund of useful conversation. That is what decided me to have instructive readings during my frugal dinner and my frugal supper, in place of the boredom of saying nothing, or of saying trivial things which leave not a trace.[38]

No doubt the main readers on these occasions would have been his secretaries, Jean-Louis Wagnière or Simon Bigex. Socially, Voltaire's secretaries occupied a middle rank in his household, distinct both from the family (*les maîtres*) and from the ordinary servants. This distinction was observed at meal-times: they ate with the *maître d'hôtel*, not with Voltaire and Mme Denis. When Voltaire gave house-room to a certain Claude Gallien, a ne'er-do-well who may well have been an illegitimate son of Richelieu, he had to assure Richelieu that Gallien never ate with the family, but always with the *maître d'hôtel* and the secretaries. But this was just Voltaire's social rule; Pierre-Michel Hennin, the French Resident in Geneva, had a different one, and when Claude Gallien went to work for him as a secretary, Hennin expected him to eat at the same table as the *maîtres*.[39]

When he had been left on his own, at Ferney, in the spring of 1768,

Voltaire had battened down the hatches. He wrote to Marie-Elisabeth Fontaine:

Here I am, all alone with Father Adam, having once had two hundred people to supper, and put on plays. The hubbub does not suit me; solitude becomes me better. I shall put all my papers in order, and that will take time. Ferney is the most beautiful retreat for fifty leagues in any direction. You would not believe how much more beautiful the château and the gardens are now, but I do not receive anyone. Flocks (*volées*) of English turn up, but I shut the door in their face. My taste for solitude has become my dominant passion.[40]

He reflected wryly, as in the letter to Mme du Deffand quoted earlier, that his previous hospitality had earned him precious little thanks.

For the past fourteen years I have been the inn-keeper of Europe [*l'aubergiste de l'Europe*], and I have wearied of this profession. I have received three or four hundred Englishmen in my home, who are all so in love with their country that almost none of them has remembered me after their departure, apart from a Scottish priest named Brown, who reproached me with going to confession, which is certainly rather hard. I have had in my house French colonels with all their officers for more than a month. They serve the King so well that they have not even had the time to write, either to Mme Denis or to me. I have built a château and a church, and I have spent five hundred thousand francs on these profane and sacred works. But finally, illustrious debtors, of Paris and Germany, seeing that such magnificence was not suitable for me, thought it appropriate to put me on short commons to make me behave myself [*ont jugé à propos de me retrancher les vivres pour me rendre sage*]. All of a sudden, therefore, I almost find myself reduced to plain philosophy. [41]

In July 1768, Voltaire told Mme Denis that he had had the main door of the château double-locked, and was seeing no one.[42] But after a while the solitude began to tell on him. In September that year he wrote to François de Caire, a locally based French engineer, to invite him and his wife to dinner, adding that he hoped they would not be too scandalised to find him in his dressing gown.[43] A little later, he wrote to Pierre-Michel Hennin to enlist his help in the entertainment of a visiting duke of Braganza.

Since, Sir, you are placing this poor invalid under the necessity of putting on a suit and shoes, in order to receive a duke of Braganza, it is only fair that it should be you who do the honours of the country and receive him in my cottage. I had taken the liberty of inviting him for Tuesday, but since, unfortunately, Tuesday is my day for cassia, I ask him, and you, as a kindness, that it should be for Wednesday. Please have the charity to succeed in this negotiation.[44]

(Voltaire took the laxative once a week, but in such quantity, it would appear, that it had the effect of a violent purgative.)

By October, Voltaire's solitude had become even more lonely. Father Adam, now his only companion in the château, had found a mistress in the village, and went to see her every day. Voltaire teased him mercilessly about his love-life and his hypocrisy; and each day at dinner, he would get Wagnière to read out loud an act of Molière's comedy *Tartuffe* (a satire on hypocrisy), interjecting mordant comments about people who try to reconcile love and piety.[45]

That autumn, Voltaire was also wrestling with the painful knowledge that Damilaville was seriously, probably fatally ill. After his death from throat cancer in December 1768, Voltaire wrote to d'Alembert: 'I shall regret Damilaville all my life. I loved the boldness of his soul; I had hoped that at the end he would come and share my retirement. I did not know that he was married and a cuckold. I learn, with astonishment, that he had been separated from his wife for twelve years. He will surely not have left her a large inheritance.'[46] And to Mme Denis: 'I weep bitter tears for Damilaville; nature had made that man for me. I even imagined that he would come and retire to Ferney. Now he is dead; he will never be replaced.'[47]

In June 1768, Voltaire had congratulated Alexandre d'Hornoy on his efforts in getting payment of some of the money he was owed:

'Thank you for your visits to this abbé de Blet, which have been not unfruitful, since they produced a good sum from M. le maréchal de Richelieu. The payments by M. de Lézeau are assured, and I have every reason to believe that the affair of the inheritors of Mme la princesse de Guise will soon be concluded.'[48] Voltaire's early optimism turned out to be premature, however. Eight months later, in February 1769, Richelieu was still turning a deaf ear to demands for further payments, and nothing had yet been received from the heirs of the Guise family who were ten years behind with theirs.[49]

And yet Voltaire's resources seemed greater than ever: by the spring of 1769, his allowances to his family and others had risen to £32,000 a year, and in April of that year he told Mme Denis that, once the refinancing of the Wurtemberg account was settled, as he was sure it would be, she ought to be able to count on *rentes viagères* of nearly £50,000 a year.[50] Which seems to imply aggregate flows of income to Voltaire, to Mme Denis, and to other members of the family, of around £98,000 a year.

Nevertheless, Mme Denis's extravagance seems to have been more than a match for Voltaire's generosity. In April 1769, Voltaire wrote to Laleu: 'I request you, Sir, with the greatest urgency, to do the impossible, and to transfer £3,000 to Mme Denis. We shall settle up easily, you and I, for the rest, and for the honoraria that I owe you. I have the honour to be, with unbreakable attachment, Sir, your very humble and very obedient servant.'[51]

In the summer of 1769, Voltaire wrote to Cardinal Bernis in Rome, on behalf of Father Adam, to ask permission for him to be allowed to wear a wig. 'It is not for my burned-out brain that I ask this favour, it is for another old man (a one-time so-called Jesuit, begging your pardon), who serves me as almoner. This almoner is from Lorraine, he has made no vow to catch colds, he is ill, and subject to violent rheumatisms; he will pray to God with all his heart for Your Eminence, if you will have the goodness to use the authority of the vicar of Christ to cover the skull of this poor devil. I can have no other almoner; he has been with me for ten years; it would be impossible to find another who would suit me so well.'[52] Bernis gave his permission; but it was blocked by Bishop Biord.[53]

One reason for Voltaire's great solitude in 1768–9 was that his adoptive daughter Marie-Françoise Corneille, her husband Claude Dupuits, and their daughter Adélaïde had left for Paris with Mme Denis. Did she take them to keep her company? Or were they caught up in the quarrel between Mme Denis and Voltaire? Much later, Voltaire wrote to Mme Denis that 'Dupuits has admitted to me that it was he who contributed to your leaving so early.'[54] The real meaning of this allusion is still unclear. What is clear is that the continued absence from Ferney of the Dupuits family during the rest of 1768 was indirectly symptomatic of the rift between Voltaire and Mme Denis. So when Marie-Françoise and her family returned to Ferney, in February 1769, it must have seemed to Voltaire an event vibrant with hope. He wrote to Mme Denis: 'Dupuits, his wife and his little daughter have arrived, and they are well and lively. They are in their estate at Maconnex, in Siberia, surrounded everywhere, like me, with two feet of snow. Our consolation is that in the mountains, the snow is eighteen feet deep.'[55]

Negotiations with Mme Denis began soon afterwards, but at first she put forward proposals which implied an alternative to a simple return to Ferney. Voltaire was clearly upset: 'There is, my dear niece, in your letter of 28 February, a word which pierced my heart. You want an estate half a league from Ferney. The children are coming to dinner today. I embrace you with the greatest tenderness.'[56]

For several more weeks, Voltaire and Mme Denis remained at cross purposes over her future plans. But towards the end of April 1769, she wrote him a letter that was unusually solicitous for his personal welfare.

I am worried about your health. I am sure that the type of life you have chosen is not designed to be good for it. You have less need for company than others, I agree, but why sadden yourself deliberately, and kill yourself with work without any relaxation, other than going to Mass, and no recreation apart from Father Adam? You were born gay, nature gave you all her gifts, don't lose your gift of gaiety.

You reproach me with having made your house too lively. There was a time when it did not displease you. Yes, there were many people on our theatre days; but would you have preferred us to perform your plays to empty chairs? In the end, I did it for you, thinking that it would please you and relax you. You seem to have changed your way of thinking.

You know, my dear friend, that you obliged and forced me to leave your home. That is what made me leave, with death in my heart. That moment is always with me, it poisons my life, and it seems just as new as on the first day. Yet I reproach you with nothing, for I have never ceased to miss you and love you.[57]

By June, Voltaire and Mme Denis were beginning seriously to discuss their future. She suggested that she should move to Geneva. What Voltaire did not know was that Mme Denis was in secret correspondence with Pierre-Michel Hennin, the French Resident in Geneva, with whom she seems to have had a far closer relationship than she could publicly admit. She wrote to Hennin in early August:

It is a century, Sir, since I had any news from you.* My friendship for you cannot accommodate itself to such a long silence. How are you? How are your affairs? Do you hope to teach reason to a man who has none [Voltaire]? I am currently in great discussions with the boss [*le patron*]. The proposition that we put forward, you and I, to let me live in Geneva, has put him in a frightful rage, and has finally brought him to propose that I return to Ferney. He even admitted that he was very bored this past winter, which gave me a certain pleasure. He told me to come when I could. I have not given up the idea of Geneva. You are my only resource, in case I should be too unhappy if I go to Ferney. Do not speak of any of this. Do not doubt the sentiments and the inviolable attachment with which I have the honour to be your friend for life.[58]

Voltaire rejected the Geneva proposal: 'The idea of being separated from you is frightful, and the idea of seeing you in Geneva while I was at Ferney is no less frightful. The best would be for me to finish my life with you, either at Ferney or in some suburb of Paris.'[59]

---

*Voltaire was of course aware that Mme Denis had long been friendly with Hennin. See letter 11592. The question was, how friendly?

By now it was almost becoming accepted that Mme Denis would return to Ferney, though she kept her options open for a few more weeks. Voltaire would have liked to fetch her from Paris in October, but his health was so feeble that he would have to await her arrival at Ferney.[60] When she finally agreed to rejoin him, Voltaire told her: 'Your plans overwhelm me with joy.'[61]

But he went on to object to some of the details of her plans.

The idea of bringing a coachman from Paris makes me shudder. I have only cart-drivers, but they are excellent coachmen on occasion. Your Parisian horses would never want to draw loads of hay. I hear that you no longer have Maton [her lady's maid]. You would be surprised at the *femme de chambre* you could find here, the most adroit, the cleanest, the best seamstress [*couturière*], the most elegant tailor. But a man-about-town [*un monsieur*], a lackey from Paris, would horrify our rustic household. A Parisian lackey who is good for nothing except to stand at the back of a coach is a monster in my eyes. We shall make our arrangements when you have made up your mind.[62]

Inevitably, Mme Denis bridled at his terms, and continued to insist on her own.

I feel from your last letter that it would be very difficult for me to make plans for my return, since you are not yet decided. You say, my dear friend, that you want me to tell you my conditions. Surely, I should never have imagined that I should talk of conditions to you, but I shall take the liberty to respond.

You say that you have a horror of Parisian lackeys. Nevertheless, I must have a lackey, as well as a lady's maid, for the journey. I would wish, with all my heart, that my sex, my age, my strength, and my status, could have allowed me to make the journey on foot with a little package on my back. But you surely understand that, whether on foot or on horseback, I must have someone for the journey. Maton is still with me. And yet, if I leave, I shall not take her with me. Here, she has her husband and her children, and she could not abandon them. Therefore, I should take Agathe, who asks nothing better than to come. I am quite sure, my dear friend, that the *femme de chambre* who lives with you is excellent, but she is accustomed to look after a young man, and there is a furious difference between the condition of a young man and that of an old woman. You can see that that would not be fair or feasible.

As for the coachman, how could I do without him? You tell me, not only that there will be no more parties, but that I shall have no company. I should certainly be very unhappy to attract a single human being to your home, if it displeases you. But it is an additional reason why I should sometimes be able to look for company elsewhere. At Ferney, I should count on leading quite the opposite kind of life from the one I used to lead, that is to say, that I should go out often, but I would never invite anyone to your home, since it displeases you. You like solitude. For relaxation, I would go to visit a dozen persons whom I know and like. Whenever you wanted me, obviously you would always have the preference over them, and I should be only too happy to see you and to hear you.

I should like to ask your kindness, to allow me not to get involved in your household arrangements, and to let me have, quite simply, my three servants and my two horses; my lackey to clean my apartment, to polish it, to serve me, and to stand behind the coach; my *femme de chambre*; and my coachman to drive me. It seems to me, my dear friend, that those things are not expensive in the country, and that three servants are not too much for a woman of my age. Tell me what you think, but be sure that you are dearer to me than life itself.[63]

Voltaire tried to insist on his terms, but only half-heartedly, and he sought to change the subject; he knew he was beaten.

I only proposed a *femme de chambre* for you, in case you did not have one. The woman Nollet is full of skills and very helpful. We do not see Adam at all, except at meal-times, and for playing chess. That's Ferney in a nutshell. The easiest and wisest course would be to spend the winter together in Paris, and the summer at Ferney. Or perhaps the southern climes of France would suit us. It is with that in mind that I have rearranged a carriage into a kind of sleeping car [*une dormeuse*], where we should be very comfortable. We should be followed by a good wagon which would contain everything we need. All of that is ready. Hyères in Provence, Montpellier in Languedoc, even Toulouse could have attractions for you; and in the month of May you would come home to a delicious Ferney. All of this is possible, and I shall only do what will please you ... The embarrassing and delicate situation I find myself in with M. le duc de Wurtemberg will require a bit of economy during the first months of our establishment. I have had to give him £100,000 which he owed me. He will pay me back in four years. This affair is good and certain.[64]

Good and certain? Maybe. By this time, August 1769, Wurtemberg's accumulated unpaid debt to Voltaire amounted to £105,600; but the duke was not yet ready to back up his promises of payment by providing irrevocable assignments of his revenues from his tenants or bailiffs.[65] As a result, Voltaire backed away from his earlier projects for delightful three-month excursions, whether to Paris (as Mme Denis suggested) or to the south (his idea), because he needed to stick around at Ferney in order to nail down the Wurtemberg refinancing. 'The crisis I am in with the agents of M. de Wurtemberg will scarcely allow me to get away before the month of November.'[66]

In the middle of September 1769, Mme Denis started to plan her departure from Paris. She told Pierre-Michel Hennin (but not Voltaire): 'Yesterday I received a very pressing letter from the boss [*le patron*] telling me to come. I count on setting off in the first days of October. I beg you to say nothing of this to anyone, I am not even telling *le patron*. I shall then sort things out with the man in question as well as I can.'[67] But on 18 September, Mme Denis did write to Voltaire to tell him, though she still kept her options open as to exact dates: 'Whatever happens, I shall have the happiness of embracing you during the month of October. Neither of us should travel later than that.'[68]

By the time Voltaire received this letter, he had finally also received some at least of the revenue assignments he had asked for from Wurtemberg, though he worried that the tenants on whom these assignments were drawn might not produce enough income to meet his payment schedule.[69] Being at least partly freed from this financial worry, he now reverted to his earlier idea of spending the winter in Toulouse, where he hoped that his long campaign for the exoneration of the Sirvens might at last be entering its final phase. He wrote to Mme Denis:

You should come home at the end of October; or if you prefer, I would travel to meet you at Lyon, and lead you, bags and baggage (*armes et bagages*) to Toulouse, where the winters are very temperate, and you should return in the spring to your lovely dwelling.

You will understand that I should not propose Toulouse if I were not sure of being very well received there. The Parlement has become the protector of the Sirvens, and only seeks to expiate the horror of the condemnation of the Calases. I do not know how it has happened, but my opinion counts for something in that town. I have told them that I should be travelling as an invalid, and that I would pay no visits.[70]

But he changed his mind five days later:

I begin to fear that the Sirven affair may not be finished before St Martin's Day [11 November], and that my health will not allow me to travel to Toulouse, despite the pressing invitations they send me. Could you please go to M. de Laleu [Voltaire's lawyer] and ask for the contract with the prince and princess of Guise. As far as I remember, one can only ask for up to five years of arrears; which is really cruel, since they owe more than ten. If all our affairs go like this, we shall not have enough to put on plays.[71]

Mme Denis arrived at Ferney on 28 October 1769, and of course she came with her carriage, with her two horses, and with her three servants. Voltaire alluded laconically, but without comment, to the fact of her arrival in a letter to d'Alembert: 'Mme Denis, my very dear and very great philosopher, brings me your letter of the 15th. I should have liked even better to talk with you in Paris; but the sad state I am in has not allowed me to travel.'[72] In no other letter does Voltaire refer to her return; and even in this one, he makes no reference to his feelings about her or about their reunion. Three months later, Mme Denis wrote to Guillaume-Claude de Laleu, Voltaire's lawyer in Paris: 'My uncle is fairly well, for which I have reason to be very glad. I am being patient. He is very pleased with my return, and I do not think that he will suggest another trip to Paris in the near future.'[73]

So: Mme Denis tells us that Voltaire is very pleased that she is back; but Voltaire himself does not tell us that he is pleased to have her back; and Mme Denis tells us that she is being patient, but not that she is pleased to be back. It is an enigmatic end to an enigmatic separation.

But perhaps it is mainly enigmatic on the part of Mme Denis. Voltaire had repeatedly given her the option to stay in Paris, if she wanted; she knew what life at Ferney was like, yet she chose to return there. After her return, she recedes once more behind Voltaire's shadow, and we hear little more about how she feels. As for Voltaire, it seems clear that he is very glad to have her back, not because he says so, but because, in the weeks and months after her return, he becomes more gay and lively, in word and deed.

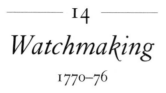

14

Watchmaking

1770–76

One of the casualties of the running battle between Voltaire and Bishop Biord was that the bishop banned Father Adam from saying Mass, so Voltaire looked around for alternatives.* He found them in a small neighbouring community of a dozen Franciscans or Capuchins (*Capucins*), some of whom came to say Mass for him at Ferney from time to time. In recognition of their services, Voltaire applied to the duc de Choiseul for a government subsidy for the community;[1] Choiseul generously obliged, and arranged a pension for the Franciscans of £600 a year.[2] In gratitude for their good fortune, the Franciscans wrote to the head of their order in Rome, Father General Amatus Alambella and urged that he should give Voltaire's generosity appropriate recognition.

Their recommendation had comical consequences which Voltaire milked for all he was worth. For in February 1770, he received notification from Alambella, that he would now receive the titles of Spiritual Child, Benefactor, and Temporal Father of the order of Saint François.

For a sceptical mocker of the Church, this was the best joke to have come Voltaire's way for years. Over the next few weeks, he took maximum advantage of this satirical turn of events, and lost no opportunity to describe himself as an honorary Franciscan, signing

---

*There is a curious contradiction in Voltaire's account. He told Richelieu, in 1765, that Father Adam had been banned from saying Mass (letter 8676). But now he tells Mme Denis, in 1768, that Father Adam has been banned by the bishop (letter 11002). Perhaps the earlier ban was only temporary; perhaps it applied to the church but not to Voltaire's home. It is not clear.

many letters as 'Friar François, unworthy Capuchin' or '✝ Friar V, unworthy Capuchin'. He wrote to Mme du Deffand: 'My God, Madame, did you know that I was a capuchin? It is a dignity which I owe to Mme de Choiseul. Just see how God takes care of his elect, and how grace performs conjuring tricks before reaching the target. The Father General has sent me my letters patent from Rome. I am a capuchin in the spiritual and in the temporal sense, besides being also temporal father of the Franciscans of Gex.'³

It is hard to imagine how this clerical slip-up occurred; presumably the correspondence in Rome had been handled by some low-level bureaucrat. Yet it is difficult to believe that there could have been any bureaucrat, however lowly, who did not know Voltaire's name and his reputation as a sceptical enemy of the Catholic Church. In any event, when word of Voltaire's new Franciscan titles got out, as he made sure it would, it provoked gales of laughter among the sceptics and free-thinkers in Paris. The French government quickly decided it must try to put a stop to this tomfoolery, and the comte de Saint-Florentin, the interior minister, wrote to the head of the Franciscan order to ask for an explanation. In reply, Alambella denied that he had ever sent letters patent to Voltaire, or that, if he had sent them, he hadn't signed them. Within weeks, Voltaire's brief incarnation as an honorary Franciscan friar was at an end, though for some time he continued on occasion to describe himself as 'Friar François'.⁴

By the middle of February, however, Voltaire was beginning to tire of his little joke, not least because he now had much more serious matters on his mind, starting with the eruption of a new wave of political violence in Geneva between the oligarchs of the *Petit Conseil* and the lesser orders.

In principle, the warring classes of Geneva had seemed to have patched up their previous political quarrel two years earlier, in March 1768, partly through French mediation, partly as a result of French pressure culminating in the military blockade. That settlement, which very slightly reduced the political power of the oligarchs, and for the first time gave social and economic privileges to the working class *natifs* at the bottom of the social pile, held up, more or less, for about a year. But in mid-1769 the patricians simply revoked that part of it which had given new advantages to the *natifs*, and by early February 1770 violence broke out again between the haves and the have-nots. Voltaire wrote to his eminent lawyer friend, Élie de Beaumont:

I do not know, my dear Cicero, if the disorders of Geneva will prevent my letter from getting to the post. Yesterday the *bourgeois* killed three *habitants*, and people say that they have killed another four this morning. According to the customs of Geneva, the losers are hanged, and it is said that they will hang three or four *habitants*, whose companions have already been killed. The whole city is up in arms, everything is in a state of combustion in this wise republic.[5]

The political combustion in Geneva would inevitably have damaging repercussions for Ferney, since it was heavily dependent on supplies from Geneva. The French blockade of 1767, which had been intended to put pressure on Geneva, had in fact created more difficulties for Ferney and the rest of the province of Gex than for Geneva itself. For though Gex was part of France, its natural communications and trading relationships were with Geneva, not with the French hinterland, and the blockade had shown how difficult it was for Gex to get supplies from other sources. As a result, Voltaire had had the idea that France in general, and Gex in particular, would be much better served in terms of trade and communications if the little French fishing village at Versoix, on the shores of Lac Léman, and just to the north-east of Geneva, could be developed into a substantial town and trading port. He had put this idea to Pierre de Buisson, the chevalier de Beauteville and France's chief mediator in the quarrels of the Genevans; it was quickly taken up by the prime minister, the duc de Choiseul, and he soon set construction work in train.[6]

The Genevan authorities and merchants were deeply hostile to this project. Versoix would face them with direct commercial competition, and undercut their trading dominance in the hinterland outside Geneva. More important, perhaps, it could undermine their political dominance at home. For the mere existence of a rival commercial centre just up the lake was likely to attract labour from

Geneva, and also offer an alternative political haven for those lower-order Genevans who were dissatisfied with the restrictive terms of their existence in Geneva. This political and economic challenge, which was actively promoted by Voltaire and consciously accepted by the French authorities, was one of the factors behind the latest wave of political conflict inside Geneva.

As soon as Versoix looked like becoming a reality, a number of the dissatisfied *natifs* of Geneva sought to move there. Voltaire reported to Pierre-Michel Hennin, the French Resident: 'When people started to talk of building Versoix, eighteen *natifs* came to bring me their signatures, undertaking to build houses there. I sent their propositions on to M. le duc de Choiseul.'[7]

On 19 February 1770, Voltaire reported that the Geneva authorities were threatening to hang all who tried to withdraw to Versoix.[8] Two days later he wrote: 'They have just cut the throats of those *habitants* who had submitted their names to the Ministry with a view to moving to Versoix. They have killed, among others, an old man of eighty who was walking in the street in his dressing gown. They have wounded, with blows from their rifle butts, a pregnant woman who is likely to die from it. Two thousand *habitants* will leave this den of discord.'[9] In a letter to Mme du Deffand he added: 'They killed four or five persons in their dressing gowns; as for me, who pass my life in a dressing gown, I find it appalling that they have so little respect for night-caps.'[10]

Indeed, some of the protesters had already fled Geneva and had been given French residence permits by François de Caire, the chief French engineer for the construction of Versoix, as well as provisional lodging on French territory, in country houses owned by rich Genevans.[11] Voltaire wrote to Caire, recommending that he should get Georges Auzière, an assembler of watch-cases and a leading spokesman for the *habitants* and *natifs*, to write a report declaring that he and his companions had been persecuted, and several of them murdered, solely because they wanted to set themselves up in Versoix.

The problem was that the town of Versoix had not yet been built, though some progress had been made with the port. As a result, many of those *natifs* and *habitants* who originally wanted to move to

Versoix found that they had to look elsewhere, and increasingly they gravitated to Ferney; the Dufour family of Genevan watchmakers was one of the first to arrive there. Ten days after the outbreak of violence in Geneva, Voltaire reported that sixty families had taken refuge in the neighbourhood, some of them in Ferney itself.

The Genevan authorities tried to persuade the French government not to admit the émigrés from Geneva, and sent Philibert Cramer, brother and partner of the publisher Gabriel Cramer, on a diplomatic mission to Paris. When Voltaire heard this, he wrote to Choiseul to discredit Philibert's mission. 'Master Cramer, who is being sent to you by the Council of Geneva, has not been instructed to tell you the truth. He has been my publisher, and he is councillor of state in the noble republic of Geneva. Proud as I am of that, I should not answer for it that he will not seek to deceive you if you honour him with an audience.'[12]

Voltaire was particularly afraid that Philibert Cramer might persuade Choiseul that the emigrants from Geneva were indigent idlers who would become a burden on the French State. He wrote to François de Caire:

I beg you urgently, Sir, not to say to M. le duc de Choiseul at this time that the emigrants need money. That would be to run down our little colony [Versoix], which we should represent with a more smiling face. Otherwise, the emigrants would only seem to be beggars driven out of their republic, coming here to ask for charity. Cramer counts on passing them off as seditious blackguards who have neither hearth nor home (*ni feu ni lieu*). Those steps which we would like to take to help the watchmakers from Geneva could turn out only to run them down and ruin them. This is not the time to ask for money for foreigners. We must wait. We can find help, and I have an idea which I shall have the honour to communicate to you.[13]

In fact, Choiseul refused to see Philibert Cramer, and told him he was wasting his time.[14]

Voltaire's idea, or rather his first idea, was that since the new arrivals were useful, able-bodied workers, France should employ them in the building of Versoix. He even thought of putting some of his own money into the development of the new town, and put his name down for one of the new houses, on condition that it was in a most favoured position. Unfortunately, not for the first time, the finances of the French State were in difficulties, leading among other things to delays in developing Versoix. It was in order to ease these difficulties, in March 1770, that the Abbé Terray, the new *Contrôleur Général* or finance minister, confiscated, or at least suspended payment on, a number of government securities, including one category called *rescriptions*, in which Voltaire had invested a large amount of money. Voltaire complained bitterly and repeatedly at this confiscation, not least because, as he said, the money he had invested in *rescriptions* was virtually his only freely disposable capital: he had a very large income, but it came essentially from *rente viagère* loans, which would expire with his death.

Pierre-Michel Hennin, the French Resident, sounded out Choiseul to see if there were any way of reimbursing Voltaire, at least in part: 'M. de Voltaire, in the fervour of his first enthusiasm, would have given capital for the construction of Versoix, but unfortunately he has £240,000 in *rescriptions* and very little in cash. He has however promised to make some advances. If it were possible to discount his *rescriptions*, we could easily commit him to put up the wherewithal to employ, immediately, a very large number of workers.'[15] Nothing came of this suggestion, however, and until the end of his life Voltaire never stopped complaining at the confiscation, which he regarded as illegal.

Voltaire's second idea, which was a variant of the first, was more interesting and more feasible. The immigrants from Geneva were not just labourers: many of them were skilled craftsmen from the large watchmaking industry in Geneva. So why not set them up in business as independent watchmakers? And since there seemed no prospect that Versoix would be built soon enough to house them, why not set them up in business in Ferney? In any case, quite a few of the *natifs* had already arrived in Ferney, since there was nowhere for them to live in Versoix.

Voltaire pursued this idea with extraordinary rapidity and dynamism, despite the fact that he was now seventy-six years old; that he knew nothing about watches, or industry, or business in general; and that he had until very recently been prejudiced, as a landowner, against the pull of manufacturing employment on his peasants.

One reason why Voltaire was, at this moment, open to the idea of a watch industry in Ferney was that he had already embarked on a manufacturing venture on his estate. This was a tiny silk industry, which he had started up the previous year (1769), during the absence of Mme Denis in Paris, and which was not only involved in the cultivation of silkworms and the production of silk, but also in the weaving of silk garments.

To begin with, he had kept it a jokey little secret. In July 1769, he wrote to the duchesse de Choiseul to ask her to send him one of her slippers, without telling her why.[16] Assuming that Voltaire was leading her on with some kind of joke, Mme de Choiseul sent him a simply enormous slipper. Voltaire replied: 'Madame Gargantua: I have received the slipper with which it has pleased Your Greatness to gratify me. It is as long as the foot of a king; it is clear that you must be seven foot three inches tall. That is a most advantageous height.'[17] The following month, September, Voltaire sent her a pair of silk stockings. 'Madame Gargantua: Forgive the great liberty, but it is my silkworms which have given me the wherewithal to make these stockings, it is my hands which have worked at making them, in my home, with the son of Calas; these are the first stockings made in this part of the country.'[18]

Not long before she returned to Ferney, Voltaire wrote to Mme Denis: 'I have amused myself this summer in raising silkworms; I have made silk; I have made a few stitches in a pair of stockings that we are knitting for you. But this work takes longer than [the writing of] a tragedy; we have been knitting for a month, and we are still only halfway there.'[19] In January 1770, Voltaire revealed that he had now converted his theatre for the cultivation of the silkworms; this would be the first of many transformations of the Ferney theatre building for other purposes.[20]

Voltaire's first reference to 'the manufacture of watches at Ferney' comes in March 1770, shortly after the outbreak of violence in Geneva and the arrival of the first artisan immigrants in Ferney.[21] By early

April, the Ferney watchmaking industry was up and running. On 9 April, Voltaire wrote to François de Caire, the chief engineer at Versoix:

You will know that I am sending to Monseigneur le duc de Choiseul a box of watches for Spain, made before my very eyes, in less than six weeks, at Ferney, and that we shall have eight or ten more boxes in under three months. Auzière has brought me his master-work of eloquence [his draft report on the persecution of the *natifs*], and I told him that he would have done better to bring me a balance wheel for a watch. Woe to whoever does not work at his trade! What we need is a town, houses, artisans, freedom, money, but no fortresses. I salute and embrace my dear commandant.

Friar François, unworthy Capuchin.[22]

Voltaire's vigour in launching his watch industry is all the more remarkable in that his health, never good, at this time went through a bad patch. He wrote for advice to Michel-Philippe Bouvart, the Paris doctor who was looking after Mme d'Argental:

An old man of seventy-three, and long subject to a scurvy humour, which has always reduced him to extreme thinness, which has removed almost all his teeth, which sometimes attacks his tonsils, which often causes rumblings in his gut, insomnia, etc., begs Mr Bouvart to have the kindness to write, at the bottom of this note, if he thinks that goat's milk could provide some relief.

It is perhaps ridiculous to hope for a cure at this age; but the patient, having some business which cannot be finished in less than ten months, takes the liberty to ask if goat's milk could keep him going until then? He asks if there is any evidence that goat's milk, with some absolutely necessary purgatives, has done any good in such a case?[23]

In his covering letter to d'Argental, Voltaire adds: 'I know [Bouvart] has not prescribed goat's milk for Mme d'Argental; but since I am more dried up, older, and weaker than her, I am determined to try goat's milk, and that M. Bouvart should agree. I ask for your protection: plead for my goat, I beg you.'[24] Evidently M. Bouvart did not approve of goat's milk, however, for Voltaire wrote to d'Argental at the end of April: 'I have just received a kind message from M. Bouvart, and I have now given up my goat, my dear angel.'[25]

Though Voltaire frequently asserted his rational belief in freedom of conscience and freedom of trade,[26] his innate conviction was that his new enterprise could only succeed with the official patronage of the State. Early in April he wrote to the duchesse de Choiseul to ask for her husband's support, without which, he said, his venture would be doomed.

Just as soon as [Choiseul] agreed that we could admit emigrants, I immediately invited emigrants into my hovels, and scarcely did they start work but they made enough watches to send a small box to Spain. I throw myself at your large feet to beg you to favour this despatch, so that this parcel shall leave without delay for Cadiz. I am writing passionately to M. de La Ponce [Choiseul's secretary] about this affair, on which depends a trade of £300,000 a year.

Your servant, Friar François, capuchin more unworthy than ever V—[27]

It is striking that, within weeks of launching his new project, Voltaire should have leapt to the conclusion that this could be a substantial business. He could not possibly have known at this early stage that his watchmakers would produce sales of £300,000, since they had only just started work at Ferney, and he knew nothing of the trade or its markets. In the event, his estimate proved conservative: in 1775, he claimed that his watchmakers had total sales of £450,000 or £500,000 a year; in 1776, he reckoned the turnover at £500,000–600,000 a year.[28]

Voltaire did not achieve these figures without extraordinary efforts on his own part. When he started out, in February 1770, he almost certainly did not foresee that this new business would require him to be, not just the overall manager, co-ordinator and organiser, but also the financier, the virtual bank manager, the sponsor, the builder of homes and factory space, the buyer of precious metals and other raw materials, as well as the international sales manager. But the fact that he did take all this on, with considerable success, is testimony to the vitality of his mind and the vigour of his spirit. And all this despite the fact that he was an ill old man.

It is an interesting question where Voltaire's renewed vitality and vigour had come from. One clue is to be found in a letter he wrote to Gaspard-Henri Schérer, his banker in Lyon, in February 1770. 'I appeal to your kindness, Sir. I should like to have a dozen pints of excellent lavender water; two pounds of good sealing wax; two thousand gilt nails for armchairs; and a barrel of good drinkable wine from the Dauphiné or the Beaujolais. I know nobody to whom I can address these little errands. If you had at hand someone who could take it on, I should be very obliged to you.'[29] This is the first time for many months, or even years, that Voltaire had written this kind of exuberant shopping list. It seems obvious that such a list could only have come from the demands of the recently returned Mme Denis, and it is tempting to imagine that it was partly her presence which had given him a new lease of life.

A different clue appears in a letter Voltaire wrote to Pierre-Michel Hennin in April 1770: 'The reason that I did not reply to my very amiable Resident is that I was dead. We have all been ill with a catarrh which is no good at all for people who are 77½ years old. But the prosperity of the hamlet of Ferney has revived me; for I now have about forty workers employed in teaching Europe how to tell the time.'[30] In other words, Voltaire was thoroughly excited by his new venture.

The best watches were expected to be made of gold, and often ornamented with precious stones; so one of Voltaire's first tasks was to locate reliable supplies of gold. In mid-April, he wrote to Jean-Joseph marquis de Laborde, the King's banker:

I am establishing a considerable manufacture. If it should fail, I should lose only the money which I have lent to it, interest-free. If you could indicate to me some method of procuring Spanish gold, in ingots or coins, you would do me a great service. We should only need about 1,000 louis worth [£24,000] each year. The workers say that gold is much too expensive in Geneva, and that they lose too much if they melt down gold coins. All this is far from my ordinary occupations, but I have the pleasure of multiplying by ten the inhabitants of my hamlet, to grow wheat where thistles grew before, to attract foreigners, and to show the King that I know how to do something else besides writing the *Histoire du Siècle de Louis XIV* and a few verses.[31]

After his first enquiry to Laborde, Voltaire turned for his gold requirements to his usual supplier of all and sundry, the banker Gaspard-Henri Schérer. Quite soon he arranged for his leading watchmakers to have drawing rights on his accounts with Schérer in Lyon: 'Dufour & Céret will never draw on you without asking my permission first, and with every letter of credit I shall give you advance notice. I hope the help I am giving them will put them in a position where they can make their manufacture prosper.' He also asked Schérer to find him sales representatives in Lyon and Milan; which he did.[32]

Voltaire's relationship with the watchmaking enterprise was to begin with entirely disinterested in money terms. As he told Mme du Deffand later that year: 'I have done it purely out of vanity. They say that God created the world for his own glory. We must imitate him as far as possible.'[33] But if Voltaire provided his watchmakers with interest-free finance, it was because he could afford to. His latest financial inventory from Guillaume-Claude de Laleu, his Paris lawyer, showed that in Paris alone he had *rentes* of more than £50,000 a year, in addition to his income from loans to the duc de Wurtemberg and a number of German princes, and his assets in Lyon and Geneva.[34] And it appears that the duc de Richelieu, and perhaps the successors of the Guise family, were now paying at least some of the interest they owed.

About the same time, Voltaire gave a vivid picture of the turbulent activity in Ferney, in a letter to the marquis de Jaucourt, who had previously been billeted on him as a commander of the blockading French troops.

My very generous and very dear commander, I have established in the hamlet of Ferney a little annexe of the manufacture of watches of Bourg-en-Bresse. Our theatre auditorium, which you remember, has been transformed into workshops. There, where once we recited verse, we are now melting gold and polishing cogs. We must build new houses for the emigrants. All the workers of Geneva would come here if we were in a position to house them. We must remember that everyone nowadays wants a gold watch, from Peking to Martinique, and that before there were only three great manufacturing centres, London, Paris and Geneva. Sensitive and tolerant souls will be happy to learn that sixty Huguenots live so well with my parishioners that it would not be possible to guess that there are two religions here.

FRIAR FRANÇOIS[35]

In Paris, meanwhile, Voltaire's friends were preparing a little surprise for him: they planned to commission a lifesize statue of the *patriarche*. The idea first came from Suzanne Curchod, wife of the rich Protestant banker Jacques Necker, and hostess of a brilliant avant-garde literary salon in Paris. On 17 April 1770, Mme Necker gave a dinner for seventeen *philosophes*, including d'Alembert, Diderot, Grimm, Helvetius, Marmontel, Morellet and Saint Lambert, in short the cream of the cream of the French Enlightenment. She outlined her proposal at the end of the meal, and they enthusiastically endorsed it. Jean-Baptiste Pigalle, the famous sculptor, was then shown into the room: he had been primed in advance, and was able to show them a rough clay model, which they immediately accepted. The statue was expected to cost between £12,000 and £15,000, including a fee of £10,000 for Pigalle. They had thought of limiting the subscription to men of letters, with the inscription *To the living Voltaire, by men of letters his compatriots*; but then they decided to open the list without restriction, in the expectation that the great and the good from all over Europe would be keen to contribute.[36]

At first Voltaire was flattered but embarrassed. 'It is not likely, my dear philosopher,' he wrote to d'Alembert, 'that it will be *To the living Voltaire*; it will be *To the dying Voltaire*, for I am coming to my end. It would not be bad if Frederick joined the list of subscribers; it would save the generous men of letters some money, of which they do not have much. In any event, he owes me some reparation.'[37] All the beau monde of Paris society were keen to subscribe to Voltaire's statue, at the standard price of two louis each; Frederick subscribed 200 louis, or £4,800.[38]

When Voltaire heard that Pigalle intended to come and model him in the flesh, he expressed concern. 'My modesty, and my reason, Madame', he wrote to Mme Necker, 'made me believe that the idea of a statue was just a good joke; but since it is serious, allow me to speak to you seriously. I am seventy six years old, and I am barely emerging from a great sickness which for six weeks maltreated my body and my soul. M. Pigalle is due, they say, to come to model my face. But then, Madam, I should need to have a face; yet one can scarcely guess where it is. My eyes are sunk three inches deep; my cheeks are like old parchment badly stuck on bones which hardly hold together. The few teeth I had are gone. What I tell you is not *coquetterie*, it is the simple truth. No one has ever sculpted a man in such a state. M. Pigalle will think he is being made fun of, and as for me, I have so much pride that I should never dare appear in his presence. After all, what does it matter to posterity if a block of marble looks like one man or like another?'[39]

Voltaire's protestations were in vain. Pigalle visited Ferney in June, and spent a week sketching and modelling Voltaire's head. It seems that the modelling sessions were carried out in the open, in full view of the curious. Voltaire reported to Mme Necker. 'When the people of my village saw Pigalle setting out some of the instruments of his craft, they said, *"Hey, look, he's going to cut him open; this will be fun"* [*"Tiens, tiens,* disaient-ils*, on va le disséquer, cela sera drôle"*]. It is thus, Madame, as you know, that men are amused by any spectacle. It is for the same reasons that people go to the marionettes, to the comic opera, to High Mass, to a burial. My statue will make some philosophers smile.'[40]

Within a few days, Pigalle made a preliminary model of Voltaire's head. 'M. Pigalle has made me speaking and thinking, even though my age and my illnesses have somewhat deprived me of thought and words. He even made me smiling; it must be at all the stupidities that one does every day. He is as good a man as he is an artist. He has the simplicity of true genius.'[41]

It sounds as if Voltaire was on good form during these modelling sessions; that is certainly what Pigalle told his friends after he returned to Paris. But when Voltaire heard, he was indignant, claiming that he was really very ill. 'My dear prophet,' he told Melchior Grimm, 'M. Pigalle, though the best man in the world, is slandering me most strangely. He goes about saying that I am well, that I am as plump as a monk. I was just trying to be gay in his presence, exercising my smiling muscles [*les muscles buccinateurs*] to be polite to him.'[42]

Voltaire's good-humoured acceptance of the statue project was spoiled only by the name of Jean-Jacques Rousseau. Considering his celebrated hate-letter to Voltaire and the vitriol of their ensuing quarrel, Rousseau was surprisingly anxious, even determined, to subscribe to the Pigalle statue. When Voltaire learned that Jean-Jacques had already paid over his two louis, he was enraged, and insisted that the money be returned and that Rousseau's name be excluded from the subscription list. It was only after some weeks of argument that d'Alembert was able to persuade him not to make a scandal, and to accept Rousseau's homage with good grace.[43]

There was one characteristic of the statue which raised eyebrows at the time, and has raised eyebrows ever since: Pigalle intended to sculpt Voltaire virtually naked. According to René Pomeau, this had always been the intention of the sponsors, right from the beginning.[44] Strangely, this fact does not figure in Voltaire's correspondence at the time. When Pigalle visited him in the spring of 1770, it was essentially to model his head and face. Voltaire said that his head and face did not deserve to be sculpted; he did not say this about his body because of course Pigalle did not ask Voltaire to sit for him in the nude. For the purpose of modelling the body of the statue, Pigalle used an old soldier from Les Invalides, after he got back to Paris.

Voltaire may have known all along that he was to be sculpted naked. But it was not until a year later that he alluded to the fact, and he did so in terms that clearly imply that the question of nudity had only recently arisen, and was controversial. He wrote to d'Alembert on 18 March 1771: 'Here is another quarrel. Mme Necker has complained bitterly to me that Pigalle wants to make me completely naked. Here is my reply: you decide on my effigy; it is up to you to give me a suit of clothes, if that's what you want. Be sure that, clothed or not, I am all yours.'[45]

The question was not to be disposed of so easily, however, and the controversy continued. Nine months later, in December 1771, Voltaire declared that Pigalle, as the artist, must have complete freedom to decide. 'I can only admire the classicism of the works of M. Pigalle: whether naked or clothed, it's all one to me. However I am presented, I shall not inspire any naughty thoughts in the minds of the ladies. We must leave M. Pigalle the absolute master of his statue. In matters of fine arts, it is a crime to place restrictions on genius. It is not for nothing that it is represented with wings: it must fly where it will and how it will.'[46]

The finest sculptures of Voltaire are probably those by Jean-Antoine Houdon, whose best-known statue of him, fully clothed and seated, is in the Comédie Française,*[47] where his plays, once so dominant, are no longer performed. By contrast, Pigalle's statue of Voltaire naked, with a pen in one hand and his modesty protected only by a sheet of parchment, remains an unloved oddity. Pigalle did not complete the statue until 1776, and the marble reality proved just as controversial as the original concept. At first there was no agreement where it should be placed. No one wanted to give it house-room; so it stayed in Pigalle's studio. Later it passed to Voltaire's heirs, the family of Mme Denis. In 1806, they gave it to the Académie Française, where it was virtually hidden away, in despised obscurity, for 150 years. It was not finally exhibited in the Louvre until 1962.

Meanwhile, in Ferney, the inflow of immigrants led to some social friction, both locally and with the *genevois*. One such noisy incident took place between one of Voltaire's servants and the guards at the Geneva city gates, as Voltaire reported to Pierre-Michel Hennin, the French Resident at Geneva, in June 1770:

*In the upstairs bar, known as the Foyer Pierre Dux

Go and get stuffed, go and scratch your arse with the arse of the Resident, you've got bread in your pockets for the French dolts, you come from those French buggers at Ferney, etc., etc.

Those, Sir, are the very words of the Philippic pronounced today by the youth, against Dalloz, errand-boy of Ferney, who was carrying, not bread for the dolts, but a little trout for our supper. These gallantries happen too often. I have not seen the arse of Dalloz, and I doubt if it is worthy to scratch yours. Frankly, these compliments of the Genevans are getting too strong.[48]

When Hennin queried whether his name had really been bandied about in this exchange of insults, Voltaire assured him it was so. 'The most amiable of Residents will see by the enclosed that his white and dimpled buttocks were certainly compromised with the buttocks of Dalloz, who is too ignorant to have invented such a story. Your servants were just passing by, and may well have not heard all the compliments, since Dalloz was insolently detained in the guard-house for a good half-hour.'[49]

The 'youth' referred to by Voltaire was in fact Sergeant Raisin of the Geneva guard at the gate of the city. Raisin was censured for his insults, and jailed for three days; but the Geneva authorities sought to take proceedings against Dalloz as well, for refusing to allow the guard to inspect the cart he was driving, and for doing some insulting of his own.[50] Voltaire asked Pierre-Michel Hennin not to allow Dalloz to be tried before a Geneva magistrate because, as he explained: 'We do not expect any justice from these people.' Hennin promised to administer justice himself. 'You are too good, Sir, and Dalloz is an animal. I send him to you, even though he is ill. As I am too. He still swears that that there was some arse in this affair. Mine is in a piteous state. It was not made for being sculpted by Pigalle.'[51]

But the upside of the new inhabitants of Ferney was that the village was starting to be big enough to support some shops and traders. At the end of July, Voltaire complained to Louis-Gaspard Fabry, mayor of Gex, that the local butcher was too disorganised; yes, he had good beef, but he could not keep his accounts, since he did not know how to write. 'Perhaps we shall have to bring in another one.' He also told Fabry that he was in a great hurry to finish a building in which he would house various merchants 'who will provide the whole region with all the things which cost too much in Geneva'.[52] Two weeks later, a new butcher arrived in Ferney.

The butcher who is now established in Ferney, for the first time in the history of this hamlet, has been useful, despite his ignorance and poverty. He supplies all the region. It just shows, obviously, that all it requires is will, to escape dependence on Geneva. Also, there is a fairly intelligent merchant who wants to set up in business here. But if he is to succeed, we must present a report to the government, to show the pernicious advantages given until now to foreigners, at the expense of the nation, which explains why everything is cheaper in Geneva than in Gex.[53]

Towards the end of 1770 the inhabitants of Ferney decided they needed a public fountain or drinking trough. Voltaire passed on their request to Fabry. 'I imagine that it only needs a word from you to authorise the inhabitants of Ferney to set up a water supply. We count on decorating our little village with a fairly pretty fountain.'[54] Fabry did nothing, however, and three weeks later Voltaire wrote again. 'The village of Ferney needs a public fountain more than ever; not just for the community, but for all the carters and farm workers, to water their horses and their cattle. I am not sure if we need a decree from the King's Council for drinking water. I assumed that it only needed a word from you for the village to be allowed to spend its own money on such an indispensable work.'[55]

By the following spring (1771), the fountain had been built; but some of the villagers were reluctant to pay for it. Voltaire asked Fabry to impose the costs in proportion to the local property tax. 'The inhabitants demanded the building of the fountain with the greatest insistence, but now some of them are reluctant, not merely to pay, but even to come to a meeting. The fountain builder is demanding payment. Please send us an official order, which we shall pass on to each individual, and if there are some too poor to pay (which we do not believe), we shall pay for them without difficulty.'[56]

*

Within weeks of the start of the watchmaking enterprise, early in the spring of 1770, Voltaire had begun to concentrate seriously on finding customers and markets for his watches. His immense initial advantage in this task was that he already knew personally many of the best placed people, both in France and abroad, and he proceeded ruthlessly to milk his contacts. But he soon saw that he would not be able to keep his rapidly growing colony in business by selling watches one by one: he needed markets, agents, representatives.

One of his first overtures was to his friend Cardinal Bernis, French ambassador to the Vatican in Rome. He explained that his aim in setting up his watchmakers in Ferney was not a game or a charitable exercise; he intended to establish an industry which would compete with Geneva; and he wanted Bernis's help in tapping the Rome market.

Our watches are very well made, very handsome, very good, and cheap. The good work which I beg your Eminence to undertake is just to deign to look out an honest merchant in Rome, who would agree to be our representative. I answer for it that it would be worth his while. The manufacturers will send him a consignment just as soon as you let us know.[57]

Bernis proved a great disappointment. He did not even bother to reply until seven months later, and when he did, on 19 December 1770, his letter was merely a tissue of feeble excuses for his unhelpfulness. 'I have done what I could, my dear colleague, to establish here with confidence the commercial branch for your watchmakers that you suggested. It is just not possible. You can understand that I cannot and must not answer for the good faith of possible agents. This country has no trade ...'[58]

Voltaire was angry, and showed it.

I have seen by your silence, about the colony I have built, that you are not helping me at all. I cannot avoid telling you that you have given me infinite pain. I have not deserved this hardness on your part. You seem to have believed that my colony was nothing more than poetic licence. It is, on the contrary, a very real and very substantial colony, composed of three manufactures, protected by the King, and especially by M. le duc de Choiseul. No other French ambassador has failed to take energetic steps to find us agents in foreign countries. You are the only one, not only who did not have that kindness, but who disdained to reply. What would it have cost you to have got someone to speak a word to the French consul in Rome? May Your Eminence please accept, if he please, the respect and extreme anger of the hermit of Ferney.[59]

If Voltaire claimed to Cardinal Bernis that none of the other French ambassadors had failed to help him, this was not the story he told to others; he complained to d'Argental that some of them did not appear to have made any very great efforts for him.[60] One notable exception was Pierre Paul, the marquis d'Ossun, French ambassador to Spain, to whom Voltaire was particularly grateful. Spain was a large potential market and it was also of course the gateway to Cadiz and trade with the Indies.[61]

Naturally, Voltaire also approached Catherine the Great, and his sales pitch to her was a mixture of obsequiousness, deviousness and cheek. In November 1770, he wrote to her to say that his watchmakers had just finished a watch decorated with diamonds and bearing her portrait, which they trusted she would allow them to send her. It was only in succeeding sentences that he let it emerge that Catherine was expected to pay for this watch, as well as for others which she might like to have to give away as presents. He assured her that the watches from Ferney were half the price of those from London or Paris.[62] Four months later, in March 1771, he told the marquis d'Ossun that Catherine had ordered £20,000-worth of watches from Ferney.[63] In June that year, he wrote to inform Catherine that his watchmakers had just sent her an enormous consignment of watches; he suggested that she need only pay half the £40,000 invoice right away; he was sure the watchmakers would be only too happy to wait a year for the rest.[64] Another ten days on, and Voltaire reckoned that the value of total recent deliveries to St Petersburg amounted to £60,000.[65]

One reason for the escalation in sales was that, despite Voltaire's claim that his watches were cheaper than those from Paris or London (as they may have been), some of the watches he sent to Catherine were really very expensive: a consignment sent in April 1771 included watches costing 80 louis, or £1,920.[66]

Voltaire also looked for sales opportunities in Turkey, which had long been a significant market for watches; so good, in fact, that there was even a little colony of Swiss watchmakers in Constantinople. Ironically, Voltaire had for some years adopted the role of sycophantic, not to say vulgar, cheerleader for Catherine's military campaigns against the Turks, and he repeatedly urged her to press on to victory against them. Yet now he seems to have experienced no difficulty in accommodating the contradiction between his political prejudices and his commercial interests. 'I used to be very interested in the troubles of Turkey,' he told Richelieu, 'that is to say that I hoped passionately that they would be driven out of Europe. But now I shall come to terms with them, for I have put together a little company which has strong links with Constantinople.'[67] Voltaire's determination to sell watches was totally single-minded; in June 1771, he reported that recent sales to Constantinople had amounted to £30,000.[68]

By the end of 1770, Voltaire had established his main export markets in Spain, Turkey and Russia, a list which he later extended to include Holland and Italy.[69] He also explored such exotic markets as Algeria and Tunisia.[70] At the same time, he worked hard at finding domestic customers for his watches. Having sold some to Louis XV,[71] he turned to the duc and duchesse de Choiseul and boldly set out his wares.

I take the liberty to importune you, to ask if we could take the extreme liberty to send, from our monastery to Mme la duchesse de Choiseul, the six watches which we have just made at Ferney. We believe they are very pretty and very good; but of course, every author has a good opinion of his own works.

We have thought that, on the occasion of the wedding [of Marie-Antoinette to the Dauphin, the future Louis XVI] and the accompanying fêtes, these examples of our manufacture could be given as gifts, either to artists who performed at these fêtes, or to persons attached to madame la dauphine. Their cheapness will no doubt please M. l'abbé Terray, since there are two watches which cost only 11 louis each, while the most expensive, decorated with diamonds, is only priced at forty-six louis. The one with the portrait of the King in enamel, with diamonds, is only twenty-five, and the one with the portrait of Monseigneur the dauphin, with a hand with diamonds, is only seventeen. They would all cost well over a third more in Paris.

Friar François, Unworthy Capucin

PS The prices are marked on a little piece of parchment attached to the watches; when you want to start one, you must remove a small piece of paper which stops the plate and the balance-wheel.[72]

Voltaire also turned to d'Argental. 'Here is a very honest price list of the watches. People cannot do better than come to us; we are good workmen and very reliable. If one of your foreign ministers wants cheap watches, let him write to Ferney. Help our enterprise, my dear angels, we have twenty families to feed.'[73] The price list, from the firm of Dufour & Ceret, ranged from three louis for a watch in smooth silver, four louis for a watch in engraved or *guillochée* silver, fouteen louis for a silver repeater watch, and forty-two louis for the best repeater gold watch. Dufour & Ceret said they would give a two-year guarantee for all watches costing more than eight and a half louis.[74]

When Voltaire said that Ferney watches were inexpensive, some of his Paris friends assumed that they must be very cheap; Voltaire quickly disabused them. 'It is just as impossible, my dear Baron,' he wrote to the marquis de Thibouville, 'to get a repeater watch for four louis as it is to get a sturgeon in Paris for four sous; so I seriously advise you to give up the idea.'[75]

By the autumn of 1771, Ferney had spawned four different watch-making companies or partnerships;[76] and it was an indicator of the rapidity of the commercial success of the colony that it was becoming difficult for Voltaire to keep track of the financial transactions. He wrote to his banker, Schérer, in November:

Would you please, Sir, do me the kindness to send me the names of those who have taken Spanish gold from you, for which I am answerable. It is true that we agreed between us that you would not give gold to our dealers except on a note from me, but I am afraid that someone may have taken advantage of your kindness. It is necessary, to put some order into my affairs, that I should have a little account of the gold that you kindly entrusted to them. Also, please specify the date by which they should pay you.[77]

When word reached Paris of Voltaire's watchmaking industry, and of the relative cheapness of his high-quality products, many of the grand Parisian jewellers bought up Ferney watches and put their own names on them, with a mark-up which Voltaire reckoned at 50 per cent.[78] But in January 1772, Voltaire decided he needed to put this Paris trade on a more systematic footing, by setting up a regular sales agency; and he suggested to d'Argental that the agency should be run by Mme Lejeune, the wife of the bookseller, and notorious for her role in the book-smuggling escapade of December 1766.[79] Voltaire's suggestion was evidently accepted because the following month he sent Mme Lejeune a consignment of watches made by Guillaume-Henri Valentin, one of the master watchmakers at Ferney; he told her that Valentin would supply her at cost, and she could sell them at any price she chose, and keep the profit.[80]

Unfortunately, Lejeune and his wife did not keep their side of the bargain, and a year later, in January 1773, Voltaire wrote to d'Argental to complain. 'I present a petition in the name of Valentin and company, against Lejeune and his wife, to whom they have long entrusted several watches. Master Valentin has written them several letters without getting a single reply. I urgently beg my angels to speak to Lejeune, and sort out the matter. Valentin's company is the least rich in Ferney, it has suffered several setbacks, and another would bring it down.'[81] Mme Lejeune was evidently accepting consignments of Valentin's watches, but whether or not she was succeeding in selling them to customers in Paris, it seems that she was not paying Valentin for them.

It was not just Mme Lejeune who was not paying, however. As we saw, Louis XV had agreed in 1770 to take six of the first watches made at Ferney, but three years later, he had still not paid for them.[82] 'My colony,' Voltaire wrote to d'Alembert, 'had supplied watches decorated with diamonds for the marriage of M. le Dauphin. They have not been paid for, and the consequences fall on me. What I feel about these fine gentlemen of Paris is indescribable. These fine gentlemen are right to detest *la philosophie*, which condemns and despises them.'[83] The following month he again complained, to Richelieu, that the watches had still not been paid for; he admitted that the enamel portraits painted on the cases had been badly executed, but he nevertheless asked for payment. 'If you could push your kindness as far as to have payment made for these two watches to Messrs Céret & Dufour, I should be most obliged. They are the poorest members of the colony.' [84]

There were also setbacks in the export trade. 'A marquis of Genoa named Vial or Viale made an approach to one of our manufacturers, and unfortunately to the poorest, and he ordered watches and jewels for the court of Morocco. I was very mistrustful of Moroccans and of marquises. The noble Genoese Viale did not behave nobly; he went completely bankrupt, and did not even deign to reply to the letters which my craftsmen sent him. This sad adventure falls entirely on me, and it is not the only one. The craftsmen in question are called Servand & Boursault. They are very honest people, fathers of families.'[85] It would appear from the rueful admission 'This sad adventure falls entirely on me' that Voltaire expected that he personally would have to indemnify the firm of Servand & Boursault for their loss.

Of course, Valentin & Company, and Céret & Dufour, and Servand & Boursault could not all be the poorest members of Voltaire's colony; but when Voltaire was making some kind of tearful appeal, he was always liable to pathetic exaggeration.

When Mme Lejeune failed to pay for her watches, Voltaire did what he should have done from the beginning: he appointed as his Paris representative the man at the top of his profession, Jean-Antoine Lépine, the King's watchmaker.[86] (This Jean-Antoine Lépine was a brother-in-law of Pierre Augustin Caron de Beaumarchais who started life as a watchmaker, who became famous as a playwright and the author of *The Marriage of Figaro*, and who later financed the first posthumous edition of Voltaire's complete works.) Three months later, in January 1774, Lépine set up an office in a house in Ferney ('at my expense,' says Voltaire), and in June he despatched Joseph Tardy, also one of the King's watchmakers, to manage this Ferney office on a permanent basis. The watch trade between Ferney and Paris was evidently booming.[87]

Within a year of the launch of the Ferney watchmaking industry, in the spring of 1771, Voltaire plunged into an abrupt depression, since he feared that the viability of his enterprise would be undermined by a change in the tax rules. When he had originally moved to Ferney, he had secured tax exemptions from the authorities in Versailles, largely through his good relations with the then prime minister, the duc de Choiseul. But in December 1770, Choiseul suddenly fell from power, and Voltaire feared that the new ministry might be much less friendly; in particular he worried that the confiscation of his investments in French government assets a year earlier, by the abbé Terray, might be an ominous precedent.

In reality, there was no immediate sign that the new ministry, under Chancellor René-Nicolas de Maupeou, would be particularly unfriendly to the Ferney enterprise; but Voltaire was born and bred to the unpredictable realities of absolutism, and he was convinced that political and therefore commercial survival depended on patronage at court. As he told d'Argental in October 1771: 'My colony, which is no longer protected, causes me acute alarms.'[88]

Voltaire's fears were not entirely illogical. The watchmakers' general tax exemption, like Voltaire's interest-free loans, may have been a necessary incentive at the beginning, to help them launch their businesses. But it was less easy to justify in economic terms after they had become financially successful. As we have seen, the take-off in sales terms was rapid, and by 1773 Voltaire was writing that 'the watchmakers whom I set up at great expense are doing a prosperous trade'.[89] And though at the start Voltaire had lent money to the watchmakers without interest, he did not go on doing so indefinitely. In 1776, when some of his leading watchmakers had become very prosperous, he charged interest of 7 per cent, which was substantially above the normal deposit rate for the time of 4 or 5 per cent.[90]

Despite the gruelling demands of the development of his watchmaking industry, Voltaire continued to write plays throughout the

1770s, as he had always done, but now with very little public success. If he was disappointed, he was not deterred. As he wrote to Mme du Deffand in 1772: 'I wanted to write verse as they wrote it a hundred years ago. I should like you to judge.'[91] He knew he must seem a little absurd, going on writing plays in old age, long after his work was out of fashion. 'You will tell me that it is quite ridiculous at my age to write plays for the theatre. I already know it all too well; but you should not rebuke a man for having a temperature. What else can one do in the middle of the snow, if not write tragedies?'[92]

Voltaire was much revived, in June 1772, by the arrival of a local acting troupe at the nearby theatre of La Châtelaine, on the border between Ferney and Geneva. 'We have a theatre company near the Geneva frontier, that is to say, very close to the city. But of course the pleasure of seeing provincial actors is not the same as being an actor oneself.' Yet according to his neighbour Mme Louise-Élisabeth Gallatin, Voltaire seems to have greatly enjoyed his visits to La Châtelaine.

> He is very well. Two days ago he went to the playhouse at La Châtelaine. They were putting on *Nanine* [by Voltaire]. The actors had announced that our friend would be there, and such a large crowd of people came that more than three hundred had to be turned away. Those who stayed had difficulty in seeing him, since they had put gauze round his box. He was pleased with the actors, and he made them come to him, so that he could tell them how to act *Adélaïde de Guesclin* [also by Voltaire], which they will put on next week. Since he didn't get ill from having been to *Nanine*, we hope to persuade him to go to *Adélaïde de Guesclin* as well.[93]

Voltaire was even more encouraged when he heard from Henri-Louis Lekain, the leading actor of the Comédie Française, that he planned to visit Ferney later that year.[94] But Voltaire warned him that the company at La Châtelaine would probably not be able to pay him more than 100 écus (£300) per performance.[95] In July Voltaire went again to La Châtelaine, to see a performance of *Zaïre*; the following day, he told d'Argental that the local actors had been excellent, and that their performance had made him weep.[96] He went to *Olympie* in August, another wonderful performance, he said, with a beautiful young actress ('completely new, completely simple, completely naïve'), and she too made him weep.[97] Tears, for Voltaire, were the touchstone of a tragedy.

In September 1772, Lekain arrived at Ferney, and stayed for a fortnight; he performed six times at La Châtelaine, in three of Voltaire's plays. Voltaire was full of enthusiasm, and at one performance was heard to shout: 'Bravo! Bravo!' He told d'Alembert that Lekain 'has enchanted the whole of Geneva'.[98] When Lekain left Ferney to return to Paris, he planned to stop off in Lyon to earn some extra money with a few freelance performances. Voltaire wrote to Richelieu to ask him to allow Lekain to delay his return until 12 October, but this time Richelieu would have none of it.[99] 'M. le maréchal de Richelieu,' Voltaire wrote to d'Argental, 'tells me that he will have him put in prison if he is not back in Paris by 4 October. This does not seem to me fair dealing, or true justice. You had always told me that he could return on the 8th and everyone would have been happy; he could easily reach Paris by 8 October'.[100]

In August 1772, Voltaire was busy writing and rewriting his new tragedy *Les Lois de Minos*, and he hoped that Richelieu (to whom he dedicated it) would arrange for it to be put on in the theatre at Bordeaux, if not in Paris. As governor of Guyenne in south-west France, as well as a patron of the Comédie Française, Richelieu was a key figure in the control of public theatre. But d'Alembert brutally disabused him on this score. D'Alembert loathed and despised Richelieu, describing him as 'an ancient doll' and a 'wizened prostitute', and he wrote to tell Voltaire the harsh truth about Richelieu's disloyalty.[101]

He asked Lekain to produce a list of twelve tragedies to be performed at the festivities of the court and at Fontainebleau. Lekain brought him the list, in which he had included, quite rightly, four or five of your pieces. Richelieu crossed them all out, with the exception of *L'Orphelin de la Chine* [*The Orphan from China*], which he had the kindness to keep. I leave you, my dear master, to make your own reflections on this subject. In truth, I am sorry that you should have been so deceived by a man so vile. If you wanted to seek support at court, you could choose a hundred people, the least of whom would command more credit and respect than him. You would be disgusted with your misplaced confidence in him, if you could see how far he is despised, even by his servants.[102]

Voltaire was shocked. 'If he is guilty of the little infamy of which you speak,' he replied, 'I admit I am a great dupe; but in my place you would have been just as great a dupe as I. The only lesson I shall draw from my deception will be to have no hope in future; but that, they say, is the fate of the damned. In the last resort, however, I have feelings; and I will confess that the treachery you tell me about causes me great pain.'[103]

In his distress, Voltaire turned for help to Mme de Saint-Julien, a young and charming woman, a regular visitor to Ferney, and the latest in a long line of Voltaire's affectionate female friends. She was also well connected at court.

Your friend, M. le maréchal de Richelieu, has inflicted the greatest pain on my heart, which has been so tenderly attached to him for more than fifty years. At first he overwhelms me with kindness about *Les Lois de Minos*, he has never been so enthusiastic; but the moment after he overwhelms me with his disgust, he treats me like his mistresses. Find him, speak to him, make him blush if he is guilty, make him turn again, bring me back my traitor.[104]

Despite what he now knew of Richelieu's brutal indifference, Voltaire continued to plead with him in his usual tone of servility. 'My hero is committed on his honour to protect my theatrical productions. I shall always count on your indulgence towards me. *Les Lois de Minos* and *Sophonisbe* are spectacles with plenty of action. I therefore reiterate my very humble and very pressing prayer to you, to be kind enough to order our masters, the actors, to perform these two plays towards the end of your year in office.'[105]

Richelieu simply ignored Voltaire's reproachful appeal. D'Argental urged Voltaire not to be so imprudent as to betray any ill-humour towards Richelieu, but instead to turn to the duc d'Aumont and the duc de Duras, who were due to take over from Richelieu in the New Year, as the duty supervisors of the Comédie Française. Voltaire followed his advice, and *Sophonisbe* was duly performed at the Comédie Française in January 1774. It was a flop, however, hissed and booed, and taken off after four performances.

But Voltaire's disappointment with his tragedies was offset by the growth of his watchmaking industry, and the equally rapid growth of the Ferney village and estate.[106] 'Florian is beautifying Ferney by bringing here his third wife.* I have built him a little house which is exactly like a pavilion at Marly, but even prettier and cooler. We have four or five houses in this style; we are bringing up a little descendant of Corneille aged twelve [the daughter of Marie-Françoise Corneille], whom we have known since her birth. We are busy encouraging five or six hundred craftsmen, who will be very useful. That is my situation at the age of eighty, without a word of exaggeration.'[107]

The place continued to expand rapidly throughout that year, as witness the admiring description the following January, 1775, by Paul-Claude Moultou, a Protestant pastor from Geneva:

Ferney is a very fine château, solidly built, with magnificent gardens and terraces. Not a day passes but M. de Voltaire plants more trees, which he looks after himself. The village is composed of about eighty houses, all very well built. The ugliest, seen from the outside, are finer than the most superb of the villages in the Paris region. There are about eight hundred inhabitants. Three or four of the houses belong to good bourgeois citizens; the rest are for watchmakers, carpenters, artisans of every type. Of these eighty houses, at least sixty belong to M. de Voltaire. He is certainly the creator of that place; he does the most immense good.[108]

The reason why Voltaire was able to build so many houses, according to Moultou, was that his income about this time was in the

---

*Marie Elizabeth, sister of Mme Denis, fell ill in 1770, and died in February 1771. Her husband the marquis de Florian quickly remarried.

region of £150,000 a year; and since less than half of this was required for the running costs of the household, the remaining £90,000 or so could be spent on house-building and the development of the estate.[109]

In August 1775, Voltaire boasted: 'The other day we were twelve at table, all of us inhabitants of Ferney, each with his house and his garden. We have several libraries. I may add that, in addition to the *philosophes*, we have a colony of watchmakers who do a trade of about five hundred thousand francs a year. Right now, we are building a dozen new houses.'[110] And by the end of the year, Voltaire was getting so carried away by the rapidity of the development of Ferney that he was beginning to sound like a property speculator. 'I am convinced that our property will double in price within a year. It is already starting to be worth much more than before. The simple term *freedom of trade* revives every kind of industry, lifts all hopes, makes the earth more fertile.'[111]

By 1776, Voltaire decided to build a new theatre in a large storehouse barn in the village.[112] One reason was that he now found that the theatre at La Châtelaine, six miles away, was too far for him to go; moreover, for the past six years his former theatre in the château of Ferney had been given over to various other activities, such as the manufacture of silk, lace and watches.

In any case, Ferney's development was now so rapid that it was becoming more of a town than a village. It was perhaps partly for this reason that Voltaire decided to create the new theatre in the town rather than bring the old theatre in the château back into service. Moreover, Voltaire's health was becoming increasingly fragile and he probably no longer wanted, at his age, to have to put up with large crowds of spectators traipsing through his home.

The plan was that the troupe from La Châtelaine would perform in the new Ferney theatre two days a week, and in their own theatre the rest of the time.[113] Gallier de Saint-Géran, the director of the troupe from La Châtelaine, proposed that Voltaire should invite Henri-Louis Lekain to come down from Paris to inaugurate his new theatre, in the summer of 1776. Voltaire passed on the request to d'Argental, and it was accepted by the authorities: Lekain duly arrived in July, and gave a number of performances in the new Ferney theatre.

One of the other causes for which Voltaire had canvassed so persistently in recent years, initially through his friend the duc de Choiseul, the then prime minister, was the preservation of various forms of tax exemption. He had managed to secure a number of concessions for the province in 1770, but he knew that once they heard of the growing prosperity of Ferney and its watchmakers, the tax farmers would be bound to try to take their cut. And so it proved: by 1774 they were already sniffing around, and provoking panic among the watchmakers. 'Despite the kindnesses of M. Turgot [finance minister in the new government], the officials of the new gold assay tax office have been here, upsetting the colony which I set up at such expense, and a hundred fathers of families are close to abandoning me.'[114]

Fortunately, however, Turgot offered the region of Gex two significant economic concessions: the removal of the high tax on salt, exacted through a private monopoly operated by the tax farmers; and the release of the inhabitants from the traditional *corvée* or community service labour, mainly for road maintenance.[115] The local inhabitants were delighted by the lifting of the *corvée*; the irony, however, was that the roads at Ferney were suffering from a shortage of labour: 'Two of our labourers are dead, and there are almost no others. We have only watchmakers here.'[116]

Salt in France was a monopoly commodity controlled by the tax farmers, and they kept its price artificially high, much higher than in, say, Geneva. Inevitably, the tax farmers were furious at Turgot's proposal to remove their monopoly, and they demanded compensation for loss of revenue. At the same time, the employees of the tax farmers were just as furious at the prospective loss of their jobs, and they engaged in gangster-like intimidation of the local population.[117]

At first, the tax farmers demanded compensation of £50,000 a year. Voltaire proposed offering £15,000;[118] Turgot supported the tax farmers in principle, and proposed a figure of £30,000 a year.[119] By December, with time running out, Voltaire decided it was necessary to give way, and on 12 December 1775, he went in person to Gex, to recommend Turgot's figure to a large public meeting of the provincial Estates-General. Pierre-Michel Hennin, French Resident at Geneva, described the event to his minister:

M. de Voltaire thought that some people would oppose the useful project for which he had worked with such zeal, and he resolved to go to the Estates. When he arrived, they made him sit, and everyone gathered round him. He said to them: '*Gentlemen, we have many favours to ask, but I believe that above all we should accept the good offer which has been made to us today, and which we have so long asked for.*' He then read a letter from M. Turgot. The representative of the clergy then thanked M. de Voltaire in the most honest manner, for his care for the province, and declared that his order was unanimously in favour of accepting the terms of the decree of the Council; the other orders did the same, they drew up the protocol, and the deputies signed it; they asked M. de Voltaire to help the Estates with his advice on the allocation of the tax [for paying the £30,000], and to continue looking after the interests of the province.

He went out, and as soon as the people gathered in Gex knew that the project had been accepted, there were cries of *Vive le Roi, Vive M. de Voltaire*, they decorated his horses and filled his carriage with laurels and flowers. He was escorted on horseback by his bourgeoisie from Ferney; and in all the villages through which he passed there were the same acclamations and the same profusion of laurels. This would have been a really brilliant day for a man indifferent to the happiness of his fellows or to his own glory, and even more for M. de Voltaire who, one can say, combines these two sentiments to excess.[120]

Two days later, on Thursday 14 December 1775, Voltaire wrote to his friend Mme de Saint-Julien:

I have never had a more beautiful story to relate. Everything was done, everything was written as I wished. A thousand inhabitants of the region were close by, listening; and they sighed for this moment, as if for their salvation, despite the £30,000. There was a cry of joy throughout the whole province.

But you will see that there is no pure joy in this world. For while we were gently passing our time in thanking M. Turgot, and while the whole province was busy drinking, the gendarmes of the tax farmers, whose time runs out on 1 January, had orders to sabotage us. They marched about in groups of fifty, stopped all the vehicles, searched all the pockets, forced their way into all the houses, and caused every kind of damage there in the name of the King, and made the peasants buy them off with money. I cannot conceive why the people did not ring the tocsin against them in all the villages, and why they were not exterminated. It is very strange that the *ferme générale*, with only another fortnight left for them to keep their troops here in winter quarters, should have permitted or even encouraged them in such criminal excesses. The decent people were very wise, and held back the ordinary folk who wanted to throw themselves on these brigands, as if on mad wolves.[121]

This meeting of the Estates-General was a personal triumph for the eighty-one-year-old Voltaire, and a spectacular tribute to his moral standing as a benefactor, not just of the inhabitants of his own estates at Ferney, but of the province as a whole. But when, in recognition of his efforts, the Estates-General gave Voltaire the honorific title of *Commissionnaire*, to advise them on taxation, Louis-Gaspard Fabry, the mayor of Gex, was eaten up with envy, and accused Voltaire behind his back of trying to take over the running of the whole province.[122]

Of course, the idea was ridiculous: but the irony of the situation was that Voltaire, who had previously argued that the watchmakers needed tax exemption for the sake of their economic viability, now proposed a progressive tax regime to finance the salt tax compensation, in which rich watchmakers would pay more than poor peasants. He wrote to François de Fargès de Polizy, the deputy finance minister:

May I beg you, Sir, in an idle moment, just to ask M. le Contrôleur Général to have a look at this little article, in which I ask on behalf of our Estates-General the favour of leaving them the freedom to allocate the £30,000 for the poor *fermiers généraux*.

The fact is that in general agriculture in our canton is a burden on the landowners, and that a man who has no team for ploughing his field, and who hires another man's plough and his labour, loses £12 per acre. A big merchant watchmaker can make £30,000 per year. Is it not right that he should contribute something to help the country which protects him? Everything comes from the earth, no doubt, it produces metals as well as wheat; but a watchmaker does not use 30 sous worth of copper and iron in the movement of a watch which he sells for fifty gold louis. As for the gold from which the case is made, and the diamonds with which it is often decorated, it is well known that our agriculture does not produce them.

We propose, Sir, to charge no more than six francs per head for each master watchmaker, and the same from the other merchants and innkeepers.[123]

Voltaire's phrase 'everything comes from the earth' was an allusion to the contemporary economic theory that all wealth ultimately derived from the land, and that therefore agriculture should bear the weight of all taxation. It was a convenient theory for those whose income did not derive from the land; but as Voltaire's analysis here demonstrates, it was increasingly absurd and indefensible in the emerging world of industrialisation and international trade.

In the summer of that year (1776), Voltaire reported with satisfaction the increasing prosperity of his colony: 'We currently have eighteen buildings under construction. It is like the *Thousand and One Nights*, and what makes it all the more fabulous is that the old man who has exhausted himself in all these frivolities has not asked for the smallest help from the government for the establishment of a colony which is now doing a trade of five or six hundred thousand francs a year.'[124]

That year, however, Turgot was removed from his position as *Contrôleur Général*, and after his departure the French authorities became increasingly keen to tax the prosperity of Voltaire's watchmaking industry in Ferney. In June, the Finance Ministry decided that the £30,000 needed for the salt buy-out must be provided two-thirds by the landowners and one-third (£10,000) by industry, that is to say, by the watchmakers of Ferney. After protests, the watchmakers' share was reduced to £6,000. But by October 1776, ten months after the negotiation of the new salt régime, Jacques Necker, the new finance minister, was moving to revoke the Ferney watch-makers' general tax exemptions, and to tax them like any Frenchmen. Voltaire assumed that political and national prejudice was at work: Jacques Necker was a Protestant financier from Geneva, and Voltaire took it for granted that the move was designed to prevent unfair competition.[125]

A week later, the situation had worsened.

Our colony of Ferney is not so happy, it is persecuted, almost annihilated. All the craftsmen are going off, one after the other, because M. l'Intendant [the governor of Burgundy] has re-imposed the old feudal tax [*la taille*] and the community service labour [*la corvée*]. The five hundred thousand francs that I spent on the houses I built are just five hundred thousand francs thrown into the Lake of Geneva. I am in danger of dying as I ought have lived, in the poverty associated with the trade of a man of letters.[126]

In practice, of course, the watchmaking colony of Ferney was not almost annihilated, though the summer of 1776 was probably the high-watermark of its prosperity. Watches went on being made there for as long as Voltaire was alive, and even after he died, two years later, the industry continued to survive. It would not start to decline until the nineteenth century.

15
Last Campaigns
1770–78

By the end of the 1760s, Voltaire was suffering from campaign fatigue, and he did not want to get involved in any more 'human rights' cases. Or so he said. Through his intense efforts between the years 1762 and 1765, he had secured the spectacular if posthumous rehabilitation of Jean Calas. The parallel case of the Sirven family proved much slower and more difficult, and was not resolved for several more years. From 1765 onwards, in addition to the long-drawn-out Sirven case, Voltaire had grappled painfully and fruit-lessly with two new and in some ways even more horrific affairs: the cases of the Chevalier de La Barre and of Lally Tollendal. So when, in August 1769, he learned of a new case of a scandalous miscarriage of justice, he no longer felt that he had the energy to challenge it. Not surprisingly: he was seventy-five years old.

The new case was that of a well-to-do farmer called Martin, from the village of Bleurville, near Bar-le-Duc, east of Paris. In 1769, a man was murdered on the highway not far from Martin's house. A footprint on the scene seemed to match one of Martin's shoes. A wit-ness saw the murderer run off. When this witness was confronted with Martin, he did not recognise him. But Martin was quoted as saying: 'Thank God! He did not recognise me!' It was on the strength of these ambiguous but damaging words, but apparently without any other evidence in confirmation, that a local judge con-demned Martin to be tortured, and then to be put to death by being broken on the wheel. The sentence was confirmed by the central criminal court in Paris, and carried out that summer. Very shortly afterwards, however, on 26 July 1769, another man, condemned to death for a different crime, confessed just before his execution (also by being broken on the wheel) that it was he who had been guilty of the earlier murder as well.

Some preliminary enquiries into the Martin affair convinced Voltaire that a grotesque injustice had indeed taken place. But he decided that he could not take it on because he already had too much on his plate. 'I have enough with Sirvens, without getting mixed up with Martins as well. I cannot be the Don Quixote of all those who are hanged or broken on the wheel. On every side I see nothing but the most barbarous injustices: Lally and his gag, Sirven, Calas, Martin, the chevalier de La Barre; they sometimes appear before me in my dreams. People seem to believe that our century is merely ridiculous; in fact, it is horrible.'[1]

Even though Voltaire said that he had decided not to campaign on behalf of Martin, he nevertheless continued his enquiries for several weeks, through his friend d'Alembert, though his great-nephew the lawyer Alexandre d'Hornoy, and through his lawyer friend Charles-Frédéric-Gabriel Christin, until he was satisfied that he had got to the bottom of the facts of the matter. It seems possible that the vigour of Voltaire's enquiries may, indirectly, have acted like a campaign on Martin's behalf. At all events, by the following spring, in March 1770, he noted: 'The attorney-general is engaged in rehabilitating Martin. Yet Martin himself is still broken, and his family is still reduced to beggary.'[2]

Despite Voltaire's desire not to get involved in any additional campaigning, events conspired against him. Later that year, another judicial scandal erupted, as horrific as it was flagrant, and Voltaire was unable to remain silent. This was the case of François-Joseph Monbailli, of St-Omer in northern France, who was accused of having killed his mother. Monbailli and his wife Anne-Thérèse lived with Monbailli's widowed mother, and slept in a room next to her bedroom. On the morning of 27 July 1770, the mother was found dead. She was widely known to be a heavy drinker of spirits, and probably died from a fall, perhaps caused by apoplexy; yet rumour insistently put it about that she had been murdered by Monbailli and his wife.

No meaningful evidence against the defendants was produced in the local court of St-Omer. As for motive, it was clear that they could not have killed the mother of Monbailli in the hope of inheritance, since she left more debts than assets. So the court of St-Omer judged that Monbailli should be held in prison until the necessary evidence could be found.

But popular clamour against Monbailli proved too strong: the public prosecutor of the superior court at Arras appealed against the decision of the court of St-Omer, and demanded a more severe sentence. Monbailli was submitted to torture, both '*ordinaire*' and '*extraordinaire*'; he continued to protest his innocence. It is not even clear if, apart from torturing Monbailli, the prosecution ever tried to find any significant evidence against him; it certainly produced none. Nevertheless, on 9 November 1770, the court of the Council of Arras condemned Monbailli and his wife to death.

Ten days later, on 19 November 1770, Monbailli was executed as a parricide: his right hand was cut off, his arms and legs were broken on the wheel, and his body was burned on a pyre. The execution of Monbailli's wife was postponed since she was pregnant.

Voltaire was alerted, and persuaded to intervene on behalf of the victims. It was a short, almost effortless campaign, because the prosecution case against Monbailli was so transparently non-existent. Voltaire appealed to the Chancellor, René-Nicolas de Maupeou, and in 1771 published (under his own name, significantly) a ten-page pamphlet called *La Méprise d'Arras* (The Error of Arras), in which he exposed the absurdity of the trial. The following spring, in May 1772, Mme Monbailli was acquitted and her husband 'rehabilitated'.

'You know the reparation they have made for the error of Arras. But what reparation! The judges should have gone on their knees to beg forgiveness from the widow of that innocent man, and they should have given her a pension of half their assets,'[3] he wrote indignantly to François Marin, who was now director of the *Gazette de France*.

Voltaire's next campaign was for the liberation of the serfs of Saint-Claude, and he pursued it for the next five years, until he was eighty-one; he got nowhere with it.

Saint-Claude is a small town in an area of six parishes in the Jura, not far from Ferney. When France had acquired the Franche-Comté from Spain, by the Treaties of Nijmegen in 1668–9, Louis XIV permitted the inhabitants to keep their traditional economic customs. One of these customs was feudal serfdom, and by a quirk of history it still survived into the eighteenth century in the case of a Benedictine monastery at Saint-Claude. In 1742 the monastery was dissolved, and replaced by an open community of some twenty canons of the Abbey of Saint-Claude; but the canons continued to enforce their rights of servitude over the local population of some twelve thousand people.

The essential principle of the serfdom of Saint-Claude was that all property, and the product of all work, and therefore ultimately all the inhabitants, belonged to the canons of Saint-Claude. Anyone who was born in Saint-Claude was a serf; if a man lived in Saint-Claude for a year, he became a serf; if a man or woman from outside married a serf, he or she became a serf; if a man moved away from the area, his 'property' was forfeit; if a son failed to live in his father's house and eat at his father's table throughout the father's life, then at the father's death he would be driven out of the house. In short, as Voltaire repeatedly said, it was a régime of legalised slavery.

Voltaire's intervention on behalf of the twelve thousand serfs of Saint-Claude in 1770 coincided with his involvement that same year with the project to develop Versoix as a trading port. It was in some sense part and parcel of his growing preoccupation, not just with the welfare and improvement of Ferney and its estate, but more broadly with the economic and social development of his region as a whole.

In 1770, Voltaire set his lawyer friend Charles-Frédéric-Gabriel Christin, who had originally come from Saint-Claude and was now Voltaire's bailiff at Ferney, to work up the legal case for the serfs. With Christin's help, he wrote two pamphlets and numerous letters appealing for the abolition of serfdom in the Jura, which he sent to the French government; he badgered the duc de Choiseul, he badgered the duchesse de Choiseul. In vain; they did not respond.[4]

When the duc de Choiseul fell from power in December 1770, Voltaire did his best to get on good terms with the new key figure in the King's ministry, the Chancellor, Maupeou. He was delighted when Maupeou closed down the Parlements and sent all the lawyers and judges into exile, replacing them with newly appointed law-courts. He conveniently overlooked the fact that Maupeou had come from a long career as a leading judge in the Paris Parlement, and that it was he who had signed the decree confirming the death sentence on the chevalier de La Barre in 1766. Indeed, it was only much later, in 1775, that Voltaire learned just how decisive a role Maupeou had played in securing the necessary majority to enforce the death sentence on La Barre.[5]

Voltaire tried to stay on friendly personal terms with the Choiseuls, now exiled to their estate. But the duchesse de Choiseul reacted to Voltaire's worldly adaptability with angry contempt; she wrote to Mme du Deffand: 'How pitiful he is, this Voltaire, how cowardly! He excuses himself, he accuses himself (*il s'excuse, il s'accuse*),* he drowns in his own spittle, as a result of having spat when he shouldn't have. He sings a recantation, he blows hot and cold. He does not know what he is doing; he is disgusting and pitiful.'[6]

Voltaire wrote to Mme du Deffand to protest his innocence of any disloyalty to the Choiseuls:

I do not in the least believe I am failing them, if I detest absurd and bloody pedants. Like the whole of Europe, I loathed the assassins of the chevalier de La Barre, I loathed the assassins of Calas, I loathed the assassins of Sirven, and I loathed the assassins of the comte de Lally [in each case, the old Parlements]. They have done nothing but evil, and they have produced nothing but evil. You hate the *philosophes*, and I hate the bourgeois tyrants. I have forgiven you your fury against *philosophie*, so forgive me mine against the gang of lawyers.[7]

It was not often that Voltaire allowed his rage to spew out so violently.

When the dust had settled at court, Voltaire returned to his

---

*cf. the modern French expression 'Qui s'excuse, s'accuse' (whoever excuses himself, accuses himself).

campaign on behalf of the serfs of Saint-Claude. He wrote to Chancellor Maupeou on the subject, and in 1771 and 1772 he drafted three more formal appeals which he sent to the government. To no avail: Maupeou simply strung him along with soft and soothing words.[8] After the death of Louis XV, Voltaire sent a new appeal to the French government in 1775; and another in 1776; still in vain.[9]

In January 1778, four months before his death, Voltaire wrote to Christin: 'I tremble on every side for our poor dear people of Saint-Claude. I am really afraid that they may be devoured by the Pharisees and publicans. Where will they find refuge? They have no protection, no asylum. I am horrified and discouraged by everything I see. I shall soon die, detesting the persecutors, and loving you.'[10]

In 1779, the year after Voltaire died, Louis XVI issued an edict freeing all the serfs in the royal domains; unfortunately, the edict did not apply to property belonging to the Church, so the twenty canons of Saint-Claude still retained their feudal rights. The serfs of Saint-Claude were not finally freed until the Revolution, in 1789; their descendants put up a statue of Voltaire in Saint-Claude nearly a hundred years later, in 1887, in recognition of his efforts on their behalf.

After 1770, Voltaire did not engage in any new 'human rights' cases, but he did attempt, over the next few years, to resuscitate two of the central cases of the 1760s, those of La Barre and Lally Tollendal. He was now in his late seventies.

In all of Voltaire's campaigns, the case which had moved him most was that of the nineteen-year-old Jean-François Le Febvre, chevalier de La Barre, executed in 1766 for blasphemy. At the time, he had made little effort to get the verdict and sentence quashed: he had exposed the scandal in his pamphlet *Relation de la Mort du Chevalier de La Barre*,[11] but it seemed to have no effect, and Voltaire went no further.

Seven years later, however, in 1773, he started a new campaign of rehabilitation; not primarily for the dead La Barre, but for La Barre's young friend Gaillard d'Étallonde, who had escaped to Prussia before the trial started, and who had been condemned to death *in absentia*.

Gaillard d'Étallonde was now pursuing a successful career as an officer in the Prussian army, and he was in little danger of any judicial pursuit by the French authorities. But his death sentence *in absentia* meant that he had lost his legal rights in France, and in particular his right to inherit the property bequeathed to him by his dead mother. In order to recover those rights, he needed a legal rehabilitation through a reversal of the Abbeville verdict. In 1773, he asked Voltaire to help him. Voltaire persuaded the King to give him a year's leave of absence, and invited him to come and stay at Ferney, to pursue his case in France. D'Étallonde arrived at Ferney in April 1774, and stayed there for sixteen months, until August 1775.

The main difficulty Voltaire faced, in this case as in every other, was that the law-courts refused to release the trial documents. Eventually, by dint of harassing friends and lawyers in Abbeville and Paris, Voltaire succeeded in accumulating 6,000 pages of trial records. But he admitted in January 1775 that 'this is not nearly enough', for he had come to the conclusion that he could not get the verdict overturned unless he could prove that Belleval and Duval de Soicourt had manipulated the trial and suborned the witnesses.[12] 'Such a trial would last four or five years, would exhaust the purses of the litigants and the patience of the judges, and I should be dead of decrepitude before we should have obtained a judgement which would put things right. The revision of the Calas affair lasted three years; that of Sirven lasted seven years; and I shall probably be dead in six months.'[13]

After a while, it began to seem possible that d'Étallonde could secure a royal pardon as an act of clemency; but this would involve some humiliating plea-bargaining, and Voltaire was determined not to settle for anything less than the overturning of the original verdict. However, this would require overturning the original verdict on La Barre as well, and that would be much harder.

Voltaire wrestled with these difficulties for well over a year. In the summer of 1775 he composed an appeal to the French King, ostensibly written by d'Étallonde, under the title *Cri du Sang Innocent* (Cry of Innocent Blood), which was based in part on the 6,000-page trial records, and in which he denounced the scandal of the 1766 trial.[14] Voltaire was quite nervous about how this pamphlet would be received at court: Louis XV had died the previous year, and one of the first acts of the new King, Louis XVI, had been to recall the old Parlements which had briefly been exiled by Maupeou. Since it was the old Parlements which had been responsible for the original verdicts on Lally and La Barre, Voltaire feared that the new ministry might react badly to any appeal against those verdicts. So he released only a handful of copies of the *Cri du Sang Innocent*, and distributed them privately to a few trusted friends, including d'Argental, d'Alembert and Condorcet, as well as to Anne Robert Jacques Turgot, Louis XVI's new finance minister and one of Voltaire's old acquaintances.

But these copies were never delivered because they were seized by the postal censors. When Voltaire learned of this, he was highly alarmed and wrote to d'Alembert:

Your letter of 11 July has petrified me. You say that you have not heard any news from me for a long time. I see that the packets I sent to M. de Vaines [a senior official in Turgot's ministry] have not been delivered. There was one for you, and another for M. Condorcet. Perhaps my rather bold appeal might not be well received at the present time. It is designed to be read by fair and enlightened people more than by lawyers; and perhaps it should not be known to Church people. You cannot imagine how anxious this makes me.[15]

In fact, no great harm came from the *Cri du Sang Innocent*, but no good either: the King simply ignored Voltaire's appeal. A month later Frederick decided that, since Voltaire seemed to be making no progress in his appeal for d'Étallonde, his young officer had been on leave long enough; and at the end of August 1775, Voltaire sent him back to Prussia and his army career.

In 1787, that is, twenty-one years after the original Abbeville trial, Gaillard d'Étallonde made a new application for his rehabilitation in France. This time he was offered a deal: he could have his sentence reversed, but the price was to be a recantation and a repudiation of his offences. D'Étallonde duly obliged, and for good measure threw in a denunciation of Voltaire's malign influence on him and on his young friends. In December 1788, his sentence was formally wiped out by the Parlement of Paris. Not long afterwards, Gaillard d'Étallonde died; he was only thirty-nine. Voltaire did not witness this moral betrayal, for by that time he had already been dead more than ten years.

In the case of Lally Tollendal, Voltaire's original campaign had come to a halt in 1766 for lack of information. It was not until four years later that he was prompted to take up the case again, by the appearance of a certain chevalier Trophime Gérard Lally-Tollendal, Lally's nineteen-year-old natural son. Young Lally-Tollendal had decided to try to secure the rehabilitation of his father, and in 1770 he sent Voltaire a long report, refuting point by point all the accusations against Lally; yet his illegitimate birth disqualified him from any formal attempt to seek legal redress. His first step had to be to get himself legitimised as Lally's son, which he achieved in 1772.

He then turned again to Voltaire for support, and Voltaire undertook to help and advise him. As in the Sirven affair, progress was extremely slow. But by this time, public opinion was beginning to be influenced by Voltaire's writings on the subject, in his updated history of the reign of Louis XV and his *Fragments sur l'Inde*. In 1776, Voltaire received a long letter from an eyewitness in Pondicherry, confirming that Lally had not in fact sold out to the English, as had been claimed at his trial, and that his actions had been fully justified in the prevailing difficult circumstances of the Seven Years War. Armed with this new information, young Lally-Tollendal lodged a petition for the quashing of the Lally verdict. In 1777, the King's Council ordered the opening of an enquiry; and on 25 May 1778, it voted, by a large majority, to overturn the Lally verdict.

And yet this did not automatically lead to rehabilitation for Lally: for that to happen, as in the Calas and Sirven affairs, the case had to be retried. It *was* retried, in Normandy, two years later, in 1780; but the Rouen Parlement confirmed the original verdict of the Paris Parlement. Young Lally-Tollendal did not give up, and he secured a second quashing, and another retrial, in Burgundy three years later, in 1783; but the Dijon Parlement again confirmed the original verdict. In fact, Lally Tollendal was never formally rehabilitated: the Parlements which had repeatedly sentenced him to death were swept away, six years later, by the Revolution. Although, in old age, Voltaire largely gave up his individual 'human rights' campaigning, he made one last effort to grapple with the general problem of penal reform. In February, 1777, the *Gazette de Berne* offered a prize of 50 louis, provided anonymously by a member of the Société Economique de Berne, for the best essay on the reform of criminal law. When Voltaire learned of the project, he immediately doubled the prize money, and set to work to compose an essay on the subject himself. He completed his sixty-page treatise, entitled *Le Prix de la Justice et de l'Humanité* (The Prize of Justice and Humanity), towards the end of that year, when he was eighty-three.[16]

Voltaire had previously published two general works on aspects of the penal system, his *Traité sur la Tolérance* 'on the occasion of the death of Jean Calas', in 1762; and his *Commentaire sur le livre des Délits et des Peines*, the commentary on the seminal work of penal reform by Cesare Bonesana, marquis de Beccaría, in 1766. He had also published a number of other works of general relevance to the subject, though specifically concerned with the details of individual cases: the *Pièces Originales*, of 1762, setting out the Calas case; the *Relation de la Mort du Chevalier de La Barre*, of 1766; and the *Avis au Public sur les Parricides imputés aux Calas et aux Sirven*, also of 1766, in which he relaunched the appeal for the Sirvens; and of course the more recent *Méprise d'Arras*.

In his new work, Voltaire returned to many of the ideas familiar in his previous books, as well as in those of authors like Montesquieu and Beccaría, not to mention a number of English writers: the idea that the law is made by men and not by God, and can therefore be changed by men; the idea that the law must be proportional; that it must be socially useful; that it is better to prevent crime than to punish; that it is better to avoid capital punishment; that torture should be virtually always avoided; that the accused should have access to a legal defence; that the innocent should be protected.

But Voltaire's views on penal reform, though well ahead of his time, and certainly far ahead of the practices of his time, were nevertheless more cautious than, say, those of Beccaría. He went much further than he had done before in condemning torture, but not quite all the way, and also in condemning capital punishment, but not as far as Beccaría. The main characteristics of the essay are typically Voltairean: it is liberal, anecdotal, combative, sceptical, lively, episodic, disputatious, rhetorical, and in the last resort improvisational. It was more of a tract for prompting questions about the defects in existing legal systems than a comprehensive and systematic programme of reform. In short, the significance of this, 'the most comprehensive and the most radical' of Voltaire's legal works,[17] may lie less in the details of the essay than in the fact that Voltaire was still, after a quarter of a century, campaigning for a reform of the French justice system.

In 1776, Voltaire opened his new theatre in Ferney, and Henri-Louis Lekain came down from Paris to inaugurate it. On the surface, the opening was a great success, but it seems clear that Voltaire did not really enjoy Lekain's visit. 'Everything worked out much better than I could have hoped. Lekain came and made Ferney famous. But miserable me, I scarcely saw any of these festivities even once. I was, and am, not only in a crisis of business and grief, but weighed down with maladies which are besieging my end.'[18]

Voltaire blamed his ill-humour on his deteriorating health. What was really upsetting him, however, was the increasingly painful contrast between the steady decline in the popularity of his own rather old-fashioned and formalistic tragedies, and the growing fashion in Paris for Shakespeare's plays, a fashion that had recently been stimulated by the publication of the first two volumes of a complete translation of the plays by Pierre Prime Félicien Le Tourneur.

Ever since he had first come upon them during his English exile fifty years earlier, Voltaire had been haunted by Shakespeare's plays. Even at that time, he had felt a deep ambivalence towards Shakespeare, with a mixture of admiration for the beauty of his language, his brilliance and inventiveness, and contempt for his vulgarity and his failure to observe any of the formal rules of dramatic discipline.

Here is what Voltaire had written about Shakespeare in 1734, in the *Letters Concerning the English Nation* which he published after his exile in England. Voltaire wrote two-thirds of this book in English, including Letter XVIII quoted below.

Shakespear boasted a strong, fruitful Genius: He was natural and sublime, but had not so much as a single Spark of good Taste, or knew one Rule of the Drama. I will now hazard a random, but, at the same Time, true Reflection, which is, that the great Merit of this Dramatic Poet has been the Ruin of the *English* Stage. There are such beautiful, such noble, such dreadful Scenes in this Writer's monstrous Farces, to which the Name of Tragedy is given, that they have always been exhibited with great Success. Time, which only gives Reputation to Writers, at last makes their very Faults venerable. Most of the whimsical, gigantic Images of this Poet, have, thro' Length of Time, acquir'd a Right of passing for sublime.[19]

Over the years, the element of contempt in Voltaire's attitude to Shakespeare gained the upper hand, and by 1776 had hardened into almost hysterical denunciation. In July of that year, Voltaire wrote to d'Argental to report the arrival of Lekain, but virtually the whole of his letter was devoted to a frothing condemnation of Shakespeare and of the new translations by Le Tourneur.

I must tell you how upset I am for the honour of the theatre, against a certain Tourneur, who is said to be Secretary of the Office for Publishing (*La Librairie*), but who does not seem to me the Secretary of good taste. Have you read two volumes by this miserable fellow, in which he wants to make us treat Shakespeare as the only model of true tragedy? He calls him *the god of the theatre*. He sacrifices all Frenchmen, without exception, to his idol, as they used to sacrifice pigs to Ceres in the old days. He does not even deign to mention Corneille and Racine; these two great men are merely wrapped up in the general proscription, without their names even being mentioned.

What is frightful is that this monster has a following in France; and the height of calamity and horror is that it was I who once was the first to speak of this Shakespeare, it was I who was the first to show the French some pearls that I had discovered in his enormous dung-heap.[20]

Ten days later, Voltaire talked with Lekain, and he concluded that the situation on the Shakespeare front was even worse than he had thought. As he wrote to d'Argental:

My dear angel, the abomination of desolation* is in the temple of the Lord. Lekain, who is just as angry as you, tells me that all the youth in Paris are on the side of Le Tourneur, that the scaffolds and brothels of the English stage are taking over the theatre of Racine and the beautiful scenes of Corneille, that nothing grand and decent has been left in Paris by the harlequins from London, and that finally they are going to put on a tragedy in prose, in which there is a company of butchers who will have a marvellous effect. I have seen the end of the reign of reason and taste.[21]

So great was Voltaire's rage, in the summer of 1776, that he had rather lost interest in Lekain's visit, and was working on a full-scale denunciation, not of Le Tourneur, but of Shakespeare. This was his *Lettre à l'Académie Française*, which he hoped would be read out at a formal session of the Académie on 25 August, the Feast of Saint Louis, and therefore the official feast-day of Louis XVI. But his first draft was so violent that d'Alembert, as *secrétaire perpetuel*, had to ask him to soften it.

'I can see, my dear friend,' replied Voltaire, 'that I have not worked enough on my declaration of war against England; it can only work, through your skill in changing words, in short, by all your professional secrets. What is amusing in my text is surely the contrast between the admirable passages from Corneille and Racine, and the language of the brothel and the fish-market, which the divine Shakespeare continually puts into the mouths of his heroes and heroines. I leave it entirely up to you.'[22]

One of Voltaire's objections was that Shakespeare used crude words on stage. 'My principal intention, and the true aim of my work,' he wrote to his young protégé La Harpe, 'are that the public should be properly informed of the excesses and infamous turpitude of his language. Of course, one cannot say out loud in the Louvre

*Daniel 9:27; Matthew 24:15

what one says every day so boldly in London: M. d'Alembert will not abase himself by singing out, before the ladies, *the two-backed beast, son of a whore, piss, deflower*, etc. But he can pause at these sacramental words, and by suppressing the word itself, alert the public that he dare not translate Shakespeare in all its energy.'[23]

After some cuts and revisions, Voltaire's *Lettre* was agreed by the members of the Académie Française and read out by d'Alembert in his little gravelly voice[24] at a formal public session. The *immortels* were so entertained that d'Alembert had to read out several passages more than once; but the English visitors present were not amused. The King was displeased, too, since he had given his official approval to Le Tourneur's project, and he refused permission for Voltaire's *Lettre* to be printed.[25]

All in all, the episode of the *Lettre à l'Académie Française* was an extraordinary manifestation of Voltaire's fixation with his ideal of rule-based and well-behaved verse drama. But Shakespeare, like Corneille, survived Voltaire's criticisms; in fact, Shakespeare's *Hamlet* has been performed more often at the Comédie Française than any of Voltaire's plays.

After the death of Louis XV, on 10 May 1774, Voltaire started thinking that he might now perhaps be able to return to Paris. Of course, he had alluded to the idea, on and off, on many previous occasions in his long exile near Geneva; but it had almost always been in wistful terms, implying that he knew it was not really possible. But as soon as the news reached him of Louis's death, he began to talk more seriously about going home to Paris, and he wrote to d'Argental almost immediately:

I do not want to die without having the consolation of having seen my angels. It is only my miserable health which can prevent me from making a little trip to Paris. There was a little trouble between me and the late departed [Louis XV], a trouble about which most of the public knew nothing, a verbal trouble, a trouble which leaves no trace behind. It seems to me that I am a sick man who can take the air anywhere, without a prescription from the doctors.

And yet, I should like it to be secret. I think it is easy to hide in the crowd. There will be so many great ceremonies, so many big troubles, that nobody will think about mine.[26]

Voltaire seems to be implying that his exile had been due to nothing more than a personal difference between him and the late King, and that therefore the death of the King had removed the only political obstacle to his return. If this is what he thought, he was deceiving himself. The court at Versailles continued to regard Voltaire as a troublesome and perhaps a dangerous individual; moreover the new King was afraid of Voltaire, and worried about the damage that he might do, not by returning to Paris, but just by dying at his home at Ferney.

In July 1774, two months after his accession, Louis XVI gave instructions that, on the death of Voltaire, the authorities should enter his château and seize all his manuscripts and other documents, and send them to Versailles for the personal attention of the King. These instructions were sent to Henri Bertin, the foreign minister, and to Pierre-Michel Hennin, the French government's representative in Geneva, among others.

For Hennin, these instructions were deeply embarrassing, both personally and politically. During his nine years as French Resident in Geneva, since 1765, he had been a frequent visitor to Ferney, and a warm friend of Voltaire; he had absolutely no desire to play the part of police bailiff after Voltaire's death. For three months he made no comment. Then, in October 1774, he wrote a long minute to Bertin, the foreign minister, giving a string of reasons why he thought the instructions as they stood were ill-advised and probably counter-productive.

First, he said, the authorities would find virtually no unpublished manuscripts. 'Knowing M. de Voltaire's turn of mind as I do, I dare assert that we should not find any of his manuscripts, apart from whatever he was working on at the moment of his death. For the past many years, scarcely has he started a work than the first sheets are already at the printer; he told me a hundred times that he had *emptied the sack*.' In addition, said Hennin, such an operation would

undoubtedly cause a large public scandal, as well as diplomatic friction with King Frederick of Prussia, Empress Catherine of Russia,
and the princes with whom he corresponded, when they learned
that their letters to Voltaire had simply been confiscated to satisfy the
curiosity of Louis XVI.[27]

Hennin proposed an alternative approach which would be more
diplomatic and less autocratic. On Voltaire's death, Mme Denis
should be instructed not to remove any of Voltaire's documents; she
should be urged to submit them all for examination by two familiar
friends whose task would be to winnow out any which might be
dangerous. Hennin suggested that these two friends should be himself and Henri Rieu, a Geneva man of letters and a frequent visitor
to Ferney. Hennin's counter-proposals received no formal reply. In
the end, the King's concern turned out to have been pointless: when
Voltaire died in 1778, he was in Paris, and almost all his letters and
other manuscripts were still at Ferney; but no attempt was made to
seize them.[28]

In the meantime, however, Voltaire started to have second
thoughts about going back to Paris, on the grounds that he was not
yet well enough. When he wrote to d'Argental in July 1774, two
months after the death of Louis XV, he again said he wanted to go to
Paris, but that his weakness and his business commitments would
force him to postpone the trip for another two months.[29] By the end
of the year, Voltaire's reluctance was becoming obvious. D'Argental
and other Paris friends wrote urging him to visit them, but Voltaire
reacted by shrinking back from the effort and the strain.

Ah! My dear angel, my dear angel! I must rebuke you. M. de Thibouville,
M. de Chabanon, Mme du Deffand, all tell me that I am coming to see
you in the spring. Yes, I want to come, but I shall only go to see you,
dear angel that you are. I cannot show myself to others than you. I am deaf
and blind, or just about. I pass three-quarters of the day in my bed, and the
rest beside the fire. I always have to have on my head a large bonnet, without which my brain would be exposed. I take medicine about three times
a week, and I speak with great difficulty, having no more teeth, Thank
God, that I have eyes and ears. Judge, according to this fine portrait,

which is quite faithful, if I am in any state to go to Paris in a snowstorm.

I could not avoid going to the Académie, and I should die of cold at the first session. Could I close my door to all the riff-raff of the rascally so-called men of letters, who would have the stupid curiosity to come and look at my skeleton? And then, if I should have the idea, at the age of eighty-one, of dying in your city of Paris, just imagine what embarrassment, what scenes, what absurdity!

So be very careful, my dear angel, not to authorise this frightful rumour that I am coming to see you in the spring. Just say, as I shall say explicitly, that there is no truth in it.[30]

The following year, however, any travel plans Voltaire might have had were put on hold when Mme Denis went through a long period of illness. She was normally of robust health, and of more than robust appetite: in March 1774, Voltaire had regretted that he had been too unwell to eat some red partridges which had been sent to him, whereas Mme Denis, 'greedier than ever', had found them excellent.[31] So when she fell ill in April 1775, Voltaire was alarmed: 'Alas! Mme Denis has been in bed for a month, overwhelmed by an inflammation of the chest, and they have twice applied plasters. I am dying quite quietly in my own quarters without plasters and without doctors.'[32] (Voltaire could not resist the temptation to draw attention to his own ailments.)

Mme Louise-Suzanne Gallatin, Voltaire's neighbour and a warm friend, gives a touching commentary on his sadness at Mme Denis's illness. 'Our friend is well, but at this time he is in great grief, for his niece Mme Denis is very ill. She has been his friend, his companion, he never leaves her, and I am terribly sorry that I am in no position to go and share his grief. But I have news of him twice a day.'[33] At the end of April 1775, Mme Gallatin reported that Mme Denis was still very ill. 'Our friend is still in good health, but his niece is not yet out of danger. He never leaves her, and stays in her room all the day long, to make sure that she takes her medicine in his presence.'[34]

By early May 1775, Mme Denis was still ill, but her condition seems to have been improving. Voltaire wrote to Mme Saint-Julien: 'If you come to the furthest limits of Burgundy, you will give life to

Mme Denis and me. She is still rather ill, but as for me, I am incurable. You will find the uncle and the niece, each in their own corner of their hospital; and Father Adam in his attic, solely concerned with his breakfast, dinner and supper. Our house is a Lazar-house. Only you could make it bearable.'[35]

Father Adam did not enjoy his attic and his three square meals a day for very much longer, however. At the end of the following year, in November 1776, Voltaire drove him out, after nearly fourteen years as his resident almoner. Why he did so is not at all clear; in general, Voltaire was an inordinately indulgent and loyal employer. It seems that Adam had a tendency to quarrel with the servants, so perhaps it was Mme Denis who wanted him gone. At all events, Voltaire dismissed him abruptly, and he took refuge in the home of a nearby curé. He was seventy-one years old.

By the middle of May 1775, Mme Denis had recovered, and Voltaire was planning a large convalescence party for her. He wrote to Christin, his lawyer friend who was masterminding the campaign for the serfs of Saint-Claude. 'My dear friend, it is a pity that you are not at Ferney. You would take part in the fête which we are giving on the 18th for the convalescence of Mme Denis. We shall have infantry companies, and rosettes, and kettledrums, and violins, and three hundred guests sitting down in the open air.'[36] On 18 May 1775, the party duly took place, and Voltaire gave a joyous account of it: 'I can tell you about the very beautiful and very agreeable fête which our colony gave yesterday for the convalescence of Mme Denis. Not only did we have cavalry and infantry, cannons, kettledrums, side-drums, trumpets, oboes, clarinets, and a table with two hundred place-settings in the garden, but very pretty and very short toasts in verse and prose, and all followed by a little comedy.'[37]

By mid-August 1775, Voltaire told Alexandre d'Hornoy, Mme Denis's overweight lawyer nephew, that she now seemed to be quite well, and had completely recovered her appetite. 'Mme Denis has regained all her strength, and she is now managing four meals a day; she could even keep up with you.'[38] Two years later, Voltaire reported that his niece had stopped drinking: 'She has recovered her health, and will long keep it, because she has become sober (for fear of dying). She is the first woman I have seen exercise any self-control.'[39]

Once Mme Denis had recovered, in August 1775, Voltaire decided to adopt the line that he was perfectly free to go to Paris, but that he preferred to stay where he was. He wrote to Michel Paul Guy de Chabanon, a literary friend of d'Alembert:

My most amiable friend, I thank you right away for having wanted to cure me of my passion for my retirement, but I cling more than ever to this passion, which my age and my ailments have made necessary for me. What! You would like to invite an old hobbler into a ballroom? That is not sensible, my dear friend. In any case, you know perfectly well that you must let nobody suspect that I have the smallest need of any special favour to come and dance in your ballrooms with my crutches. There is nothing to prevent me from being so silly, if I wanted to. There has never been a formal ban out against me.[40]

By this time, the main obstacle to a return to Paris was not Mme Denis's health, but Voltaire's. For many years, Voltaire had talked constantly of his ailments. This was partly out of self-pity, partly out of self-mockery, and partly for the sake of narrative entertainment; he knew that the state of his health would be received, at his age, and from his distance in exile, as significant news, especially by those who cared for him. But his ailments were not imaginary. Like many people at that time, Voltaire was often ill, and his illnesses became more frequent and more acute as he got older. In his sixties, he complained of hydropsy, colic, scurvy, paralysis, snow blindness, loss of teeth and deafness, but above all of constipation (*l'article de la garderobe*), and he made a permanent running bawdy joke of all the many absurd, much-debated, and largely ineffectual remedies for dealing with it, from rhubarb and cassia to goat's milk.

Other people may not always have taken Voltaire's complaints of ill-health entirely seriously because what they noticed, much of the time, was his energy and above all his gaiety. Sometimes Voltaire claimed that he was only cheerful out of politeness. In 1766 he had written to Richelieu: 'I beg my hero's pardon for not writing in my own handwriting, and I beg his pardon again for not writing gaily;

but I am ill and sad. I have never been gay except by pretence. Whoever writes tragedies and histories must naturally be serious, however French he may be.'[41]

In 1768 he had written to the *philosophe* Jean-François Marmontel: 'My dear friend, the patriarch is still suffering; and if he is satirical in the intervals of his sufferings, he owes his life to the practice of gaiety, which is the best practice. But however much I may put on an appearance of gaiety, deep down I am very sad.'[42]

In 1770, after the visit of the sculptor Pigalle, Voltaire wrote to Melchior von Grimm: 'My dear prophet, M. Pigalle, though the best man in the world, is slandering me most strangely. He goes about saying that I am well, that I am as plump as a monk. I was just trying to be gay in his presence, exercising my smiling muscles to be polite to him.'[43]

It is possible that Voltaire's gaiety may have been partly assumed for the sake of politeness. A more plausible explanation is that Voltaire genuinely enjoyed company, and that the presence of other people amused and stimulated him: and there is no doubt that Voltaire enjoyed the company of women, especially when they were young and pretty.

There was a celebrated episode at the end of 1772, when an eighteen-year-old girl visited Voltaire in his room, and he fainted three times in succession. This girl was apparently notorious for the freedom of her conduct, and the rumour rapidly spread that Voltaire had passed out trying his luck with her. The story was almost incredible; but the literary world was so excited by the whiff of scandal that even Diderot, who seldom communicated with Voltaire, was moved to write to him. 'Sir and dear master, here they are saying unbelievable things about you. That a young woman should have had the vanity to sleep with the unique man of the century does not surprise me too much, I should even be edified. But you ... I could not believe that sort of madness, it must be just a story. Story or not, reassure us about your health.'[44]

Louise-Suzanne Gallatin was a regular and solicitous visitor to Ferney, and her frequent letters give a lively picture of Voltaire's health and happiness. Despite his frequent bouts of illness, the most remarkable feature of her accounts is his gaiety and vitality. Here is her story of a trip Voltaire made to Geneva in July 1775.

Our friend is very well. He came one day to Geneva. As there was a jam of carriages at the city gate, he got quite impatient, and got down from his carriage and walked as far as the gate-house. As soon as they saw him, everyone wanted to follow; and the crowd was so great that he had difficulty getting through. He had the pleasure of hearing people shout: '*I want to see him too!*' All the windows were full of people. I think he was very flattered.[45]

In his late seventies, Voltaire started to suffer from new ailments which were much more serious, including apoplexy, gout and urine retention (*strangurie*). Some of these conditions, like gout and strangury, were extremely painful and, for periods, incapacitating. It may be that his increasingly frequent attacks of strangury were in fact early symptoms of the prostate cancer which eventually killed him. When Voltaire complained of some ailment, whether it was indigestion, snow blindness, gout, insomnia, apoplexy, constipation, urine retention or piles, he may have been exaggerating, but he was generally not inventing. And in many cases, his symptoms were indirectly confirmed by others.

Voltaire's first attack of strangury seems to have occurred in February 1773, when he was seventy-nine. He complained to Gabriel Cramer, his printer, that his urine retention was preventing him from working: 'The old invalid cannot send you anything today, he has been bathed, bled, and dosed for a frightful strangury.'[46]

Voltaire's account was confirmed by Hennin.

M. de Voltaire is rather ill, and I begin to fear for him. Two weeks ago he got up in the middle of the night, when it was very cold, without stockings and without underwear, to light his fire and work. He caught cold, which attacked his bladder, and from there he had a retention of urine. He treated himself in his own way for the next four days, and when they sent for [Doctor] Cabanis, he had a high fever, an inflamed strangury, in short he was in a bad way. Cabanis put him in the bath for four hours, cared for him, his urine returned, and he was a bit better. Whether because he wanted a distraction, or because he had something urgent he had to do, he began to work harder than ever. His legs started to swell, he had some indigestion, he cannot sleep, today he has a temperature. If this incident has any bad consequences, he will have been the victim of false medical ideas. At the height of his crisis, he purged himself from his medicine with an enema of soap; since then he has surely dosed himself secretly with many personal remedies; he eats a lot in the evening, in order to sleep. In short, he makes up his own treatments because he is not yet afraid.[47]

In March 1773, Voltaire wrote to Claude-François Passerat, a doctor acquaintance:

You make me love life, Sir, through the interest you deign to take in my ailments. I no longer have a temperature, but I am not getting better. For the last two months, I have been suffering from insomnia on top of everything else. I attribute it to the gout, which wanders all over me, sometimes in my feet, sometimes in my knees, sometimes in my hands, and which finds itself everywhere so poorly housed that it does not stay long in any one place. I must endure all this with patience, and thank nature for not having sent me gravel, or stone, or apoplexy, or dysentery, or gangrene. She has somewhat hardened my ears, but she has not hardened my heart.[48]

Four years later, however, nature did send him a severe attack of apoplexy. As he told Richelieu in March 1777: 'A few days ago, I lost my memory for two days, and I lost it so completely that I could not find any word in the language. Never has nature played such a brutal trick on a member of the Académie Française. It is quite ridiculous that I should endure an apoplexy, considering how thin I am.'[49]

It is perhaps not surprising, therefore, that for several years Voltaire remained ambivalent about the prospect of setting out on a long and stressful journey to Paris. In the middle of 1777, however, he started to talk openly about visiting Paris because he now had two practical reasons for thinking of going. The first was that he was working on a pair of new tragedies, *Irène* and *Agathocle*, and he wanted to see them performed at the Comédie Française.[50]

The second reason was the marriage between Charles Michel, the marquis de Villette, and Reine Philiberte Rouph de Varicourt. She was the teenage daughter of an impoverished local noble family, and so beautiful and so charming that in January 1776, when she was nineteen, Voltaire decided to take her into his household. He called her 'Belle et Bonne' (Beautiful and Good), and her affection for him became essential to his happiness.

Villette, by contrast, was a middle-aged libertine, whose disordered life included a scandalous reputation for homosexuality; but Voltaire found him amusing and witty. He had visited Voltaire on previous occasions but when he arrived at Ferney towards the end of September 1777, he at once fell in love with 'Belle et Bonne', and almost immediately decided to marry her. Parisian society was scandalised that any well-born young lady should be contaminated by association with the notorious Villette, but Voltaire was delighted by the match and hoped that she would 'convert' Villette to normal heterosexuality. They were married at Ferney on 19 November, and Voltaire placed a diamond necklace round the neck of his 'Belle et Bonne'.

Villette owned a large house in Paris, and the day after the wedding he was already announcing that they should all – that is, he, 'Belle et Bonne', Voltaire and Mme Denis – go to Paris within the next two months.[51] With the New Year, the plan took concrete shape: the Comédie Française agreed to stage *Irène* in the spring; and Voltaire prepared for his return to Paris – a journey from which he was never to return.

16

Return to Paris

1778

The journey to Paris was planned for early February 1778, and it is clear that for a month at least Voltaire had been quite excited by the prospect. Paul-Claude Moultou, a Protestant pastor from Geneva and a familiar visitor at Ferney, gives a vivid picture of his enthusiasm and vitality. 'Voltaire is so infatuated, so taken in by what surrounds him, that he really wants to have this play performed in Paris. Just imagine, my friend, the force of this man: he read, no, he declaimed, the whole of this tragedy to us before supper, after that he had supper with us, he frolicked around like a child until two in the morning, and then he slept seven hours without waking once.'[1]

At the last moment, however, Voltaire seemed to dither. On Tuesday 3 February, Mme Denis set out for Paris, with Villette and 'Belle et Bonne', but without Voltaire. He wrote to d'Argental that morning: 'I am in despair not to be accompanying our travellers. But I have not the strength for one hundred leagues.' Yet in another letter written that same evening, he said that he himself would leave 'on Thursday, or Friday at the latest, for Dijon'; but not, apparently, for Paris.[2]

It is not entirely clear what was going on in Voltaire's head. One theory is that he was playing a game of hide-and-seek in order to conceal his real intentions from the French authorities, but this does not seem likely. Voltaire had very recently received reassurances from an impeccable source at Versailles that there was no *lettre de cachet* out against him in the files. 'Some church-goers have put it about that there was against me, in some office or other, a piece of paper that they call *littera sigilli* [letters of proscription]; I can assure you that there is no such thing.'[3]

The most likely explanation for Voltaire's apparent dithering is the simplest: Voltaire was old and of very uncertain health, and when the moment arrived, he hesitated before the rigours of a long journey in the depths of winter. In short, for a day or two, he simply vacillated between staying and going.

But only for a day or two. On Thursday 5 February 1778, Voltaire set off for Paris, accompanied by Wagnière and his cook, in his specially adapted sleeping carriage (*la dormeuse*), which was kept warm by a portable stove. On the road, Voltaire caught up with Mme Denis and the Villettes, and five days later, on Tuesday 10 February, they all reached Paris and went straight to the Hôtel de Villette, at the corner of the rue de Beaune and the quai des Théatins on the Seine (now named quai Voltaire). But even before settling into the set of rooms provided for him, Voltaire set out on foot to see his old friend d'Argental, who lived not far away, on the quai d'Orsay. He evidently cut quite a comical figure, in his long sable fur coat (a present from Catherine the Great), his large old-fashioned wig topped off by a red bonnet, and his walking stick with a handle in the shape of a crow; but if he attracted attention, he was not recognised; he had been away so long, and no one expected to see him. When he found that d'Argental was not at home, Voltaire returned to the rue de Beaune, where d'Argental soon came to find him. The two old men embraced; it was their first meeting for twenty-eight years, for d'Argental had never once visited Voltaire in his exile.

By one of those wonderful ironies, the Hôtel de Villette was a house with which Voltaire had once been intimately familiar, over fifty years earlier. At that time, it had belonged to the marquis and marquise de Bernières, and Voltaire in his late twenties had rented an apartment from them; he had also enjoyed a love affair with the marquise, Marguerite Madeleine. In 1778, however, Voltaire would probably not have recognised the house, since it had been substantially modified and enlarged by Villette.

The day after his arrival, the Hôtel de Villette was besieged with visitors and well-wishers from every walk of life. Mme du Deffand, the blind literary hostess, sent her secretary to observe the scene, and he told her that some three hundred people called at the house that day: the visitors were marshalled by Mme Denis or 'Belle et Bonne', while Voltaire kept to his room, working on revisions to *Irène*. When a new caller was announced, Voltaire would emerge, wearing a dressing gown and night-cap, exchange a few words with the visitor, and then withdraw again to his study.

According to Mme Denis, the crowds of visitors kept coming, day after day. 'I have been in such a great agitation since I have been here that I have not had the time to recognise myself. As soon as we arrived, I was obliged to receive the whole of the court and the whole of the town. It started at nine in the morning, and did not stop until ten at night. My uncle would come to the salon several times during the day, and from time to time withdraw to his room. It went on like this for ten or twelve days.'[4]

In the first few days after his arrival in Paris, Voltaire's visitors included a ceremonial delegation from the Académie Française on the Thursday; a deputation from the Comédie Française on the Saturday; and visits by the two rival composers, Christoph Willibald von Gluck and Niccolò Piccini, in quick succession on the Sunday; they may not have realised that Voltaire had no interest in, or appreciation of, music.

On Monday 16 February, he was visited by Benjamin Franklin, the celebrated statesman from the recently founded United States. 'He has seen Mr Franklin, who brought his little grandson, and asked the old man [Voltaire] to bless him. The old man gave his blessing in the presence of twenty people, and pronounced these words for a blessing: *God and Liberty*.'*[5]

The social round did not stop Voltaire from working hard on improving his tragedy *Irène*. Before leaving Ferney, he had been told that the play had been much admired by the Comédie Française actors, and that the duc de Duras had given virtually *carte blanche* permission for its performance.[6] But many of Voltaire's friends had

---

*In the letter Voltaire writes *'Dieu et la Liberté'* but in fact he pronounced the blessing in English.

serious reservations, even if they kept quiet about it; only Condorcet had the courage to spell out to him all its shortcomings. Voltaire was shaken, but contrite and submissive: 'I had thought ... I had imagined ... Unfortunately, I was mistaken ... I accept a large part of the truths which you have had the kindness to tell me.'[7] He obediently set about revising the tragedy, and said he was sorry the actors at the Comédie Française had been shown what was, he could see now, no more than a first sketch of the play.[8]

In the days immediately after his arrival, according to Mme du Deffand, he stayed up two nights in succession working at it,[9] and on the Sunday, five days later, he summoned the actors of the Comédie Française for a first rehearsal at the Hôtel de Villette. Voltaire asked Mme du Deffand to attend the rehearsal, but she declined. 'He invited me; but it will be between eleven o'clock and midday, and as that is often the time when I start to sleep, it is doubtful that I can be there.'

The stresses of work and the hectic social round, coming on top of the strains of the journey, quickly took their toll of Voltaire's failing health. Even Mme du Deffand, for all her blindness, could sense how ill he was. 'He pretends that he will go home this Lent, but I do not think he can; he has pain in his bladder, he has haemorrhoids, and they said yesterday that he was losing his balance; his extreme vivacity sustains him, but it is wearing him out; I should not be astonished if he should die soon.'[10]

On Thursday 12 February, Voltaire felt unwell and sent for Dr Théodore Tronchin, now practising in Paris. Tronchin called the next day, but the remedies he prescribed did no good. Five days later, on Tuesday 17 February, Voltaire again appealed to Tronchin for help.

The aged Swiss, whom Monsieur Tronchin had the kindness to come and see at M. de Villette's, wishes to point out that the continuous alternation between strangury and incontinent urination (*diabète*), with a total and complete cessation of peristaltic movement in the entrails, is fairly disagreeable and a bit dangerous. And that a machine so dislocated cannot survive more than a few more days except with the kindness of Monsieur

Tronchin. The old invalid would be very glad to be able to talk for a moment with Monsieur Tronchin, before making his farewell.[11]

This time Tronchin did not respond to Voltaire's appeal; Voltaire wrote to him again the next morning, Wednesday 18 February: 'One is ashamed to importune Monsieur Tronchin for one's little miseries, but the aged traveller from Ferney may well be condemned. The strangury has started again, and is now in control; the feet and legs are swollen; otherwise, he would use his legs to come and embrace Monsieur Tronchin at the Palais-Royal.'[12] The day passed, presumably with Voltaire in great pain; but Tronchin did not call. That evening Voltaire sent a further letter.

The aged invalid dares once more to tell his saviour Monsieur Tronchin: that the phlegms [*les glaires*] which sometimes pass by his urethra get absorbed [*congromelées*] into his entrails, and pass into his blood; that he cannot alleviate the cessation of the peristaltic movement, except by taking the pills of Mme Denis; and that he asks Monsieur Tronchin's permission to go on taking them, and to take a little quinine before meals. He wishes to do nothing without Monsieur Tronchin's advice, and begs him to send word.[13]

Voltaire's description of his symptoms is hard to translate, since some of the words he used have no recognised meaning. Modern medicine would tend to interpret Voltaire's reference to *glaires* as an alarming indication of pus or infection coming from his cancerous prostate or bladder. In those days, Tronchin had no means of arriving at such a diagnosis. But it is also clear, from things that he said and wrote at the time, that Tronchin was dismissive of Voltaire's ailments, impatient at Voltaire's wilful reluctance to take his advice, and unsympathetic to Voltaire as a human being.

Tronchin's hostility can be traced back to the political conflicts in Geneva in 1770, when Voltaire had gradually sided with the lower orders against the Tronchins and their patrician friends. In any case, Tronchin's worldly interests lay with the court and the *ancien régime*, not with Voltaire and the *philosophes*. His attitude was eloquently conveyed in the note which he left at the Hôtel de Villette around this time. 'I should very much have liked to say to M. le marquis de Villette, face to face, that M. de Voltaire has been living, since his arrival in Paris, on the capital of his strength, and that all his true friends must wish that he should live only on his income. At the rate things are going, his strength will soon be exhausted; and we shall be witnesses, if not accomplices, of the death of M. de Voltaire.'[14]

In short, Tronchin did not wish to take Voltaire's symptoms at all seriously, and he preferred to pretend that his patient was merely suffering from over-exertion. To ram home his indifference, and his impatience with the treatment Voltaire was receiving at the Hôtel de Villette, he passed the text of this grim diagnosis to the *Journal de Paris*, which published it two days later. This was obviously a scandalous violation of the most basic principles of medical ethics, since it implied that Villette would be to blame if anything happened to Voltaire, and it marked open hostility in relations between Tronchin and Villette.

The antagonism between Villette and Tronchin was only the most acute manifestation of the poisonous atmosphere of manoeuvrings and machinations developing in Voltaire's entourage. Of the entire household, Wagnière was probably the only member who was completely loyal to Voltaire; Wagnière and Mme Denis had long disliked each other; and Wagnière also disliked Villette. And then, in the wings, there was the muffled struggle for Voltaire's soul, between the Catholic Church and the *philosophes*, with the Church hoping to extract a recantation and a confession from him, and the *philosophes* hoping to prevent any such thing.

D'Alembert obviously thought that Voltaire might be dying, and he worried that he could be harassed into submitting to the last rites of a Christian death. At Ferney, Voltaire had his own church, and even his own ready-prepared mausoleum; but here in Paris he was much more exposed to the forces of conformity, and he seems to have been afraid that the Church might deny him a respectable burial. On 18 February, d'Alembert wrote to Théodore Tronchin to ask him to make sure that Voltaire was kept calm. 'The most important thing you now have to do is to tranquillise him, if it is possible, on his state (real or supposed). Yesterday I passed some time alone with him, and he seemed to me very fearful, not only about his state, but also about the disagreeable consequences which could follow. No doubt you understand me, my dear and illustrious colleague: it is the moral disposition of our old man, above all, which needs your care and your attention.'[15]

The Catholic Church could not long be kept at bay, however. On Friday 20 February, just ten days after Voltaire's arrival in Paris, Voltaire received an ingratiating letter from a certain abbé, Louis-Laurent Gaultier, requesting an interview. 'Many people, Sir, admire you and write your praises in fine verses and elegant prose. I desire with the deepest part of my heart to be among your admirers. I shall have that advantage, if you wish it, it depends on you, I am sure. There is still time. I should say more if you were to permit me to talk with you. Although the most unworthy of all ministers, I should not say anything unworthy of my ministry.'[16]

Voltaire may have judged, from the tone of the letter, that Gaultier was a modest and unsophisticated fellow; and that just as he had got the better of two modest churchmen in 1768 and 1769, so now he had a good chance of getting the better of the abbé Gaultier, without having to meet the full demands of the Church. Voltaire breezily agreed to a meeting.

Your letter, Sir, appears to me that of an honest man, and that is enough to decide me to receive the honour of your visit, on any day and hour that suits you. I am eighty-four years old, and I shall shortly appear before the God who created all the worlds. If you have anything special to tell me, and which is worth the trouble, I shall make it a duty and an honour to receive your visit, despite the sufferings which weigh me down.

I have the honour to be, Sir, your very humble and very obedient servant,

VOLTAIRE, Gentleman in Ordinary of the King's Chamber.[17]

If Gaultier thought Voltaire's reply was a model of self-satisfied impertinence, he kept it to himself, and duly turned up at the Hôtel de Villette the next morning, Saturday 21 February. Little of consequence took place at their short meeting: Gaultier told Voltaire who he was, and Voltaire was relieved to learn that the abbé had come on his own initiative, not as the emissary of his church superiors. Afterwards Voltaire commented to Wagnière that Gaultier was 'a good idiot'; presumably he now felt he could count on being able to outmanoeuvre the man at a later meeting.[18]

Voltaire was not in control of the march of events, however. That afternoon, he conducted a heavy rehearsal of *Irène* which left him exhausted. Four days later, on Wednesday 25 February, while sitting up in bed and dictating to Wagnière, he had a sudden and violent haemorrhage, with blood pouring out of his mouth and nose. Tronchin was called, and this time he came; he bled Voltaire, and the haemorrhage diminished. But Voltaire was still spitting blood, and he continued to spit blood for the next three weeks. On the same day, Voltaire wrote to Gaultier to ask him to visit; but Wagnière suppressed the letter, in case Voltaire should seem to have shown weakness. But the haemorrhage must have shaken Voltaire's confidence, for he wrote to Gaultier again the next day, to ask him to come as soon as possible. This time, there was no trace of his previous insolence. 'You promised, Sir, to come and hear me, I beg you to be so kind as to give yourself the trouble of coming to see me as soon as you can.'[19]

News of Voltaire's physical deterioration, and of Gaultier's visit, had by this time reached the church hierarchy. Christophe de Beaumont, the ultra-conservative archbishop of Paris, and one of Voltaire's *bêtes noires* for the past thirty-two years, wrote to Gaultier to commend him for his efforts to bring about the conversion of Voltaire. But he urged him to keep quiet about it; 'for if the project of conversion that you have in mind were to become publicly known, and if word of it reached either M. de Villette, or even M. de Voltaire himself, nothing more would be needed to wreck the good work that you are undertaking.'[20]

The abbé Gaultier did not respond immediately to Voltaire's request; when he did return to the Hôtel de Villette, four days later, on Monday 2 March, he brought with him a prepared text, which was presumably a formal declaration of Christian faith, and some kind of recantation of Voltaire's anti-Christian writings. Voltaire was not to be caught so easily: he brushed aside Gaultier's text, and called in Wagnière to give him pen and paper, so that he could write his own declaration.

I the undersigned declare that, having been attacked four days ago with a vomiting of blood at the age of eighty-four, and not having been able to drag myself to church, and M. le curé of Saint-Sulpice having kindly added to his good works that of sending to me M. l'abbé Gaultier, priest, I confessed to him, and that if God disposes of me, I die in the holy catholic religion in which I was born, hoping that the divine mercy will pardon all my faults, and that if I had scandalised the mother Church, I ask pardon from God and from her.[21]

Although Gaultier dismissed this declaration as not meaning anything much, he nevertheless gave Voltaire absolution; and he would have proceeded to complete Voltaire's formal reconciliation with the Church by giving him communion, but that Voltaire refused, on the grounds that he was still spitting blood; Gaultier was persuaded to leave the room, and the house.

Voltaire seems to have thought that the essential issue was now settled. With his formal absolution by Gaultier, he had secured what he believed would be enough to ensure a 'Christian' burial. But his declaration had made no meaningful concessions to the key beliefs of Christianity; and by refusing communion he thought he had prevented any allegations, either by the devout or by the *philosophes*, that he had finally succumbed to the Catholic Church.

Various churchmen continued to yap at Voltaire's heels, most notably Jean-Joseph Faydit de Tersac, the curé of the local parish church of Saint-Sulpice. On 4 March 1778, Tersac wrote Voltaire an obsequious letter, asking for a meeting. But if he thought that he could win Voltaire over by referring to Christian doctrine as 'the sublime philosophy of the Evangelist', or by finessing the question of the divinity of Christ in the phrase 'divine wisdom clothed in our nature', he was much mistaken.[22] From now on, Voltaire felt that he had no more business to transact with the Church. On Tuesday March 3, the day after he had given Voltaire absolution, Gaultier returned; he was not admitted. He called again; he was still not admitted. Ten days later, he wrote a pathetic letter, assuring Voltaire of his deepest good wishes, and begging for another meeting. Voltaire replied curtly: 'The master of the house has ordered his door-keeper not to admit any ecclesiastic except M. le curé de Saint-Sulpice; when the invalid has recovered a bit of health, he will have pleasure in receiving M. l'abbé Gaultier.'[23]

Despite Tronchin's recommendations that he rest, Voltaire continued to wear himself out with the preparations for the staging of *Irène*. On Tuesday 10 March, he held another rehearsal at the Hôtel de Villette; that night he had another haemorrhage. Five days later, on Sunday 15 March, the actors held a dress rehearsal at the Comédie Française; Voltaire was too ill to take part, so it was conducted by Mme Denis.

The first performance of *Irène* was scheduled for the following evening, but Voltaire was still too ill to attend. Of course, it may also have been first-night nerves which kept him away; throughout the performance, he waited impatiently, in a state of extreme excitement and anxiety, for messengers from the theatre, who reported in detail how each act had gone. The play was a triumphant success, but the strain for Voltaire was too much. The next day, and the day after, he was exhausted and received no one.

By the end of the week, however, he had recovered somewhat, and on Saturday 21 March, he went out sightseeing in a carriage, his first such outing since arriving in Paris. But that evening, he wrote to Tronchin, complaining of his maladies. 'As I told you, my dear saviour, my vomiting of blood is only one of the symptoms of my illness. The root of it is a stubborn strangury, accompanied by an invincible constipation. That is what makes my feet swell, and which makes me fear a hydropsy which will finish me off, for one day one must finish. Count on it that I shall end my days as a Tronchinian.'[24]

The high point of Voltaire's stay in Paris came on Monday 30 March, with his double apotheosis: a special session of the Académie Française in the afternoon, followed by the sixth performance of *Irène* at the Comédie Française in the evening.

In the early afternoon, he left the Hôtel de Villette by carriage for the Académie Française, which at the time was based in the Louvre. In an unprecedented gesture, all the academicians present came to greet him at the door – all, that is, but the bishops and other church-men, who had stayed away from any contamination by the scan-dalous old *philosophe*. Voltaire was asked to preside over the meeting, and to accept his appointment as the Académie's new director; and Voltaire's friend d'Alembert, the permanent secretary (*secrétaire per-pétuel*) of the Académie, read a eulogy in which he compared Voltaire with Racine and Boileau.

After the session, Voltaire wanted to see the modest official apart-ment provided upstairs for the *secrétaire perpetuel*, but there was no time. He had to hurry on to the Comédie Française at the Tuileries, where the curtain was due to go up at 5.30 p.m.

His appearance in the auditorium provoked a tumult of pro-longed applause, which delayed the start of the performance for over twenty minutes. When the play started, it was constantly interrupt-ed by cries of adulation for Voltaire. After it had finished, the cur-tain was raised again to reveal a bust of Voltaire on a pedestal in the middle of the stage, surrounded by the cast of actors, each of whom in turn placed a wreath on the head of the statue. When Voltaire left the theatre, he was confronted by an enormous crowd, and his car-riage horses could only proceed at a walking pace. Someone in the crowd shouted out: 'He's the one who wrote *Oedipe, Mérope, Zaïre*' [titles of three of his best-known tragedies]. Another voice cried: 'Long live the defender of the Calas family!'[25]

A week later, on 6 April, when Voltaire was walking from the Hôtel de Villette to the Académie Française, a voice in the crowd called out: 'That's M. de Voltaire; he is the defender of the poor and the oppressed, he saved the family of the Calas and the Sirven.'[26] Madame du Deffand, an old if cynical and increasingly conservative friend of Voltaire, wrote to Horace Walpole: 'The honours which he has received here are unbelievable . . . He is followed in the streets by the people, who call him *The man of the Calas* [*L'homme aux Calas*].'[27]

These successive waves of adulation may even have done Voltaire some good physically, for his health seems to have enjoyed a brief period of remission. During April and the first week of May, he made numerous outings. He attended four working sessions at the Académie Française, partly to discuss his plan for a new dictionary; after one of these sessions, he went a second time to the Comédie Française, to see a performance of his tragedy *Alzire*. He paid three visits to the duc d'Orléans, whose grand establishment included a private theatre. He attended a meeting at the Masonic Lodge of the Neuf Sœurs. He went to a ceremonial session at the Académie des Sciences. He called on Mme du Deffand. He called on Suzanne de Livry, one of the mistresses of his youth. He went twice, or perhaps three times, to sit for the sculptor Jean-Antoine Houdon.

Even Théodore Tronchin seems to have been impressed. On 6 April, he reported to his cousin François Tronchin that Voltaire now seemed full of vigour. 'Your old neighbour is making a frightful uproar here, and is well despite his unbelievable fatigues. I have seen some madmen in my life, but I have never seen any as mad as him. He counts on living to at least a hundred. The other day he called on me at half past seven in the morning; I was still in bed. He stayed for a long time, during which a crowd of four hundred people gathered outside my door.'[28]

In fact, two months after arriving in Paris, Voltaire was enjoying life in the city so much that he even rented a house in the rue de Richelieu, as if he expected to be around for quite some time. His rationale for this seemed to shift. Sometimes he implied that he would divide his time between Ferney (in the summer) and Paris (in the winter), sometimes that he would make Paris his permanent home. His doctor, Théodore Tronchin, retailed the second of these stories: 'He says that he will go home to Ferney after the Quasimodo [the Sunday after Easter, in this case 26 April] to arrange his affairs and those of his colony. After that he will come back and settle in Paris. He is buying a house.'[29] Either way, Voltaire seemed to be assuming that he had plenty of life ahead of him.

One reason why Voltaire was thinking of returning to Ferney was that when he had set off rather suddenly in February, he had evidently expected that he would soon return, for he had left his affairs and his papers in some haphazard disorder. Since then, time had passed, however, and he felt the need to tidy things up. Voltaire's plans were not shared by Mme Denis who had no intention of leaving Paris. 'My uncle plans to make a trip to Ferney. It is not decided that I should go with him.'[30] But then she was warned by the marquis de Thibouville that Voltaire must at all costs be prevented from leaving Paris, even briefly, for he had heard word that the authorities would prevent his ever returning. Mme Denis seized on this report as a pretext for getting rid of Wagnière. If it was now unsafe for Voltaire to return to Ferney, even briefly, then someone else had to be sent back to tidy up the everyday problems of the estate, and who better than Wagnière?

On Sunday 26 April, Voltaire and Mme Denis signed over to Wagnière a power of attorney for managing Ferney. Four days later, on 30 April, Wagnière left Paris, and he arrived at Ferney on 7 May. The following days and weeks were filled with conscientious letters from Wagnière to Voltaire relating in detail all his loyal services. It is not clear if Voltaire had made any attempt to resist Mme Denis's plan to send Wagnière back to Ferney. What is clear is that Wagnière's absence was Voltaire's deepest sadness in the four weeks of life that remained to him; he missed him, he regretted his departure, he wanted him to come back. A month later, on 25 May, Mme Denis and her nephew Alexandre d'Hornoy agreed to recall Wagnière from Ferney. But by then it was too late.

Five months earlier, in October 1777, Voltaire had written fom Ferney to his military friend in Angoulême, the marquis d'Argence: 'The trees we have planted remain, and we are leaving. All that I would ask of nature is to let me leave without pain; but it does not seem she will show me that mercy after having made me suffer for nearly eighty-four years. And yet I must still thank her for having given me life.'[31]

Nature did not show Voltaire 'that mercy', however. He was now not only very ill, but dying in increasing pain. At the beginning of May he wrote to Tronchin: 'The old invalid of the quai des Théatins throws himself into the arms of M. Tronchin; he is suffering unbearable pains; he may not have a high temperature, but he has an agitation in the pulse and in the blood which increases all his torments; he has not slept at all for the past fifteen nights; his state is horrible, nothing relieves him, his only hope is in Monsieur Tronchin; he hopes he will have pity on him.'[32]

Yet despite his sufferings, Voltaire continued to deal in detail with business affairs, as if he expected to be around for quite some time. In the first half of May, he sent Wagnière a series of letters, giving detailed instructions for the management of the estate, or listing the books and papers he was to send to Paris. 'Send my books by the carters. They will arrive when they can. I shall let you know to whom you should address them; but once more, my dear friend, it is you I need most. Come back as soon as you can. I cannot do without you, nor without my books. If you do not come back very soon, I shall set off, dead or alive, to find you.'[33]

On Thursday 7 May, Voltaire made his last effort at normal activity, when he went to the Académie Française for another plenary meeting to discuss the plan for a new dictionary. Mme Denis commented: 'My uncle is very well, he goes to the Académie, where he shouts like the very devil. He wants to get them to make a new dictionary; but these gentlemen are balking at it, for they are afraid that it will give them too much trouble.'[34] Mme Denis must have known that Voltaire was far from being 'very well', but she seems to have been briskly indifferent to the seriousness of his condition. On Saturday 9 May, Voltaire was too ill to attend a new meeting at the Académie Française. The following day he felt a little better, well enough to go for a walk; but when he got home, he was exhausted and went to bed with a high temperature, which became worse as the evening wore on. At first Mme Denis made no effort to call Tronchin; later Villette sent out to a nearby apothecary for some calming potion. When Tronchin was finally called, later that night, he prescribed a pain-killing medicine, which was probably some form of opium. Voltaire may well have taken far more of it than the prescribed doses, for it seems he was in delirium for the next two or three days.

That same Sunday, 10 May, Théodore Tronchin wrote to his cousin François that Voltaire was dying, and his letter eloquently conveyed his deep aversion and contempt for his patient: 'Now that Voltaire is near his end, people are beginning to talk, to evaluate all the damage he has done to society, which even those who are not infinitely severe are comparing to the wars, plagues and famines which for the past several thousand years have desolated the earth.'[35]

In mid-May, the Catholic Church made a fresh attempt to drag a valid confession and retraction out of Voltaire. This time the attack was led by Jean-Joseph Faydit de Tersac, the curé de Saint-Sulpice; he told Voltaire's family that he would not give Voltaire a Christian burial unless he first provided a full recantation of his anti-Christian sins. Some among Voltaire's friends were tempted to make a trial of strength: the curé had no right to deny burial since Voltaire had not been excommunicated and had already received an absolution (of sorts) from the abbé Gaultier. But the political authorities were extremely anxious that Voltaire's death should not precipitate a major public scandal, so they pressed the church authorities to agree a compromise way out. If anything was needed to underline the farcical nature of this negotiation, which had nothing to do with Christianity and everything to do with hypocrisy and public order, it was the fact that the negotiators included not just the church authorities, but also the chief of police; a Communist régime could not have done better.

The final compromise, hammered out on Saturday 23 May, a week before Voltaire's death, was grotesquely *grand Guignol*. The curé of Saint-Sulpice could not be compelled to give Voltaire a Christian burial. On the other hand, Voltaire's corpse could not be taken elsewhere for burial. Yet Voltaire was too ill to be moved while still alive. Therefore he would be allowed to die at the Hôtel de Villette. Once he had died, his corpse would be removed for burial at Ferney. But in order to satisfy everybody's hypocrisy, it would be necessary to pretend, for the purpose of that last journey, that Voltaire was still alive.

Voltaire's state of mind, as he was dying, became and long remained a subject of great controversy between liberals and Catholics in France. Some weeks after his death, Théodore Tronchin was to imply that Voltaire had died in a state of despair and dementia; and his account was subsequently used by anti-liberal Catholic propagandists to claim that Voltaire the unbeliever had been punished by dying amidst the torments of all the devils of hell. Now, those who wish to believe in devils are at liberty to do so. There is no evidence, however, that Voltaire gave any signs of dementia: great pain, but not madness. On the contrary, his letters, especially those to Wagnière dealing with practical matters, show that his mind remained lucid and rational right up until the end. In the early hours of Sunday 24 May, six days before his death, Voltaire wrote his final letter to Wagnière:

I am dying my dear Wagnière, it seems quite difficult that I can avoid it. I am really punished for your departure, for having left Ferney, and for having taken a house in Paris. I embrace you tenderly, my dear friend, and with sadness.[36]

This was almost the last letter that Voltaire wrote. The very last, written two days later, and four days before his death, dealt appropriately with one of his outstanding 'human rights' cases. Voltaire had heard that the young chevalier Trophime-Gérard de Lally-Tollendal had been given permission to appeal against the condemnation of his father, and he wrote him a warm three-line note to congratulate him. 'The dying man has been revived by learning this great news; he embraces M. Lally most tenderly. He can see that the King is the defender of justice; he will die content.'[37]

Despite the face-saving compromise already negotiated, Faydit de Tersac and the abbé Gaultier made yet another attempt to extract a declaration of faith out of Voltaire. On Saturday 30 May 1778, they were brought to the bedside of the dying man. When Faydit de Tersac asked him explicitly whether he believed in the divinity of Jesus Christ, Voltaire is said to have replied: 'In the name of God, Sir, do not speak to me any more about that man, and let me die in peace.' Some scholars question the authenticity of this remark, though it is quoted by both Condorcet and the abbé Duvernet. What is not in serious doubt, despite malicious rumours spread at the time and much later by his ultra-right-wing enemies, is that Voltaire did not succumb to the pressure of his Catholic persecutors, neither did he die in fear of the torments of hell.[38]

He died at eleven o'clock at night, on Saturday 30 May 1778.

The agreed plan, according to the compromise agreement, was that Voltaire's corpse would be taken to Ferney, dressed up as if he were still alive. But there were obvious difficulties in this scenario. Any number of mishaps could occur on a journey which would take five days or more, and there was every risk that the bishop of Annecy, with whom Voltaire had frequently been in conflict, might seek to prevent burial at Ferney. Voltaire's family therefore decided on different arrangements.

The day after he died, Sunday 31 May, Voltaire's corpse was opened for an autopsy, and then embalmed. That evening, after dark, Voltaire's elegant star-spangled carriage, with his body, now fully dressed again and propped up as if he were still alive, set off, followed in a second carriage by Alexandre d'Hornoy, Voltaire's great-nephew. But instead of driving south-east in the direction of Geneva and Ferney, the convoy travelled due east in the direction of the abbey of Scellières near Troyes, in Champagne.

For Alexandre Jean Mignot, Voltaire's nephew, was the abbot of the abbey of Scellières, and he had decided to use his position to ensure Voltaire's burial in sanctified ground. He had gone on ahead of the funeral cortège, arriving at the abbey in the evening of 31 May. He explained the position to the prior, and he claimed Voltaire's right to Christian burial by producing various certificates which had previously been extracted from Faydit de Tersac and Gaultier. The prior made no difficulty, and when the funeral cortège arrived on Monday 1 June, everything was ready for an all-night vigil, and for a formal funeral Mass the following day. They were just in time. The following day, the bishop of Troyes, alerted to what had happened, wrote to the prior forbidding him to bury Voltaire; but by then Voltaire was already buried.

His body remained in the vault in the centre of the abbey de Scellières for the next thirteen years, until, in 1791, the French Revolutionaries decided to canonise Voltaire for their own purposes.

They had his remains removed from the Abbaye de Scellières, and they gave him a spectacular reburial on 11 July, 1791 in the Panthéon in Paris, with the full works of revolutionary pomp, twelve white horses and all.

Although Voltaire was not a revolutionary, the Revolutionaries nevertheless paid well-judged homage to his achievements. On the catafalque bearing his coffin, there were three inscriptions.

The first read: 'He avenged Calas, La Barre, Sirven and Monbailli.'

The second read: 'Poet, philosopher, historian, he gave a great impetus to the human spirit, and prepared us to be free.'

The third read: 'He combated atheists and fanatics. He inspired tolerance. He reclaimed the rights of man against serfdom and feudalism.'[39]

—— *Afterword* ——

If Voltaire's paradox is that he is today both famous and unfamiliar, much of the explanation lies, as so often in France, with the French Revolution.

The Revolutionaries tried to co-opt Voltaire (and, later, Rousseau) posthumously for their own purposes. But in the nineteenth century, diehard French ultra-conservatives refused to accept the Revolution, and they blamed Voltaire and Rousseau for having brought it about. There was even a popular little ditty whose recurrent refrain 'C'est la faute à Voltaire, c'est la faute à Rousseau' (It's all Voltaire's fault, it's all Rousseau's fault) was still being trotted out many decades later; Victor Hugo quoted it in his novel *Les Misérables* and that was in 1862.

The idea is, of course, absurd. At the limit, Rousseau's *Contrat Social* may have given some threadbare plausibility to this afterthought; but in Voltaire's case, there was nothing remotely similar to pin on him, since his political views were, as we have seen, decidedly conservative.

Except for one thing: his insistent calls for toleration, and his constant campaigning against superstition and fanaticism, against Christianity and the repressive alliance between Church and State, in short against *L'Infâme*. It is this which explains the nineteenth-century hostility of the French extreme right towards Voltaire, for they tended to be not just ultra-conservative politically, but also ultra-Catholic.

Edgar Quinet, one of the leading nineteenth-century French historians of the Revolution, increasingly found himself asking not

'Why did it happen?' but 'Why did it fail?' After all, a ten-year revolution followed by a fifteen-year revolutionary empire ought to have been solidly entrenched; yet it was followed by a century of violent oscillations from right to left and back again, as if nothing had been settled after all. Quinet was himself forced into exile after the *coup d'état* of the tinpot emperor Napoléon III.

Quinet's answer to his own question was that the problem of religion was in a sense more fundamental to individual liberty than the problem of politics; and that the French Revolution had failed to bring about a stable political settlement at the end of the eighteenth century because the French Reformation had failed in the seventeenth century.

In England, the Protestant Reformation had succeeded. Despite the violent traumas of the Civil War, the Protestant settlement prepared the way for an important degree of individual liberty in matters of religion, and for an essential degree of separation between politics and religion; it had therefore made possible a stable political settlement. In France, by contrast, Louis XIV had capitulated to the Catholic fanatics, and had revoked the principles of religious tolerance for Protestants which had been so boldly accorded by Henri IV in the Edict of Nantes a hundred years earlier. In 1789, therefore, the Third Estate was confronting not just the absolutism of the monarchy, but the absolutism of the monarchy combined with the absolutism of the Catholic Church. If the Revolution failed to produce a stable settlement, it was because these two problems could not be tackled at once. In fact, it is arguable that there has still not been a reformation in France: a truce, perhaps, and a face-off between the Catholic Church and the lay State, but not a real reformation.[1]

Voltaire might well have recognised Quinet's analysis of the failure of the Revolution, in terms of the failure of the Reformation in France. If Voltaire had a hero, it was Henri IV, precisely because he had inaugurated a régime of religious tolerance between Catholics and Protestants, and he had celebrated him in his very early epic poem, *La Henriade*; if Voltaire had a nightmare, it was the feast of Saint-Bartholomew on 24 August 1572, when thousands of Protestants were massacred by fanatical Catholics; if Voltaire had a *bête noire* it was the absolutism of the Catholic Church. And though Voltaire never directly challenged the legitimacy of the Bourbon monarchy, neither did he cease to proclaim his belief that the pluralism and liberty of conscience of Protestant England were the source of its prosperity and Enlightenment.

After Voltaire's death, the marquis de Condorcet took on the task of editing a new complete edition of his works. It was a massive undertaking, lasting ten years (1779–89) and running to seventy volumes; and for the last volume, Condorcet appended a biography of Voltaire. Condorcet was one of Voltaire's most admiring disciples; yet as we saw in an earlier chapter, he could not resist including quite strong criticisms of Voltaire's lack of courage and his obsequiousness towards the powerful. 'He was often seen to expose himself to the storm, almost with temerity, but seldom to stand up to it with firmness; and these alternations of audacity and weakness have often afflicted his friends, and prepared unworthy triumphs for his cowardly enemies.'[2]

But if Condorcet's *Vie de Voltaire* is interesting and valuable, it is mainly for the light it sheds on the relative importance which he attached to the various aspects of Voltaire's life. Naturally, Condorcet provides an admiring survey of Voltaire's writings. But he gives priority to the stories of Voltaire's 'human rights' cases, and adds: 'Who would think, in reading these details, that this is the life of a great poet, of a fertile and tireless writer? We have forgotten his literary glory, as he had forgotten it himself. He seemed to recognise only one glory, that of avenging humanity, and rescuing victims of oppression.'[3]

—— *Endnotes* ——

The endnotes are intended almost exclusively for the purpose of identifying sources and references. For this reason, the general reader should not feel obliged to look to the back of the book every time he or she sees an endnote number.

By far the most frequent type of endnote is a reference to Voltaire's letters, prefaced simply by the word 'Letters'. I have used the text of the complete thirteen-volume *Correspondance* in the edition of the Bibliothèque de la Pléiade, in which the letters are numbered in chronological sequence. This edition is based on the so-called Definitive Edition of Theodore Besterman.

In all cases, the translations are my own.

CHAPTER I
Prologue

1. Letters, 14481
2. Letters, 2029
3. Letters, 2170
4. Letters, 2318
5. *Mémoires pour servir à la Vie de M de Voltaire* (composés en 1759, publiés seulement en 1784)
6. *Histoire du Docteur Akakia et du Natif de Saint-Malo*; in *Mélanges*, Bibliothèque de la Pléiade, 1981, 1995

CHAPTER 2
Money

1. Letters, 3483, 3489
2. Letters, 3548
3. Letters, 3551
4. Letters, 3553
5. Letters, 3658
6. Letters, 3667
7. Letters, 3658
8. Letters, 3565
9. Besterman, *Voltaire*, Longman, 1969, p. 335
10. Letters, 3568
11. Letters, 3592
12. Letters, 3594
13. Letters, 4822, 4832, 4835, 4989
14. Letters, 4994
15. Letters, 9092
16. Letters, 3706, 3711
17. Letters, 3715
18. Letters, 3739
19. Letters, 3751

CHAPTER 3
Geneva

1. Letters, 3856
2. Letters, 3912
3. Letters, 3900
4. Letters, 3919
5. Letters, 3694
6. Letters, 4104
7. Letters, 4052
8. Letters, 4074
9. Letters, 4301
10. Letters, 3926
11. Letters, 3929
12. Letters, 3968
13. Letters, 3970
14. Letters, 4018
15. Letters, 4027
16. Letters, 4028, 4029
17. Letters, 4030
18. Letters, 4032
19. Letters, 4046
20. Letters, 4047
21. Letters, 4056
22. Voltaire, *Letters Concerning the English Nation*, Oxford World's Classics, 1994, 1999, Letter 23
23. Letters, 4040
24. Letters, 4051
25. Letters, 4061
26. Letters, 4071
27. Letters, 4085
28. Letters, 4163
29. Letters, 4048, 4246
30. Letters, 4153
31. Letters, 4163
32. Letters, 4221
33. Letters, 4224 and note p. 1382
34. Letters, 4410
35. Letters, 4132
36. Letters, 4164
37. Letters, 4145
38. Letters, 4468
39. Letters, 4326
40. Letters, 4409
41. Letters, 4491; and ('lavement …') 5101

42. Letters, 4735
43. Letters, 4443
44. Letters, 4629
45. Letters, 4568
46. Letters, 4530
47. Letters, 4734

CHAPTER 4
Candide *and the English Admiral*

1. Voltaire, *Dictionnaire Philosophique*, GF-Flammarion, 1997
2. Letters, 4305
3. Letters, 4643
4. Letters, 3791
5. Letters, 4282
6. Letters, 4309
7. Letters, 8728
8. Pope, *Essay on Man*, edn I, 294
9. Letters, 4265, 4269
10. Letters, 4473
11. Letters, 4286
12. Letters, 4601
13. Letters, 4605
14. Letters, 4614
15. Letters, 4630
16. Letters, 4621
17. Letters, 4684 and note p. 1528
18. Letters, 4493
19. Letters, 4640
20. Letters, 4654 and note p. 1494
21. Letters, 4781; also see Voltaire's much later recollection in 1766, Letters, 9558
22. Letters, 4678, 4682, 4900, 4945
23. Letters, 5109
24. *Candide ou l'Optimisme*, ch. XXIII
25. *Précis du Siècle de Louis XV*, pp. 1527–8, in *Oeuvres Historiques*, Bibliothèque de la Pléiade, 1958
26. Letters, 4660

27. Letters, 4661
28. Letters, 4666
29. *Histoire du Parlement de Paris*, p. 105
30. *Histoire du Parlement de Paris*, pp. 106–7
31. Michel Foucault, *Surveiller et Punir*, Gallimard, 1975, trans. as *Discipline and Punish*, Penguin, 1991
32. Letters, 4683
33. Letters, 4712
34. Letters, 4831
35. Letters, 5761, 5927, 6330
36. Letters, 4738, 4777
37. Letters, 4965, 4985
38. Letters, 5062; and René Pomeau, *La Religion de Voltaire*, Librairie A-G Nizet, 1995, p. 307
39. Letters, 5199
40. Deloffice et Courier (eds.), *Voltaire et sa 'grande amie'*, pp.284, 289
41. Letters, 5446
42. Letters, 5441
43. *Candide ou l'Optimisme*, ch. XXX

CHAPTER 5
L'Infame

1. Letters, 5287
2. Pomeau, *Voltaire en son Temps*, Fayard/Voltaire Foundation, and I, p. 891
3. Letters, 5271 and note p. 1261
4. Letters, 5288
5. Letters, 5333
6. Letters, 5224 and note p. 1243
7. Letters, 5400, 5539, 5554, 5619
8. Letters, 5539, 5619
9. Letters, 5390, 5393, 5435, 5552, 5553, 5555, 5580
10. Letters, 6859

11. Letters, 12103 and note p. 1306
12. Letters, 5272
13. Letters, 5295, 5309, 5311, 5312, 5323, 5331, 6471
14. Letters, 5663
15. Letters, 5774
16. Letters, 5832
17. Letters, 5301
18. Letters, 5288, 5321
19. Letters, 5349
20. Letters, 6542
21. Pomeau, *Voltaire en son Temps*, II, p. 34
22. Letters, 5503, 5505
23. Letters, 5595
24. Letters, 5515, 5522
25. Letters, 5618
26. Letters, 5522
27. Letters, 5534
28. Letters, 5546
29. Letters, 5596
30. Letters, 5610
31. Letters, 5698
32. Letters, 5489
33. Letters, 5524
34. Letters, 5529
35. Letters, 5610
36. Letters, 5665
37. Letters, 5688 and note p. 1418
38. Letters, 5703
39. Letters, 5573
40. Letters, 5494 and note p. 1346
41. Letters, 5615
42. Letters, 5721
43. Letters, 5724
44. Letters, 5733, 5734
45. Adapted from Revelations, 3: 16
46. Letters, 5493
47. Letters, 6225
48. Letters, 6221
49. Letters, 6212
50. Letters, 6248

51. Letters, 6255
52. Letters, 6261
53. Letters, 5967
54. Letters, 6247
55. Letters, 6835
56. Letters, 6797
57. Letters, 5659
58. Letters, 5704
59. Letters, 5968
60. Letters, 6281
61. See René Pomeau, *La Religion de Voltaire*
62. Letters, 6627 and note p. 1315
63. Letters, 5488
64. Letters, 5353
65. Letters, 8676, 8760
66. Letters, 9376
67. Letters, 6206
68. Letters, 5704

CHAPTER 6
The Adoption of Mlle Corneille

1. Letters, 6311
2. Letters, 6376
3. Letters, 6377
4. Letters, 6387
5. Letters, 6389
6. Letters, 6412
7. Letters, 6544
8. Letters, 6439
9. Letters, 6532
10. Letters, 7344
11. Letters, 6465
12. Letters, 6532
13. Letters, 6470
14. Letters, 6507
15. Letters, 6456
16. Letters, 6518
17. Letters, 8692
18. Letters, 6849
19. Letters, 6602, 6968
20. Letters, 6752

21. Letters, 6578
22. Letters, 6601
23. Letters, 6840
24. Letters, 6601
25. Letters, 6671, 6786
26. Letters, 6754
27. Letters, 6674
28. Letters, 7590
29. Pomeau, *Voltaire en son Temps*, II, p. 93
30. Letters, 6682
31. Letters, 6785
32. Letters, 6825
33. Letters, 6791
34. Letters, 7103
35. Letters, 7108
36. Letters, 6999
37. Letters, 7133
38. Letters, 7157
39. Letters, 7289
40. Letters, 7145
41. Letters, 7148
42. Letters, 7151
43. Letters, 7174
44. Pomeau, *Voltaire en son Temps*, II, p. 94
45. Letters, 8295
46. Letters, 8369 and note p. 1399
47. Letters, 8619
48. Letters, 8446
49. Letters, 8437
50. Letters, 8461
51. Letters, 8467, 8468
52. Letters, 8305, 13121, 13539
53. Pomeau, *Voltaire en son Temps*, II, p. 94–5
54. Letters, 6977; Pomeau says the *petite rente* was for £13,096, *Voltaire en son Temps*, II, p. 92
55. Letters, 7499
56. Letters, 6600, 7285
57. Letters, 7532

58. Letters, 7540
59. Letters, 7539
60. Letters, 7551
61. Letters, 7590
62. Letters, 7583
63. Letters, 7650
64. Letters, 7642

CHAPTER 7
The Calas Affair

1. Letters, 6838
2. Matthew, 18: 20
3. Letters, 6939
4. Letters, 6940
5. Letters, 7075
6. See David D. Bien, *The Calas Affair*, Princeton, 1960, pp. 15–17
7. Pomeau, *Voltaire en son Temps,* II, p. 119, quoting Marc Chassaigne, *L'Affaire Calas,* Paris, 1929
8. Letters, 7082
9. Letters, 7094
10. Letters, 7096
11. Letters, 7097
12. Letters, 8738 (1March 1765 to Damilaville)
13. Letters, 7101
14. Letters, 7116
15. Letters, 7099
16. Letters, 7112
17. Letters, 7120
18. Letters, 7135
19. Letters, 7162 and note p. 1488
20. Letters, 7170
21. Letters, 7162
22. Letters, 7184
23. Letters, 7244
24. Voltaire, *La Méprise d'Arras* (1771), Édition Moland, CD-ROM
25. Letters, 7227
26. Letters, 7237
27. Letters, 7268

28. Letters, 7232
29. Letters, 7238
30. Letters, 7246
31. Letters, 7306
32. Letters, 7316 and note p. 1532
33. Letters, 7318
34. Letters, 7351
35. Letters, 7444
36. Letters, 7496
37. Letters, 7656, 7678
38. Letters, 7699
39. Letters, 7687, 7862
40. Letters, 7662
41. Letters, 7739
42. Letters, 7833
43. Letters, 7440
44. Letters, 7536
45. Letters, 7709
46. Voltaire, *Traité sur la Tolérance* in *Mélanges,* p. 563
47. Voltaire, *Traité sur la Tolérance* in *Mélanges,* p. 572
48. Voltaire, *Traité sur la Tolérance* in *Mélanges* p. 599
49. Voltaire, *Traité sur la Tolérance* in *Mélanges,* pp. 616, 618
50. Letters, 8042
51. Letters, 8015
52. Letters, 8020 and note p. 1297
53. Letters, 7792
54. Letters, 7814
55. Letters, 8071
56. Letters, 8095
57. Letters, 8118, 8119
58. Letters, 8143
59. Letters, 8143
60. Letters, 8144
61. Letters, 8240
62. Letters, 8196
63. Letters, 8231
64. Letters, 8265, 8357
65. Letters, 8253

66. Letters, 8220
67. Letters, 8242, 8261
68. Letters, 8106, 8161
69. Letters, 8204
70. Letters, 8206, and Pomeau, *Voltaire en son Temps,* II, pp. 130–31
71. Letters, 8020 and note p. 1297; 8125, 8233, 8258, 8354
72. Letters, 8354
73. Letters, 8346
74. Letters, 8341; for Voltaire's regret at Mme de Pompadour's death on 15 April, see Letters, 8280
75. Letters, 8354

CHAPTER 8
The Swiss Marmot

1. Voltaire, *Dictionnaire Philosophique*, GF-Flammarion, 1964
2. Letters, 8401, 8481, 8482
3. Letters, 8541 and note p. 1449, 8551
4. Letters, 8489
5. Letters, 8615
6. Letters, 8498
7. Letters, 8524, 8525, 8527
8. Letters, 8441
9. Letters, 8770
10. Letters, 8761, 8776
11. Letters, 8777
12. Letters, 8810
13. Letters, 8341 and note p. 1392; 8830 and note p. 1202; 8837
14. Letters, 8837
15. Letters, 8851
16. Letters, 9412 (9 May, 66)
17. Letters, 7435
18. Letters, 7664
19. Letters, 7704, 7706
20. Letters, 8736

21. Voltaire, *Avis au Public*, in *Mélanges* pp. 809–29; and in *L'Affaire Calas*, Gallimard, Folio Classique, 1996, pp. 204–30
22. Letters, 8841
23. Letters, 9474, 9475, 9476, 9529
24. Letters, 9474
25. Letters, 12617

CHAPTER 9
Ferney

1. Letters, 8656
2. Letters, 8690
3. Letters, 8737
4. Letters, 8700
5. Letters, 8564
6. Letters, 8715
7. Letters, 8705
8. Letters, 8728
9. Letters, 8709
10. Letters, 8722
11. Letters, 8722, note p. 1498-9
12. Letters, 8746
13. Letters, 8785
14. Letters, 8780, 8785, 8787
15. Letters, 8815
16. Letters, 8337
17. Letters, 8215
18. Letters, 8338; 'man of sorrows': Isaiah, 53: 3
19. *Boswell on the Grand Tour*, ed. Frederick Pottle, Heinemann, vol. 1, 1953, pp. 285–6
20. Letters, 8719
21. Letters, 9041
22. Letters, 9158
23. Letters, 9137
24. Letters, 9102
25. Letters, 8676
26. Letters, 8763
27. Letters, 8730
28. Letters, 4211

29. Letters, 8878
30. Letters, 9042
31. Letters, 9043
32. Letters, 9043 and note pp. 1240–41
33. See Frank A. Kafker, *The Encyclopedists as Individuals*, Voltaire Foundation, 1988
34. Letters, 8887
35. Letters, 8918
36. Letters, 9043 and note p. 1241
37. Letters, 9044
38. Letters, 9055, and 9070 and note p. 1250
39. Letters, 9066
40. Letters, 9069
41. Letters, 9082
42. Letters, 9097, see Ch. 5; 5494 and note p. 1346
43. Letters, 8178
44. Letters, 9809
45. Letters, 9781
46. Letters, 9788
47. Letters, 8811
48. Letters, 8837
49. Letters, 8844
50. Melchior Grimm, *Correspondance Littéraire*, 15 December 1768, quoted in Frank A. Kafker, *The Encyclopedists as Individuals*, Voltaire Foundation, 1988, p. 85
51. Pomeau, *Voltaire en son Temps,* II, p. 190
52. Peter Gay, *The Enlightenment*, Norton, 1966, I, p. 19
53. Denis Diderot, *Correspondance*, quoted in Frank A. Kafker, *The Encyclopedists as Individuals*, Voltaire Foundation, 1988, p. 86
54. Letters, 8744
55. Letters, 8742
56. Letters, 8915

57. Letters, 9040
58. Letters, 9092
59. Letters, 9111, 9119
60. Letters, 9138
61. Letters, 9141
62. Letters, 9150; *On Crimes and Punishments* (*Dei Delitti e delle Pene*), by Cesare Beccaría, was first published in 1764.
63. Letters, 9222
64. Letters, 10893
65. Letters, 5502
66. Letters, 5517, 6012, 6427, 6491, 6523
67. Letters, 6523
68. Letters, 7428, 7541, 8222
69. Letters, 8303
70. Letters, 11002
71. Letters, 11020
72. Letters, 11083
73. Letters, 14818

CHAPTER 10
Beccaría and the Commetaire

1. Letters, 11517
2. See Marcello T. Maestro, *Voltaire and Beccaría as Reformers of Criminal Law*, Columbia UP, 1942, p. 11
3. Letters, 7862
4. Maestro, *Voltaire and Beccaría as Reformers of Criminal Law*, pp. 34–50
5. Letters, 9125
6. Letters, 9150
7. Cesare Beccaría, *On Crimes and Punishments*, trans. David Young, Hackett, 1986
8. Cesare Beccaría, *On Crimes and Punishments*, p. 81
9. Letters, 7217; Beccaría: *Del disordine e de' rimedii delle monete*

nello stato di Milano nell'anno 1762

10. Quoted in Maestro, *Voltaire and Beccaría as Reformers of Criminal Law*, pp. 68–9
11. Letters, 9480
12. Letters, 9545, 9622
13. Voltaire, *Commentaire sur le livre des délits et des peines*, in *Mélanges*, pp. 769–807; also in *L'Affaire Calas*, ed. Jacques van den Heuvel, Folio Classique, pp. 235–84
14. Voltaire, *Commentaire sur le livre des délits et des peines*, in *Mélanges*, pp. 802–6
15. Louis Philipon de la Madelaine, *Discours sur la Nécessité et les Moyens de Supprimer les Peines Capitales*
16. Letters, 12129

CHAPTER 11
The Execution of the Chevalier de La Barre

1. Letters, 5878
2. Voltaire, *Précis du Siècle de Louis XV*, ch. XXXIV, in *Oeuvres Historiques*, Bibliotheque de la Pléiade; also see Voltaire, *Fragments Historiques sur l'Inde*: 'd'avoir trahi les intérêts du roi, de l'État et de la Compagnie des Indes, d'abus d'autorité, vexations et exactions', Edition Moland, CD-ROM
3. Pomeau, *Voltaire en son Temps*, II, pp. 471–2
4. Letters, 9422
5. Letters, 9439
6. Letters, 9441
7. Letters, 9442

8. Letters, 9460
9. Voltaire, *Précis du Siècle de Louis XV*, in *Oeuvres Historiques*, ch. XXXIV, Bibliothèque de la Pléiade, pp. 1499–1506; Voltaire, *Fragments sur l'Inde*, chs. XVIII, XIX, Edition Moland CD-ROM
10. Letters, 9464
11. Letters, 9478
12. Letters, 9512 and note pp. 1390–91; these details are from Voltaire's early 'letter' account. Pomeau confirms that Dumaisniel de Saveuse was a suspect and son of Belleval; he does not mention Douville de Maillefer, except in a back-of-the-book note.
13. Letters, 9936 and note pp. 1512–13; ('soon': either April 1767 or April 1768); 10061 and note pp. 1556–7, 10088
14. Marc Chassaigne, *Le Procès du Chevalier de La Barre*, Victor Lecoffre, 1920, p. 141
15. Voltaire, *Relation de la Mort du Chevalier de La Barre*, in *Mélanges*, p. 765
16. Pomeau, *Voltaire en son Temps,* II, pp. 241–8
17. Letters, 9471
18. Letters, 9482
19. Letters, 9487
20. Letters, 9488
21. Letters, 9499
22. Letters, 9501
23. Letters, 9512, and note pp. 1390–91
24. Letters, 9513
25. Letters, 9569, 9578, 9583
26. Voltaire, *Relation de la Mort du Chevalier de La Barre*, in *Mélanges*, pp. 755–67

27. Letters, 13536
28. Letters, 13957
29. Voltaire, *Relation de la Mort du Chevalier de La Barre*, in *Mélanges*, p. 762
30. Voltaire, *Relation de la Mort du Chevalier de La Barre*, in *Mélanges*, pp. 763, 766–7
31. Letters, 9524
32. Letters, 9578
33. Letters, 9528
34. Letters, 9535
35. Letters, 9650
36. Letters, 9559
37. Letters, 9562
38. Letters, 9545
39. Letters, 9591

CHAPTER 12
The Blockade

1. Letters, 9406
2. Letters, 7193
3. Letters, 6054, note p. 1560
4. Letters, 7818
5. Letters, 7889
6. Letters, 7935
7. Voltaire, *Sermon des Cinquante* in *Mélanges*, p. 253
8. Letters, 8629
9. Voltaire, *Le Sentiment des Citoyens* in *Mélanges*, p. 715
10. Letters, 8646
11. Letters, 9147
12. Letters, 9150
13. Letters, 9174
14. Letters, 9191
15. Letters, 9211
16. Letters, 9200
17. Voltaire, *Idées Républicaines*, sections XIII. XXV, XXXIX, XLIII, in *Mélanges*
18. Letters, 9268

19. Letters, 9697, 9704
20. Letters, 9405
21. Letters, 9408 and note p. 1363
22. Letters, 9408 and note p. 1364
23. Letters, 9408 and note p. 1364
24. Letters, 9417
25. Letters, 10059
26. Letters, 9765
27. Letters, 9795
28. Letters, 9798
29. Letters, 9813
30. Letters, 9820
31. Letters, 9837
32. Condorcet, *Vie de Voltaire*, Quai Voltaire, 1994, p. 151
33. Letters, 9844
34. Letters, 9850 and note pp. 1490–91
35. Letters, 9849
36. Letters, 9883
37. Letters, 9907
38. Letters, 9921
39. Letters, 9829
40. Letters, 9777, 9779, 9787, 9808
41. Letters, 9831
42. Letters, 9831
43. Letters, 9835
44. Letters, 9874
45. Letters, 9895
46. Letters, 9902
47. Letters, 10048
48. Letters, 10045
49. Letters, 10313, 10333
50. Letters, 10292
51. Letters, 10297
52. Letters, 10410
53. Letters, 10486
54. Letters, 10607
55. Letters, 10613
56. Voltaire, *Correspondance Choisie*, Livre de Poche, Classiques Modernes, note p. 925; Peter Gay,

Voltaire's Politics, Yale UP, 1959, 1988, p. 231
57. Letters, 10619, 10620

CHAPTER 13
Solitude

1. Letters, 10589 and note pp. 1251–2
2. Letters, 11184
3. Letters, 11192 and note pp. 1454–5
4. Letters, 10640 and note pp. 1265–7
5. Letters, 10660
6. Letters, 10617
7. Letters, 10627, 10629
8. Letters, 10645
9. Letters, 10591
10. Letters, 10373
11. Letters, 10422
12. Letters, 9735
13. Letters, 10575
14. Letters, 10606
15. Letters, 10585
16. Letters, 10607
17. Letters, 10724
18. Letters, 10589
19. Letters, 10690
20. Letters, 10694
21. Letters, 10675
22. Letters, 10680
23. Letters, 6145
24. Letters, 10707
25. Letters, 10610
26. Letters, 10613
27. Letters, 10807
28. Letters, 10703 and note p. 1284
29. Letters, 10703 and note pp. 1283–5
30. Letters, 10703
31. Letters, 10819 and note p. 1320
32. Letters, 10806

33. Letters, 11153
34. Letters, 11142 and note p. 1432, 11144 and note p. 1433, 11153 and note p. 1447, 11167, 11180 and note pp. 1447-9, 11186, 11187, 11233, 11234, 11256
35. Pomeau, *Voltaire en son Temps*, II, p. 326
36. Letters, 11233
37. Letters, 11126
38. Letters, 11407
39. Letters, 10520
40. Letters, 10620
41. Letters, 10660
42. Letters, 10842, 10877
43. Letters, 10913
44. Letters, 10924
45. Letters, 10929 and note p. 1356
46. Letters, 11029
47. Letters, 11030
48. Letters, 10808
49. Letters, 11114
50. Letters, 11123, 11162
51. Letters, 11164
52. Letters, 11251
53. Letters, 11338 and note pp. 1501–2
54. Letters, 11365
55. Letters, 11114
56. Letters, 11124
57. Letters, 11192 and note p. 1454
58. Letters, 11351, note p. 1506–7
59. Letters, 11261
60. Letters, 11308
61. Letters, 11332
62. Letters, 11332
63. Letters, 11365 and note pp. 1511–12
64. Letters, 11365
65. Letters, 11363
66. Letters, 11370
67. Letters, 11413 and note p. 1530

68. Letters, 11423 and note p. 1534
69. Letters, 11420
70. Letters, 11423
71. Letters, 11428
72. Letters, 11462
73. Letters, 11575 and note p. 1134

CHAPTER 14
Watchmaking

1. Letters, 11483
2. Letters, 11500
3. Letters, 11607
4. Letters, 11582, 11591, 11596, 11597, 11598, 11607, 11610, 11613, 11619, 11625, 11626, 11628, 11632, 11643, 11644, 11689, 11690, 11691, 11723, 11737
5. Letters, 11591
6. Letters, 9933
7. Letters, 11592
8. Letters, 11599
9. Letters, 11605
10. Letters, 11607
11. Letters, 11606
12. Letters, 11643
13. Letters, 11642
14. Letters, 11654 and note p. 1156
15. Letters, 11652 and note pp. 1155–6
16. Letters, 11326
17. Letters, 11360
18. Letters, 11394
19. Letters, 11407
20. Letters, 11550
21. Letters, 11650
22. Letters, 11690
23. Letters, 11627
24. Letters, 11628
25. Letters, 11720
26. For example, Letters, 11857
27. Letters, 11691
28. Letters, 14237, 14274, 14659

29. Letters, 11601
30. Letters, 11708
31. Letters, 11702
32. Letters, 11749, 11796, 11861
33. Letters, 12003
34. Letters, 11575
35. Letters, 11723
36. Pomeau, *Voltaire en son Temps*, II, pp. 348–9
37. Letters, 11714 and note p. 1178
38. Letters, 11729
39. Letters, 11748
40. Letters, 11793
41. Letters, 11797
42. Letters, 11867, 11871
43. Letters, 11801, 11840 and note pp. 1219–20, 11871
44. Pomeau, *Voltaire en son Temps*, II, p. 349
45. Letters, 12317
46. Letters, 12604
47. In the upstairs bar, called the Foyer Pierre Dux
48. Letters, 11785
49. Letters, 11787
50. Letters, 11785 and note p. 1203
51. Letters, 11789, 11791
52. Letters, 11884
53. Letters, 11903
54. Letters, 12048
55. Letters, 12078
56. Letters, 12414
57. Letters, 11737
58. Letters, 12126 and note p. 1315
59. Letters, 12126
60. Letters, 11867
61. Letters, 11859, 11917, 11924
62. Letters, 12029
63. Letters, 12292
64. Letters, 12433
65. Letters, 12439
66. Letters, 12364

67. Letters, 11904 and note p. 1241
68. Letters, 12439
69. Letters, 12210, 12381, 12430
70. Letters, 11966
71. Letters, 11783, 11842
72. Letters, 11738
73. Letters, 11746
74. Letters, 11761 and note p. 1194
75. Letters, 12379
76. Letters, 12520
77. Letters, 12574
78. Letters, 12430, 12520, 13893
79. Letters, 12664
80. Letters, 12700
81. Letters, 13108
82. Letters, 13289
83. Letters, 13296
84. Letters, 13327
85. Letters, 13348
86. Letters, 13478
87. Letters, 13596, 13791
88. Letters, 12540
89. Letters, 13331
90. Letters, 14666 and note p. 1162
91. Letters, 12972
92. Letters, 13149
93. Letters, 12831 and note p. 1580
94. Letters, 12834, 12835
95. Letters, 12871
96. Letters, 12852, 12853
97. Letters, 12912
98. Letters, 12931 and note p. 951
99. Letters, 12938, 12945, 12952
100. Letters, 12956
101. Letters, 13169 and note pp. 1041-2
102. Letters, 13296 and note pp. 1087–8
103. Letters, 13296
104. Letters, 13299
105. Letters, 13327

106. Letters, 14745, 14746, 14766, 14771, 14783, 14785, 14821
107. Letters, 13902
108. Letters, 13998 and note p. 852
109. Pomeau, *Voltaire en son Temps,* II, pp. 456–7 (Moultou to Meister, D 19217)
110. Letters, 14237
111. Letters, 14402
112. Letters, 14561 and note p. 1111
113. Letters, 14561 and note p. 1111
114. Letters, 13888
115. Letters, 14257, 14265, 14313
116. Letters, 13246
117. Letters, 14262, 14306
118. Letters, 14313, 14316
119. Letters, 14340 and note p. 1011
120. Letters, 14392 and note pp. 1032–3
121. Letters, 14389
122. Letters, 14432 and note pp. 1048–9
123. Letters, 14488
124. Letters, 14659
125. Letters, 14766
126. Letters, 14752

CHAPTER 15
Last Campaigns

1. Letters, 11381, 11393, 11517
2. Letters, 11624
3. Letters, 12784
4. (1770) *Au Roi en son Conseil* and *Nouvelle Requête*
5. Letters, 14102
6. Letters, 12337 and note p. 1378
7. Letters, 12372
8. Letters, 12378 and note p. 1397; (1771) *La coutume de Franche-Comté*; & *Supplique des Serfs*; (1772) *La Voix du Curé*

9. (1775) *Extrait d'un Mémoire* & (1776) *Supplique à M. Turgot*
10. Letters, 15153
11. Voltaire, *Relation de la Mort du Chevalier de La Barre*, in *Mélanges*, pp. 755–68
12. Letters, 14004
13. Letters, 14006
14. Voltaire, *Cri du Sang Innocent*, in *L'Affaire Calas*, pp. 341–50
15. Letters, 14213
16. Voltaire, *Le Prix de la Justice et de l'Humanité*, Édition Moland, CD-ROM
17. Peter Gay, *Voltaire's Politics*, p. 284
18. Letters, 14695
19. Voltaire, *Letters concerning the English Nation,* Letter XVIII, p. 87. The French equivalent is: Voltaire, *Lettres Philosophiques*, in *Mélanges*
20. Letters, 14682
21. Letters, 14691
22. Letters, 14701
23. Letters, 14706
24. Letters, 12501
25. Letters, 14714 and note p. 1186
26. Letters, 13740
27. Letters, 13904 and note pp. 1312–16
28. Letters, 13904 and note pp 1312–16; Pomeau, *Voltaire en son Temps*, II, pp. 438–9; J. Goulemot, A. Magnan, D. Masseau, eds., *Inventaire Voltaire*, Quarto Gallimard, Paris, 1995, p. 631
29. Letters, 13797
30. Letters, 13982
31. Letters, 13653
32. Letters, 14089
33. Letters, 14089 and note pp. 903–4

34. Letters, 14120 and note p. 917
35. Letters, 14131
36. Letters, 14142
37. Letters, 14152
38. Letters, 14240
39. Letters, 14886
40. Letters, 14228
41. Letters, 9583
42. Letters, 10999
43. Letters, 11867, 11871
44. Letters, 13079 and note p. 1008, 13257 and note p. 1073
45. Letters, 14221 and note p. 959
46. Letters, 13168
47. Letters, 13162 and note p. 1038
48. Letters, 13215
49. Letters, 14912
50. Letters, 14754, 14766
51. Pomeau, *Voltaire en son Temps*, II, p. 559

CHAPTER 16
Return to Paris

1. Letters, 15146 and note p. 299
2. Letters, 15176, 15177
3. Letters, 15175
4. Letters, 15250 and note p. 351
5. Letters, 15189
6. Letters, 15145 and note p. 298
7. Letters, 15151
8. Letters, 15155
9. Letters, 15187 and note p. 321
10. Letters, 15187 and note p. 321
11. Letters, 15189
12. Letters, 15191
13. Letters, 15192
14. Letters, 15192 and note p. 322
15. Letters, 15192 and note p. 323
16. Letters, 15203 and note p. 326
17. Letters, 15203
18. Pomeau, *Voltaire en son Temps*, II, p. 579

19. Letters, 15212
20. Letters, 15214 and note p. 330
21. Pomeau, *Voltaire en son Temps*, II, p. 583
22. Letters, 15217 and note pp. 332–3
23. Letters, 15221 and note pp. 334–5
24. Letters, 15230
25. Pomeau, *Voltaire en son Temps*, II, p. 599
26. Pomeau, *Voltaire en son Temps*, II, p. 604
27. Pomeau, *Voltaire en son Temps*, II, p. 738
28. Letters, 15259 and note p. 353
29. Letters, 15259 and note p. 353
30. Letters, 15253 and note pp. 351–2
31. Letters, 15077
32. Letters, 15264
33. Letters, 15269, 15268
34. Letters, 15267 and note p. 357
35. Letters, 15270 and note p. 359
36. Letters, 15283
37. Letters, 15284
38. Condorcet, *Vie de Voltaire*, p. 147; Pomeau, *Voltaire en son Temps*, II, p. 624
39. Quoted in Goulemot, Magnan, Masseau, eds., *Inventaire Voltaire*, 1995

Afterword

1. See François Furet and Mona Ozouf, eds., *Dictionnaire Critique de la Révolution Française*, Flammarion, 1988, pp. 1041–52; and Dale K. van Kley, *The Religious Origins of the French Revolution*, Yale UP, 1996, pp. 369–75
2. Condorcet, *Vie de Voltaire*, p. 151
3. Condorcet, *Vie de Voltaire*, p. 132

Bibliography

Works by Voltaire

Oeuvres Historiques, Gallimard, Bibliothèque de la Pléiade, Paris, 1958
Correspondance, Gallimard, Bibliothèque de la Pléiade, Paris, 1977–1992, 13 vols.
Romans et Contes, Gallimard, Bibliothèque de la Pléiade, Paris, 1979
Mélanges, Gallimard, Bibliothèque de la Pléiade, Paris, 1981, 1995
Romans et Contes, Livre de Poche, Classiques Modernes, Paris, 1994
Romans et Contes, Classiques Garnier, Paris, 1958
Correspondance Choisie, Livre de Poche, Classiques Modernes, Paris, 1997
Deloffre & Cornier (eds.), *Voltaire et sa « grande amie »* : *Correspondance complète de Voltaire et de Mme Bentinck*; Fayard/Voltaire Foundation, Oxford, 2003
Voltaire en sa Correspondance, Aphorismes, L'Escampette, Paris 1995
Dictionnaire de la Pensée de Voltaire, ed. Versaille, Editions Complexe, Paris 1994
Mémoires, Livre de Poche, Paris, 1998
Letters Concerning the English Nation, Oxford World's Classics, Oxford, 1994, 1999
Lettres Philosophiques, Gallimard, Folio Classique, Paris, 1986, 1999
Dictionnaire Philosophique, GF-Flammarion, Paris, 1964
L'Affaire Calas, ed. Jaques van den Heuvel, Gallimard, Folio Classique, Paris, 1975, 1996
Œuvres complètes: Édition Louis Moland, Paris, Garnier, 1875, available on CD-ROM, published by Daniel Boudin, Tournon-Saint-Martin, France 36220

Other works
Contemporary Writings

Jean Antoine Nicolas de Caritat de Condorcet, *Vie de Voltaire*, Quai Voltaire, Paris, 1994
Mme de Graffigny, *Correspondance*, vol. 1, 1716–39, Voltaire Foundation, Oxford, 1985
Mme du Deffand, *Lettres à Voltaire*, Rivages Poche, Paris, 1994

Biographical Works

René Pomeau, *Voltaire*, Seuil, Paris 1955, 1989, 1994

René Pomeau, ed., *La Politique de Voltaire*, Armand Colin, Paris, 1963, 1994

René Pomeau, *La Religion de Voltaire*, Librairie A-G Nizet, Paris, 1969, 1995

René Pomeau, *Voltaire en son Temps,* 2 vols., Fayard/Voltaire Foundation, Oxford, 1985–94, 1995

Theodore Besterman, *Voltaire*, Longman, London, 1969

John Hearsey, *Voltaire*, Constable, London, 1976

Haydn Mason, *Voltaire*, ELEK Granada, London, 1981

A. J. Ayer, *Voltaire*, Faber and Faber, London, 1986

A Voltaire Encyclopaedia

Jean Goulemot, André Magnan, Didier Masseau, eds., *Inventaire Voltaire*, Quarto Gallimard, Paris, 1995

Voltaire's Private Life

Jean-Daniel Candaux, ed., *Voltaire chez lui*, Genève-Ferney, Geneva, 1994

J. Berchtold & M. Porret, *Être Riche au Siècle de Voltaire*, Librairie Droz, Geneva, 1996

Christiane Mervaud, *Voltaire à Table*, Desjonquères, Paris, 1998

Voltaire and the English

Frederick Pottle, ed., *Boswell on the Grand Tour*, 2 vols., Heinemann, London, 1953–55

André M. Rousseau, *L'Angleterre et Voltaire*, 3 vols., Voltaire Foundation, Oxford, 1976

Haydn Mason, ed., *Voltaire and the English*, Voltaire Foundation, Oxford, 1979

Voltaire's Contes

Roger Pearson, *The Fables of Reason*, Clarendon Press, Oxford, 1993

Human Rights and Penal Reform

Marc Chassaigne, *Le Procès du Chevalier de La Barre*, Victor Lecoffre, Paris, 1920

Marcello T. Maestro, *Voltaire and Beccaría as Reformers of Criminal Law*, Columbia UP, 1942

David D. Bien, *The Calas Affair*, Princeton UP, 1960
Michel Foucault, *Discipline and Punish*, trans. Sheridan, Penguin, London, 1977, 1991
Cesare Beccaría, trans. David Young, *On Crimes and Punishments*, Hackett, Indiana,1986

Catholics and Protestants

Janine Garrison, *Protestants du Midi*, Bibliothèque Privat, Toulouse, 1980, 1991
Nicole Castan, *Justice et Répression en Languedoc,* Flammarion, Paris, 1980
Dale K. van Kley, *The Damiens Affair*, Princeton UP, 1984
Dale K. van Kley, ed., *The French Idea of Freedom*, Stanford UP, 1994
Dale K. van Kley, *The Religious Origins of the French Revolution*, Yale UP, 1996

The *Encyclopédie*

L'Encyclopédie de Diderot et d'Alembert, on CD-ROM, Editions Redon, Marsanne
Frank A. Kafker, *The Encyclopedists as Individuals*, Voltaire Foundation, Oxford, 1988
Paul Ledieu, *Diderot et Sophie Volland*, Clermont Serveau, Paris, 1925
Denis Diderot, ed., Jean Varloot, *Lettres à Sophie Volland*, Gallimard, Folio Classique, Paris, 1984
P. N. Furbank, *Diderot*, Secker & Warburg, London, 1992

The Enlightenment

Peter Gay, *Voltaire's Politics*, Yale UP, 1959, 1988
Peter Gay, *The Enlightenment*, Norton, New York, 2 vols., 1966 and 1969, 1995 and 1996
Jonathan Israel, *Radical Enlightenment*, OUP, 2001
Robert Darnton, *The Business of Enlightenment*, Harvard UP, 1979
Robert Darnton, *The Great Cat Massacre*, Basic Books, Vintage Books, 1984, 1985
Robert Darnton, *The Kiss of Lamourette*, Faber and Faber, London, 1990
Robert Darnton, *The Forbidden Best-sellers of pre-Revolutionary France*, HarperCollins, London, 1996, 1997
Haydn Mason, *French Writers and their Society,* 1715–1800, Macmillan, London, 1982
Haydn Mason, ed., *The Darnton Debate*, Voltaire Foundation, Oxford, 1998
Daniel Roche, *France in the Enlightenment*, trs. Goldhammer, Harvard UP, 1998, 2000

Jean-Jacques Rousseau, *Les Confessions*, Gallimard, Folio Classique, Paris, 1959, 1973

Maurice Cranston, *Jean-Jacques Rousseau*, Chicago, 3 vols., 1982, 1991, 1997

French Politics

J. H. Shennan, *The Parlement of Paris,* Eyre & Spottiswoode/Sutton, London, 1968, 1998

E. Le Roy Ladurie, *The Ancien Régime*, trans. Greengrass, Blackwell, Oxford, 1991, 1998

John Hardman, *French Politics 1774–1789*, Longman, London, 1995

Julian Swann, *Politics and the Parlement of Paris,* CUP, 1995

The French Revolution

Alexis de Tocqueville, *L'Ancien Régime et la Révolution*, Gallimard, N.R.F., Paris, 1952

François Furet, *Penser la Révolution Française*, Gallimard, Folio Histoire, Paris, 1978

François Furet and Mona Ozouf, eds., *Dictionnaire Critique de la Révolution Française*, Flammarion, Paris, 1988

Simon Schama, *Citizens*, Knopf, New York, 1989

Keith Michael Baker, *Inventing the French Revolution*, CUP, 1990

Index